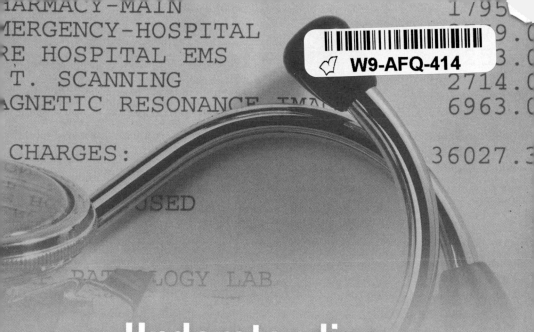

Understanding
Value-Based Healthcare

Christopher Moriates, MD
Assistant Clinical Professor of Medicine
University of California, San Francisco
San Francisco, California
Director of Implementation Initiatives, Costs of Care, Inc

Vineet Arora, MD, MAPP
Associate Professor and Director of
GME Clinical Learning Environment Innovation
University of Chicago
Chicago, Illinois
Director of Education Initiatives, Costs of Care, Inc

Neel Shah, MD, MPP
Assistant Professor
Harvard Medical School
Cambridge, Massachusetts
Founder and Executive Director, Costs of Care, Inc

Mc
Graw
Hill
Education

New York   Chicago   San Francisco   Athens   London   Madrid   Mexico City
Milan   New Delhi   Singapore   Sydney   Toronto

Understanding Value-Based Healthcare

1 2 3 4 5 6 7 8 9 0   DOC/DOC   19 18 17 16 15

ISBN 978-0-07-181698-4
MHID 0-07-181698-4

This book was set in Chaparral Pro Regular by MPS Limited.
The editors were James Shanahan and Christina M. Thomas.
The production supervisor was Catherine Saggese.
Project management was provided by Ruchika Abrol of MPS Limited.
The designer was Eve Siegel.
RR Donnelley was printer and binder.

This book is printed on acid-free paper.

Library of Congress Cataloging-in-Publication Data
Understanding value-based healthcare / editors, Christopher Moriates, Vineet Arora, Neel Shah.

p. ; cm.

Includes bibliographical references and index.

ISBN 978-0-07-181698-4 (alk. paper) — ISBN 0-07-181698-4 (alk. paper)

I. Moriates, Christopher, 1982- , editor.   II. Arora, Vineet, editor.   III. Shah, Neel (Obstetrician/Gynecologist), editor.

[DNLM: 1. Delivery of Health Care—economics—United States—Case Reports. 2. Costs and Cost Analysis—United States—Case Reports.   3. Economics, Medical—United States—Case Reports.   W 84 AA1]

RA410

338.4'73621

2014046528

We sincerely thank all of our fellow physicians, medical trainees, nurses, pharmacists, and allied health professionals that we work with every day and those that have helped shape our lives. This book was written for you and we sincerely hope that you will find it useful. Most of all, we thank our patients, who have taught us more lessons than could ever be captured in a textbook, and whom we dedicate this book to.

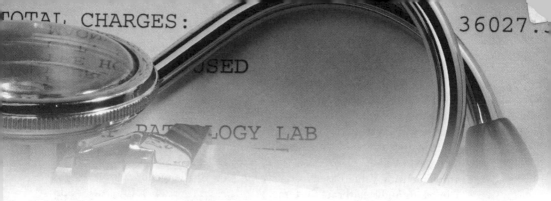

Table of Contents

Guest Authors/Contributors

David Margolius, MD
Chief Resident
Department of Medicine,
University of California, San Francisco
San Francisco, California
National Team Advisor,
Primary Care Progress

Andrew F. Morris-Singer, MD
President and Founder,
Primary Care Progress
Affiliate Instructor, Family Medicine,
Oregon Health & Science University,
Portland, Oregon
Lecturer
Department of Global
Health & Social Medicine,
Harvard Medical School
Boston, Massachusetts

Cynthia D. Smith, MD
Senior Physician Educator
American College of Physicians
Philadelphia, Pennsylvania
Adjunct Associate Professor
Perelman School of Medicine
at the University of Pennsylvania
Philadelphia, Pennsylvania

Steven E. Weinberger, MD
Executive Vice President and
Chief Executive Officer
American College of Physicians
Philadelphia, Pennsylvania
Adjunct Professor of Medicine
University of Pennsylvania
Philadelphia, Pennsylvania
Senior Lecturer on Medicine
Harvard Medical School
Boston, Massachusetts

Foreword

Robert M. Wachter, MD

*Professor and Associate Chair of Department of Medicine,
University of California, San Francisco*

A couple of years ago, I was speaking to a group of medical students at my institution, the University of California, San Francisco. The setting was a small seminar, and we were running through a variety of topics related to health policy. The students asked me about the changes I'd seen over my 30 years of clinical practice, and where I saw the healthcare system headed during their professional lifetimes. I decided that this was a great opportunity to shake them out of their youthful complacency.

"You folks need to be prepared for a career that will be massively different from mine," I said. "You will be under relentless pressure to deliver the highest quality, safest, most satisfying care ... at the lowest possible cost." I spoke these words slowly and solemnly, my words heavy with gravitas.

After a few seconds, one of the students raised his hand and asked a question that was at once naïve and profound. "What exactly were *you* trying to do?" he said.

I think of that student's question every time I consider the state of our healthcare system. Today's clinicians and administrators may be unsettled, even overwhelmed, by all the pressures they now find themselves under to deliver high-value care: more stringent regulations and accreditation requirements, public reporting of various value-related measures, value-based purchasing initiatives, new payment models such as bundling and accountable care organizations, even Yelp reviews and apps that offer cost and quality data with a single click. It's certainly a lot to take in. Yet what is odd, even bizarre, is not that we are now under such pressure. What is odd is that, until recently, we were not.

The indictment against our healthcare system—particularly the American system, though other countries' systems are facing similar pressures—is well known and largely accurate. Evidence accumulated over the last generation finds that we do poorly on virtually every measure of healthcare value. Variations are enormous and clinically indefensible. We deliver evidence-based care only about half the time. Medical errors are rampant, and tens, perhaps hundreds, of thousands of people die each year from preventable harms. Patients are frequently unhappy with their care, usually with justification. Access is sporadic and unpredictable. And if all of that weren't bad enough, the costs of care are bankrupting the government, and, increasingly, corporations and individuals, too.

The field of patient safety has taught us that most errors are committed by good, competent people working in dysfunctional systems. And so it is with healthcare value: while there are certainly instances of low-value care delivered by clinicians who are incompetent or even dishonorable, most low-value care is delivered by good clinicians working in dysfunctional systems. Here, of course, I'm not simply referring to the healthcare delivery system, such as clinics or hospitals. Just as important are the systems that determine the environment in which care is delivered: the system of training young physicians and other clinicians, the system of capturing key data and making it available to both clinicians and patients at the point of care, the system of regulating medicine, the malpractice system and, of course, the payment system. In light of this overwhelming complexity, efforts to improve value need to be broad-based, innovative, and interdisciplinary. Moreover, such efforts involve knotty measurement problems and often profound ethical and political ones. This means that there will not be a magic bullet for improving healthcare value, no healthcare value checklist.

Which is where this book comes in. As the authors note, there are other resources focusing on the individual elements of value: cost, quality, access, patient safety, and patient experience. And there are books that explore many of the contextual determinants, such as the payment and regulatory systems. But, until now, there has not been a single book that brought together each of these domains in the service of helping clinicians and non-clinicians understand and improve healthcare value.

The authors have done a masterful job in weaving together the appropriate resources and educational techniques. There are case studies to illustrate key points. Foundational information, such as the nuts and bolts of health insurance or of costs and charges, are presented at the level of detail needed to understand these topics, while skillfully avoiding the temptation to wander into some very tall weeds. Charts and graphs help illustrate key points. The book is written in a style that manages to be both authoritative and utterly accessible.

Perhaps most impressively, the book is deeply practical. The authors have unmatched experience implementing programs designed to improve value in their own institutions, and in many others across the country. In sharing these experiences, they manage to draw universal lessons that will be helpful to everyone—from the young clinician-educator trying to teach her students about value, to the practicing physician, nurse, or pharmacist beginning a value-improvement program, to the healthcare administrator or policymaker trying to understand this vital new agenda. Given the complexity of the topic and the diverse needs of these audiences, this is a singular achievement.

For those of us who work in, or care about, healthcare, improving value is the defining issue of our generation. This is not simply an academic matter, nor is it one whose impact is limited to the healthcare system. Yes, high value in healthcare is about whether a woman's breast cancer is treated effectively and compassionately. And it's about whether a child can see the right provider to get her vaccines and treat her strep throat. And it's about whether an elderly man with angina receives the appropriate medical therapy and does not receive an unnecessary stent.

But as healthcare costs crowd out other national priorities for societal spending, high-value care is also about whether our schools have enough teachers, our streets have enough policemen, and our businesses have the resources they need to compete in a global market—while still providing excellent care and maximizing the health of the population. It is not hyperbole to say that the healthcare value agenda is about the overall viability of our civilization, and the preservation of our way of life.

Remarkably given the importance of this issue, until now, we lacked a roadmap to attack it. With this book, we now have one. That makes it essential reading for everyone who cares about making our system better.

Foreword

Steven E. Weinberger, MD, FACP
Executive Vice President and Chief Executive Officer,
American College of Physicians

It is difficult to find an issue that simultaneously has as much financial impact on individuals, families, corporate America, and both state and federal governments as the cost of healthcare. As President Obama concisely made the case to attendees at the 2009 annual meeting of the American Medical Association: "Make no mistake: The cost of our healthcare is a threat to our economy. It is an escalating burden on our families and businesses. It is a ticking time bomb for the federal budget. And it is unsustainable for the United States of America." These days in Washington, DC, there is little consensus across the political spectrum about virtually anything—except perhaps the magnitude of the problem of healthcare costs and the urgency with which it must be addressed.

In general, when we pay more for the same type of product or service, we expect to get something of higher quality or more value. Unfortunately, that principle does not hold when we are talking about healthcare. Despite healthcare expenses approaching $3 trillion and 20% of GDP, our health outcomes are no better—and in many cases worse—than those in industrialized countries that spend far less per capita on healthcare. I will not recount the many factors responsible for the relatively high cost and low value of healthcare in the United States, which are covered so beautifully and comprehensively in this authoritative treatise that links the care that patients receive and the dollars that individuals, organizations, and government spend to get that care.

A major theme throughout this book is waste—dollars spent that provide no benefit to patients, that is, care that is overused or misused. I can provide my own personal experience as a patient when, several years ago, I had a torn medial meniscus in my knee. After it became clear that my symptoms were not resolving on their own, my orthopedist and I agreed that it made sense for me to have arthroscopic surgery. When setting a date for the surgery, the scheduler told me that I first needed to complete my preoperative testing, which included a chest radiograph, an electrocardiogram, and a battery of blood tests. Fortunately, I am healthy, and there was nothing in my medical history to suggest that any of these tests would be of value to me, to my care, or to the orthopedist who would be performing the arthroscopy. None of these tests is individually enormously expensive, but when we add them up and then multiply by the number of individuals across the country who have unnecessary preoperative testing, we are now talking about "real money."

I can also provide my perspective as a physician who speaks frequently about high-value care and the problem of overuse and misuse. When I first gave talks on the topic, focusing on overused diagnostic testing, I was concerned about getting pushback or at least excuses from physicians: concerns about malpractice liability because of a missed diagnosis; patients who expect "high-tech" diagnostic services; a commitment to do everything for patients and not worry about costs, etc. To my surprise, this has not been the reaction. Instead, the overwhelming response from physicians in the audience is to recount their own stories—speaking as physicians who feel that they (and their colleagues) are overusing or misusing care, as patients who have had their own personal experiences, or as family members of individuals who have suffered from overused care or its exorbitant cost.

The three authors of this book have done a superlative job in covering the critical topics relating to healthcare costs and value. Their comprehensive presentation of data and literature citations is accompanied by many stories that illustrate the problems we are confronting and must address. They have successfully conducted a "root cause analysis" of the problem and, not unexpectedly, have identified and discussed many contributing factors. But most important, they have not just thrown up their hands in frustration, but instead have nicely detailed the solutions and tools that are being applied—and must be expanded and extended—to treat this critical problem. Their practical approach focuses on several important areas: the training environment; the role of patients; cost-effective medication prescribing; appropriate screening; and use of financial incentives (or penalties) to change the behavior of physicians and other healthcare providers.

Now the ball is in our court. We must take the messages delivered in this book and apply them to the care we deliver to our patients. As individuals and as a nation, we generally strive to become #1. But being #1 in healthcare costs is not a desirable goal. Being #1 in healthcare value—which I like to define as the benefit of care we provide relative to its costs and harms—is the goal to which we should strive. It is the responsibility of each and every one of us who are part of the healthcare system to do our part in achieving this goal. We owe it to ourselves, our patients, our profession, and our society.

Introduction/Preface

How To Read and Use This Book

We hope that everyone with a stake in making healthcare delivery work better will find this book useful. That being said, we wrote it with a primary audience in mind: the people who spend their days (and nights) caring for patients. At the beginning of the 21st century, healthcare professionals are able to deploy an extraordinary range of medical capabilities. The problem is that sometimes our capabilities stretch beyond what we are able to afford financially, physically, and morally. As the adage goes, just because we *can* do something does not always mean that we *should* do something.

The irony of our modern predicament is that even as scientific knowledge and technology have enhanced our prowess in some ways it has actually added to our fallibility in others. Healthcare has gotten more specialized, more nuanced, more complicated. Where complexity exists, so do opportunities to mess up. As a result, for those of us on the frontlines, applying our capabilities appropriately is increasingly becoming an uphill struggle.

For patients, our misfires can be devastating. Every day, patients are blindsided by bankruptcy-inducing medical bills. Every day, patients are subjected to intensive end-of-life treatments that overlook the fact that most people have other goals besides simply living longer. These occurrences are seldom flagged as "medical errors," but they still represent significant harms. In many cases these harms can be avoided, not by passing legislation, but by improving our processes of care.

This book is an extension of that insight. It is not an introduction to healthcare policy. It is not an introduction to healthcare economics. It is not an introduction to healthcare finance. Those books already exist. We are instead focused on *value-based care*—the idea that healthcare needs reform not only in the halls of government or the suites of executives but in the wards and clinics where care is provided. Value-based care requires that those of us who care for patients optimize healthcare outcomes while also taking direct and specific responsibility for costs and patient experiences.

Parts I and II lay the groundwork for understanding value-based care by identifying several failure points in the clinical environment. We discuss why healthcare pricing is opaque (*Chapter 3*), and what this means for how we define and measure value (*Chapter 4*). We discuss the unconscionable disparities in how healthcare resources are distributed (*Chapter 7*) and how inadequate investments in primary care (*Chapter 9*) restricts access to basic services. We then talk about what these failures mean for frontline clinicians—the implications of being faced with too much to do in too little time, all while balancing discomfort with uncertainty, fears about malpractice, and concerns regarding fulfilling patient expectations (*Chapter 10*).

Then we talk about what we can do about it. We can supply a pipeline for change by embedding the principles of value-based care into the apprenticeship of health professional education (*Chapter 11*). We can improve patient experiences by tracking patient-reported outcomes and engaging in shared decision-making (*Chapter 12*). Sometimes, improving care is just a matter of choosing our treatment options more wisely (*Chapter 13*). In other cases, there are opportunities for us to be on-the-ground leaders of change within our own practices or institutions, developing projects and programs, and redesigning care pathways (*Chapter 16*).

Some of the concepts in this book are relatively new and others are surprisingly old. Nonetheless, efforts to embed them into the practice of healthcare remain at the earliest stages. That is where you come in. It is not enough to have a healthcare system that is capable. We need to have a healthcare system that performs. We need to have a healthcare system where those who spend their days and nights caring for patients are leading from the front rather than trailing from behind. If you are reading this, we know you are up to the task.

About Costs of Care, Inc

Costs of Care is a 501c3 nonprofit formed in 2009 and directed by the authors of this book. Our goal is to leverage insights from frontline clinicians that improve the value of healthcare delivery. The "Stories From the Frontlines" that appear in each chapter were submitted to Costs of Care by real patients, nurses, and physicians whose insights inform many of the ideas in this book, and continue to motivate our ongoing efforts to inspire, educate, and support clinicians in the practice of value-based care. We invite you to join us and hundreds of other clinical leaders at www.CostsOfCare.org, in order to share the opportunities you are seeing and the challenges you are encountering along the way.

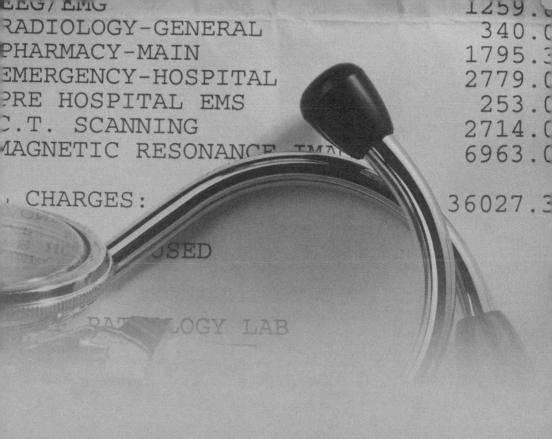

PART I

Introduction to Value in Healthcare

CHAPTER 1

The Current State of Healthcare Costs and Waste in the United States

*M*s Avery Jones shuffles through the magazines in the waiting room, looking for one she has not yet read. She recently lamented to her grandson that these days she seems to spend more time sitting in medical offices than doing anything else. She is an 82-year-old woman who has lived most of her life as a committed elementary school teacher. She is now retired, widowed, and carries a long list of medical diagnoses, including congestive heart failure (CHF), atrial fibrillation, chronic obstructive pulmonary disease (COPD), osteoporosis, arthritis, and chronic kidney disease. She regularly sees her primary care provider (PCP), her cardiologist, her pulmonologist, and a nephrologist. She is prescribed a total of 12 medications, some of which are taken twice per day. She has to pay a few hundred dollars out-of-pocket each month for her medications, which places a significant strain on her fixed retirement budget. Unbeknownst to her, some of her brand-name prescriptions have effective, cheaper generic alternatives readily available, which would save her more than a hundred dollars each month.*

Today she is scheduled to get an echocardiogram that was ordered by her pulmonologist to assess her chronically worsening shortness of breath. As they place the ultrasound probe on her chest to start the echocardiogram, she realizes that this is the exact same test that she had undergone a few weeks ago, when it was ordered by her cardiologist to "check on her CHF." It occurs to her now that she was never told the results of that test. Her multiple physicians use different electronic medical record systems (in fact, her pulmonologist still uses paper charts), and they never seem to know what tests the other has ordered. One time she asked her nephrologist why she needed to have blood work done when she had just had blood drawn a few days prior by her PCP, and she was told that it was "better to just have it done here again so that it is in our system."

At her last cardiology appointment her cardiologist told her that she may need a pacemaker with an automatic implantable cardioverter-defibrillator (AICD). He warned that without it she could possibly "die from a sudden heart arrhythmia." This worried her a great deal; however, when she mentioned this to her PCP he just shrugged and told her that she didn't need this done because her "QRS is not yet wide." She does not know what this means but her doctor seemed to be in a rush and so she didn't ask him to clarify. She trusts both her PCP and her cardiologist dearly and is not sure what she is supposed to do.

Healthcare in the United States is fraught with complexity, fragmentation, inefficiency, unexplained variation, and waste. In order to navigate this complexity in ways that make care more affordable, safe, and convenient, patients and their caregivers will need to understand how to deliver and receive high-value care. This will require understanding the origins and root causes of our health system shortfalls, being able to recognize existing sources and types of waste, and learning new methods of delivering care. We have written this book for clinical caregivers and focus our attention on topics of direct relevance to those who provide clinical care.

High-value care typically refers to maximizing the "quality divided by cost" equation—or, in other words, producing the best health outcomes and patient experiences at the lowest cost (see Chapter 4).[1-3] Despite the seemingly simple and, perhaps, cold appearance of this definition, it is important to realize that there are many intricacies to best capture health outcomes and costs in a way that truly matters to all players in the healthcare system, including, most importantly, our patients. While clinicians may innately focus on issues related to overuse such as the avoidance of unnecessary antibiotics, patients may view the creation of value solely in terms of an enriched experience in the way they receive care.[4] It is vital that neither of these goalposts gets overlooked in our quest to improve the overall value of healthcare delivered in our country. This book will aim to explore healthcare value from many different perspectives, often grappling with real tensions between the many stakeholders in our system. Ultimately, however, our goal is to provide tools for clinicians to better deliver the best possible care at lower costs.

As bleakly illustrated by Ms Jones' situation, the current healthcare system infrequently delivers on this promise. Ms Jones' care demonstrates the all-too-common scenario of unnecessary and redundant tests, ordered by well-meaning but inadequately informed clinicians, working in disconnected systems that do not effectively communicate. The effect of these problems is care that is less convenient, safe, humanizing, and affordable for Ms Jones. As she sits in a darkened examination room, wearing a thin cotton gown, sacrificing her time to receive a test that she did not need, she can take little comfort in the fact that she is not alone: up to one-third of healthcare may not actually make patients healthier.[5] And among Medicare patients, around half of echocardiograms, imaging stress tests, pulmonary function tests, and chest computed tomography scans are repeated within 3 years.[6] By some estimates, more than 40% of services delivered to Medicare patients provide minimal clinical benefit, thus are considered low-value care.[7]

Ms Jones was also given conflicting recommendations without the knowledge or tools to make an appropriate decision. Her physician recommended an invasive treatment (an AICD) that may not actually benefit her. In fact, as many as 22% of AICDs—which are pacemakers that are implanted into the chest wall and have the ability to shock patients' hearts directly if the machine senses specific dangerous heart rhythms—are inserted in circumstances that are counter to the recommendations of professional society guidelines.[8]

All of this waste and inefficiency in the current healthcare system is astounding, and hardly defensible.

As the Institute of Medicine (IOM) recently pointed out[5]:

- "If banking were like healthcare, automated teller machine (ATM) transactions would take not seconds but perhaps days or longer as a result of unavailable or misplaced records.
- If home building was like healthcare, carpenters, electricians and plumbers each would work with different blueprints, with very little coordination.
- If shopping was like healthcare, product prices would not be posted, and the price charged would vary widely within the same store, depending on the source of payment.
- If automobile manufacturing was like healthcare, warranties for cars that require manufacturers to pay for defects would not exist. As a result, few factories would seek to monitor and improve production line performance and product quality.
- If airline travel were like healthcare, each pilot would be free to design his or her own preflight safety check, or not to perform one at all."

This book will outline the emerging concept of value in healthcare, delineate areas of current medical waste and unsustainable costs of care, and provide evolving tools and strategies to improve the medical care that is delivered in the United States.

A LOT OF BUCKS, NOT A LOT OF BANG: THE HEALTHCARE COST AND QUALITY CRISIS

In the United States, healthcare costs have exploded over the last few decades. Approximately $2.5 to $3 trillion is spent annually in the United States on healthcare, equaling nearly 18% of the gross domestic product (GDP) in 2011 (Figure 1-1).[9] The real issue is that despite spending more than anywhere else in the world, by a wide margin, our outcomes are actually subpar. The United States "ranks at or near the bottom in both prevalence and mortality for multiple diseases, risk factors, and injuries."[10]

Perhaps the easiest and most relevant comparison is that to our closest neighboring country to the north. Total health spending per capita in the United States is 82% more than in Canada ($7960 vs $4363 per year, in 2009)[11] (Figure 1-2), yet

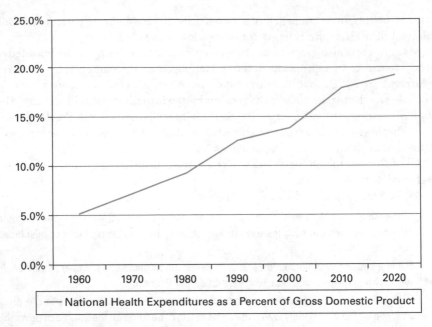

Figure 1-1. National health expenditures as a percentage of gross domestic product. (Data from Centers for Medicare & Medicaid Services, Office of the Actuary. National Health Expenditures. 2013. http://www.cms.gov/Research-Statistics-Data-and-Systems/Statistics-Trends-and-Reports/NationalHealthExpendData/NationalHealthAccountsHistorical.html. Accessed July 14, 2013.)

Americans are not any healthier. In 2000, the World Health Organization ranked the health systems of its 191 member states.[12] Canada ranked 30th overall. The United States was 37th.

The Commonwealth Fund has created a health system scorecard that includes 42 performance indicators for comparing national spending rates with domestic and international quality benchmarks. In 2011, the US health system scored 66 out of 100.[13] In school terms, this is a failing grade. Put bluntly, by most measures the United States is spending a lot of bucks on healthcare, but unfortunately not getting a lot of bang.

From a national health policy perspective, this is seen as a large opportunity for improvement in many ways, including how clinicians practice. For example, according to Stanford health services researcher Dr Arnold Milstein, if the average clinician in the United States practiced the way the best clinicians practice (in terms of health gained per dollar spent), our per capita spending might drop overnight by 15% to 30%.[14]

Although clinicians may increasingly recognize an ethical duty to address societal healthcare spending (see Chapter 6), arguments focused on the national

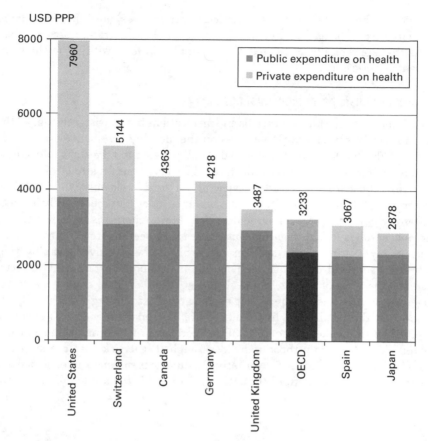

USD PPP

Figure 1-2. Total health expenditures per capita. (Data from OECD (Organization for Economic Co-operation and Development). Health expenditure per capita. In: Health at a Glance 2011. OECD Publishing; 2011. http://www.oecd-ilibrary.org/social-issues-migration-health/health-at-a-glance-2011/health-expenditure-per-capita_health_glance-2011-60-en. Accessed January 3, 2013.)

GDP may not be the most compelling to those on the frontlines of every-day patient care. It is not that the statistics we just cited do not draw gasps of horror. They do. Clinicians understand that the exponentially growing trend lines with numbers in the trillions foretell a bleak national financial future. However, many walk away feeling uninformed about how to really change their individual practice. This may be due to the fact that healthcare providers do not go to medical or nursing or pharmacy school to treat the national GDP. They are instead appropriately passionate about treating the individual patients sitting in front of them. However, as discussed below, healthcare costs and wasteful spend-ing do indeed affect individual patients. The financial harm to patients and their families can be substantial,[15-17] and clinicians can take responsibility for helping alleviate this problem.[18] Part of the challenge will be to reframe cost conversations that are typically abstracted to the population level within the clinician-patient relationship.

Healthcare costs harm individual patients

Lack of money to pay for medical bills and medications has consistently topped the list of financial concerns for Americans on the monthly *Consumer Reports* index survey.[19] This has led approximately half of all patients to take steps to decrease their *out-of-pocket costs*, many of which could be dangerous (Figure 1-3).[19,20]

Medical bills are now a leading cause of personal bankruptcy in the United States,[21,22] and increasingly medical insurance does not necessarily protect patients from the high costs of medical care. More Americans than ever before are now enrolled in *high-deductible insurance plans* (see Chapter 2). At the same time, many routine health services are arbitrarily expensive, meaning that seemingly simple decisions that physicians make about testing could directly lead to thousands of dollars in out-of-pocket costs.[17,23] Even among Medicare-covered patients, the out-of-pocket costs can be astounding. In 2008, it was found that during the last five years of life, personal expenditures averaged $38,688 for individuals, and $51,030 for couples in which one spouse died.[24] Incredibly, it isn't only those unlucky enough to get sick that are suffering from high healthcare costs. Skyrocketing insurance *premiums* are too expensive for most Americans to afford (Chapter 2).[25] In 2011, the annual premium for

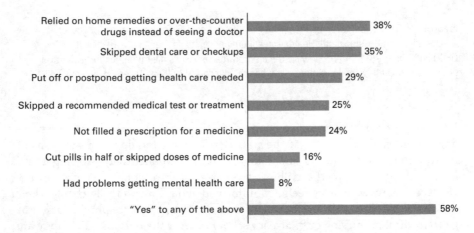

Figure 1-3. Putting off care because of costs. (Kaiser Polls: Health Insurance/Costs—Kaiser Family Foundation (Conducted May 8-14, 2012). http://www.kff.org/kaiserpolls/ins_costs.cfm. Accessed December 5, 2012.)

employer-sponsored family health coverage cost $15,073, a large burden even for middle-class families.[26] This strain on household budgets can cause further erosion of personal health, and clearly leeches resources from other imperatives of daily living.

Since 2009, we have collected (via the Costs of Care Essay Contest, described in Chapter 5) more than 400 personal accounts from physicians, nurses, and patients from all over the United States that illustrate the financial and physical harms that result from the current healthcare system. These stories also present many high-yield opportunities for caregivers to improve the value of care delivery. Some of these first-person accounts are included throughout this book as "Story From the Frontlines," to give voice to the many that are personally affected by the issues in this book, and to regularly remind all of us of the real-life high stakes at play.

HEALTHCARE WASTE

"In very large measure, improving care and reducing waste are one and the same thing," said Dr Donald Berwick, founder of the Institute for Healthcare Improvement (IHI) and former administrator for the Centers for Medicare and Medicaid Services (CMS).[27] A study by Dr Berwick and RAND policy analyst Dr Andrew Hackbarth estimated that approximately $476 to $992 billion is wasted in US healthcare annually.[28] Around the same time, the IOM independently placed their own estimate squarely in the center of this range, at $750 to $765 billion.[5,29] This waste represents up to more than 30 cents on every healthcare dollar spent. The effect on taxpayer funds is substantial, with at least $166 to $304 billion of Medicare and Medicaid spending squandered each year.[28]

Warren Buffett, the famous American businessman, investor and philanthropist, has likened healthcare costs to "a tapeworm eating at our economic body."[30] National healthcare expenditures, particularly those that are considered waste, divert major resources from other important domestic priorities, such as education, infrastructure (roads, railroads, and bridges), basic research, and other public goods. It drags down our global competitiveness in business, and thwarts social programs to support small businesses. Indeed, healthcare waste is detrimental at the individual, family, community, state, and national levels.[5]

There are multiple contributors to healthcare waste. Using the categories recognized by the IOM,[5] these include

- Unnecessary services (those that add to expenses without improving health)
- Inefficient care due to systems errors and failures of coordination
- Prices that are excessively high
- Excessive administrative costs
- Fraud
- Missed prevention opportunities

Unnecessary services

As clinicians, when looking at the IOM pie chart of healthcare waste (Figure 1-4), our eye is most drawn to that upper right quadrant where the slice for "unnecessary services" resides. This is not only because, at $210 billion, unnecessary services comprise the biggest proportion of the pie, *but* also because this is the area that individual clinicians have the most direct control over every day that they care for patients. Whenever a physician places pen to a prescription pad (or enters an order into a computer system), she is liable to be contributing to the $210 billion spent each year on services that do not make patients any healthier. These are medications, tests, and procedures that are not evidence-based, go outside of guidelines, and, in a minority of cases, are known to cause net harm (eg, elective back surgery in certain situations), but are done anyways.

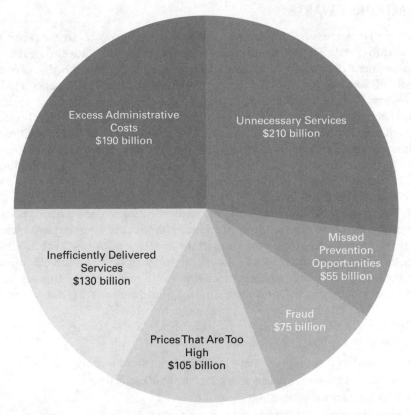

Figure 1-4. Sources of waste annually in US healthcare. (Reproduced, with permission, from IOM (Institute of Medicine). *Best care at lower cost: the path to continuously learning health care in America.* Washington, D.C.: National Academies Press; 2013.)

As discussed throughout this book, the problem of overuse has become pervasive in US healthcare.[31,32] Recently, this culture of overuse has become a hot topic in the medical literature,[33-35] and the popular press has begun to explain the problem of overtesting and overtreatment to the public.[36-38]

Let's briefly consider the example of using a computed tomography angiography (CTA) scan to diagnose pulmonary embolism (PE)—a potentially life-threatening blood clot in the lungs that can be difficult to diagnose from symptoms alone. The story of CTA scans and PEs demonstrates the complicated relationships between overuse, overdiagnosis, technology, and the lack of a sufficient evidence-base to guide decisions.

While some patients with PE dramatically suffer cardiovascular collapse and acute heart failure, others with ultimately clinically significant PEs may present with very vague complaints and lack clear objective findings on examination.[39] In fact, the possibility of an underlying PE is discussed nearly daily on medicine and surgical hospital rounds. Despite this focus, there are many gaps that remain in our knowledge for appropriately diagnosing and treating PE. This has led to PE being called "a metaphor for medicine in the evidence-based medicine era."[40] At first glance this sounds like a compliment since most modern clinicians worship at the altar of "evidence-based medicine," but Dr Vinay Prasad and his colleagues from Northwestern University and colleagues warn that they actually consider PE a metaphor "not because it represents a great success, but because it captures all the complexity of medicine in the evidence-based era."[40]

For many years the incidence of PE was stable at about 62 cases per 100,000 population.[41] Then in 1998, CTA became widely utilized for the diagnosis of PE. Over the next 8 years, the number of PEs diagnosed nearly doubled. However, despite these rapidly increasing number of PEs found and treated, the effect on mortality was very small. We were diagnosing and treating twice as many PEs, but we weren't really saving many more lives. This pattern is consistent with *overdiagnosis*.[41]

It would be one thing if we simply weren't making much of a difference, but in fact overdiagnosis frequently can lead to significant harms.[42] As we began treating more patients for PEs with blood thinners, or anticoagulants, the rate of major bleeding complications increased rather dramatically—from 3.1 to 5.3 per 100,000.[41] Furthermore, the harms associated with CTAs are not trivial. They include excess radiation, which has been linked to future cancer risk[43,44]; exposure to intravenous contrast, which puts patients at risk for allergic reactions and kidney failure[45,46]; and moderate financial costs. According to some estimates, as many as one-third of the more than 1.5 million CTAs performed annually to rule-out PE may be avoidable.[47]

While tests like excessive CTAs are relatively expensive and dramatic, even small-ticket items, such as inappropriate repeat cholesterol tests ("lipid panels"), can have large effects on the health system due to the high-volume of these lab draws.[48,49] And the cost is not only monetary. The effects of these extra tests should be seen through the eyes of the patient: "The price to a patient asked to take 1 or 2 additional hours off of work to sit in the laboratory waiting room may not be modest at all."[48]

There are many different drivers for overuse, including medical culture, fee-for-service payments, and fear of malpractice litigation (all of which will be further investigated throughout this book).[33] But it is clear that patients also play an important role. In 2010, *The New York Times* described an internist in Boca Raton, Florida, named Dr Robert Colton, who said that his patients come in demanding treatments that are unnecessary.[36] He said that some patients come in with a reported chief complaint of, "I need an MRI." And Dr Colton, when asked what he does in these situations, said, "I do the damn test. There is no incentive for me, Rob Colton, to reduce overutilization. If the person wants it, what are you going to do, say no?"[36] (Chapters 10 and 12 explore how to engage patients in high-value care shared decision making.)

Some have pointed out that, in general, American patients tend to inordinately favor and embrace high-technology options, are shielded in many cases from the true costs of these options due to third-party payer insurance, and may be improperly swayed by direct-to-consumer marketing.[33] This "perfect storm" for overutilization, as University of Pennsylvania Bioethicist Ezekiel Emanuel and Stanford Economist Victor Fuchs have called it, has helped lead to overutilization becoming one of the most important contributors to the high healthcare costs in the United States.[33]

Story From the Frontlines—"Uncertainty and Challenges of Being an Informed Patient"

The patient—blue-eyed, red-haired, and healthy but worried looking—guided the doctor's hand to just below the angle of her jaw, where a small lump was barely palpable. She had first noticed the swollen lymph node after a cold and thought nothing of it at the time. But five months later, it was still there. She knew it was nothing, but she couldn't shake the thought that it might be related to the skin cancer she had had cut off of her shoulder one year earlier. After all, melanoma can spread through the lymphatic system, and her dermatologist checked carefully for swollen lymph nodes at every appointment to make sure the cancer had not escaped the scalpel and metastasized.

Melanoma is a terrifying disease. When caught early, it is easily treated by surgical excision. When caught late, however, it is universally fatal. The doctor smiled at the anxious 20-something-year-old woman in front of him, told her it was most likely nothing, and then wrote her orders for a CT scan to look for more inflamed lymph nodes. You're young, he told her, and if I were you, I would want this test to make absolutely sure that the cancer has not spread. For the doctor, that was the end of it—another satisfied patient, reassured by the advanced technology of modern medicine.

As a medical student, I have witnessed many discussions between healthcare providers about this type of hyper-vigilant patient. These conversations usually go something like this: "Mr. Smith's cough is probably just a cold, but he wants an x-ray to make sure it's not pneumonia." Or "Susie's headache is probably just a migraine, but her mom wants her to get a lumbar puncture [spinal tap] to make sure it's not a serious infection." Doctors and residents may express reservations, but if the test or treatment is reasonably justifiable, they frequently bow to the patient's wishes. After all, medicine is no longer the paternalistic discipline it once was; doctors today are supposed to enable patients to make their own decisions, not simply tell them what to do. And why not order a test if there is a possibility, even a small one, that it will reveal useful information—especially if the patient's insurance will cover the costs?

For the patient in this case—me—that visit was not the end of things. I walked out of the doctor's office feeling temporarily reassured; after all, he told me it was probably nothing, and I could always get the CT scan if I wanted to. But as the days went by, I found myself worrying more and more. Weren't the CT orders sitting on my desk at home proof that there was something to worry about?

On the other hand, I did not want a CT scan. Though I was lucky enough to have insurance that would have covered the costs of the scan 100%, I knew that CT scans were expensive, and I did not want to undergo a test that would take time out of my busy schedule, expose me to radiation, and add to the social burden of healthcare costs.

So I made an appointment with a dermatologist. She listened to my story, felt the lymph node, and then looked me dead in the eye and told me that there was absolutely nothing to be worried about. The lymph node was soft, it moved around—unlike cancerous nodes—and it was on the wrong side and the wrong place to be related to the cancer that I had had on my shoulder. In five minutes, she was in and out the door and I was on my way, without a single test having been done. This time, armed not with test orders but with more information about why I should not worry, I felt infinitely more reassured.

Doctors often talk about patients coming into clinic "with an agenda." They feel at odds with these patients, many of whom push for extensive testing. Yet in the end, the ultimate goal of most patients is not the testing itself—it is the answers that testing will provide. A provider who takes the time to fully explain the benefits and drawbacks of testing is likely to find that patients are much less desirous of exhaustive testing than they originally seem. In doing so, they are doing a favor for both the patient and the healthcare system that bears the cost of unnecessary testing.

—Erin Plute. "Uncertainty and Challenges of Being an Informed Patient." Costs of Care, 2013. (www.costsofcare.org)

Failures of care delivery and coordination: preventable errors, care fragmentation, and inefficiency

Another important area of healthcare waste includes the preventable complications and inefficiencies that result from failures in care delivery and coordination.

Errors and preventable complications

When a commercial airplane crashes in the United States, it immediately makes international news and triggers investigations and public response. Luckily, these airline crashes have become extremely rare, and the risk of dying in an airplane is now around 1 in 45 million flights.[50] In contrast, in 1999 the IOM famously revealed that as many as 98,000 Americans may die annually as a result of preventable medical errors,[51] and this was memorably translated into the gut-gripping "jumbo jet crash each day" analogy. The outrage was both immediate and warranted. But now more than a decade-and-a-half later, the progress overall to improve patient safety has been rather disappointing.[52,53]

Adverse events may still occur in up to one-third of all hospital admissions, causing costly complications both physically and financially.[54] According to one large national study that examined claims databases for about 24 million insured patients (including both private insurance and Medicare), more than 1.5 million preventable adverse events occurred in hospitalized patients in 2008, resulting in $19.5 billion in excess costs that year.[55]

Care fragmentation

As clinical care has become more complicated and specialized, it is increasingly common for patients to see multiple providers in different medical specialties, often located in different practices and healthcare systems. A Medicare patient sees on average seven different physicians.[56] But that is nothing compared to what happens when these patients get hospitalized. The typical hospital patient is seen by more than 15 clinicians during a single hospital stay.[57,58] Only a few decades ago the average was around two to three clinicians during a hospitalization. It is no wonder that three-quarters of hospital patients now are unable to identify the clinician in charge of their care.[59]

This care fragmentation does not only affect patients. The typical primary care provider coordinates with an average of 229 physicians across 117 different practices.[60] If this sounds overwhelming and unworkable, that is because it usually is (see Chapter 9).

Inadequate care coordination leads primary care providers to frequently lack important information at the time of a patient's clinic visit.[61] And that is if the patient even makes it to clinic. About one-fifth of Medicare patients are readmitted within 30 days of hospitalization, and more than half of these patients do not see any outpatient providers between these hospitalizations.[62] Imagine being discharged from the hospital after a weeklong stay for shortness of breath resulting from congestive heart failure. A few days after arriving home you find that you aren't sure if you are taking your new medications correctly, so you call your primary care provider for advice. Instead you find out that your doctor was not even aware that you were ever admitted to a hospital. He does not seem to know anything about what happened during your hospitalization, the results of your tests, or the new medications that you were prescribed. The sad reality is that direct communication rarely occurs between hospital and primary care providers.[63] This creates an unfair, incredibly challenging, and unsafe situation. It is not surprising that the top complaint patients have traditionally reported about their hospital care is related to continuity and transitions.[64]

Operational inefficiencies in care deliveries

Poorly functioning work processes are characterized by unnecessary pauses and rework, delays, established workarounds, and a process that participants feel is illogical.[65] Unfortunately, a patient is likely to find a number of these situations during just 1 day spent in any average US hospital. In fact, those who work in hospitals quickly become adept at figuring out workarounds to complete otherwise complicated, or even broken, workflows.[66-68] These workarounds may be essential to effective care delivery in some instances,[69] but they also often pose significant risks to patient safety.[70] One common example is the upfront ordering of advanced imaging for patients in an emergency department (ED) prior to obtaining a surgical consultation "just in case the surgeon might request it," thereby avoiding a potential bottleneck downstream. This may improve patient flow through the ED, but may also expose the patient to an unnecessary test, with unintended costs and consequences.

Complicated workflows and necessary workarounds create costly inefficiencies and variations in care delivery. An inpatient asking what time their CT scan will happen today is likely to be met with shrugged shoulders and the response: "it depends."

The inefficiency in hospital care delivery has created a system where nurses spend less than one-third of their working time performing direct patient care.[71] Intern physicians spend even less time interacting with patients. In one study, interns spent 12% of their work day directly with patients and more than 40% with computers.[72] This does beg the question about whether physicians are now training to take care of actual patients, or rather (as Stanford physician Dr Abraham Verghese put it) "iPatients."[73]

Inefficiencies are certainly not confined to the hospital. Just think about the wasted time routinely found at the beginning of most office encounters: "We in medicine actually institutionalized the waste of waiting," Dr Gary Kaplan from Virginia Mason Medical Center noted during his lecture at the Association of Academic Medical Colleges Integrating Quality meeting in 2013 (*paraphrased*). "We created 'waiting rooms' where patients rush to arrive and then sit and wait for us."

The waste of inefficiently delivered services—which includes preventable errors and complications, care fragmentation, unnecessary use of higher-cost providers, and operational inefficiencies at care delivery sites—cost up to $130 billion in the United States annually.[5,29]

Chapter 16 will discuss modern strategies applied by health systems to improve efficiencies and reduce waste.

Excessive administrative costs

It is hard to imagine that anybody becomes a health professional because they love sitting at a desk and filling-out paperwork. Yet, many clinicians spend multiple hours each week directly interacting with health plans and performing other administrative tasks related to our payment system. Nursing and clerical staff usually devote even much larger amounts of time to this tedious chore.[74] In the United States, physician practices spend approximately $83,000 per physician per year on insurance company interactions.[75] This is four times as much as Canadians.[75] The discrepancy is at least partially due to the fact that American health services need to coordinate with multiple different insurance companies on behalf of their patients. Most patients under the age of 65 obtain health insurance from their employer who has purchased their insurance plan from a private insurer (see Chapter 2). This means that more than 1.5 million unique employers are purchasing insurance plans from more than 1200 insurers in the United States.[76] The costs of dealing with this excessive insurance paperwork are substantial. To the tune of 11% of premiums dedicated to administrative overhead.[77]

"To understand how this could be different," wrote Stanford economists Alain Enthoven and Victor Fuchs,[77] "consider that Kaiser Permanente signs one annual contract for the coverage of more than 400,000 employees and dependents with the California Public Employees Retirement System (CalPERS), and CalPERS administrative costs are on the order of 0.5% of premium."

Insurance paperwork costs beyond benchmarks, insurers' administrative bottlenecks, and inefficiencies due to care documentation requirements are estimated to cost an excess $190 billion each year in the United States.[5,29] The private and public insurance systems will be discussed further in Chapter 2.

Pricing failures

We have outlined in this chapter a number of reasons why healthcare costs so much in the United States. But health economists Gerard Anderson, Uwe Reinhardt, Peter Hussey, and Varduhi Petrosyan put it a different way in the rather blunt title of their 2003 *Health Affairs* study: "It's the prices, stupid."[78]

Despite Anderson and colleagues' headline-catching study title, prices do not explain all of the differences between America and other countries. But it is indeed true that Americans pay more for most health services than any other country. For instance, an MRI in the United States may cost $1080, whereas the same test would cost $280 in France.[79]

There is clear evidence that medical services in the United States are overpriced and are seemingly immune to normal market forces. In a properly functioning market, the price of a service should be equal to the actual cost of production plus a reasonable profit. But, as will be discussed in Chapter 3, the prices of many medical services in the United States plainly exceed this standard.[80]

The terms "price," "cost," "charge," and "reimbursement" will be differentiated and discussed in detail in Chapter 3, along with a conversation about price variation and current efforts to achieve price transparency.

Fraud

During the mid-2000s, a group of people set up an AIDS clinic in Miami, Florida that billed for millions of dollars in infusion treatments for HIV-related illnesses. The only problem: the clinic never actually saw a single patient.[81,82]

The crooks stayed one step ahead of authorities by quickly moving on and opening up at least 29 shell companies and phantom clinics across multiple states. By using stolen identities and bribing physicians to use their names, the thieves were submitting Medicare bills at the rate of $100,000 per week, eventually swindling an estimated $70 million from the government before the US Federal Bureau of Investigations (FBI) finally caught them.[81]

This case was indeed sensational, but other cases of fraud have led to even more than just financial harms. Rarely, predator physicians purposefully perform unnecessary operations solely to collect from insurers.[83] One widely reported case was that of a 22-year-old semi-pro baseball player who was told that he had something wrong with his heart and that "if he wanted to live to age 30" he needed to undergo an operation to have a pacemaker placed. He knew that it would cut his baseball career short, but he trusted the doctor and underwent the operation. Months later he found out that the operation was never warranted and that the cardiologist who performed it had been convicted of billing Medicare for dozens of unnecessary heart procedures.[83]

Most healthcare fraud is neither as dramatic nor as frankly malicious as these cases, but it costs us dearly regardless. Several schemes are used to defraud the healthcare system, including billing for services not rendered, "upcoding" of services or items ("upcoding" is using a billing code for a procedure or diagnosis that is more complex than the actual procedure or diagnosis and that results in higher reimbursement), providing explicitly unnecessary services, and receiving kickbacks. A common area of abuse is with durable medical equipment, such as wheelchairs. The FBI estimates that healthcare fraud costs the country an estimated $80 billion per year.[84]

Missed prevention opportunities

We have already touched upon the rampant overuse of medical services, but it turns out that there is also a big problem of underuse for certain medical interventions as well. Americans receive only half of the preventive, acute, and chronic care recommended by clinical guidelines.[85] This may be due to the fact that primary care providers are faced with too many patients, too many recommendations, and too little time. It would take 21 hours a day for a primary care provider to provide all of the care recommended to meet their patients' acute, preventive, and chronic disease management needs (Figure 1-5).[86] With the race to see more patients and with less time to address all of their concerns, it may be understandable that the opportunities to tackle preventive services—such as appropriate immunizations, screening, and counseling—could too often get lost in the shuffle.

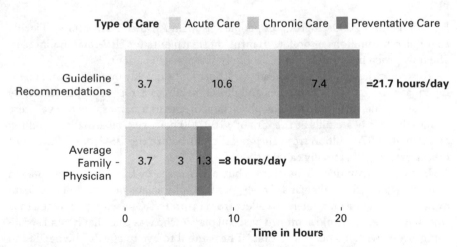

Figure 1-5. Time requirements for a primary care provider to treat a standard patient panel. (Data obtained from Yarnall KSH, Østbye T, Krause KM, Pollak KI, Gradison M, Michener JL. Family physicians as team leaders: "time" to share the care. *Prev Chronic Dis*. 2009;6(2):A59.)

Although it may be an impossible task, these missed prevention opportunities are costly both physically and financially. As the popular adage goes, "an ounce of prevention is worth a pound of cure." Inadequate disease prevention in the United States results in greater illness and premature deaths. On a population level, improvements in health in the United States have not kept pace with that of other wealthy countries.[87] *Morbidity* (the relative incidence of a particular disease) and chronic disability now account for nearly half of the US health burden.[87] Too many Americans are overweight, lack recommended vaccinations, or have uncontrolled blood pressure.

Disease prevention is largely the domain of primary care providers. Therefore, in order to shift the focus toward prevention, we will need more primary care providers in the United States and we must deliver more support for these frontline clinicians in performing these vital tasks (see Chapter 9).

In monetary terms, missed prevention opportunities could be resulting in $55 billion in wasteful healthcare spending annually.[5,29]

THE "VALUE" SHORTFALL: INADEQUATE HEALTHCARE SAFETY, QUALITY, AND OUTCOMES DESPITE RISING COSTS

This chapter may paint a bleak picture of the current state of affairs in healthcare and the resultant "value shortfall" (Figure 1-6). Indeed, the system may be sick but it is not yet terminal. The Institute for Healthcare Improvement has provided a framework for the United States to achieve high-value care through linked goals

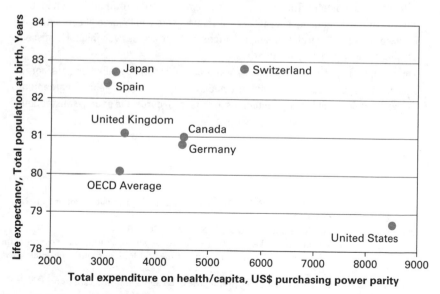

Figure 1-6. The value "shortfall." (Data obtained from OECD.)

that they call the "triple aim" (see Chapter 4). The purpose of the triple aim is to simultaneously improve the patient experience of care, improve the health of populations, and reduce per capita costs of care.

If we do not act, then too many patients will continue to experience unnecessary harms. Healthcare costs and waste will continue to grow, taking away from other important national priorities. And some patients will continue to have physical ailments replaced by equally distressing personal fiscal strains.

It does not need to continue this way.

This book will provide tools and resources to help transform the way care is delivered at the bedside by clinicians, at organizational levels, and on the national scale by way of major health policy levers.

KEY POINTS:

- Healthcare delivery in the United States has become increasingly complex, fragmented, inefficient, and expensive.
- Healthcare expenditures are growing at an unsustainable rate for both the nation and for individual families. Currently, the United States spends more than 18% of its gross domestic product (GDP) on healthcare, and medical bills are the leading cause of personal bankruptcy.
- Approximately one-third of all healthcare costs—more than $750 Billion—are considered to be wasteful. These excess costs can be categorized into (1) unnecessary services, (2) inefficient care due to systems errors and failures of coordination, (3) excessive administrative costs, (4) prices that are excessively high, (5) missed prevention opportunities, and (6) fraud.
- The specific definition for healthcare value can differ widely whether considered from the perspective of the patient, provider, or payer. There is general agreement that value should include cost, outcomes (or quality of care), and patient satisfaction.

References:

1. Curfman GD, Morrissey S, Drazen JM. High-value health care—a sustainable proposition. *N Engl J Med*. 2013;369(12):1163-1164.
2. Porter ME. What is value in health care? *N Engl J Med*. 2010;363(26):2477-2481.
3. Owens DK, Qaseem A, Chou R, Shekelle P. High-value, cost-conscious health care: concepts for clinicians to evaluate the benefits, harms, and costs of medical interventions. *Ann Intern Med*. 2011;154(3):174-180.
4. Rosenbaum L. The whole ball game—overcoming the blind spots in health care reform. *N Engl J Med*. 2013;368(10):959-962.

5. Institute of Medicine. *Best Care at Lower Cost: The Path to Continuously Learning Health Care in America*. Washington, DC: National Academies Press; 2012.

6. Welch HG, Hayes KJ, Frost C. Repeat testing among Medicare beneficiaries. *Arch Intern Med.* 2012;172(22):1745-1751.

7. Schwartz AL, Landon BE, Elshaug AG, Chernew ME, McWilliams J. Measuring low-value care in medicare. *JAMA Intern Med.* 2014;174(7):1067-1076.

8. Al-Khatib SM, Hellkamp A, Curtis J, et al. Non-evidence-based ICD implantations in the United States. *JAMA.* 2011;305(1):43-49.

9. Fuchs VR. The gross domestic product and health care spending. *N Engl J Med.* 2013;369(2): 107-109.

10. Woolf SH, Aron LY. The US health disadvantage relative to other high-income countries: findings from a national research council/institute of medicine report. *JAMA.* 2013;309(8): 771-772.

11. OECD. Health expenditure per capita. In: *Health at a Glance 2011*. Paris, France: OECD Publishing; 2011. http://www.oecd-ilibrary.org/social-issues-migration-health/health-at-a-glance-2011/ health-expenditure-per-capita_health_glance-2011-60-en. Accessed January 3, 2013.

12. World Health Organization. *The World Health Report 2000: Health Systems: Improving Performance*. Geneva: World Health Organization; 2000.

13. The Commonwealth Fund Commission on a High Performance Health System. *Why Not the Best? Results from the National Scorecard on U.S. Health System Performance*. New York, NY: The Commonwealth Fund; 2011.

14. Milstein A. Code Red and Blue—Safely Limiting Health Care's GDP Footprint. *N Engl J Med.* 2013;368(1):1-3.

15. Brill S. Bitter pill: why medical bills are killing us. *Time*. http://healthland.time.com/2013/02/20/ bitter-pill-why-medical-bills-are-killing-us/print/. Accessed February 21, 2013.

16. Zafar SY, Peppercorn JM, Schrag D, et al. The financial toxicity of cancer treatment: a pilot study assessing out-of-pocket expenses and the insured cancer patient's experience. *The Oncologist.* 2013;18(4):381-390.

17. Schoen C, Collins SR, Kriss JL, Doty MM. How many are underinsured? Trends among U.S. adults, 2003 and 2007. *Health Aff.* 2008; 27(4): w298-309.

18. Moriates C, Shah NT, Arora VM. First, do no (financial) harm. *JAMA.* 2013;310(6):577-578.

19. Gill L. Risky prescription drug practices are on the rise in a grim economy. Consumer reports. http://news.consumerreports.org/health/2011/09/risky-prescription-drug-practices-are-on-the-rise-in-a-grim-economy.html. Accessed November 15, 2012.

20. Kaiser Polls: Health Insurance/Costs—Kaiser Family Foundation (Conducted May 8-14, 2012). http://www.kff.org/kaiserpolls/ins_costs.cfm. Accessed December 5, 2012.

21. Himmelstein DU, Warren E, Thorne D, Woolhandler S. MarketWatch: illness and injury as contributors to bankruptcy. *Health Aff.* 2005; W5: 63-73 (Suppl Web Exclusives).

22. Himmelstein DU, Thorne D, Warren E, Woolhandler S. Medical bankruptcy in the United States, 2007: results of a national study. *Am J Med.* 2009;122(8):741-746.

23. Wharam JF, Ross Degnan D, Rosenthal MB. The ACA and high-deductible insurance—strategies for sharpening a blunt instrument. *N Engl J Med.* 2013;369(16):1481-1484.

24. Kelley AS, McGarry K, Fahle S, Marshall SM, Du Q, Skinner JS. Out-of-pocket spending in the last five years of life. *J Gen Intern Med.* 2013;28(2):304-309.

25. Banthin JS, Cunningham P, Bernard DM. Financial burden of health care, 2001-2004. *Health Aff.* 2008;27(1):188-195.

26. Kaiser Family Foundation. *Employer Health Benefits 2012 Annual Survey*. Kaiser Family Foundation. 2012;242. http://ehbs.kff.org/. Accessed November 16, 2012.

27. Berwick DM. The moral test. Institute for Healthcare Improvement 23rd Annual National Forum. 2011.http://www.ihi.org/knowledge/Pages/Presentations/TheMoralTestBerwickForum2011Keynote. aspx. Accessed November 15, 2012.

28. Berwick DM, Hackbarth AD. Eliminating waste in US health care. *JAMA*. 2012;307(14):1513.

29. Institute of Medicine (U.S.). *The Healthcare Imperative: Lowering Costs and Improving Outcomes: Workshop Series Summary*. Washington, DC: National Academies Press; 2010.

30. Stempel J. Buffett: health care tapeworm drags on economy. *Reuters*, March 1, 2010. http://www. reuters.com/article/2010/03/01/us-berkshire-buffett-idUSTRE62022120100301. Accessed January 22, 2013.

31. Caverly TJ, Combs BP, Moriates C, Shah N, Grady D. Too much medicine happens too often: the teachable moment and a call for manuscripts from clinical trainees. *JAMA Intern Med*. 2014; 174(1):8-9.

32. Sirovich BE, Woloshin S, Schwartz LM. Too little? Too much? Primary care physicians' views on US health care: a brief report. *Arch Intern Med*. 2011;171(17):1582-1585.

33. Emanuel EJ, Fuchs VR. The perfect storm of overutilization. *JAMA*. 2008;299(23):2789-2791.

34. Emery DJ, Shojania KG, Forster AJ, Mojaverian N, Feasby TE. Overuse of magnetic resonance imaging. *JAMA Intern Med*. 2013;173(9):823-825.

35. Kale MS, Bishop TF, Federman AD, Keyhani S. Trends in the overuse of ambulatory health care services in the united states. *JAMA Intern Med*. 2013; 173(2):142-148.

36. Kolata G. Law may do little to help curb unnecessary care. *The New York Times*, March 29, 2010. http://www.nytimes.com/2010/03/30/health/30use.html. Accessed July 7, 2013.

37. Consumer Reports. Unnecessary tests can drive up costs, harm patients. *The Washington Post*, July 25, 2011. http://www.washingtonpost.com/national/consumer-reports-unnecessary-tests-can-drive-up-costs-harm-patients/2011/06/02/gIQAIMJ9YI_story.html. Accessed November 15, 2012.

38. Parker-Pope T. Overtreatment is taking a harmful toll. *Well (New York Times)*. http://well.blogs. nytimes.com/2012/08/27/overtreatment-is-taking-a-harmful-toll/. Accessed November 15, 2012.

39. Stein PD, Beemath A, Matta F, et al. Clinical characteristics of patients with acute pulmonary embolism: data from PIOPED II. *Am J Med*. 2007;120(10):871-879.

40. Prasad V, Rho J, Cifu A. The diagnosis and treatment of pulmonary embolism: a metaphor for medicine in the evidence-based medicine era. *Arch Intern Med*. 2012;172(12):955-958.

41. Wiener RS, Schwartz LM, Woloshin S. Time trends in pulmonary embolism in the United States: evidence of overdiagnosis. *Arch Intern Med*. 2011;171(9):831-837.

42. Moynihan R, Doust J, Henry D. Preventing overdiagnosis: how to stop harming the healthy. *BMJ*. 2012;344:e3502.

43. Einstein AJ, Henzlova MJ, Rajagopalan S. Estimating risk of cancer associated with radiation exposure from 64-slice computed tomography coronary angiography. *JAMA*. 2007;298(3): 317-323.

44. Miglioretti DL, Johnson E, Williams A, et al. The use of computed tomography in pediatrics and the associated radiation exposure and estimated cancer risk. *JAMA Pediatr*. 2013; 167(8): 700-707.

45. Mitchell AM, Kline JA. Contrast nephropathy following computed tomography angiography of the chest for pulmonary embolism in the emergency department. *J Thromb Haemost*. 2007;5(1):50-54.

46. Maddox TG. Adverse reactions to contrast material: recognition, prevention, and treatment. *Am Fam Physician*. 2002;66(7):1229-1234.

47. Venkatesh AK, Kline JA, Courtney DM, et al. Evaluation of pulmonary embolism in the emergency department and consistency with a national quality measure: quantifying the opportunity for improvement. *Arch Intern Med*. 2012;172(13):1028-1032.

48. Covinsky KE. The problem of overuse. *JAMA Intern Med*. 2013;173(15):1446.

49. Drozda JP Jr. Physician performance measurement: the importance of understanding physician behavior: comment on "correlates of repeat lipid testing in patients with coronary heart disease". *JAMA Intern Med*. 2013;173(15):1444-1446.

50. DePillis, L. Worried about a San Francisco-type plane crash? They almost never happen anymore. *The Washington Post*, July 7, 2013. http://www.washingtonpost.com/blogs/wonkblog/

wp/2013/07/07/worried-about-a-san-francisco-type-plane-crash-they-almost-never-happen-anymore/. Accessed July 7, 2013.

51. Institute of Medicine. *To Err Is Human: Building a Safer Health System*. Washington, DC: National Academies Press; 1999.

52. Landrigan CP, Parry GJ, Bones CB, Hackbarth AD, Goldmann DA, Sharek PJ. Temporal trends in rates of patient harm resulting from medical care. *N Engl J Med*. 2010;363(22):2124-2134.

53. Downey JR, Hernandez-Boussard T, Banka G, Morton JM. Is patient safety improving? National trends in patient safety indicators: 1998-2007. *Health Serv Res*. 2012;47(1, pt 2):414-430.

54. Classen DC, Resar R, Griffin F, et al. "Global trigger tool" shows that adverse events in hospitals may be ten times greater than previously measured. *Health Aff*. 2011;30(4):581-589.

55. Shreve J, Van Den Bos J, Gray T, Halford M, Rustagi K, Ziemkiewicz E. *The Economic Measurement of Medical Errors*. Schaumburg, IL: The Society of Actuaries; 2010.

56. Pham HH, Schrag D, O'Malley AS, Wu B, Bach PB. Care patterns in Medicare and their implications for pay for performance. *N Engl J Med*. 2007;356(11):1130-1139.

57. Gawande A. Cowboys and pit crews. *The New Yorker*, May 26, 2011. http://www.newyorker.com/online/blogs/newsdesk/2011/05/atul-gawande-harvard-medical-school-commencement-address.html. Accessed January 3, 2013.

58. Vidyarthi AR, Arora V, Schnipper JL, Wall SD, Wachter RM. Managing discontinuity in academic medical centers: strategies for a safe and effective resident sign-out. *J Hosp Med*. 2006;1(4):257-266.

59. Arora V, Gangireddy S, Mehrotra A, Ginde R, Tormey M, Meltzer D. Ability of hospitalized patients to identify their in-hospital physicians. *Arch Intern Med*. 2009;169(2):199-201.

60. Pham HH, O'Malley AS, Bach PB, Saiontz-Martinez C, Schrag D. Primary care physicians' links to other physicians through Medicare patients: the scope of care coordination. *Ann Intern Med*. 2009;150(4):236-242.

61. Van Walraven C, Taljaard M, Bell CM, et al. Information exchange among physicians caring for the same patient in the community. *CMAJ*. 2008;179(10):1013-1018.

62. Jencks SF, Williams MV, Coleman EA. Rehospitalizations among patients in the Medicare fee-for-service program. *N Engl J Med*. 2009;360(14):1418-1428.

63. Kripalani S, LeFevre F, Phillips CO, Williams MV, Basaviah P, Baker DW. Deficits in communication and information transfer between hospital-based and primary care physicians: implications for patient safety and continuity of care. *JAMA*. 2007;297(8):831-841.

64. Leatherman S, McCarthy D. *Quality of Health Care in the United States: A Chartbook*. New York, NY: The Commonwealth Fund; 2002. http://www.commonwealthfund.org/usr_doc/leatherman_chbk_520.pdf. Accessed March 15, 2014.

65. Cain C, Haque S. Organizational workflow and its impact on work quality. In: Hughes RG, ed. *Patient Safety and Quality: An Evidence-Based Handbook for Nurses. Advances in Patient Safety*. Rockville, MD: Agency for Healthcare Research and Quality; 2008. http://www.ncbi.nlm.nih.gov/books/NBK2638/. Accessed July 13, 2013.

66. Debono DS, Greenfield D, Travaglia JF, et al. Nurses' workarounds in acute healthcare settings: a scoping review. *BMC Health Serv Res*. 2013;13:175.

67. Halbesleben JRB, Savage GT, Wakefield DS, Wakefield BJ. Rework and workarounds in nurse medication administration process: implications for work processes and patient safety. *Health Care Manage Rev*. 2010;35(2):124-133.

68. Koppel R, Wetterneck T, Telles JL, Karsh B-T. Workarounds to barcode medication administration systems: their occurrences, causes, and threats to patient safety. *J Am Med Inform Assoc*. 2008;15(4):408-423.

69. Yang Z, Ng B-Y, Kankanhalli A, Luen Yip JW. Workarounds in the use of IS in healthcare: a case study of an electronic medication administration system. *Int J Human-Computer Studies*. 2012;70(1):43-65.

70. Spear SJ, Schmidhofer M. Ambiguity and workarounds as contributors to medical error. *Ann Intern Med*. 2005;142(8):627-630.

71. Hendrich A, Chow MP, Skierczynski BA, Lu Z. A 36-Hospital Time and Motion Study: how do medical-surgical nurses spend their time? *Perm J.* 2008;12(3):25-34.
72. Block L, Habicht R, Wu AW, et al. In the wake of the 2003 and 2011 duty hours regulations, how do internal medicine interns spend their time? *J Gen Intern Med.* 2013.
73. Verghese A. Culture shock—patient as icon, icon as patient. *N Engl J Med.* 2008;359(26): 2748-2751.
74. Casalino LP, Nicholson S, Gans DN, et al. What does it cost physician practices to interact with health insurance plans? *Health Aff (Millwood).* 2009;28(4):w533-w543.
75. Morra D, Nicholson S, Levinson W, Gans DN, Hammons T, Casalino LP. US physician practices versus Canadians: spending nearly four times as much money interacting with payers. *Health Affairs.* 2011;30(8):1443-1450.
76. Cebul RD, Rebitzer JB, Taylor LJ, Votruba ME. Organizational fragmentation and care quality in the U.S. healthcare system. *J Econ Perspect.* 2008;22(4):93-113.
77. Enthoven AC, Fuchs VR. Employment-based health insurance: past, present, and future. *Health Aff.* 2006;25(6):1538-1547.
78. Anderson GF, Reinhardt UE, Hussey PS, Petrosyan V. It's the prices, stupid: why the United States is so different from other countries. *Health Aff (Millwood).* 2003;22(3):89-105.
79. Klein E. Why an MRI costs $1,080 in America and $280 in France. *The Washington Post—Blogs.* 2012. http://www.washingtonpost.com/blogs/ezra-klein/post/why-an-mri-costs-1080-in-america-and-280-in-france/2011/08/25/gIQAVHztoR_blog.html?tid=pm_business_pop. Accessed November 15, 2012.
80. Experts in Chronic Myeloid Leukemia. Price of drugs for chronic myeloid leukemia (CML), reflection of the unsustainable cancer drug prices: perspective of CML experts. *Blood.* 2013.
81. Putting the Brakes on Health Care Fraud. FBI. http://www.fbi.gov/news/stories/2012/november/putting-the-brakes-on-health-care-fraud/putting-the-brakes-on-health-care-fraud. Accessed July 14, 2013.
82. Grow B, Bigg M. Special report: Phantom firms bleed millions from Medicare. *Reuters,* December 21, 2011. http://www.reuters.com/article/2011/12/21/us-shellcompanies-medicare-idUSTRE7BK0PY20111221. Accessed July 14, 2013.
83. Eisler P, Hansen B. Doctors perform thousands of unnecessary surgeries. *USA Today,* June 20, 2013. http://www.usatoday.com/story/news/nation/2013/06/18/unnecessary-surgery-usa-today-investigation/2435009/. Accessed July 14, 2013.
84. Federal Bureau of Investigations (FBI). Health Care Fraud. http://www.fbi.gov/about-us/investigate/white_collar/health-care-fraud/health_care_fraud. Accessed July 14, 2013.
85. McGlynn EA, Asch SM, Adams J, et al. The quality of health care delivered to adults in the United States. *N Engl J Med.* 2003;348(26):2635-2645.
86. Yarnall KSH, Østbye T, Krause KM, Pollak KI, Gradison M, Michener JL. Family physicians as team leaders: "time" to share the care. *Prev Chronic Dis.* 2009;6(2):A59.
87. Murray CJL, Abraham J, Ali MK, et al. The state of US health, 1990-2010: burden of diseases, injuries, and risk factors. *JAMA.* 2013;310(6):591-606.

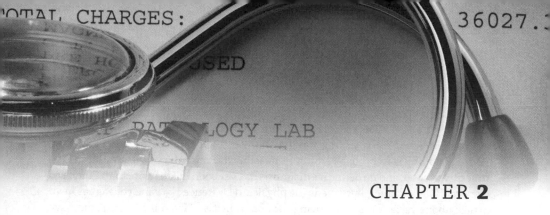

Paying for Healthcare in the United States

Mr James Green is a 28-year-old man living in San Diego, California. He splits his nights between working as a server at a small restaurant, and his true passion—playing guitar in a local rock band. He is currently uninsured, but has always been healthy. This evening he was waiting tables at the restaurant when he began to have pain in his lower abdomen. He tried to ignore it and keep working but it steadily worsened. By the time he returned home from his shift, he was clenching his belly, uncomfortable and worried. Not knowing what to do or how worried he should be, he typed, "belly pain" into a search engine on the Internet. A list of "searches related to belly pain" returned[1]:

- *Appendicitis:* "A serious medical condition in which the appendix becomes inflamed and painful."
- *Gastroenteritis:* "Inflammation of the stomach and intestines typically resulting from bacterial toxins or viral infection."
- *Stomach flu:* "A short-lived stomach disorder of unknown cause, popularly attributed to a virus."
- *Irritable bowel syndrome:* "A widespread condition involving recurrent abdominal pain and diarrhea or constipation, often associated with stress, depression, anxiety, or previous intestinal infection."

James does not know if his abdominal pain could be something urgent like appendicitis or something "short-lived" like the stomach flu. He becomes very anxious about the emergency department (ED) and how much it might cost. This episode of abdominal pain could cost him about $100 for a simple urgent care visit, a couple thousand dollars for imaging, or tens of thousands of dollars for surgical treatment, and he has no way to know which it will be. He decides that he will try to "tough it out" a little longer. He lies down in bed, but by the middle of the night he is vomiting and curled over in pain. He calls a friend and asks him to come urgently to bring him to the hospital. He ultimately is diagnosed with a ruptured appendix from untreated appendicitis.

Adding to Mr Green's initial uncertainty about access to care and how much it may cost is the fact that once a patient like him with severe abdominal pain arrives at the ED, he really has no way of knowing whether the care that his physician is ordering—and he is paying for—is the most appropriate for his condition. "Price shopping is improbable, if not impossible, because the services are complex, urgently needed, and no definitive diagnosis has yet been made," notes San Francisco General Hospital emergency medicine physician Dr Renee Hsia and colleagues in an article about variation in ED pricing for appendicitis.[2] "Even if a patient did have the luxury of time and clinical knowledge to 'shop around,' we found ... hospitals charge patients inconsistently for what should be similar services."

WHY WE NEED HEALTH INSURANCE

In the early 20th century, physicians often individually negotiated fees with patients based on their ability to pay.[3] During this time, out-of-pocket cash payment for medical care was the norm, and by far the most common method of reimbursement.[4] In cases where patients had limited ability to pay, physicians would barter or informally subsidize care by charging wealthy patients more and poor patients less.[3] On the surface, this seems to make the most sense since virtually every other service or commodity that we purchase in the United States is paid for "out-of-pocket." However, since that time, the complexity and cost of healthcare delivery have increased exponentially. This has made critical services too expensive to pay for in cash for most citizens and challenging to anticipate.

Compared to other service industries, healthcare is exceptional for a number of reasons. The first is that many people consider basic healthcare a necessity rather than a luxury. If healthcare is indeed a basic need, then a social contract to insure affordable care is appropriate. This is why health insurance differs from other forms of insurance, such as homeowner's insurance, which is seen as an optional safeguard and therefore an individual responsibility. The challenge has always been in defining how much healthcare is actually "needed."

In addition, as shown in the case of Mr James Green, the need for and cost of healthcare services are challenging to predict, making it difficult (and often impossible) to adequately plan for these expenses. Even under "more predictable" healthcare scenarios, such as a planned pregnancy where it would be conceivable for one to save for the eventual delivery costs, it is still rarely possible to know whether the cost will be a few thousand dollars for a routine delivery, tens of thousands for needed emergent care, such as a surgical cesarean delivery ("C-section"), or hundreds of thousands for a prolonged stay for the newborn in a neonatal intensive care unit to treat an unforeseen problem. It is this uncertainty that underlies why we buy health insurance. Health insurance is important "not just because healthcare is expensive (which it is)," stated Harvard health economists Katherine Baicker and Amitabh Chandra.[5] "Lots of other things are expensive, too, including housing and college tuition, but we don't have insurance to help us purchase them because they are not uncertain in the way that potentially needing very expensive medical care is."

Another barrier to simple out-of-pocket purchasing of healthcare is that patients strongly rely on healthcare professionals to help guide their decisions. Under many circumstances they cannot make the purchasing decisions on their own since they require specialized knowledge. *"Mr. Smith, would you like me to treat your pneumonia with azithromycin, doxycycline, levofloxacin, ceftriaxone or intravenous piperacillin/tazobactam?"* This is not a fair question to ask a patient that does not have adequate knowledge about the potential risks and benefits of each of these medications, or the most likely microorganism causing their pneumonia.

In the United States, we have health insurance exactly because of the great uncertainty of who will need expensive and potentially life-saving care and when they will need it. We can confidently predict that some of us will be in an accident and need emergent surgical procedures, some of us will contract deadly infectious diseases requiring treatment, and some of us will develop cancer and will require expensive chemotherapy and radiation treatments. We just can't predict who will need this and when. At its most basic level, all insurance is designed to mitigate risk of financial catastrophe. Insurance ideally spreads this predictable population-level risk among the entire group so that the unlucky afflicted individuals can afford to have these vital therapies when they need it. The idea is that life-saving therapy should not necessarily deplete one's life savings. One of the great challenges in modern healthcare, however, is that health insurance may also be necessary to make noncatastrophic and routine care affordable, and that different patients may carry very different healthcare risks.

HOW DID WE GET HERE: A BRIEF HISTORY OF HEALTH INSURANCE IN THE UNITED STATES

Private insurance

During World War II, companies in the United States faced a labor shortage, but due to wage and price controls in place they were unable to compete for workers by promising increased wages. Instead, they began to offer insurance as a benefit to entice employees.[4] Thus the "fringe benefit" of employer-sponsored health insurance was born. Following the war, unions began to negotiate for health benefits, and a series of federal rules were enacted regulating how employer-sponsored insurance would be treated with respect to federal taxes and labor negotiations. This led to a rapid increase in private insurance.[6] The number of persons enrolled in private health plans catapulted between 1940 and 1950 from 20.6 million to 142.3 million.[7] At its peak in the year 2000, employer-sponsored insurance covered 66.8% of all nonelderly Americans.[7]

Currently, the majority of Americans under the age of 65 obtain health insurance from more than 1.5 million different employers, who in turn purchase insurance plans from more than 1200 different insurers.[8] This has led private insurance in the United States to be a decentralized and nonstandardized system. As discussed further in Chapter 3, this insurance system is built on separate "negotiated fees" to providers. This means that different health plans will pay different rates for the same care to different providers; and providers will accept different rates for the same care from different plans. The question of "how much does surgery for appendicitis cost," may not be met with an answer, but rather with the questions, "for whom, when, and where?"

These complexities and issues have led prominent Princeton health economist Uwe Reinhardt to state, "If we had to do it over again, no policy analyst would recommend this model."[7] Regardless, it is the world that we live in and the model that we now must work with.

Who really pays for employer-based health insurance?

Although private insurance companies administer the vast majority of employer-based insurance, this system is actually floating on a substantial government subsidy. While employers pay most of the health insurance premiums for their employees, this expense is tax-deductible, resulting in roughly $260 billion annually in foregone tax income for US state and federal governments (in 2009).[9] This is by far the largest of the tax expenditures by the federal government.[9]

In addition, despite the term "employer-sponsored insurance," employees themselves actually pay for their health insurance in the form of foregone wages and other benefits. For example some employers will offer their employees the choice of either receiving health insurance as a pretax benefit or receiving a higher salary. "In 2005, the average premium for family coverage of healthcare was $10,880, which, for the first time, was the equivalent of the wages paid annually to a minimum-wage worker," health care policy expert Dr David Blumenthal has pointed out.[7] "Thus, nested within the compensation package of each American worker with family coverage is the equivalent of another worker paid the minimum wage." Increasing medical costs (premiums plus out-of-pocket expenses plus taxes devoted to healthcare) have led to stagnant real incomes for US families over the past decade.[10]

Individual private insurance. An alternative to employment-based health insurance is individual private insurance. Individual insurance is a relatively small but growing market. This is partially driven by the relentless skyrocketing annual premiums that have led employers, particularly small businesses, to no longer offer comprehensive benefits.[11] In 2009, 11 million nonelderly Americans had private individual health insurance at some time during the year.[12]

Individual insurance generally costs more than employer-based insurance due to additional administrative and marketing costs and the higher risks that insurers bear with these policies.[11,13] In addition, individuals have less bargaining power in negotiating premium fees compared with larger employers—a fact that motivated the formation of *health insurance exchanges* under the Patient Protection and Affordable Care Act (ACA), detailed below. More than half of adults who tried to purchase individual insurance in 2007 found it very difficult to impossible to find a plan they could afford, and 36% said they were turned down or charged a higher price because of a preexisting condition.[11] As many as three-quarters of those seeking coverage in the individual insurance market between 2004 and 2007 did not end up buying a plan, most often because the premium was too high.[11] Traditionally, these plans also tend to have less generous benefits than employment-related insurance, such as higher deductibles and *copayments* (Table 2-1 for insurance term definitions) and lower likelihood of prescription drug coverage.[12] This ultimately leads to higher out-of-pocket costs for patients.[14]

Table 2-1 **Common health insurance terms and definitions**

Health Insurance Term	Definition
Accountable Care Organization (ACO)	Groups of doctors, hospitals, and other healthcare providers, who come together voluntarily to give coordinated high-quality care.
Beneficiary	The person that receives any of the benefits of the insurance coverage.
Capitation	The payment of a fee to a healthcare provider providing services to a number of people, such that the amount paid is determined by the number of total patients.
Coinsurance	The amount a beneficiary must pay for medical care after they have met their deductible. For instance, the insurance company may pay for 80% of an approved amount, and the patient's coinsurance will be for 20%.
Copayment	The flat fee that a beneficiary must pay each time they receive medical care. For example, a patient may pay a $10 copay for every doctor visit, while the insurance plan covers the rest of the cost.
Coverage limits	The maximum amount that a health insurance plan may pay for certain healthcare services. Some health insurance policies may also have a maximum annual or lifetime coverage amount. After any of these limits are reached, then the policyholder may have to pay for all remaining costs.
Deductible	The amount the beneficiary must pay each year before their health insurance coverage plan begins paying.
Exclusions/limitations	Services that are not covered by a plan. These must be clearly defined in the plan literature.
Fee-for-service (FFS)	A payment system where healthcare services are unbundled and paid for separately.

(Continued)

Table 2-1 **Common health insurance terms and definitions** (*Continued*)

Health Insurance Term	Definition
Formulary	An insurance providers list of covered drugs.
Health Maintenance Organization (HMO)	A form of managed care in which all care is received from participating providers within the network. A referral from a primary care provider needs to be obtained prior to seeing specialists.
Health reimbursement account (HRA)	An account established by an employer to pay an employee's medical expenses. Only the employer can contribute to a HRA.
Health savings account (HSA)	An account established by an employer or an individual to save money toward medical expenses on a tax-free basis.
High-deductible health plan (HDHP)	A plan that provides comprehensive coverage for high-cost medical events but features a high deductible coupled with a limit on annual out-of-pocket expense.
Individual health insurance	Insurance coverage purchased independently (as opposed to as part of a group), usually directly from an insurance company.
Medicaid	A federal program administered by individual States to provide healthcare for certain poor and low-income individuals and families.
Medicare	A federal insurance program that provides healthcare coverage to eligible individuals aged 65 and older and certain disabled people (such as those with end-stage renal disease).
Network	A group of physicians, hospitals, and other providers who participate in a particular managed care plan.
Out-of-pocket maxima	The maximum amount that an insured person can pay, after which the insurance plan pays all further covered costs. Out-of-pocket maxima may be limited to a specific benefit category (such as prescription drugs) or can apply to all coverage provided during a specific benefit year.
Preferred provider organization (PPO)	A form of managed care in which insurance policyholders have more flexibility in choosing physicians and other providers than in an HMO. Both participating and nonparticipating providers may be seen, however the out-of-pocket expenses paid by the policyholder will vary.
Premium	The amount the insurance policyholder pays to belong to a health plan. In general under employer-sponsored health insurance, the employee's share of premiums is usually deducted from their pay.

Sources: Agency for Healthcare Research and Quality. Questions and Answers About Health Insurance. http://archive.ahrq.gov/consumer/insuranceqa/qaglossary.htm. Accessed August 15, 2013; Medicare.gov. Accessed August 31, 2013; Bodenheimer T, Grumbach K. *Understanding Health Policy: A Clinical Approach*. 6th ed. New York, NY: McGraw-Hill Medical; 2012.

In summary, due to multiple economic factors, an increasing number of Americans are seeking private individual health insurance, and thus may be at great risk for higher premiums and exposure to out-of-pocket costs.[11,14]

Government-financed insurance

In a system where the majority of insurance is employment based, naturally as Americans age and retire they would no longer be covered. This leaves those who generally need healthcare the most—the elderly—without any insurance. In fact, in the late 1950s, less than 15% of the elderly had health insurance.[15] In addition, those that are unemployed, and therefore often poor, are also left out of an employment-based market. In response to these significant gaps, President Lyndon B. Johnson enacted tax-financed government health insurance in 1965, aiming to provide affordable care for the elderly (Medicare) and the poor (Medicaid).[16]

Although the creation of Medicare and Medicaid occurred in the 1960s, it is important to highlight that discussions of public insurance have dominated congressional debate since at least the 1930s. Shortly following his first election in 1932, President Franklin D. Roosevelt decided not to pursue universal healthcare.[7] Although President Roosevelt had led the expansion of other government programs and had assigned a group to work on proposals to add healthcare reform to the Social Security Act, this met staunch resistance from the medical establishment, including prominently from the American Medical Association (AMA) who denounced "socialist medicine."[17] Despite the resistance, some see this as the most likely opportunity to have established national universal healthcare in the United States. Of interest, the father-in-law of President Roosevelt's son was famous neurosurgeon Dr Harvey Cushing, who notably opposed the enactment of federal health insurance on its merits, and may have also affected President Roosevelt's stance on the matter.[7]

Medicare

Medicare is a federal health insurance program for all people aged 65 and older, regardless of income or medical history. It also provides coverage for those under 65 years if they have end-stage renal disease, or are blind. In 2012, Medicare covered approximately 50 million Americans, representing one-sixth of the total population.[18] The Medicare program is structured into four parts (Table 2-2: Medicare Parts A-D).

Medicare plays a fundamental role in providing healthcare coverage for elderly Americans.[19] About 40% of people on Medicare have at least three chronic medical conditions, and almost a quarter of Medicare beneficiaries have cognitive impairments.[20] These patients frequently visit physicians, obtain expensive healthcare services, and often require hospitalization. In fact, almost 50% of Medicare beneficiaries are hospitalized at least once over a 4-year period.[21]

Despite its noble mission to provide affordable healthcare for the elderly, "Medicare by itself offers only limited protection against economic ruin."[19]

Table 2-2 Medicare parts A-D

	Description	Coverage	Premium Payments	Portion of Benefit Spending
Medicare Part A	Hospital insurance plan largely financed through social security taxes from employers and employees.	Covers inpatient hospital stays, skilled nursing facility stays, home health visits, and hospice care.	Most people do not pay a premium as long as they or their spouse paid Medicare taxes while working. If one does not qualify for "premium-free Medicare Part A," then they may pay up to $441 each month (2013). Benefits are subject to a deductible ($1184 for each benefit period [2013]) and coinsurance.	Accounts for 31% of total benefit spending (2012)
Medicare Part B	Outpatient services insurance financed by federal taxes and monthly premiums from beneficiaries. Covers people that are eligible for Medicare Part A and elect to pay the Medicare Part B premium.	Covers physician visits, outpatient services, preventive services, and home health visits. Also covers required durable medical equipment, such as wheelchairs and walkers.	Most people will pay a standard premium amount ($104.90 [2013]), however this amount may be adjusted up or down based on the beneficiaries' income. Subject to deductible ($147 [2013]).	Accounts for 20% of total benefit spending (2012)

Medicare Part C	The "Medicare Advantage Program," through which beneficiaries can enroll in a private health plan (such as an HMO) and receive all Medicare-covered benefits.	Plans may cover Part A, Part B, and/or Part D services.	Subject to premiums and deductibles determined by the private health plan, which vary.	Accounts for 22% of total benefit spending (2012)
Medicare Part D	The voluntary, subsidized outpatient prescription drug benefit.	Provides coverage for outpatient prescription drugs.	Most Medicare Prescription Drug Plans charge a monthly premium that varies by the plan (this is paid in addition to the Medicare Part B premium). Deductibles vary between Medicare drug plans, but may not exceed $325 (2013). The plans include copayments and/or coinsurance for prescription drugs, and many include "tiers" for different medications (see Chapter 13).	Accounts for 11% of total benefit spending (2012)

Sources: Medicare.gov (accessed August 31, 2013); Bodenheimer T, Grumbach K. Understanding Health Policy: A Clinical Approach. 6th ed. New York, NY: McGraw-Hill Medical; 2012.

During the last 5 years of life, average out-of-pocket expenditures for patients with Medicare were almost $40,000 for individuals and more than $50,000 for couples in which one spouse dies.[22] This is at least partially due to the fact that the "basic benefit lacks a cap on out-of-pocket spending, so beneficiaries are exposed to the risk of open-ended cost sharing, which can generate substantial financial strain (or deplete assets for surviving spouses)."[19] In fact, the end-of-life expenditures described above exceeded baseline total household assets in a quarter of all patients, and 43% of patients' spending surpassed their nonhousing assets.[22]

On a national level, Medicare spending was estimated in 2012 to account for 21% of total national health spending.[18] Medicare spending per person is rising slower than private insurance, but the elderly population is growing. It is projected that the Medicare population will grow from 50 million to 81 million Americans by 2030.[20] The Medicare solvency crisis is approaching "slowly but inexorably."[19]

Over the years, attempts to expand government-subsidized insurance via Medicare by both republican and democratic administrations (Kennedy, Nixon, Ford, Clinton) were ultimately challenged by tension between the roles of private versus public insurance.

Medicaid

Medicaid, which aims to provide health coverage for the poor, is the largest public health insurance program in the United States, covering roughly 1 in 5 Americans, and 1 in 3 children—these numbers are prior to the implementation of the ACA, which expanded eligibility to millions more poor Americans (see "The Affordable Care Act of 2010").[23] The federal Medicaid program is administered by the individual states, with the federal government paying between 50% and 76% of total state Medicaid costs, based on the financial status of the state (Medicaid pays at least 50% by law, but pays more in poorer states).[23]

To qualify for Medicaid a person must meet financial criteria for low-income and also belong to one of Medicaid's eligible groups[24]:

- Children
- Pregnant women
- Adults with dependent children
- People with severe disabilities (wheelchair-bound)
- Seniors age 65 and over, sometimes referred to as "dual-eligibles"

More than half of all Medicaid enrollees are children, but nonelderly adults (mostly working parents) make up another quarter. Without Medicaid, most of these beneficiaries would be uninsured or lack the coverage for care that they need.[23,25]

The federal government requires that a broad set of services be covered under Medicaid, including hospital, physician, laboratory, x-ray, prenatal, preventive, nursing home and home health services.[24] Medicaid improves access to care for

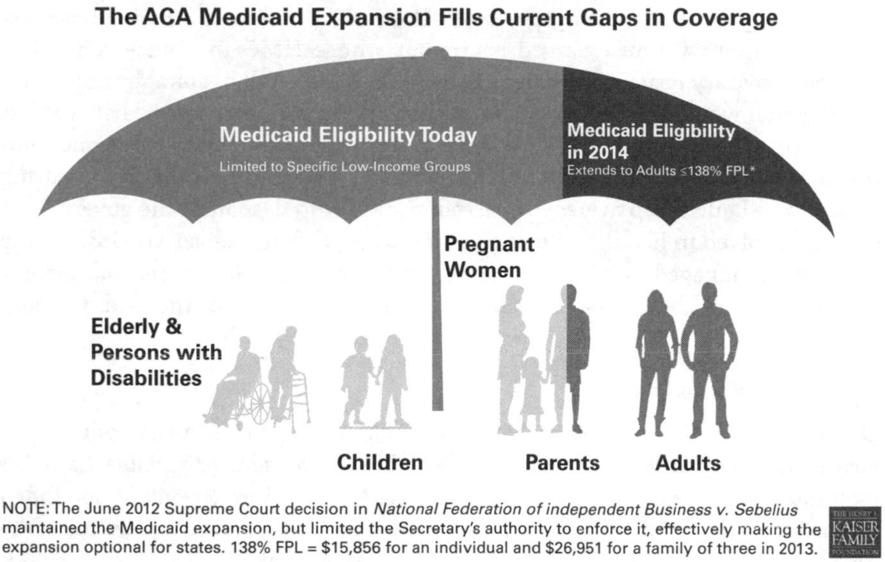

The ACA Medicaid Expansion Fills Current Gaps in Coverage

Medicaid Eligibility Today
Limited to Specific Low-Income Groups

Medicaid Eligibility in 2014
Extends to Adults ≤138% FPL*

Pregnant Women

Elderly & Persons with Disabilities

Children

Parents

Adults

NOTE: The June 2012 Supreme Court decision in *National Federation of independent Business v. Sebelius* maintained the Medicaid expansion, but limited the Secretary's authority to enforce it, effectively making the expansion optional for states. 138% FPL = $15,856 for an individual and $26,951 for a family of three in 2013.

Figure 2-1. The Medicaid expansion. (Reproduced, with permission, from The Henry J. Kaiser Family Foundation. Available at http://kff.org/health-reform/slide/the-aca-medicaid-expansion-fills-current-gaps-in-coverage/. Accessed January 16, 2015.)

a group of patients that generally would otherwise be uninsured.[26] As discussed further below, the ACA is leading to a large Medicaid expansion in most states (Figure 2-1).

Managed care and the counterrevolution

During the 1990s, managed care promised to control costs without imposing financial risk on patients. Managed care limits patients to visiting only certain doctors and hospitals, whose costs of care and treatment are being monitored aggressively by a managing company. *Healthcare maintenance organizations* (HMOs) are generally recognized as the first form of managed care.

There were some early successes, with the rate of increase in real healthcare costs falling about two percentage points below its historical trend during the 1993-1997 period.[27] This stretch of low cost-growth had not been seen since prior to World War II.[27]

However, a strong backlash by both the public and healthcare providers against managed care took hold. This led to a counterrevolution, "in part because providers disliked the increased price competition and because neither providers nor consumers liked the command-and-control utilization review methods."[27] Perhaps the public perception of the evils of the managed care system at the time was best embodied via Hollywood dramatic hyperbole. The 2002 feature film starring Denzel Washington, titled "John Q,"[28] followed a man whose son was diagnosed with an enlarged heart, but whose HMO insurance refused to cover a necessary heart transplant. John Q then took a full hospital hostage until the hospital would put his son's name on the heart donor recipient list. The "us versus them" ethos was clearly galvanized. Another example was an iconic commercial sponsored by the Health Insurance Association of America featuring "Harry and Louise," an average American couple who despaired the government getting involved in healthcare using the message "if they choose, you lose."[29] The recoil from managed care led to a strong swing of the pendulum and subsequent unrestricted healthcare practices and resultant cost growth for the next decade.

The Affordable Care Act of 2010

On March 23, 2010, President Barack Obama signed into law the comprehensive health reform legislation, the Patient Protection and Affordable Care Act (commonly referred to as "Obamacare" or "ACA").[30] As Vice President Joe Biden infamously whispered during the ceremony—and was picked up by a nearby microphone—"Mr President, this is a big [expletive] deal."[30]

The ACA is primarily aimed at decreasing the number of uninsured Americans and reducing the overall costs of healthcare. It also contains reforms hoping to improve healthcare outcomes and streamline healthcare delivery.[31]

The ACA includes numerous provisions to take effect over several years beginning back in 2010 (see timeline, Figure 2-2).

The most relevant piece of this legislation for the context of this discussion is the expansion of insurance coverage via two major mechanisms: the expansion of Medicaid coverage and the establishment of state-level health insurance exchanges. The Medicaid coverage expansion was designed to cover all adults whose family income is below 133% of the federal poverty level (approximately $15,000 for a single individual and $30,000 for a family of four) by 2014[32,33]; however, the Supreme Court ruling in 2012 allows states to choose whether or not to expand their Medicaid programs.[34]

The other major attempt under the ACA to increase health insurance access is the implementation of health insurance exchanges, which are meant to provide more organized, transparent, and competitive markets for individuals seeking to buy health insurance.[32] The idea is that these exchanges offer clear information to people to help them pick an insurance plan that best suits their needs. Health plans participating in the exchanges are also required to offer a package of "essential benefits" (such as basic maternity and newborn care). [35] The ACA provides insurance premium subsidies for people living below approximately $88,000 for a family of four (or 400% of the federal poverty limit in 2014).[31,32]

The Congressional Budget Office (CBO) originally estimated that the legislation would reduce the number of uninsured residents by 30 million, leaving 25 million uninsured residents in 2019 after the bill's provisions have all taken

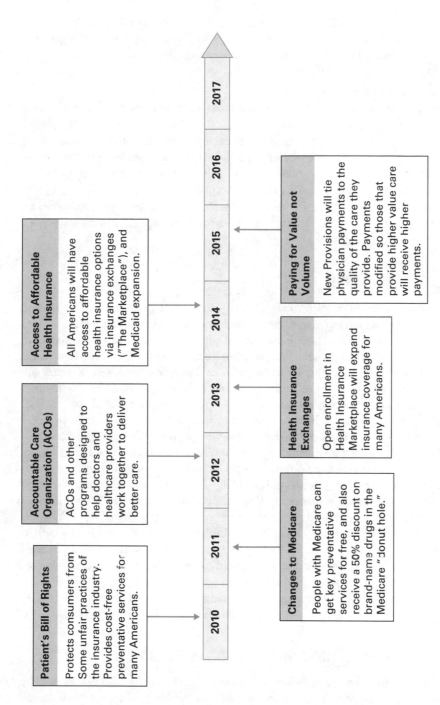

Patient's Bill of Rights

Protects consumers from Some unfair practices of the insurance industry. Provides cost-free preventative services for many Americans.

Accountable Care Organization (ACOs)

ACOs and other programs designed to help doctors and healthcare providers work together to deliver better care.

Access to Affordable Health Insurance

All Americans will have access to affordable health insurance options via insurance exchanges ("The Marketplace"), and Medicaid expansion.

Changes to Medicare

People with Medicare can get key preventative services for free, and also receive a 50% discount on brand-name drugs in the Medicare "donut hole."

Health Insurance Exchanges

Open enrollment in Health Insurance Marketplace will expand insurance coverage for many Americans.

Paying for Value not Volume

New Provisions will tie physician payments to the quality of the care they provide. Payments modified so those that provide higher value care will receive higher payments.

2010 2011 2012 2013 2014 2015 2016 2017

Figure 2-2. The Affordable Care Act—timeline. (Adapted from: Key Features of the Affordable Care Act, By Year | HealthCare.gov. http://www.healthcare.gov/law/timeline/full.html. Accessed August 13, 2013.)

effect, but in July 2012 the CBO updated the estimate by raising the expected number of uninsured by 3 million, due to the successful Supreme Court legal challenge to the ACA's mandated expansion of Medicaid.[36]

Among the remaining uninsured will be[37]

- Undocumented immigrants
- People who do not sign up for Medicaid (citizens not enrolled in Medicaid despite being eligible)
- People who feel that insurance is unaffordable (citizens not otherwise covered and opting to pay the annual penalty instead of purchasing insurance [likely mostly younger and single Americans] and citizens whose insurance coverage would cost more than 8% of household income and are exempt from paying the annual penalty)
- People who live in states that opt out of the Medicaid expansion and who qualify for neither existing Medicaid coverage nor subsidized coverage through the states' new insurance exchanges

THE UNDERINSURED

A lot of focus has been paid to the striking number of uninsured in the United States, but merely having insurance coverage does not necessarily protect patients medically or financially. There is no universally accepted definition for the term "*underinsurance*," but it generally refers to healthcare insurance that requires excessive out-of-pocket expenditures, has significant limits regarding what services are covered, or fails to cover healthcare expenses that are perceived by the insured person to be essential to his or her health.[38] Another way to think about it is that "underinsurance" occurs whenever there are potential barriers to healthcare access due to out-of-pocket costs of care for people who have health insurance.[39]

In 2007, there were an estimated 25 million Americans considered to be underinsured.[40] Of note, this does not include the 45 million Americans with no insurance at all at that time. In one study published in 2012, 1 in 6 parents reported that their child was underinsured.[41] With the surge in the number of Americans—particularly young Americans—now being enrolled in *high-deductible health plans* (see "High-deductible health plans"), the number of underinsured in the United States is at an all-time high.[40,42] A study by the Commonwealth Fund proclaimed that full implementation of the ACA could potentially reduce the number of underinsured adults by 70%,[43] although this remains to be seen.

Underinsurance and increased cost sharing is associated with less access to care, foregone medical treatments, and high financial stress for patients.[40]

EVERYBODY PAYS: COST SHARING FOR PATIENTS

Different health plans have different degrees of "cost sharing." These fees paid by individuals for specific medical services come in the form of *copays, coinsurance, deductibles*, and other *"consumer-driven health plan"* mechanisms (Table 2-1 contains definitions for common insurance terms), as discussed below.

Copays and coinsurance

A copayment is the amount paid by the insured person each time a medical service is accessed. This is technically different than coinsurance, which is a percentage payment after the deductible up to a certain limit. Coinsurance payments usually contribute to the policy *out-of-pocket maxima*, whereas copays generally do not.

Insurance companies designed these mechanisms with the idea of discouraging *"moral hazards"* with regard to unnecessary care. Moral hazards describe the situation in which one has a greater tendency to take risks (or in this case, seek unnecessary care) because they are not exposed to the costs that could incur. It is like playing roulette using someone else's stack of money—you do not feel the risk. Conversely, designing insurance that requires cost-sharing with patients can discourage *necessary* care as well. The best evidence for this is described by the famous RAND Health Insurance Experiment, which is explored in further detail below. Briefly, the experiment demonstrated that patients with the highest coinsurance rates utilized the least care. However, this cost-sharing resulted in a detrimental effect on a variety of health outcomes ranging from visual acuity to blood pressure control. Recent work suggests even small amounts of cost-sharing may deter patients from important services such as mammograms.[44]

Cost sharing strategies are typically used by payers to discourage individuals from choosing more costly services. For instance, some insurance companies set the copay percentage for non-generic drugs much higher than for generic drugs (see Chapter 13). One of the problems is that physicians—sometimes unwittingly—prescribe brand-name drugs causing patients to potentially have higher copays. In one study, 4 of 10 physicians reported that they sometimes or often prescribe a brand-name drug to a patient when a generic is available because the patient wanted it, but it was unclear how informed these patients were of the higher costs.[45]

As previously discussed, copays and coinsurance can lead to substantial out-of-pocket costs.

High-deductible health plans

A deductible is a certain amount of money that insurance policy holders must pay before their insurance begins to pay for any services. A deductible may apply to all care in a year, or it might be service-specific (ie, a health plan may have a $500 deductible for each hospitalization). High-deductible health plans (HDHPs) are defined by the US Internal Revenue Service (IRS) as plans that have "(1) a higher annual deductible than typical health plans, and (2) a maximum limit on the sum of the annual deductible and out-of-pocket medical expenses that you must pay for covered expenses. Out-of-pocket expenses include copayments and other

Table 2-3 The minimum and maximum annual deductibles and other out-of-pocket expenses for high-deductible health plans in 2013

	Self Only Coverage	Family Coverage
Minimum annual deductible	$1,250	$2,500
Maximum annual deductible and other out-of-pocket expenses	$6,250	$12,500

Source: Internal Revenue Service. *Health Savings Accounts and Other Tax-Favored Health Plans.* 2013. http://www.irs.gov/pub/irs-pdf/p969.pdf. Accessed February 8, 2013.

amounts, but do not include premiums."[46] The federally mandated minimum and maximum annual deductibles for HDHPs in 2012 are shown in Table 2-3. Note that under these plans a family could be liable for up to $12,500 in out-of-pocket medical expenses (in addition to paid premiums) during a single year.[46]

More Americans than ever before are currently on HDHPs, leading to increasing numbers of insured, nonelderly adults having difficulty paying their medical bills.[42]

Story From the Frontlines—"All This for a Migraine?"

Last year, I experienced one of the scariest moments of my life. I was a student in the Masters of Public Health Program at Brown University. After taking a break to watch a Sunday afternoon football game alone in my apartment, I sat down at my desk in an attempt to finish writing a paper. I suddenly noticed little flashes of light in my vision. I drank some water thinking that I might be dehydrated, when my lips and fingers started to tingle. I continued typing but when I looked up, all of the words that I had just typed were spelled wrong. I tried unsuccessfully to send a text message, then called my mom (who, thankfully, lives only thirty minutes away) and could barely get the words out. I sat on the floor, my heart racing, waiting for help to arrive, and panicking that I might be suffering a stroke.

I spent several anxious hours in the Rhode Island Hospital Emergency Room, eventually being seen by the attending physician, a third-year medical student, and neurologist consultant. They all suspected that I had experienced a "silent" migraine, but the neurologist suggested that I get an MRI to make sure. Since I was dealing with the US health care system, I first had to go to my primary care physician who would then make a referral so that the MRI would be covered by my health insurance.

After meeting with my primary care doctor, I received the referral; the next step was to find a testing center that was part of my "preferred provider network." Luckily, there was an imaging center at my local hospital, which was part of the preferred network. Later, I got the MRI results back from my primary doctor who said that everything looked okay and that it must have been only a migraine. Ironically, that's when the real headache started.

Several months after the migraine incident, I got a bill for close to $2000. The bill was for the MRI that I received at the hospital. I called the hospital to see what was going on and they told me that I needed to call my health insurance company. When I called the claims agency for my insurance, the agent told me that I had been charged for using an out-of-network provider (ie, I owed 70% of the total cost of the procedure). I was advised to call the hospital billing department to ask them to resubmit the claim so that they could check to see if my visit was covered within the provider network. I called the hospital and the agent said that he would pass the information on to the billing department. Thinking that everything was taken care of, I went about my normal life until I received the exact same bill in the mail. I spent the next several months on a roller coaster of communications with the hospital, insurance provider, and the insurer's claims department.

Generally, I would call the hospital and be advised to call the insurance company, who would then tell me to call elsewhere. This pattern would repeat itself over and over again.

There are times now when I am hopeful that the issue has been resolved—then I receive another bill for the original balance. As of this writing, the issue has still not been officially resolved and I continue to waste time and energy placing phone calls in a roundabout fashion due to the complex cost and reimbursement schema between providers and insurance companies.

This experience has not only tested my patience and caused me stress and anxiety about paying an outrageous bill for something that should have been covered, but has also given me perspective. I have a better understanding of how confusing and complex the costs reimbursement system in the US can be and I feel a great deal of empathy for anyone who suffers as a consequence of the bewildering morass that exists. I can see how many patients get "lost" in this system. I will be extremely wary when seeking medical care in the future and will keep this incident in mind when advising my future patients.

—Morgan Congdon. "All This For A Migraine?" Costs of Care, 2012.
(www.costsofcare.org)

Health savings and flexible spending accounts

In an attempt to give individuals more control over their healthcare spending and utilization, *health savings accounts* (HSAs) were created by the 2003 Medicare Modernization Act.[47] HSAs involve pairing HDHPs with the establishment of an account that can be funded with pretax dollars and used to pay for eligible healthcare expenditures. Accounts are akin to a bank account and contributions may earn interest. They are owned by the individual, therefore are portable even after workers leave their job.

HSAs are similar, but technically not the same, as *health reimbursement arrangements* (HRAs). HRAs involve employers (rather than the employee) making the pretax contributions to the account to be used by the enrollee.[46] The employee does not own the account in this situation, thus HRAs are not portable. A flexible spending arrangement (FSA) may receive contributions from the employee or an employer.[46] Together these plans may be referred to as *consumer-driven health plans* (CDHP).

"Sort of like anchovies or the New York Yankees, no one is neutral about CDHPs," radiologist and healthcare administrator Dr Michael Pentecost has stated.[48] "Health policy analysts either love them or hate them."

In general, they are a good deal for the young and healthy (who use less care and are unlikely to spend from their account) and a worse deal for the older and chronically ill (who use more care and are much more likely to spend from their account). The selective enrollment of young healthy patients into these plans could lead to stratification of the insurance risk pools in the market, ultimately leading to higher premiums for those who are sick.

HSAs are designed in order for patients to have "skin in the game" when it comes to using medical services. There is some evidence that CDHPs do indeed lead to less health spending, with one study showing that enrollees in HSAs spent roughly 5% to 7% less when compared with traditional health plan enrollees.[47]

HOW COST SHARING EFFECTS PATIENT BEHAVIOR

The classic RAND health insurance experiment

The RAND health insurance experiment (HIE)—a landmark randomized field trial of different insurance plans—began in 1971, led by health economist Joseph Newhouse, PhD.[49] It was a 15-year effort that cost multimillion dollars, in which 5809 patients were randomly assigned to insurance plans with different coinsurance rates, making it the largest health policy study ever.[49] The program randomly assigned people to different kinds of health plans ranging from completely free care (no cost sharing) up to "catastrophic plans" that had 95% coinsurance rates and included a maximal annual payment up to $1000 (in 1970s dollars; would be more than $6000 today). There were also intermediate groups with 25% and 50% coinsurance rates. The group followed participants' behavior between 1974 and 1982.

The study was designed to address two questions:

1. How much more medical care will people use if it is provided free of charge?
2. What are the consequences for their health?

Results

Perhaps not surprisingly, having to pay out-of-pocket for health services led to less utilization. In fact, participants in the 95% coinsurance plan used 25% to 30% fewer services than those in the free-care plan. On average, they had two fewer physician visits per year and were almost a quarter less likely to be hospitalized in a year. Despite this decrease in utilization, there was little to no effect on the health of the majority of patients. With one very important exception: low-income people with poor health ended up disproportionately going without care that they needed. The study concluded that cost sharing reduced inappropriate or unnecessary medical care (overutilization), but also reduced some appropriate or needed medical care.

As the study's primary investigator, Dr Newhouse summarized: "For most people enrolled in the RAND experiment, who were typical of Americans covered by employment-based insurance, the variation in use across the plans appeared to have minimal to no effects on health status. By contrast, for those who were both poor and sick—people who might be found among those covered by Medicaid or lacking insurance—the reduction in use was harmful, on average."[27]

The decrease in the use of medical services by the high-coinsurance group had adverse effects on some conditions such as visual acuity[50] and blood pressure control.[51] Most concerning, the rise in blood pressures is likely to translate to increased mortality in this group.

Implications

The results of the RAND HIE, which suggested that modest levels of cost-sharing among the nonpoor decreased the use of unnecessary services and did not have substantial health effects, led to the restructuring of private insurance and helped increase the stature of managed care. In many ways, this study opened the doors for increased cost sharing in the 1980s and 1990s.

Statewide Medicaid expansions

One ongoing study that provides more recent and persisting evidence of the effects of cost sharing has been dubbed "The Oregon Experiment."[52] In 2008 Oregon enrolled 10,000 uninsured low-income adults into its Medicaid program, from a lottery of almost 90,000 applicants. This set-up a natural, opportunistic randomized control trial of the effects of Medicaid coverage comparing those that were accepted and those rejected by the lottery.

During the first 2 years of this study, Medicaid coverage increased the use of healthcare services, raised rates of diabetes detection and management, lowered rates of depression, and reduced financial strain.[52] But, disappointingly there were no significant improvements in measured physical health outcomes during this time.

Other studies have looked at statewide Medicaid expansions compared to similar states without expanded coverage and found that these insurance expansions have been "significantly associated with reduced mortality as well as improved coverage, access to care, and self-reported health."[53] Of note, these Medicaid patients also spent more money on healthcare, contributing to the conclusion by health economists Katherine Baicker (Harvard) and Amy Finkelstein (Massachusetts Institute of Technology) that early results from Medicaid expansions "cast considerable doubt on both the optimistic view that Medicaid can reduce healthcare spending, at least in the short run, and the pessimistic view that Medicaid coverage won't make a difference to the uninsured."[54]

Prescription drug cost sharing

As discussed in more detail in Chapter 13, most insured patients are now covered by incentive-based prescription drug programs in which drugs are assigned to one of several tiers based on their cost to the health plan and other factors. Some plans may require beneficiaries to pay coinsurance (a percent of the total cost of the medication). This strategy is meant to incentivize the use of generic or low-cost brand-name medications.

While this may be sound in concept and even prove to be successful in many instances, a number of studies have shown some adverse effects of medication cost sharing, such as lower rates of drug treatment, worse adherence among existing users, more frequent discontinuation of therapy, and higher rates of hospitalizations and ED visits in certain populations.[55-57]

KEY POINTS:

- Most consumer goods in the United States are paid for via out-of-pocket payments, but medical care presents many inherent issues—including unpredictability and reliance on specialized knowledge—that make this an inadequate payment method for the majority of patients.
- Methods of paying for healthcare in the United States currently include (1) out-of-pocket payments, (2) individual private insurance, (3) employment-based private insurance, and (4) government-financed programs (Medicare and Medicaid).
- Due to the rising costs of healthcare benefits, insurers have enacted increasing methods for sharing costs with those that receive the benefits. Some common cost sharing mechanisms include annual deductibles, lifetime maximums, copays, and coinsurance. There are growing numbers of "consumer-based" insurance plans including health savings accounts and high-deductible insurance plans.
- Cost sharing does reduce utilization of unnecessary medical services; however, may also lead to decreased utilization of necessary services in those that are both poor and sick.

References:

1. "Belly pain"—Google search. http://www.google.com/search?client=safari&rls=en&q=belly+pain&ie=UTF-8&oe=UTF-8. Accessed August 15, 2013.
2. Hsia RY, Kothari AH, Srebotnjak T, Maselli J. Health care as a "market good"? Appendicitis as a case study. *Arch Intern Med*. 2012;172(10):818-819.
3. Starr P. *The Social Transformation of American Medicine*. New York, NY: Basic Books; 1982.
4. Bodenheimer T, Grumbach K. *Understanding Health Policy: A Clinical Approach*. 6th ed. New York, NY: McGraw-Hill Medical; 2012.
5. Baicker K, Chandra A. Myths and misconceptions about U.S. health insurance. *Health Aff*. 2008;27(6):w533-w543.
6. Enthoven AC, Fuchs VR. Employment-based health insurance: past, present, and future. *Health Aff*. 2006;25(6):1538-1547.
7. Blumenthal D. Employer-sponsored health insurance in the United States—origins and implications. *N Engl J Med*. 2006;355(1):82-88.
8. Cebul RD, Rebitzer JB, Taylor LJ, Votruba ME. Organizational fragmentation and care quality in the U.S. healthcare system. *J Econ Perspect*. 2008;22(4):93-113.
9. Gruber J. *The Tax Exclusion for Employer-Sponsored Health Insurance*. National Bureau of Economic Research; 2010. http://www.nber.org/papers/w15766.pdf. Accessed January 13, 2013.
10. Auerbach DI, Kellermann AL. A decade of health care cost growth has wiped out real income gains for an average US family. *Health Aff*. 2011;30(9):1630-1636.
11. Doty MM, Collins SR, Nicholson JL, Rustgi SD. *Failure to Protect: Why the Individual Insurance Market Is Not a Viable Option for Most U.S. Families*. New York, NY: The Commonwealth Fund; 2009. Available at http://www.commonwealthfund.org/Publications/Issue-Briefs/2009/Jul/Failure-to-Protect.aspx. Accessed January 24, 2013.
12. Hill SC. Individual insurance benefits to be available under health reform would have cut out-of-pocket spending in 2001-08. *Health Aff (Millwood)*. 2012;31(6):1349-1356.
13. Pauly MV, Nichols LM. The nongroup health insurance market: short on facts, long on opinions and policy disputes. *Health Aff (Millwood)*. 2002;Suppl Web Exclusives:W325-W344.
14. McDevitt R, Gabel J, Lore R, Pickreign J, Whitmore H, Brust T. Group insurance: a better deal for most people than individual plans. *Health Aff (Millwood)*. 2010;29(1):156-164.
15. Harris RO. *A Sacred Trust*. Baltimore, MD: New American Library; 1966.
16. Conrad P. *The Sociology of Health and Illness*. New York, NY: Macmillan; 2008.
17. Hoffman B. Health care reform and social movements in the United States. *Am J Public Health*. 2003;93(1):75-85.
18. Kaiser Family Foundation. Medicare at a glance—fact sheet. 2012. http://www.kff.org/medicare/1066.cfm. Accessed January 13, 2013.
19. Baicker K, Levy H. The insurance value of medicare. *N Engl J Med*. 2012;367(19):1773-1775.
20. Kaiser Family Foundation. Medicare's role and future challenges. *JAMA*. 2012;308(20):2072.
21. Medicare Payment Advisory Commission. *Medicare and the Health Care Delivery System: Report to Congress*. Washington, DC; 2012.
22. Kelley AS, McGarry K, Fahle S, Marshall SM, Du Q, Skinner JS. Out-of-pocket spending in the last five years of life. *J Gen Intern Med*. 2013;28(2):304-309.
23. Kaiser Family Foundation. The medicaid program at a glance—update. 2012. http://www.kff.org/medicaid/7235.cfm. Accessed January 13, 2013.
24. Medicaid Home. Medicaid.gov. http://medicaid.gov/. Accessed August 15, 2013.
25. Kaiser Family Foundation. Medicaid: its role today and under the affordable care act. *JAMA*. 2012;308(8):752-752.
26. Kaiser Family Foundation. 5 Key questions and answers about medicaid. 2012. http://www.kff.org/medicaid/8162.cfm. Accessed January 13, 2013.
27. Newhouse JP. Consumer-directed health plans and the RAND health insurance experiment. *Health Aff (Millwood)*. 2004;23(6):107-113.

28. John Q. Internet Movie Database. 2002. http://www.imdb.com/title/tt0251160. Accessed November 20, 2013.
29. Harry and Louise. Wikipedia, the free encyclopedia. http://en.wikipedia.org/wiki/Harry_and_Louise. Accessed November 20, 2013.
30. Stolberg SG, Pear R. Obama signs health care overhaul into law. *The New York Times*, March 23, 2010. http://www.nytimes.com/2010/03/24/health/policy/24health.html. Accessed August 15, 2013.
31. United States Department of Health and Human Services. Key Features of the Affordable Care Act. HHS.gov/healthcare. http://www.hhs.gov/healthcare/facts/timeline/index.html. Accessed August 15, 2013.
32. American Academy of Family Physicians. *The Affordable Care Act: Medicaid Expansion & Healthcare Exchanges.* Washington, DC; 2012. http://www.aafp.org/dam/AAFP/documents/advocacy/coverage/aca/ES-MedicaidExpansion.pdf. Accessed August 16, 2013.
33. Sommers BD, Epstein AM. Medicaid expansion—the soft underbelly of health care reform? *N Engl J Med.* 2010;363(22):2085-2087.
34. Liptak A. Supreme Court upholds health care law, 5-4, in victory for Obama. *The New York Times*, June 28. 2012. http://www.nytimes.com/2012/06/29/us/supreme-court-lets-health-law-largely-stand.html. Accessed August 17, 2013.
35. United States Department of Health and Human Services. Key Features of the Affordable Care Act, By Year. HealthCare.gov. http://www.healthcare.gov/law/timeline/full.html. Accessed August 13, 2013.
36. Congressional Budget Office. Estimates for the insurance coverage provisions of the affordable care act updated for the recent Supreme Court decision. 2012. http://www.cbo.gov/publication/43472. Accessed January 28, 2013.
37. Trumbull M. Obama signs health care bill: who won't be covered? *Christian Science Monitor.* 2010. http://www.csmonitor.com/USA/2010/0323/Obama-signs-health-care-bill-Who-won-t-be-covered. Accessed January 28, 2013.
38. Oswald DP, Bodurtha JN, Willis JH, Moore MB. Underinsurance and key health outcomes for children with special health care needs. *Pediatrics.* 2007;119(2):e341-e347.
39. Ziller EC, Coburn AF, Yousefian AE. Out-of-pocket health spending and the rural underinsured. *Health Aff.* 2006;25(6):1688-1699.
40. Schoen C, Collins SR, Kriss JL, Doty MM. How many are underinsured? Trends among U.S. adults, 2003 and 2007. *Health Aff.* 2008;27(4):w298-w309.
41. Spears W, Pascoe J, Khamis H, McNicholas CI, Eberhart G. Parents' perspectives on their children's health insurance: plight of the underinsured. *J Pediatr.* 2013;162(2):403-408.e1.
42. The Massachusetts Health Reform Survey. http://www.urban.org/health_policy/url.cfm?ID=411649. Accessed December 6, 2012.
43. Schoen C, Doty MM, Robertson RH, Collins SR. Affordable Care Act reforms could reduce the number of underinsured US adults by 70 percent. *Health Aff (Millwood).* 2011;30(9):1762-1771.
44. Trivedi AN, Rakowski W, Ayanian JZ. Effect of cost sharing on screening mammography in Medicare health plans. *N Engl J Med.* 2008;358(4):375-383.
45. Campbell EG, Pham-Kanter G, Vogeli C, Iezzoni LI. Physician acquiescence to patient demands for brand-name drugs: results of a national survey of physicians. *JAMA Intern Med.* 2013:1-3.
46. Internal Revenue Service. Health savings accounts and other tax-favored health plans. 2013. http://www.irs.gov/pub/irs-pdf/p969.pdf. Accessed February 8, 2013.
47. Lo Sasso AT, Shah M, Frogner BK. Health savings accounts and health care spending. *Health Serv Res.* 2010;45(4):1041-1060.
48. Pentecost MJ. Consumer-directed health plans: at last, data. *J Am Coll Radiol.* 2007;4(4):211-213.
49. Newhouse JP. *Free for All?: Lessons from the Rand Health Insurance Experiment.* Boston, MA: Harvard University Press; 1993.
50. Lurie N, Kamberg CJ, Brook RH, Keeler EB, Newhouse JP. How free care improved vision in the health insurance experiment. *Am J Public Health.* 1989;79(5):640-642.

51. Keeler EB, Brook RH, Goldberg GA, Kamberg CJ, Newhouse JP. How free care reduced hypertension in the health insurance experiment. *JAMA*. 1985;254(14):1926-1931.
52. Baicker K, Taubman SL, Allen HL, et al. The Oregon Experiment—effects of Medicaid on clinical outcomes. *N Engl J Med*. 2013;368(18):1713-1722.
53. Sommers BD, Baicker K, Epstein AM. Mortality and access to care among adults after state Medicaid expansions. *N Engl J Med*. 2012;367(11):1025-1034.
54. Baicker K, Finkelstein A. The effects of Medicaid coverage—learning from the Oregon Experiment. *N Engl J Med*. 2011;365(8):683-685.
55. Goldman DP, Joyce GF, Zheng Y. Prescription drug cost sharing: associations with medication and medical utilization and spending and health. *JAMA*. 2007;298(1):61-69.
56. Karaca-Mandic P, Jena AB, Joyce GF, Goldman DP. Out-of-pocket medication costs and use of medications and health care services among children with asthma. *JAMA*. 2012;307(12):1284-1291.
57. Tamblyn R, Laprise R, Hanley JA, et al. Adverse events associated with prescription drug cost-sharing among poor and elderly persons. *JAMA*. 2001;285(4):421-429.

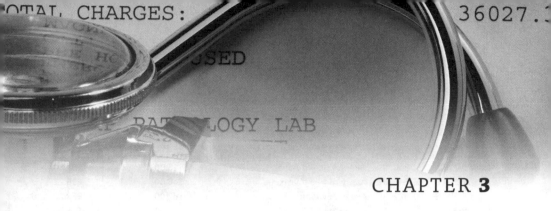

CHAPTER 3

The Challenges of Understanding Healthcare Pricing

*I*n Dr Linda Burke-Galloway's own words, "it is a unique and humbling experience when a physician becomes the patient." Her ophthalmologist (eye doctor) recommended a surgical procedure that would be necessary to preserve her vision. As a public health physician with 23 years of experience, Dr Burke-Galloway thought she knew what to expect when she went to the hospital. And she did. It's what happened after the hospital and routine recovery that floored her.

One day after work she opened an envelope containing a medical bill for $13,298.02. After blinking to make sure her vision was indeed working, she went through the individual line items and noticed equally astounding prices. $78 for a $4 antibiotic called gentamycin. $863.20 for a $192 pair of disposable forceps. And on it went.

Assuming a mistake occurred, she first verified the discrepant prices and compared them to those listed by medical supply companies. She then contacted the hospital only to find that no one knew how to address her concerns. Not the auditing department. Not the CEO's office. Ultimately, she received a jolting final response to her appeal: "...when you sign consent for a procedure, you're allowing us to charge anything we want to..." How could this be right?

In the United States, healthcare prices are opaque—hard to predict, justify, or even understand. Unlike almost everything else that Americans buy, healthcare services can seem impossible to shop for. Patients frequently make purchases without knowing the prices or even fully knowing what is being sold. When the bill arrives (weeks later) it is filled with cryptic information: diagnosis and procedure codes, unfamiliar line items, and confusing calculations involving total charges, deductibles, and copayments (Figure 3-1). As major expenses go, few of us would be willing to buy a car or house under similar circumstances. And yet

PATIENT BILL FOR SERVICES				

Patient Name
Xxxxxx Xxxx

Account Number
0000#######

Statement Date
11/18/06

Date	ICD 9	Description	Charges	Approved
09/20/06	80050	General Health Panel	$125.00	$63.50
09/20/06	84439	Assay of free thyroxine	$46.00	$16.22
09/20/06	82306	Assay of vitamin D	$62.00	$53.23
09/20/06	80061	Lipid Panel	$51.00	$24.09
09/20/06	36415	Routine venipuncture	$8.00	$0.00
09/20/06	99396	Pre. visit est. age 40–64	$154.00	$113.80
		TOTALS:	$446.00	$270.84

Claim Summary		Beneficiary Liability Summary		Benefit Period Summary	
Amount Billed:	$446.00	Deductible:	$0.00	**Fiscal Year Beginning:**	
Approved:	$270.84	Copayment:	$0.00	October 1, 2005	
Amount Owed:	**$175.16**	Cost Share:	$0.00		*Individual*
Other Insurance:	$0.00			Deductible:	$0.00
Paid to provider:	$0.00			Catastophic Cap:	$20,000
Paid to Beneficiary:	$270.84				

Figure 3-1. Anatomy of a medical bill. (Adapted idea from the Wall Street Journal.)

this is exactly how healthcare is purchased all the time. Princeton economist Uwe Reinhardt has described US healthcare pricing as "chaos behind a veil of secrecy."[1]

Clinicians are no more privy to the vagaries of healthcare pricing than patients are. In the true story above, Dr Burke-Galloway—despite decades of experience in both clinical care and public health—was bewildered by several aspects of the bill she received: the inflated prices of individual items, the total amount in the bottom line, and most of all, the inability of anyone to explain it to her. Sadly, the circumstances she found herself in are common in the United States and for many Americans the consequences are severe. Even among the insured, medical bills have become a leading cause of personal debt.[2] Carey Goldberg, a public radio journalist who covers healthcare, pointed out that "sticker shock" after receiving a medical bill is "becoming a rite of passage for Americans."[3] As Americans continue to face greater cost sharing under high-deductible plans (Chapter 2), patients will be increasingly sensitive to prices. It goes without saying that clinicians are the ones who decide what goes on the bill.

This chapter reviews the many challenges of understanding healthcare pricing in the current system, along with approaches to achieve price transparency. However, it is worth pausing for a moment to reflect on how we got here. As we discussed in Chapter 2, healthcare purchasing at the beginning of the 19th century was more straightforward. Prices were negotiated between patients and clinicians, and payments were made "out-of-pocket" with cash or in-kind bartered goods. This was possible because clinicians were self-reliant and were able to carry most of the diagnostic tools and therapies they needed in a single small bag. Because the infrastructure of hospitals was seldom necessary outside of mass casualties or epidemics, it was common and convenient for the clinician to simply travel to the patient's bedside.

At the turn of the 21st century the delivery of medicine looks very different. The small doctor's bag has been replaced by an expensive array of technologies that are not easily portable. House calls are rare and patients must typically travel to the clinicians. Moreover, large teams of care have become the norm. In observing his mother's recovery from a routine knee replacement surgery, Harvard surgeon and writer Dr Atul Gawande counted 63 different clinicians involved in her care during her short 3-day hospitalization: 19 doctors (including surgeons, radiologists, and anesthesiologists), 23 nurses, 5 physical therapists, 16 patient-care assistants, plus x-ray technologists, transport workers, and nurse practitioners.[4] This type of medicine has evolved to require the economies of scale that result from large organizations, and as a result prices are no longer determined within the confines of the doctor-patient relationship. Instead prices are separately determined through closed-door negotiations between insurance companies and provider organizations. Today clinicians seldom set prices from the bedside and patients rarely negotiate prices directly with their caregivers.

Currently, healthcare is paid for through a complex matrix of transactions that occur between providers, technology vendors, insurance companies, and other stakeholders. Each party is incentivized to charge different amounts to different customers and keep the amounts secret in order to maximize their profits. In many areas of the economy prices are determined through the meeting of supply and demand. Prices fall somewhere between the "costs of production" (ie, what it costs to deliver care) and the willingness of the customer to pay. By contrast, in healthcare multiple transactions are required to deliver a single service, thereby disconnecting prices from both what it costs to deliver care and the willingness of patients to pay. Along the way, the dollars changing hands are given different names such as "costs," "charges," "reimbursements," and of course "prices" (Figure 3-2). In each transaction the amounts are altered so that the final price bears little resemblance to the original cost of production, much in the way the final whispered message in the children's game "telephone" bears little resemblance to the original phrase. Information asymmetries between multiple stakeholders, clinical uncertainty, and lack of reliable data sources all add to the difficulty of determining prices upfront.

If this seems thoroughly confusing, don't worry. In fact, that is the point. The aim of this chapter is to explain why healthcare pricing is so hard to understand. We break this task into two components: understanding why prices appear to vary arbitrarily, and understanding why these prices are so challenging for patients to meaningfully interpret.

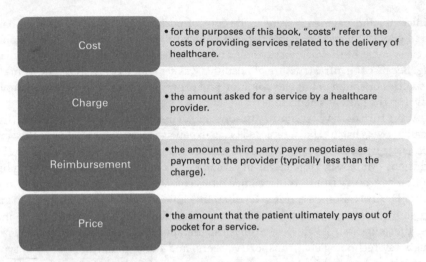

Cost
- for the purposes of this book, "costs" refer to the costs of providing services related to the delivery of healthcare.

Charge
- the amount asked for a service by a healthcare provider.

Reimbursement
- the amount a third party payer negotiates as payment to the provider (typically less than the charge).

Price
- the amount that the patient ultimately pays out of pocket for a service.

Figure 3-2. Cost, charge, reimbursement, price. (Data from the Healthcare Financial Management Association (HFMA).)

VARIABLE PRICES AND THE MULTIPLE STAKEHOLDER DILEMMA

The first step to understanding healthcare pricing requires unraveling why prices for the exact same service will vary so tremendously from provider to provider, payer to payer, and patient to patient—a problem rooted in what we call the "multiple stakeholder dilemma." In the simple 19th century approach, healthcare transactions occurred between an individual clinician and an individual patient. In the complex 21st century approach, healthcare transactions occur between large provider organizations (composed of multiple clinicians who must coordinate their efforts) and large payer organizations (composed of multiple patient "members" of an insurance company with pooled costs and financial risks). This setup introduces a "third party" to the payment relationship with different stakes in the transaction from the individual patient or the individual clinician. As a result, providers, payers, and patients are distinct parties who each evaluate costs differently (Figure 3-3).[5]

- To **providers**, costs are the expense incurred to deliver healthcare services to patients.
- To **payers**, costs are the amount payable to the provider for services rendered.
- To **patients**, costs are the amount payable out-of-pocket for healthcare services.

The perspective of clinicians, provider organizations, and delivery systems

In the 1980s, I (NS) grew up in a community of expatriate Indian Americans on the Jersey Shore, many of whom were physicians who began their careers by starting their own small private practices. When I went to medical school in the early

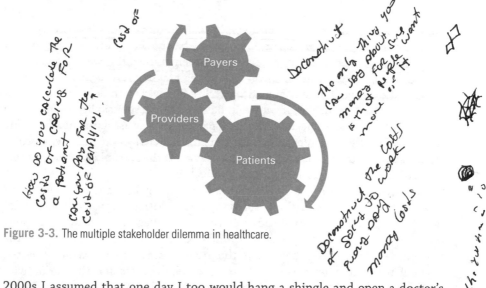

Figure 3-3. The multiple stakeholder dilemma in healthcare.

2000s I assumed that one day I too would hang a shingle and open a doctor's office. That is not what happened—graduating clinicians-in-training rarely hang shingles anymore. The majority of us will apply to a human resources department and sign corporate employment contracts. Over the last few decades, fierce competition and mounting regulatory pressure has prompted many small practices to join large provider organizations, including independent physician's associations, affiliated hospitals, and in some cases expansive multi-institutional delivery systems (California-based Kaiser-Permanente is a good example, comprised of 167,300 employees, 14,600 physicians, 37 medical centers, and 611 medical offices).[6]

One way to start understanding healthcare prices is to deconstruct the costs of delivering care at a small organization and then work our way up. In a small private practice on the Jersey Shore, the total costs of delivering care might be calculated similarly to any other business and divided into the expenses of staff salaries, short-term supplies, and long-term capital equipment investments. In theory, the expenses in each of these categories might be further divided up in order to determine the cost per patient. In practice however, parsing the cost of caring for individual patients is not straightforward. Some patients require many types of healthcare services over lengthy and unpredictable intervals of time. How do you calculate the costs of caring for a patient who receives a portion of their care at a different facility? How do you allocate the cost of an x-ray machine with a 7-year lifespan to a patient that only needs the machine for 7 minutes? For a small private practice, these calculations are cumbersome and may not be helpful in informing their business practices.

For corporations with multiple clinical and administrative departments, expenses are even more challenging to determine at the patient level. Typically, larger provider organizations will use sophisticated financial management software to track the patient's utilization of "billable items" that have discrete wholesale costs (such as medicines in the pharmacy or linens from the supply closet). However, many important costs of delivering care cannot be easily tracked this way. Costs such as the time of the nurses and the overhead of maintaining a blood bank are rarely calculated as a line item on the patient's bill. Moreover, each department—from orthopedics to waste management—may have primary responsibility for managing their own budget, which means different departments may use different accounting methods. Typically, in order to get department-level budgets to balance, a health system may create cross-department subsidies and other cost allocations that further obfuscate the patient-level costs of production.

Financial accounting in healthcare is challenging but not impossible and Chapter 4 will discuss methods for deciphering patient-level costs in greater detail. However as you can already tell, there are several immediate limitations of using the costs to the provider to understand patient prices. First, for the reasons described above, the costs to the provider are crude estimates at best—particularly for complex episodes of care. Second, the costs of caring for individual patients are mostly pieced together retrospectively after the care has already taken place. This is not helpful for a patient with a high deductible who is trying to shop for a good value. A third reason is that the costs of providing care are only loosely tied to what gets charged.

The connection between costs of providing care and the amount that gets charged is specified by a tediously long document known as the *chargemaster* (also known as a charge description master or "CDM"). Each provider organization has their own unique chargemaster, providing a comprehensive listing of tens of thousands of billable items along with the corresponding fee for each item. For hospital financial managers, the chargemaster is used to reconcile total costs with revenue.[7] For payers, the chargemaster provides the basis and starting point for negotiating the amount they will actually pay or "reimburse" for individual care (usually less than half of what is charged).[8,9]

Although the chargemaster is theoretically related to both costs and payments, in practice it does not match up with either because providers highly inflate the listed prices. These sky-high prices are commonly justified as a way of balancing the relatively low fixed reimbursement rates of government payers with the higher negotiable rates paid by private payers (more on that in a moment) (Figure 3-4).[8,10] Defenders of the chargemaster have also argued that the inflated prices are necessary to mitigate financial risk that providers bear since it can be hard to predict how costly an episode of care will be.[11] Nonetheless the chargemaster system has come under sharp criticism for being opaque and arbitrary while exposing patients like Dr Burke-Galloway to exorbitant cost. As journalist Steven Brill detailed in his attention-grabbing April 2013 *Time Magazine* cover story, "prices vary from hospital to hospital and are often ten times the actual cost of an item."[12]

Regardless of how it is justified, it is reasonable to wonder exactly how providers end up with the specific prices they list. Most providers start by estimating

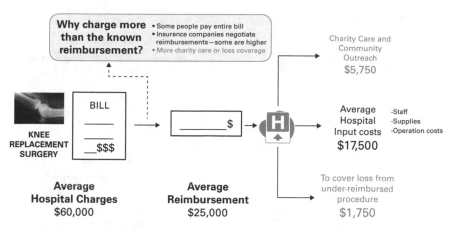

Figure 3-4. The story of how costs, charges, and reimbursements are connected.

their costs of delivering care for a particular service and then apply a "mark-up" to come up with the amount charged. The mark-up is based on a combination of the provider organization's internal financial pressures (such as a union-negotiated nurse staffing model), as well as external market pressures. Market pressures include the mix of payers (ie, how much reimbursement is coming from lower paying Medicare insurance plans verse higher paying private plans) as well as the mix of other provider organizations that are competing for the same patients. Often, the charges reflect specific market knowledge of what others are charging or paying. For example, hospitals can retrieve publically reported charge-masters from their competitors and use this information to set a ceiling on their charges so that they are not perceived as the most expensive outlier. Similarly, because Medicare typically pays much less than private payers, many hospitals use Medicare's fee schedule as a floor for setting charges.

In 2005, the Medicare Payment Advisory Commission (MedPAC) commissioned a study by the Lewin Group that examined the charge practices of 57 delivery systems representing more than 238 hospitals across the nation.[13] Most of these hospitals were affiliated, nonprofit, academic teaching institutions. Even in these settings, they found a high level of arbitrariness. Decisions about how and when to apply mark-ups varied widely based on a variety of factors, including economic inflation, specific costs of services, hospital missions, competitive forces, influence of specific payers, community perception, managed care contract terms, and administrative overhead costs. Since some of these factors could be in conflict, it is possible that charges would be kept low in one clinical arena (like childbirth) for the sake of community perception only to be inflated in another area (like neonatal intensive care) to allow cross-subsidization (Figure 3-5). The Lewin Group discovered that many hospitals did not have a strategic process for regularly

A and B: Not all costs to the provider are well-reimbursed

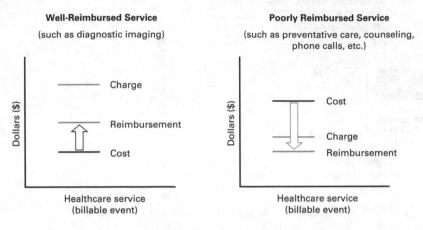

C: Different payers reimburse different amount for the same service

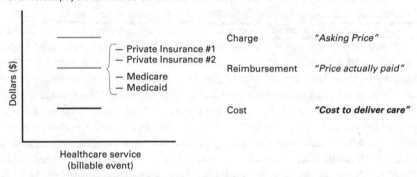

Figure 3-5. Well-reimbursed and poorly reimbursed services. (Adapted, with permission, from Mary L. Witkowski, Fellow, Value Measurement in Healthcare, Harvard Business School.)

reviewing their charges and even lost track of exactly how certain charges were historically determined. As a result, many of these hospitals struggled to explain or even rationalize the basis of their charges.

The perspective of government and private "third-party" payers

Given the arbitrariness of the chargemaster, most payers use the collective willingness to pay and overall size of their membership as leverage to negotiate steep discounts. The biggest payers of all are Medicare and Medicaid, often collectively referred to as an "800-pound gorilla" because of their power to set prices (this metaphor is rooted in the riddle, "where does an 800-pound gorilla sit?"—answer: "anywhere it wants to"). Medicare and Medicaid payment rates are adjusted annually but otherwise fixed by Congress at relatively low amounts. A 2005 study noted that on average, for every dollar of allocated cost, Medicare typically pays about 95 cents.[14] Currently, the annual adjustments are subject to a cost-control method called the "sustainable growth rate" or SGR which every year threatens to severely cut reimbursements and sends lobbyists and lawmakers on Capital Hill into a frenzied scramble for a temporary quick fix.[15] Still, even in cases when Medicare payments do not fully cover the costs of providing care, outside of the annual SGR fix, provider organizations do not have much leverage to push back.

Despite this rigidity in Medicare payments, the rates are based on the estimated costs of providing care using a process that aims to be equitable. Let's use payments for inpatient care as an example. As we described in Chapter 2, the Center for Medicare and Medicaid Services (CMS) pays for inpatient care prospectively with a flat fee per episode of care, rather than paying fee-for-service and accounting for each individual billable item. CMS defines episodes of care according to 746 distinct *diagnosis-related groups* or DRGs. According to MedPAC, CMS sets base payment amounts "for the operating and capital costs that efficient facilities would be expected to incur in furnishing covered inpatient services."[16] This base rate is first weighted by DRG to reflect the costs of caring for more severe conditions, and then adjusted according to an algorithm that includes market conditions (such as the regional cost of labor), whether or not the hospital is a teaching facility, and a number of other factors (MedPAC provides a short primer with more details on how this algorithm works on their website).[17]

Occasionally, hospitals may incur costs for caring for a particularly complex patient that are much higher than the prospective amounts allocated for the DRG. In these cases, Medicare will provide "outlier payments" based on a similarly calculated, imprecise ratio of costs to charges or "RCC."[18] Of note, despite the lack of precision, many hospital accountants and health service researchers continue to use the RCC as a basis for estimating the costs of providing care. Over the last 20 years the average hospital RCC has nearly doubled, adding to the strong sentiment that hospital charges are highly inflated (Figure 3-6).[19]

It is worth briefly mentioning here that in addition to prospective payment schedules, CMS (and many private payers) employ variety of reimbursement designs to help manage and contain the costs they face (see Chapter 15). Of course, they also employ a variety of insurance product designs (as discussed in Chapter 2), to help pass these costs along to individual patients.

Although CMS aims to compensate different providers equitably, private payers are motivated to get the best deal possible and therefore have no such intentions. It is common for payers to reimburse different amounts to different providers for the exact same service (and irrespective of the quality provided). The rates are not fixed through a formula but instead negotiated between each provider and payer. Princeton economist Uwe Reinhardt points out that although it may seem unfair, this type of "price discrimination" is commonly practiced in other industries including education where different students may negotiate different

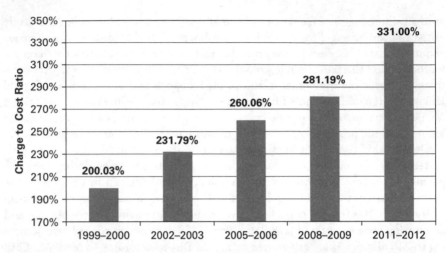

Figure 3-6. Growth in ratio of costs to charges (RCC) over time. (Adapted from National Nurses United.[19])

financial aid packages based both their ability to pay and their attractiveness to the school.[1] The problem with the use of price discrimination in healthcare brings us back to the chargemaster.

As we discussed, because the rates in the chargemaster are partly designed to offset the low reimbursement rates of Medicare and Medicaid, they end up being highly inflated. Rather than going through each billable item line-by-line, insurance companies use the size of their membership to negotiate bulk discounts from providers on lists of items. The process by which this is done has not been well characterized systematically because generally, both the providers and payers are incentivized to conduct each negotiation behind closed doors so that they can try to get a better deal during the next negotiation. Anecdotally, many hospital-insurer contracts have explicit "gag clauses" that prevent insurers from disclosing the negotiated rates. What is well known is that the end result is considerable variation in the negotiated amounts.

Cumbersome price negotiations are repeated annually, adding substantially to the administrative overhead of the prices that are ultimately passed along to the patients.[8] The secretive nature of the negotiations adds to the opacity that patients face when trying to understand how much their healthcare will cost. They also expose parties with less bargaining leverage (such as individual patients who are uninsured) to exorbitant prices. While these practices have been decried for a long time, stemming pricing variation through regulation has not been politically feasible. On occasion, however, the wide variation in prices paid to different providers for similar care has led to a stand off. In 2009 (and then again in 2011), Tufts Medical Center, a major academic medical center in Boston, threatened to drop Blue Cross Blue Shield members entirely (the state's largest private insurer) because Blue Cross was paying 20% to 40% more for the same services to a hospital only a few miles away (Figure 3-5C).[20,21] It was a colossal game of "Chicken" that played out on the front pages of the *Boston Globe*. In the end, Tufts acquiesced to taking lower payments than their competitors for providing the same care.

The perspective of individual patients and society-at-large

The mismatch between the true costs of delivering care and the inflated charge-master allows for the widespread price discrimination we see between providers and private payers. But variable pricing is only part of why individual patients are left in the lurch when it comes to shopping for care. After all, we shop for similar products with variable prices all the time, such as airline tickets. In healthcare, part of the challenge is that we also have very little information about the necessity of what we are purchasing. Patients are likely to understand that they have shortness of breath—they do not necessarily know whether they need a $50 chest x-ray or a $500 echocardiogram. Even if they know that they need an echocardiogram, there is very little reliable information available to match the price to the quality of the service at Facility A versus Facility B. Without this information, the prices are not only variable but also highly arbitrary. We explore the challenge of meaningfully interpreting price information in more detail later in this chapter.

A separate challenge is that the amount that patients will owe for care depends both on the price and their individual insurance plan design. As we described in Chapter 2, in some cases this will be the full amount negotiated by their insurance company up to a fixed amount, known as a "deductible." In other cases patients may not be exposed to any component of the cost at all. In yet other cases patients may be responsible for a small portion of the cost (either a fixed amount or small percentage of the total) known as a "copayment."

It is not only prices and plan designs that vary, but coverage policies for specific types of services can vary as well. Many insurance products have limits, exceptions, loopholes, and gaps that are challenging to understand and navigate. For example, a screening colonoscopy may be fully covered, while the biopsy for a polyp that the colonoscopy identifies may not be covered. Emergency care that is provided in state may be well-covered while emergency care provided out of state may be barely covered. Patients rarely review the fine print of their policies, particularly for nonroutine and unanticipated services. In 2013 George Lowenstein, a healthcare economist at Carnegie Mellon University, quizzed more than 200 patients with private insurance on their understanding of their policies. Only half of the respondents understood the concept of "maximum out-of-pocket expenses," let alone how much they could potentially owe.[22]

For services (or facilities) that are not covered under an insurance policy, patients are left paying the inflated chargemaster sticker price. Patients who do not have insurance will be charged the chargemaster price automatically for all services. Without the bargaining power of the insurance company, patients must individually negotiate payment after the fact. In these circumstances the final amount paid is often significantly higher than the amount that would have been paid by an insurance company with a negotiated rate. This process creates a regressive pricing system that exposes those with the least means to the greatest financial consequences.

The costs borne by patients do not start and end with what they pay for individual services. Often, a single healthcare decision will create a ripple effect of expensive future consequences. Some of these long-term consequences are the actual costs of care, such as a biopsy prompted by a false positive result (see Chapter 14) or the lifetime costs of caring for a kidney failure patient on dialysis. Other consequences include indirect costs such as a patient's foregone wages caused by missing work to receive care, or the costs of transportation between a patient's home and a healthcare facility.

Cumulatively, these "bigger picture" costs can either be considered from the perspective of individual patients or the perspective of all patients at once. When a patient is admitted to the hospital, he or she may forego wages, but in theory this loss of productivity impacts all of us. Similarly, if a patient chooses not to get a flu vaccine due to cost, they may pass along an infection that affects other members of society as well. As a result, the perspective of all patients at once is often referred to as the "societal cost" perspective.

In Chapter 8, we review some of the methods that are used to measure and understand the societal costs of healthcare decisions. Typically, the societal perspective is the one undertaken by policymakers who seek to maximize benefits to as many patients as possible. Occasionally, however, there are both real and perceived tensions between what appears to be cost-effective at the societal level and what is in the best interests of the individual patient. As we explain in Chapter 14 screening tests are designed to benefit populations, not individuals. As we explain in Chapter 6 conserving healthcare resources may benefit some members of society while harming others. The tension between the interests of the individual patient and society-at-large is an ongoing theme of this book.

INTERPRETING PRICES AND ENABLING TRANSPARENCY

The "multiple stakeholder dilemma" provides a useful framework for understanding how healthcare prices are derived and why they appear to vary arbitrarily. It does not however fully explain why healthcare prices remain so hard to interpret. Healthcare is not the only service in the marketplace with prices that are determined through complicated processes that require expert knowledge to understand. Real estate prices also vary widely. Like healthcare prices, they are settled through private negotiations with undisclosed terms. Like healthcare, it is seldom clear how different components add up to what you are paying for; one home may cost more because of a larger yard, another may cost more because of an additional bedroom. And like healthcare, costs are passed on to the buyer through an indirect mechanism that uses pooled resources of other buyers to mitigate near-term financial risk (in this case in the form a bank mortgage rather than an insurance policy).

Nonetheless, homebuyers know the overall sale price upfront. Typically, patients have no such luck. Homebuyers are able to see what similar homes sold for in the past. Patients rarely know what those who have come before them have paid. Homebuyers have access to home inspectors who can verify the quality of the construction and real estate agents to provide context for the home's fair-market value. Yet here too patients are considerably less equipped and are given little guidance from anyone on how to determine quality or value.

Why do patients have so much less agency than other types of consumers in the marketplace? In our view, the answer it is not just the way prices are derived, but the process by which healthcare is delivered. Homebuyers might not separately calculate the price of the kitchen and bathroom but they at least have an opportunity to tour the house and see all of the items they are buying before the sale is made. By contrast, patients rarely know the individual components of what they are purchasing, even in real time. A patient may experience her blood getting drawn but does not necessarily experience every individual test that is subsequently run on her blood sample.

It is common for several parallel cost-generating processes to occur behind the scenes from the patient experience—from blood testing to instrument sterilizing to clinical documentation. The technical expertise required to understand and navigate these processes makes it challenging for patients to make independent decisions about their care. In some cases, the urgency or deteriorated status of a patient's condition may not allow for any direct participation at all. Because of the ways healthcare gets delivered, patients are highly reliant on clinicians to act as their agents.

Most agents (like real estate agents) are expected to disclose the terms and rationale behind every decision they make on their client's behalf. By contrast, it is rare for clinicians to comprehensively disclose the care they are providing at a level of detail that accounts for each billable item. That being said, lack of disclosure is not entirely the clinician's fault. Although well-meaning clinicians will often do their best to disclose the most salient aspects of their decisions whenever possible, disclosing the detailed rationale behind every decision may be unduly cumbersome at the point of care. As a result, the ideal of shared decision making between patients and their caregivers is seldom achieved (Chapter 12).[23] Moreover, clinicians are rarely trained to consider financial consequences (Chapter 11). For these reasons, we believe that achieving healthcare transparency will require more than just being able to know, explain, or justify the price. We will need ways to capture pricing information as well as ways to deliver this information to patients in a form that is timely, interpretable, and actionable.

Story From the Frontlines—"Sticker Shock"

It was supposed to be a routine office visit for my patient. Unexpectedly, it turned into a real-world health economics lesson for me, the treating physician. The old adage "listen to your patients; they will always give you the answer" became exceedingly true in this case, even when it dealt with an issue beyond a medical diagnosis, such as lack of transparency regarding insurance coverage for medical procedures.

My patient had recently undergone an interventional procedure to treat severe peripheral vascular disease in order to improve his leg circulation. Usually, patients like him don't seek treatment for vascular insufficiency until the discomfort associated with activity, or claudication, is severe enough to interfere with their regular rounds of golf. That is the real motivator for these patients. The procedure was a success and a few days following the procedure he was back to his normal activities and was pleased that his leg no longer bothered him as he motored around the golf course.

My patient calmly waited until after I checked his pulses, reviewed his medications and gave him a plan for follow-up before he expressed his real concern, and it certainly wasn't about whether he could now get an extra 20 yards on his tee shot as a result of the new strength in his leg. Despite my office obtaining all the necessary private insurance pre-authorizations for the interventional procedure, he still had received a bill for approximately $10,000 related to out-of-network charges. I was baffled and my patient was disgruntled about this mix-up. After reviewing with him in the examination room the numerous sheets of paper he had received from his insurance company, it became clear what had happened.

A magical alignment of stars needs to occur for an elective procedure to be pre-approved. Emergency services are covered through a separate and more straightforward mechanism. First, the provider, or surgeon in this case, needs to be within the patient's insurance network. Appropriate professional credentialing and outcome data are submitted to the insurance company, and if acceptable, the provider can participate in the company's insurance plan. This tedious process needs to be repeated for every insurance plan in which the physician wants to participate. Second, appropriate medical record documentation needs to be submitted to the insurance company demonstrating medical necessity for the procedure. Third, the intended hospital where the procedure is being performed needs to be in-network, which is completely independent of the provider's status.

Pre-authorizations in this patient's case were obtained for both the surgeon's fee and hospital charges. The particular anesthesiologist utilized for this patient's procedure—a member of the medical team for which insurance companies don't require pre-authorization—was out-of-network. It is not customary to obtain pre-authorization for anesthesiologists since almost always the anesthesiologist is in the same network as the physician and hospital. We assume, incorrectly, that if an anesthesiologist is working in an in-network hospital and with an in-network surgeon, that they also have in-network status.

The challenge in this process is the lack of transparency surrounding patient choice regarding anesthesiologist assignment, which is often made by the operating room staff moments before the procedure. Despite the anesthesiologist meeting the patient in the holding area before the procedure, no one informed the patient about his upcoming out-of-network charge related to anesthesia services or gave the patient an option to choose another anesthesiologist who was within his insurance's network.

Fortunately, the out-of-network anesthesiologist worked with my patient to drastically reduce the cost of his services and they agreed upon a much more reasonable charge and associated payment plan. Subsequently, my office has modified the process to ensure that the anesthesiologist assigned to a patient's procedure is pre-authorized.

This patient's case was an eye-opening experience for me and helped me better understand the complex maze of healthcare reimbursement. It also enabled me to see things more clearly from my patient's perspective. I am thankful that this patient took the time to speak-up and share his financial situation with me. How many other patients have I operated on were put in this situation and suffered financially in silence? I have always prided myself on making sure my patients have a thorough understanding of their disease and upcoming procedure. Now, I take the time to make sure they also have a clear understanding of the reimbursement process. As a physician, it is not enough to relieve the physical pain of a medical problem, it is also our responsibility to help patients avoid preventable financial jeopardy.

—Grayson Wheatley. "Sticker Shock." Costs of Care, 2010.
(www.costsofcare.org)

Capturing pricing data and delivering it to patients at the right time

At some point, patients will learn the price of their care. The problem is that this information frequently arrives too late. In the continuum of healthcare delivery there are several earlier points when cost information can be more helpful, starting at the very beginning with selection of an appropriate health insurance plan. Until recently, even this task was incredibly challenging. As we described in Chapter 2, the majority of nonelderly Americans receive employer-sponsored health insurance. This amounts to approximately 149 million people receiving health insurance via one of 1.5 million employers who negotiate policies from 1200 different private insurance companies, each with their own specific policies and rates.[24,25]

These Americans typically rely on their employers to select an appropriate plan on their behalf, with highly variable results depending on their employer's generosity and ability to negotiate. Before the Affordable Care Act (ACA), an additional 19 million Americans were left to purchase insurance on their own with little available guidance on how to compare plans, and nearly 50 million Americans were crowded out of the insurance market altogether, presumably because none of the available plans were either affordable or deemed worthwhile.[26,27] Since the ACA was passed, employers have been reluctant to take on the cumbersome role of acting as a healthcare purchaser. At the same time, individual premiums have become more affordable. As a result, the number of Americans who will be directly purchasing their own health insurance is expected to skyrocket. S&P Capital IQ, a research firm serving the financial industry, predicts that by 2020 as many as 90% of the 149 million pre-ACA Americans who received health insurance from their employers will instead be shifted to government exchanges created by the new health law (Chapter 2).[28]

For the rapidly growing number of Americans who must purchase their own health insurance, the Obama administration released *Healthcare.gov* in October 2013 to provide necessary guidance for choosing an appropriate health plan. On the website, health plans are tiered from "catastrophic" at the lowest end to bronze, silver, gold, and platinum depending on the degree of coverage they provide (Table 3-1). Each plan is also required to include simplified and standardized "labeling" that makes the specific benefit structures easier to understand. Furthermore, all plans on the exchanges are guaranteed to provide a core set of benefits, ranging from preventive care to childbirth.[29] Despite these guarantees, the amount that the patient will owe will still depend on the tier of the plan. The majority of enrollees opting for more affordable plans with low premiums will face high out-of-pocket expenses when they actually need to receive care.

For the growing group of price-sensitive patients with high out-of-pocket expenses, simply knowing the degree of cost sharing in their health plan is not enough for them to fully understand their costs. They also need ways to obtain prices for anticipated services upfront. In the spring of 2013, a medical student named Jaime Rosenthal undertook a project that poignantly illustrates how challenging obtaining price estimates can be. She decided to contact each of the 20

Table 3-1 **Health exchange coverage tiers**

	Bronze	Silver	Gold	Platinum
Monthly Cost	$	$$	$$$	$$$$
Cost sharing for care you receive	Plan pays 60%, you pay 40%	Plan pays 70%, you pay 30%	Plan pays 80%, you pay 20%	Plan pays 90%, you pay 10%

US News and World Report top-ranked orthopedic hospitals in the country to find out the price of a common elective surgery called a "total hip arthroplasty." As the scripted story went, Jaime was looking for the "bundled price" (physician and hospital fees) for an acquaintance's 62-year-old grandmother who did not have health insurance but had the means to pay out-of-pocket. Jaime found that less than half of the hospitals were even able to quote a price, and for those who were the price varied by an order of magnitude (from $12,500 to $105,000).[30]

Clearly, even if you sign up for a platinum plan on *Healthcare.gov* that covers 90% of the cost of hospital care, the type of price variation that Jaime discovered would flummox the most savvy of patients trying to shop for affordable care. The patient's 10% share of the cost of a total hip arthroscopy could range from $1000 to $10,000 for similar quality care at a top ranked hospital. In response, a number of public and private resources are emerging to help patients better understand their healthcare costs upfront, and in some cases even shop for the most affordable option.

As of March 2011, more than 30 states were either considering or actively pursuing legislation to provide patients with at least some degree of upfront price transparency (Table 3-2).[31] As part of a comprehensive survey performed at that time by Harvard health policy researchers Anna Sinaiko and Meredith Rosenthal, the majority of these states could provide average or median within-hospital prices for individual services. This level of information would at least give patients a sense of the relative expensiveness of one hospital compared to another, and might steer shoppers like Jaime to a lower cost facility. Still, it does not tell them how much they will actually pay out-of-pocket. Some states such as New Hampshire do provide patients with expected out of pocket costs for both individual services (like x-rays) and bundled episodes of care (like surgeries).[32] Massachusetts additionally pairs this pricing information with high-level estimates of healthcare quality.[33] In 2013, in order to encourage other states to continue down this pathway, the Healthcare Incentives Improvement Institute (HCI3) and Catalyst for Payment

Table 3-2 States with price transparency initiatives

State	Type of Provider	Selected State-Level Price-Transparency Initiatives*	
		Information Reported	Source
California	Hospitals	Median charge by hospital for common surgeries, including digestive, female system, heart and circulatory, male system, obstetrical, skeletal, thyroid, urinary procedures. Quality data by hospital are also available elsewhere on website.	www.oshpd.ca.gov/commonsurgery
Massachusetts	Hospitals, medical groups	Both summary and detailed average costs that commercial health plans pay, by provider, for common cardiac, imaging, obstetrics, orthopedic, pulmonary, and select other procedures. Listed alongside provider-level quality information, if available.	http://hcqcc.hcf.state.ma.us
Minnesota	Clinics, medical groups, hospitals	Average payment made by insurance plans for select gastrointestinal procedures, laboratory services, mental health services, obstetrical services, office visits, surgical procedures. Quality ratings by site of care are also available at same Web page.	www.mnhealthscores.org
New Jersey	Hospitals	Average hospital charges and length of stay for most common major diagnostic categories and diagnosis-related groups.	www.njhospitalpricecompare.com
New Hampshire	Hospitals, surgery centers, physicians, other healthcare professionals	Expected out-of-pocket and total price of preventive health services, emergency visits, radiology procedures, surgical procedures, and maternity services by insurance plans (includes prices for uninsured).	www.nhhealthcost.org

*"Charges" (California and New Jersey) reflect the prices that hospitals first charge for a procedure and are much higher than the actual rates paid by public and private payers. Information is from the National Conference of State Legislatures and the individual websites listed in the table.

Source: Reproduced, with permission, from Sinaiko AD, Rosenthal MB. Increased price transparency in health care—challenges and potential effects. *N Engl J Med.* 2011;364:891-894. Copyright © 2011 Massachusetts Medical Society.

Reform (CPR) began issuing an annual report card that assigns letter "grades" to states based on their healthcare price transparency efforts.[34]

In many cases, data for these state-based initiatives are sourced from "all-payer claims databases," or APCDs, that use legislative mandates to collect, organize, and analyze private insurance claims. While the majority of states in the United States either have or are planning to build APCDs, only a small minority are currently using them to guide patient decision making, due the sensitivities in disclosing privately negotiated payment rates.[35] An alternate source of data on the highly variable and individually negotiated rates has come from providers on the other side of the transaction. Under the ACA, all providers were required to publish their chargemasters. As of January 2014, all providers in Massachusetts are required to disclose the "allowed amount" (contractually agreed amount paid by a private insurance company) or charge of an admission, procedure, or service to any patient who asks within 2 working days.[36] In California, providers have to disclose price estimates to uninsured patients and cannot bill for an amount greater than the reimbursement the hospital would receive from a government payer.[37]

Where states have not yet been able to impose price transparency measures, private organizations have stepped in. Among providers, an Oklahoma City surgery center made national headlines in July 2013 by advertising itself as a "free market-loving, price-displaying" surgical facility, starting a price bidding war among several local competing hospitals.[38] Other providers that feel they are able to offer competitive prices compared to their peers have been encouraged to do the same.[39] Among payers, several insurance companies are offering tools that guide their members toward lower cost facilities and help them estimate their out-of-pocket expenses. United Healthcare created one of the first price transparency applications for smartphones.[40]

Among patients, several crowdsourcing initiatives have emerged that allow patients to report their experiences with the value of healthcare services via credible third-party platforms. A collaboration between the Knight Foundation and several public radio stations aims to "map" regional variation in healthcare prices for specific services.[41] Even traditional consumer rating organizations such as *Consumer Reports* have started to get involved in helping patients navigate healthcare price and quality.[42] The number of companies seeking to provide patients with price transparency solutions is rapidly multiplying (Table 3-3). In 2014, a company called Castlight Health reached an initial public offering of its stock that valued the company at $3 billion.[43]

Making pricing data interpretable and actionable

Existing solutions for providing patients with the upfront price of healthcare are imperfect and not yet universally available. However, even as such services become more specific, accurate, and widely utilized in the near future, interpreting and acting on this data remains challenging. Patients cannot always predict which services

Table 3-3 Private price transparency approaches

Company	Year Founded	Approach
Castlight Health	2008	Contracts with large employers to analyze and interpret payer claims, provides Web-based suite of enterprise software applications to support patient decisions
HealthSparq	2012	Contracts with both health plans and employers to create member-facing cost and quality visualizations that are ultimately delivered through the payer member portals
Change: Healthcare	2007	Contracts with both employers and health plans to provide a member engagement platform based on analysis of proprietary claims information
Healthcare Bluebook	2008	Provides patients with free "fair price" cash payment estimates based on a distributed industry data on the amount providers accept as payment in full. Customized version provided to employers that offer high-deductible plans.
Clear Health Costs	2011	Partners with media partners to CrowdSource prices from patients who submit medical bills

Source: Data from the Healthcare Financial Management Association (HFMA).

they will need. As Johns Hopkins University Professor Gerard Anderson has put it, "without knowing which services they will need in advance, it is impossible for patients to comparison shop."[44] One price transparency company, HealthSparq, aims to mitigate some of this predictive uncertainty by contracting directly with payers. In addition to providing out-of-pocket cost estimates for individual services, HealthSparq advertises treatment level, encounter level, and service level cost estimates by taking into account the most common care pathways that other patients in the same health plan with similar conditions take.[45] With this tool, patients can see the most likely expected expenses for complex episodes of care.

Even if patients had an easy way to predict and interpret healthcare prices upfront, it would only help them select which facility to go to, and in many cases, particularly when patients are very sick, patients may not have much choice about where to go. Moreover, few solutions exist to help patients interpret and act on pricing data once they are already in the door of a healthcare facility. In the majority of cases where patients have limited agency over specific clinical decisions, it is particularly important for clinicians making decisions on their behalf to consider the value of the care they are providing. One dimension of considering value may be to understand and communicate pricing information to patients at the point of care.

As author and Stanford Professor Dr Abraham Verghese has put it, "in a healthcare system in which our menu has no prices, we can order filet mignon at every meal."[46]

Currently, clinicians appear to have very little idea how their decisions impact what patients pay for care. In one study, the vast majority of hospital medicine physicians were unable to estimate inpatient charges for routinely ordered tests within a reasonable margin of error.[47] In another study, the majority of orthopedic surgeons struggled to estimate the institutional costs of common implantable devices within the correct order of magnitude—guesses ranged from less than 50 times too low to more than 25 times too much.[48] To address this significant knowledge gap, several medical centers over the last two decades have experimented with "putting prices back on the menu." A growing number of institutions are embedding some level of cost information into the computer "order-entry" systems clinicians use, and some have been able to demonstrate modest decreases in utilization of laboratory tests.[49]

In 2014 a private company called Maven Medical partnered with Johns Hopkins University to provide real-time cost and quality analytics at the point of care.[50] In the same year the *Wall Street Journal* reported that the University of Pittsburgh Medical Center will begin selling software that "shows physicians how they can achieve the most desirable outcomes from procedures using more efficient, lower cost clinical processes and equipment."[51] The utility and efficacy of these solutions remain to be seen. Moreover, bringing price transparency to the bedside is unlikely to be a panacea by itself. Nonetheless, understanding prices is clearly a necessary component of providing the best possible care at the lowest possible cost. This information must be paired with thoughtful consideration from clinicians who are trained to provide value-based care, balancing cost information with quality, safety, and patient preferences. The remaining chapters of this book aim to provide the context and tools to do exactly that.

KEY POINTS:

- Providers, payers, and patients all consider costs from different perspectives. Furthermore, the amount that a provider charges is not necessarily related to the amount the patient pays.
- Inflated prices often result from an attempt to reconcile the relatively low and fixed reimbursements of government payers with the higher negotiable reimbursements of private payers.
- A number of public and private solutions are emerging to provide both patients and clinicians with more transparent price information.
- The complexity of clinical processes, limited patient agency, and predictive uncertainty of healthcare delivery all make existing price data challenging to interpret.

References:

1. Reinhardt UE. The pricing of U.S. hospital services: chaos behind a veil of secrecy. *Health Aff (Millwood)*. 2006;25(1):57-69.
2. Himmelstein DU, Thorne D, Warren E, Woolhandler S. Medical bankruptcy in the United States, 2007: results of a national study. *Am J Med*. 2009;122(8):741-746.
3. How To Prevent Medical Bill "Sticker Shock". Radio Boston. 2014. http://radioboston.wbur.org/2014/03/17/medical-bills-sticker-shock. Accessed March 30, 2014.
4. Gawande A. Big med. *New Yorker*. 2012. http://www.newyorker.com/reporting/2012/08/13/120813fa_fact_gawande?currentPage=all. Accessed March 30, 2014.
5. Improving price transparency: an overview of the report from the HFMA price transparency task force. http://www.hfma.org/Content.aspx?id=22275. Accessed May 4, 2014.
6. Fast Facts about Kaiser Permanente. Kaiser Permanente Share. http://share.kaiserpermanente.org/article/fast-facts-about-kaiser-permanente/. Accessed April 1, 2014.
7. Rosenberg T. Revealing a Health Care Secret: The Price. Opinionator. http://opinionator.blogs.nytimes.com/2013/07/31/a-new-health-care-approach-dont-hide-the-price/. Accessed November 17, 2013.
8. Reinhardt UE. The many different prices paid to providers and the flawed theory of cost shifting: is it time for a more rational all-payer system? *Health Aff (Millwood)*. 2011;30(11):2125-2133.
9. American Hospital Association. Hospital Statistics 2005. Chicago, IL: American Hospital Association; 2005.
10. Frakt AB. How much do hospitals cost shift? A review of the evidence. *Milbank Q*. 2011;89(1):90-130.
11. Reid G. Defending the chargemaster. Healthcare Finance News. http://www.healthcarefinancenews.com/news/defending-chargemaster?page=1. Accessed April 12, 2014.
12. Brill S. Bitter pill: why medical bills are killing us. *Time*. http://content.time.com/time/magazine/article/0,9171,2136864,00.html. Accessed November 16, 2013.
13. Dobson A, DaVanzo J, Doherty J, Tanamor M. A study of hospital charge setting practices. 2005. http://www.medpac.gov/documents/dec05_charge_setting.pdf.
14. Dobson A, DaVanzo J, Sen N. The cost-shift payment "hydraulic": foundation, history, and implications. *Health Aff (Millwood)*. 2006;25(1):22-33.
15. Lowery W. In voice vote, House approves Medicare "doc fix." *The Washington Post*. http://www.washingtonpost.com/blogs/post-politics/wp/2014/03/27/in-voice-vote-house-approves-medicare-doc-fix/. Accessed April 13, 2014.
16. Hospital Acute Inpatient Services Payment System. 2010. http://www.medpac.gov/documents/MedPAC_Payment_Basics_10_hospital.pdf.
17. MedPAC Payment Basics: Hospital Acute Inpatient Services Payment System. 2010. http://www.medpac.gov/documents/MedPAC_Payment_Basics_10_hospital.pdf.
18. Shwartz M, Young DW, Siegrist R. The ratio of costs to charges: how good a basis for estimating costs? *Inq J Med Care Organ Provis Financ*. 1995;32(4):476-481.
19. New Data—Some Hospitals Set Charges at 10 Times their Costs | National Nurses United. http://www.nationalnursesunited.org/press/entry/new-data-some-hospitals-set-charges-at-10-times-their-costs. Accessed April 28, 2014.
20. Rubenstein S. Tufts Medical Threatens to Drop Massachusetts Blue Cross Over Pay. WSJ Blogs—Health Blog. 2009. http://blogs.wsj.com/health/2009/01/07/tufts-medical-threatens-to-drop-massachusetts-blue-cross-over-pay/. Accessed November 19, 2013.
21. Zimmerman R. Talks Break Down Between Blue Cross and Tufts Medical, Patients May Need New Docs. CommonHealth. 2011. http://commonhealth.wbur.org/2011/11/talks-break-down-between-tufts-blue-cross. Accessed April 14, 2014.
22. Loewenstein G, Friedman JY, McGill B, et al. Consumers' misunderstanding of health insurance. *J Health Econ*. 2013;32(5):850-862.
23. Oshima Lee E, Emanuel EJ. Shared decision making to improve care and reduce costs. *N Engl J Med*. 2013;368(1):6-8.

24. Cebul RD, Rebitzer JB, Taylor LJ, Votruba ME. Organizational fragmentation and care quality in the U.S. healthcare system. *J Econ Perspect J Am Econ Assoc.* 2008;22(4):93-113.

25. Kaiser Family Foundation. 2013 Employer Health Benefits Survey - Summary of findings. http://kff.org/report-section/2013-summary-of-findings/. Accessed May 4, 2014.

26. US Census Bureau Health Insurance main page. http://www.census.gov/hhes/www/hlthins/. Accessed May 4, 2014.

27. America's Health Insurance Plans—Individual Market Health Insurance. https://www.ahip.org/Issues/Individual-Market-Health-Insurance.aspx. Accessed May 4, 2014.

28. Irwin N. Envisioning the end of employer-provided health plans. *The New York Times*, May 1, 2014. http://www.nytimes.com/2014/05/01/upshot/employer-sponsored-health-insurance-may-be-on-the-way-out.html. Accessed May 4, 2014.

29. Centers for Medicare and Medicaid Services. Rate review. 2013. https://www.cms.gov/CCIIO/Resources/Fact-Sheets-and-FAQs/ratereview.html. Accessed May 4, 2014.

30. Rosenthal JA, Lu X, Cram P. Availability of consumer prices from us hospitals for a common surgical procedure. *JAMA Intern Med.* 2013;173(6):427-432.

31. Sinaiko AD, Rosenthal MB. Increased price transparency in health care—challenges and potential effects. *N Engl J Med.* 2011;364(10):891-894.

32. New Hampshire Health Cost. http://www.nhhealthcost.org/. Accessed May 4, 2014.

33. MyHealthCareOptions. http://hcqcc.hcf.state.ma.us/Content/AboutTheRatings.aspx. Accessed May 4, 2014.

34. Report Card on State Price Transparency Laws—2014 | Health Care Incentives Improvement Institute, Inc. (HCI3). http://www.hci3.org/content/report-card-state-price-transparency-laws-2014. Accessed May 5, 2014.

35. Realizing the Potential of All-Payer Claims Databases. RWJF. http://www.rwjf.org/en/research-publications/find-rwjf-research/2014/01/realizing-the-potential-of-all-payer-claims-databases--creating-.html. Accessed May 4, 2014.

36. Massachusetts Medical Society Blog. Medical price transparency law rolls out: physicians must help patients estimate costs for patients. http://blog.massmed.org/index.php/2014/01/mass-medical-price-transparency-law-rolls-out-physicians-must-be-able-to-estimate-costs-for-patients/. Accessed May 5, 2014.

37. Farrell KS, Finocchio LJ, Trivedi AN, Mehrotra A. Does price transparency legislation allow the uninsured to shop for care? *J Gen Intern Med.* 2010;25(2):110-114.

38. Oklahoma City hospital posts surgery prices online; creates bidding war. KFOR.com. http://kfor.com/2013/07/08/okc-hospital-posting-surgery-prices-online/. Accessed May 4, 2014.

39. Betbeze P. Why Is Healthcare Price Transparency So Hard? http://www.healthleadersmedia.com/page-1/FIN-301946/Why-Is-Healthcare-Price-Transparency-So-Hard. Accessed May 5, 2014.

40. Health4Me Mobile App from UnitedHealthcare. http://www.uhc.com/individuals_families/member_tools/health4me_mobile_application.htm. Accessed May 5, 2014.

41. Mapping Local Health Care Prices: A Crowdsourcing Consortium. News challenge. https://www.newschallenge.org/challenge/healthdata/entries/mapping-local-health-care-costs-a-crowdsourcing-consortium Accessed May 5, 2014.

42. Consumer Reports. Best health insurance - health insurance ratings & reviews. http://consumerreports.org/cro/health/health-insurance/index.htm. Accessed May 5, 2014.

43. Moukheiber Z. Health IT Soars With Castlight Health IPO. *Forbes*. http://www.forbes.com/sites/zinamoukheiber/2014/03/14/health-it-soars-with-castlight-health-ipo/. Accessed May 5, 2014.

44. Anderson GF. From "soak the rich" to "soak the poor": recent trends in hospital pricing. *Health Aff (Millwood).* 2007;26(3):780-789.

45. HealthSparq Cost. HealthSparq, Inc. http://www.healthsparq.com/transparency-solutions/cost-estimator/. Accessed May 5, 2014.

46. Verghese A. Culture shock—patient as icon, icon as patient. *N Engl J Med.* 2008;359(26):2748-2751.

47. Graham JD, Potyk D, Raimi E. Hospitalists' awareness of patient charges associated with inpatient care. *J Hosp Med Off Publ Soc Hosp Med.* 2010;5(5):295-297.
48. Okike K, O'Toole RV, Pollak AN, et al. Survey finds few orthopedic surgeons know the costs of the devices they implant. *Health Aff (Millwood).* 2014;33(1):103-109.
49. Tierney WM. Controlling costs with computer-based decision support: an ax, a scalpel, or an illusion?: Comment on "impact of providing fee data on laboratory test ordering: a controlled clinical trial." *JAMA Intern Med.* 2013;173(10):909-910.
50. Maven Medical. http://mavenmedical.net/index.html. Accessed May 6, 2014.
51. UPMC Selling Analytics to Curb Health Care Costs. 2014. http://blogs.wsj.com/cio/2014/04/28/upmc-builds-analytics-to-curb-health-care-costs/. Accessed May 6, 2014.

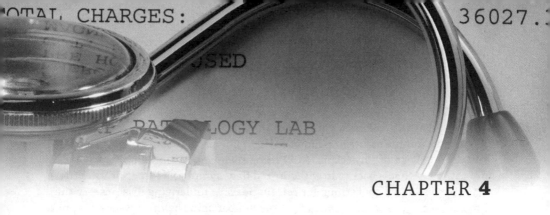

CHAPTER 4

Defining Value: Connecting Quality and Safety to Costs of Care

James Anderson, a 45-year-old accountant, regularly plays basketball and has always been healthy and active. For the past 2 weeks though he has not been able to shoot hoops due to low back pain. Two Saturdays ago, he cleaned out his garage and was moving around heavy boxes. He awoke the next morning feeling an aching pain in his low back, with an occasional intermittent sharp pain when he moved in certain positions. The discomfort seemed to be worse with bending and standing, and after lying down for long periods. After 2 weeks of using ice and heat packs, and Tylenol, with only temporary improvements, he decided to go see his doctor.

His doctor asked him a number of questions about the pain, ensuring that he did not have any bowel or bladder incontinence, fevers, weakness or numbness in his legs, or other concerning neurologic symptoms. He performed a full examination including a neurologic exam, which was completely normal except for some limited back mobility due to discomfort and some tenderness surrounding the lumbar spine region.

The physician explained to Mr Anderson that his back pain was almost assuredly "benign" and would get better slowly over about 4 to 6 weeks, but then suggested that he would order a magnetic resonance imaging (MRI) study of his back, "just to be sure."

Approximately one-quarter of American adults have had low back pain that lasted at least 1 day in the last 3 months,[1] leading low back pain to be the fifth most common outpatient complaint.[2] In the United States, we spend a lot of money on back pain. The direct expenditures annually are similar to that for diabetes and for cancer.[2,3] And yet for low back pain we are not actually making people much better. Between 1997 and 2005 the United States had rapidly increasing medical expenditures for low back pain, but there were no measurable improvements in outcomes for patients, including self-assessed health status, functional disability, work limitations, or social functioning.[2]

Expensive imaging tests are a major contributor to these excessive healthcare costs.[4] The problem is that abnormalities on imaging are as common in individuals with and without back pain. More than 57% of asymptomatic people over 60 years have abnormalities on lumbar MRIs.[5] Clinical guidelines published by the American College of Physicians (ACP) recommend against obtaining imaging in any patient with low back pain without "red flag" symptoms—specific symptoms that are considered concerning for certain possible underlying diseases—within 4 to 6 weeks of onset, since imaging of the lumbar spine before 6 weeks does not improve outcomes but does increase costs.[4,6] The American College of Radiology (ACR) agrees that imaging is frequently overused in the evaluation of low back pain and notes that most patients return to normal activity within one month regardless of imaging.[7]

Despite a mountain of evidence and clear guidelines, about 40% of family practice and 13% of internal medicine physicians reported ordering routine diagnostic imaging for acute low back pain.[8] Dr. Shubha Srinivas and colleagues from the University of Connecticut estimate that more than 3.8 million Americans receive routine imaging for low back pain each year (Figure 4-1).[9] This places patients at risk of excessive radiation (in the case of x-rays and computed tomography [CT] scans), costs, and substantial cascading downstream effects.[10] In addition, unnecessary imaging may lead to substantial out-of-pocket costs, particularly for patients like Mr Anderson who have a high-deductible insurance plan (see Chapter 2) and therefore are responsible for up to the first few thousand dollars in costs. The further downstream effects of back imaging include undue worry, perceptions of worsened back pain and/or lessened overall health status,[11] and even unhelpful spine operations.[12,13]

Routine imaging for low back pain is just one of countless examples of a costly test that does not provide higher quality care for patients.

WHAT IS "VALUE"

The meaning of "value" in healthcare—very roughly defined as the output of healthcare per unit of cost—may differ widely whether considered from the perspective of the patient, provider, or payer.[14]

"Value in healthcare depends on who is looking, where they look, and what they expect to see," Harvard cardiologist and journalist Dr Lisa Rosenbaum has suggested.[14] For clinicians, value may mean decreasing overuse and inefficiency, while improving compliance with evidence-based care. But for patients, creating value may signify enriching the patient experience and concentrating on patient-centered outcomes.[14]

These differing perspectives have created a gap that must be investigated and bridged. However, at the most basic level there is general agreement that value should include cost, outcomes (or quality of care), and patient experience. And it is clear that currently there is substantial room for improvement in all of these areas (see Chapter 1).

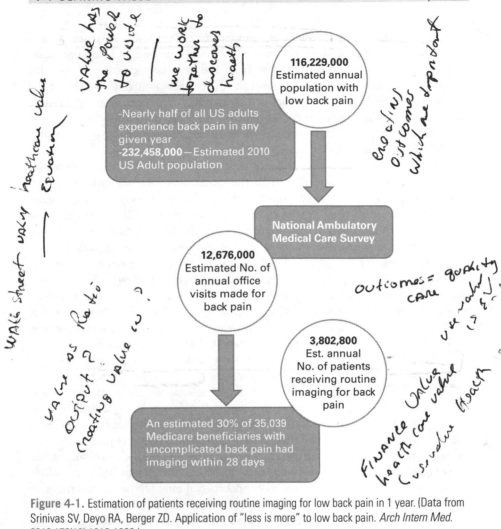

Figure 4-1. Estimation of patients receiving routine imaging for low back pain in 1 year. (Data from Srinivas SV, Deyo RA, Berger ZD. Application of "less is more" to low back pain. *Arch Intern Med.* 2012;172(13):1016-1020.)

Defining value from the perspective of patients and clinicians

We believe that clinicians should begin to consider the value of a healthcare intervention similarly to how their patients think about it. Many others have also warned that value in healthcare should consistently be defined by what actually matters to patients.[14-16] This is because when considered from the perspective of the patient, value has the power to unite the interests of all players in the healthcare system.[15] So, how do patients weigh the healthcare "value equation"?

In most instances the quality ("the numerator" of the value equation) of the recommended test/procedure/medication may be summarized as simply "what will this do for me?" Notably missing from the brief conversation above with Mr Anderson was any indication of what the potential benefits of undergoing the MRI would be for him. Patients should understand the potential benefit to them personally of recommended tests, procedures, or medications. The growing interest in measuring and addressing clearly defined *patient reported outcome measures* (PROMs) is discussed in Chapter 12.

Whether or not clinicians explicitly address benefits, one must understand that patients will automatically weigh their perceived benefit with their own values, history, and context surrounding medical care. A patient whose father died at the age of 57 from prostate cancer that was metastatic to the spine will likely view back pain very differently from someone like Mr Anderson who has never directly known anybody with cancerous bone lesions causing pain.

Clear communication between medical staff and patients is vitally important, and has been shown to improve appropriate testing by reducing underuse, overuse, and misuse.[17] In a randomized clinical trial, women who were fully counseled about testing options, had undergone exercises to clarify their personal values, and had financial barriers removed were measurably better informed and chose to undergo prenatal genetic testing less frequently than other women.[18]

As for costs ("the denominator" of the value equation), this may prove to be even more nuanced for patients and clinicians. Although weighing quality with cost is how almost all other consumer decisions are made, healthcare has traditionally not been determined this way. As we discussed in Chapter 3, this is at least partially because true healthcare costs and quality information have broadly been hidden from patients and physicians, contributing to both groups' difficulties in making rational decisions about healthcare. Furthermore, most patients are shielded from the full cost of medical purchasing decisions by their health insurance (see Chapters 2 and 3).

Some patients may not necessarily be concerned about their healthcare resource consumption. In one study, interviews with privately insured patients revealed that few of them understood terms such as "medical evidence" or "quality guidelines," and most believed that more care automatically meant higher-quality care.[19] The idea that receiving less care could actually be safer and be of higher-quality seemed counterintuitive. "I don't see how extra care can be harmful to your health," one participant said.[19] "Care would only benefit you." In fact, some patients may explicitly equate more costly care with better care. Despite a vocal contingent of patients who express this view, it is quite obvious that in many instances patients do care a lot about their healthcare costs. Indeed, healthcare costs lead many patients to postpone or skip needed care,[20] and it is increasingly clear that the financial harms alone can be substantial for patients.[21-23] Since value depends on "what matters to patients," and patients are generally concerned about the monetary costs of medical care, we believe that financial costs should be included in modern clinician risk/benefit calculations.[21]

The costs considered in the value equation should not only focus on financial costs but also include other costs potentially incurred by patients, such as possible physical harms, downstream effects, and anxiety. In the case of routine back imaging, this may include out-of-pocket costs, the logistics of missing a day of work, the story one heard from a friend about the claustrophobia of lying still in the MRI tube, and the anxiety of worrying about being "unwell."[11] These additional costs to patients may be summed in terms of the overall experience of care. Even an objectively improved outcome may not be worthwhile to a patient if it entails significant physical or psychological suffering.[24]

To be clear, this does not mean that patients in the right age and risk group should not undergo testing, such as back imaging, when warranted, but rather that clinicians should understand the personalized value equation that patients may be, perhaps even subconsciously, calculating. When recognized, the healthcare provider can help patients more explicitly navigate this calculus. Actively engaging patients in their healthcare has been shown to be associated with better health outcomes and care experiences,[25] and possibly even lower costs.[26]

Most clinicians are currently unaware of the cost of routinely ordered tests,[27] but to explain the potential options and their fiscal implications to patients, health professionals should take responsibility for knowing the financial ramifications of the care they are recommending.[21] This does not always require knowing the exact dollars-and-cents costs, but clinicians can utilize resources so to at least provide estimates within an order of magnitude. For instance, the clinician should be able to, at the very least, point Mr Anderson to a resource to check with his insurance about how much the MRI would cost him out-of-pocket (see Chapter 12 for some examples of emerging tools for cost transparency). There are also multiple emerging tools, which are discussed in Chapter 13, for clinicians to evaluate and possibly decrease out-of-pocket costs of prescription medications for their patients.

Of course, one of the best ways to deflate medical bills is to avoid interventions that do not make patients healthier—such as inappropriate back imaging. Avoiding unnecessary medical tests, procedures, and treatments is the easiest way to simultaneously improve quality of care, safety, and patient experience, and decrease costs.[28]

The differences between "value" and "cost"

Although "value" has emerged as a catchall term to encapsulate the quality, experience, and costs of care, it often gets conflated into being about costs alone. In the past, value improvement was met with skepticism by both physicians and patients, who feared it was being used simply as a euphemism for blanket cost controls.[29] Even today the terminology is confusing. Some may conjure up images of McDonald's "value meals" or the local diner's "blue plate special"—not really an appealing metaphor for a healthcare service. However, to be clear, we do not use value here as a code word for cost reduction.

The distinction between cost and value is critical (Table 4-1). Certain high-cost interventions are extremely beneficial in the right setting. An MRI scan provides excellent value for the evaluation of a suspected epidural abscess (a collection of infected pus around the spinal cord), but that same study is considered low-value when used for routine evaluation of common low back pain, since it does not improve outcomes. On the other hand, there are other interventions that are typically low-value, regardless of cost, because they do not improve patient outcomes under almost any circumstances, and even may cause harm.

Consider the routine, rather than clinically indicated, replacement of peripheral intravenous catheters (PIVs). Most hospitals require that PIVs be replaced in inpatients every 72 to 96 hours. This has been shown to be a wasteful practice with no difference in rates of infection or phlebitis (inflammation of the blood vessel) for patients compared to replacing PIVs only when they have failed or show evidence of emerging infection.[30-32] Even though the individual cost saving from saving plastic PIVs is rather minimal, this practice could likely be completely eliminated without negatively affecting patients. In fact, decreasing needle sticks would be very welcomed by patients and is likely to improve their care experience. Thus, even low-cost interventions may be of low-value and should be targeted for elimination. This means that simply concentrating on return on investment is likely an inadequate way to assess the success of healthcare strategies aimed at improving value for patients.[33] Therefore, although cost is part of the value calculation, it does not solely define it.

Simply put, value is increased either by improving the quality of care delivered to patients at similar costs, or by reducing the total costs involved in a patient's care while maintaining quality. The improvement of healthcare value, when appropriately applied, stands to benefit patients, clinicians, payers, and medical systems.

The value calculation

Ability to pay

Table 4-1 Cost, benefit, and value of medical interventions

Cost	Net Benefit	Value	Examples
High	High	Usually high-value, but depends on the situation and the relationship of costs and benefits	High-value: MRI for epidural abscess
	Low	Low	Low-value: Routine MRI for low back pain
Low	High	High	High-value: Universal HIV screening
	Low	Usually low-value, but depends on the situation and the relationship of costs and benefits	Low-value: Preoperative testing prior to low-risk surgery like cataract surgery

Defining value from the healthcare system perspective

In order to assess whether the delivery of a healthcare service is high-value, it is useful to couch value improvement efforts within the shared goals of the health system as a whole. In 2007, the Institute for Healthcare Improvement (IHI) proposed a framework for optimizing health system performance known as the "triple aim" (Figure 4-2)[28]:

- Improve the experience of care
- Improve the health of populations
- Reduce per capita costs of healthcare

These aims are interdependent and require a balanced approach.[28] If not taken together, some health systems may improve quality while generating exorbitant costs. Alternatively, haphazard application of these aims could lead to decreased costs but at the detriment of the patient experience or quality of care. Therefore, it is vital that these three goals are pursued equally and simultaneously. If a space shuttle with excellent insulation design exploded due to faulty fuel mechanics, nobody at NASA would be celebrating the good insulation; they would be lamenting the overall failure of the mission.

The triple aim has been broadly adopted as an aspiration of many health system improvement efforts but it can be challenging to implement. With many moving parts that must be tackled in tandem, it requires the dedication of frontline clinicians as well as health systems leaders. It also requires a way of defining, measuring, and prioritizing the components of the value equation at the healthcare system level.

System-based outcomes

The triple aim goals imply a focus on the bottom-line results achieved—not just the volume of services delivered or the number of patients that are cared for.[15] Harvard Business School Professor Michael Porter has helped popularize a tiered

The IHI Triple Aim

Population Health

Experience of Care   Per Capita Cost

Figure 4-2. The IHI triple aim. (The IHI Triple Aim framework was developed by the Institute for Healthcare Improvement in Cambridge, Massachusetts (www.ihi.org). Reproduced, with permission. Accessed January 30, 2015.)

"Outcomes Measures Hierarchy" with implications for both healthcare quality and patient experience[15]:

- Tier 1: Health status achieved (survival; degree of health recovery)
- Tier 2: Process of recovery (time to recovery and time to return of normal activities; disutility of care or treatment process)
- Tier 3: Sustainability of health (recovery and nature of recurrences; long-term consequences of therapy)

This hierarchy suggests a way not only of parsing outcomes that are meaningful, but also for prioritizing them. Ideally care is provided with an efficient and sustainable process (tiers 2 and 3), but improved health status (tier 1) must be demonstrated foremost.

The outcomes hierarchy is most easily applied to care where the processes of care are highly standardized. There also must be a clear endpoint where success can be declared. Osteoarthritis of the knee requiring a joint replacement provides a commonly cited example—most patients are treated similarly and in all cases the successful endpoint is a patient who can return to normal physical function without experiencing pain (Figure 4-3). The tier 1 outcome is therefore how many patients achieve this endpoint. The tier 2 outcome may be how long it takes to achieve this endpoint, and the tier 3 outcome may be how long this endpoint lasts before the patient relapses into pain and dysfunction.

While this example is fairly straightforward, the outcomes hierarchy becomes knottier to use in more complex, less predictable health conditions. Hospitals are also brimming with patients that have multiple active and overlapping health problems. They may have osteoarthritis of the knee, but they may also have congestive heart failure, diabetes, and asthma. For these patients, using "time to recovery" as a tier 2 outcome measure may not be valid, particularly when comparing their recovery to patients whose functional status is not limited by other medical conditions. When comparing outcomes at the system level we lose a lot of detail regarding each patient's prognosis and personal treatment goals. By assuming standardization in care, we sometimes overlook important patient-level differences.

Still, we clearly need to start measuring outcomes somewhere, even when the measures are imperfect. Often, we can supplement outcome measures by moving upstream in the care delivery pathway and focusing our attention on the processes of care that we suspect lead to good outcomes. Although we care most about end results, process measures are often more actionable because they inform how care can be delivered differently. Roughly, process measures are "what health professionals do to people," whereas outcome measures are "what happens to people" (also see Chapter 16).[34] An example of a process measure for a total knee replacement may be whether or not the patient received appropriate pre-operative antibiotics. Administering antibiotics before performing this type of surgery is likely to improve outcomes by decreasing infections. Nonetheless a

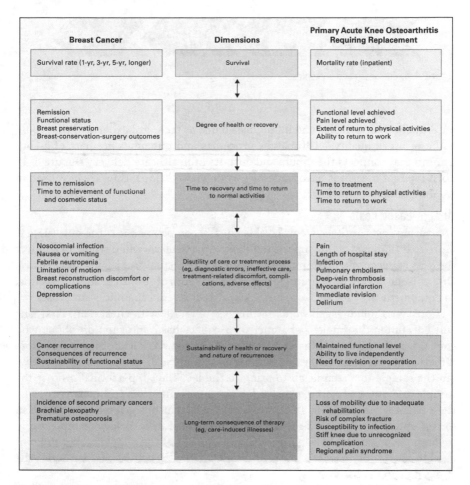

	Breast Cancer	Dimensions	Primary Acute Knee Osteoarthritis Requiring Replacement
	Survival rate (1-yr, 3-yr, 5-yr, longer)	Survival	Mortality rate (inpatient)
	Remission Functional status Breast preservation Breast-conservation-surgery outcomes	Degree of health or recovery	Functional level achieved Pain level achieved Extent of return to physical activities Ability to return to work
	Time to remission Time to achievement of functional and cosmetic status	Time to recovery and time to return to normal activities	Time to treatment Time to return to physical activities Time to return to work
	Nosocomial infection Nausea or vomiting Febrile neutropenia Limitation of motion Breast reconstruction discomfort or complications Depression	Disutility of care or treatment process (eg, diagnostic errors, ineffective care, treatment-related discomfort, complications, adverse effects)	Pain Length of hospital stay Infection Pulmonary embolism Deep-vein thrombosis Myocardial infarction Immediate revision Delirium
	Cancer recurrence Consequences of recurrence Sustainability of functional status	Sustainability of health or recovery and nature of recurrences	Maintained functional level Ability to live independently Need for revision or reoperation
	Incidence of second primary cancers Brachial plexopathy Premature osteoporosis	Long-term consequence of therapy (eg, care-induced illnesses)	Loss of mobility due to inadequate rehabilitation Risk of complex fracture Susceptibility to infection Stiff knee due to unrecognized complication Regional pain syndrome

Figure 4-3. Outcomes hierarchy examples for breast cancer and knee osteoarthritis. (Reproduced, with permission, from Porter ME. What is value in health care? *N Engl J Med.* 2010;363(26): 2477-2481. Copyright © 2010 Massachusetts Medical Society.)

100% track record of administering antibiotics does not tell you about whether or not the surgery itself was successful.

Outcomes depend on many factors aside from health services. Even if a patient presenting to an emergency department (ED) with a heart attack received "atrocious care," he still may have a good outcome—if one did nothing for this patient other than provide pain relief, he would still have a 60% to 70% chance of surviving and being able to resume his daily activities.[34] The patient's *outcome* would be considered great, but their *care* would have been appalling. In some cases process measures are much more sensitive to differences in quality of care. However, when compared to outcome measures, process measures may ignore many other

Figure 4-4. Processes and outcomes.

potentially vital variables and intangibles (such as technical expertise) that could make or break quality.[35] Ultimately, processes and outcomes are part of a con- tinuum that connects the inputs and outputs of healthcare delivery (Figure 4-4). Both types of measures have trade-offs when viewed alone, thus are best used in combination.

System-based costs

Measuring costs at the systems level is equally complex. As it turns out, there is more to it than just adding up the numbers—particularly when trying to connect the dots between where the money is going and the actual care that is taking place. One episode of care can require many different types of resources from personnel to equipment to space and supplies, each with different capabilities and costs.[36]

Consider a middle-aged woman who goes to an ED with chest pain. First, she will encounter the intake personnel who collect basic information about who she is. A triage nurse will then take her vital signs and ask basic questions before directing her toward an ED examination room. A nurse draws her blood and deliv- ers the sample to a technician to bring to the lab. The lab personnel process the sample and run tests on expensive lab machines. Another technician stops by the patient room to obtain an electrocardiogram, which is given to the physician for interpretation. A chest x-ray is obtained by a separate radiology technician and reviewed by a radiologist. Up until this point, most of the people and equipment used to care for her needed to be paid for by the health system whether or not she showed up in the ED that day.

Then the ED physician gets involved. He spends a variable amount of time examining the patient and reviewing all of the pertinent data. The decision is made to admit her to the hospital, so the ED physician calls a hospital medi- cine physician to "sign-out" the patient by describing the patient, work-up, and suspected diagnoses. The ED nurse calls the floor nurse and provides her own "hand-off" of the patient. All of this occurred before the patient was even officially admitted to the hospital, which is when things become even more complicated and idiosyncratic. How exactly should this patient's hospital encounter be prop- erly financially accounted for?

Traditionally, we haven't really tried to do this with great precision. As long as we generally get paid more than we spend, we have been content to instead bundle the money that is being spent into different categories of costs that are not always well connected to individual episodes of care. These costs are often thought of in layers, with "variable" costs on top (most connected to episodes of care), "fixed"

money not connected to care

costs at the bottom (least connected to episodes of care), and then "mixed costs" (sometimes divided into "semivariable" or "semifixed" costs) that fall somewhere in between (Table 4-2). A limited understanding of how costs connect to processes of delivering care may be at least partially responsible for why many clinical quality improvement (QI) efforts fail to deliver bottom-line results.[37]

Variable costs depend directly on the amount of care that is being delivered. Items that account for variable costs are fully "consumed" if they are used (like the disposable gloves a nurse dons before collecting a patient's blood sample). The converse is also usually true: if the item is not used, it will be available for later use, providing opportunities for savings. Variable costs include many of the items used to stock a supply closet or pharmacy shelf (catheters, bandages, medicines, etc). Because these items are within the direct control of clinicians, they are often considered ideal targets for reducing waste.

Fixed costs must be paid for regardless of the amount of care that is being delivered. Items that fall into this category also do not get fully consumed with each use and are usually considered to be fixed over some relevant range of time or activity. For example, the cost of keeping the lights on in the emergency department is fixed over the course of a shift of work. The costs of major equipment like MRI machines are fixed for a certain volume of patient care. Because fixed costs are independent from the amount of care that is taking place, they are not within the control of clinicians in the short term. Instead, fixed costs are usually

Table 4-2 Behavior of various cost layers in the healthcare system

Cost Layer	Effects of Reduction in Use	Examples
Layer 1: truly variable costs of patient care	The item is not consumed, does not need to be replaced, and is available for later use.	Supplies, medications
Layer 2: semivariable costs of patient care	The item is not consumed, but the ability to repurpose the item is limited by time. Costs of providing the service may be reduced with sufficient reduction in volume.	Direct hourly nursing, respiratory therapists, physical therapists
Layer 3: semifixed costs of patient care	The item is not consumed, but the obligation to continue to pay for the item does not change.	Equipment, operating room time, physician salaries, ancillary services
Layer 4: fixed costs not associated with patient care	Resource consumption is not altered in the short run but may be altered in the next operating cycle.	Billing, organizational overhead, finance

addressed over longer operating cycles, well beyond the planning horizon of a single episode of care.

It is sometimes challenging to isolate variable costs from the related fixed costs they get bundled with. It has been estimated that hospitals might save at least $650 per blood transfusion avoided.[38] However, transfusing blood entails more than the expense of the blood itself. There is the cost of maintaining the blood bank, the cost of the highly trained personnel that deliver the transfusion, and a host of other costs that are not necessarily within the clinician's control. Across many care delivery settings, up to 84% of total expenses may fall into the fixed costs category when the relevant range of consideration is a single episode of care.[39]

In between variable costs and fixed costs is a category of "mixed" costs that are sometimes divided into "semivariable" or "semifixed" costs. *Like variable costs, resources that generate semivariable costs are available for later use but the ability to repurpose them is limited by time.* As a result, these costs can typically only be reduced if there is a sufficient decrease in volume of services. The hourly time of nurses is sometimes accounted for as a semivariable cost. For example, a project to reduce unnecessary PIV replacements may save significant nursing time (on average, nurses spend 10 to 20 minutes total time per IV replacement; in difficult access situations it may take much longer),[40] but it would need to save enough time to warrant one less nurse for a shift to translate into real savings. Semifixed costs may be modified over a relevant range of activity but ultimately must be paid for even if resources are not used during an episode of care. Certain types of replaceable, transferable, or multiuse equipment (like a portable x-ray machine) may fall into this category.

Although many so-called "fixed" costs are not easily modifiable at the point of care, some resources are more fixed than others. As a result, the distinctions among the traditional cost layers—particularly for resources that are considered mixed costs—are not always consistent and can depend on institutional accounting preferences. In order to best identify and measure improvement opportunities, some have argued that all costs (even administrative overhead) should be treated as variable and allocated to care delivery activities.[36]

The limitation of considering most healthcare costs as fixed is that it focuses cost reduction efforts on a narrow range of variable cost resources while potentially ignoring other high-yield opportunities.[36] Harvard Business School Professor Robert Kaplan has been a particularly vocal advocate of bypassing the traditional cost layers in order to instead account for all costs (variable, mixed, and fixed) as they accrue in real time during the delivery of care. Using a method called *time-driven activity-based costing* (TDABC) the costs of space, nonconsumable equipment, and administrative overhead are all assigned minute-to-minute cost rates that are relevant to specific processes of care.[36,41]

In order to do this, the beginning point and endpoint of an episode of care are first defined. Depending on the goals of the healthcare improvement effort, multiple episodes of care might get bundled into a "care delivery value chain." For

[handwritten margin notes: "Efficiency of need", "Efficiency of money", "Industrial medicine"]

a total knee replacement, this may mean starting with the first preoperative clinical visit and ending with an episode of rehabilitation many weeks after the surgery has taken place. The care that is delivered is then broken down into discrete activities or process steps (eg, check-in, vitals and intake, physician evaluation). For each step, a cost is assigned by keeping track of who is doing which activity, what resources they use, which space they are in, and how long it takes them. Each item (personnel, resources, and space) is assigned a per-minute cost rate by bundling together all costs (fixed and variable) and then dividing by the total amount available for patient care.

This method allows you to measure the cost benefits of any process improvement efforts. Using TDABC, you might learn that an orthopedic surgeon costs $5.00 per minute while verifying the patient's medication history prior to performing the knee replacement operation. You might decide that a medical assistant who costs $2.00 per minute could instead perform this task in order to make the care process more efficient. Kaplan and his Harvard Business School colleague Michael Porter have advocated for a value measurement system that combines the outcome measures hierarchy with TDABC.[15] As health systems work steadily toward achieving the triple aim, these measurements, though imperfect, provide an important means of benchmarking our progress. *[handwritten: Efficiency = Surplus money value]*

LINKING VALUE TO QUALITY IMPROVEMENT AND PATIENT SAFETY

The patient safety and quality improvement (QI) movements of the last dozen or so years were largely galvanized by two landmark Institute of Medicine (IOM) reports, "To Err Is Human" (1999), and "Crossing the Quality Chasm" (2001).[42,43] Following "To Err Is Human," the media increasingly popularized stories to the public of horrific medical errors such as wrong limb surgeries and left behind surgical objects. The proverbial "burning platform" had been set ablaze and momentum was building for improving patient safety and quality of care, even if it was not entirely clear yet how to do so. Early efforts were fraught with missteps. Even seemingly simple interventions such as having surgeons mark the limb to be operated on led to serious unforeseen complications. Without some standardization, some surgeons marked the target limb with an "X," as in "X marks the spot," whereas others marked the opposite limb with an "X," as in "X = do not cut here."[44] Over the years, more coherent strategies for QI have emerged, but there is still much work to be done to achieve the six aims for healthcare systems set out by the 2001 IOM "Crossing the Quality Chasm" report: patient safety, patient-centeredness, effectiveness, efficiency, timeliness, and equity.[43]

To clinicians, improving the quality of care inherently depends on the effective delivery of evidence-based medicine. The problem is that there is a tremendous amount of drop-off at each stage between the translation of science into appropriate care delivery and patient experience (Figure 4-5).[45] At each step of the way, failures lead to missed opportunities, waste, and harm. Many of the goals of QI

Figure 4-5. Translating Science Into The Patient Experience. (Reproduced, with permission, from IOM (Institute of Medicine). Best care at lower cost: the path to continuously learning health care in America. Washington, D.C.: National Academies Press; 2013.)

are aimed at strengthening these connections. The goal is to more consistently and efficiently deliver advancements in science all the way to the bedside.

Despite some frustrating setbacks over the years, there have also been some significant advancements in the delivery of high-quality, safe patient care.[46] Now, representing a revolution that has been more than a decade in the making, new QI targets are largely focusing on including waste and costs into the equation, thus introducing value as the "quality dimension of our time,"[47] and proving that value really is just an extension of the patient safety and QI movements. Safe, high-quality, and affordable care tends to generally go hand-in-hand. On the flipside, medical errors, adverse events, and preventable complications lead to significant costs in morbidity and monetary measures. Adverse events during hospitalization alone result in billions of dollars in additional spending each year.[45,48,49] And efforts to improve patient safety often inherently improve healthcare value for patients.

Story From the Frontlines—"Actually, High-Tech Imaging Can Be High-Value Medicine"

"Can you hear it?" she asked with a smile. The thin, pleasant lady seemed as struck by her murmur as I was. She was calm, perhaps amused by the clumsy second-year medical student listening to her heart.

"Yes, yes I can," I replied, barely concealing my excitement. We had just learned about the heart sounds in class. This was my first time hearing anything abnormal on a patient, though it was impossible to miss—her heart was practically shouting at me.

Her mitral valve prolapse—a fairly common, benign condition—had progressed into acute mitral regurgitation. She came to the hospital short of breath because her faulty valve was letting blood back up into her lungs.

Though it was certainly frightening, surgery to fix the valve could wait a few weeks. But before doing anything, the surgical team wanted a picture of the blood vessels in her heart. If the picture showed a blockage, the surgeons would have to perform two procedures: one to fix the blockage, and another to fix her valve. If her vessels were healthy, though, the surgeons could use a simpler approach focused just on her valve.

So she came to the interventional cardiologist who was teaching me for the day. Coronary angiograms are the interventionalists' bread-and-butter procedure, done routinely to look for blockages and to guide stent placement. They involve snaking a catheter from the groin or arm through major blood vessels and up to the heart.

Under fluoroscopy (like a video X-ray), the cardiologists shoot contrast medium into the arteries, revealing the anatomy in exquisite detail. The images are recorded electronically and accompanied by the cardiologist's interpretation for anyone else who opens her medical record.

Though routine, these catheterizations aren't trivial. Whenever you enter a blood vessel, you introduce the risk of bleeding and infection. Fluoroscopy is radiation, and contrast medium can damage the kidneys. And let's not forget cost—reimbursing the interventional cardiologist, a radiology technician, and nursing staff costs Medicare almost $3,000 per case.

So I asked the cardiologist if such an invasive approach was really necessary. I knew the rationale—the surgeons needed to know if any of her vessels were blocked, so they could incorporate repairing them into their surgical plan. In a young, otherwise healthy patient, the likelihood of a blockage was low. But in open-heart surgery, "unlikely" isn't enough. They needed to know her anatomy definitively.

I still wondered if there was a less invasive approach to get the same information.

I knew I was entering delicate territory, since these catheterizations are how he makes his living. So I was surprised to hear his answer when I asked if CT angiography would've done the trick: "Probably, but the surgeons aren't comfortable with it. They only trust catheterizations."

CT angiography (CTA) is a noninvasive way to get detailed information about the anatomy of the heart. It's like a regular CT scan, except that pictures are taken after an injection of contrast medium. The total costs to Medicare were about $500 in 2009.

A study has shown that in low-risk patients with a positive stress test, starting with CTA (and catheterizing only when CTA is positive) can save an average of $789 per patient, with a small increase in radiation exposure but little change in accuracy.

Now, I'm just a medical student. I'm in no position to decide when interventions are necessary or needless. And I certainly won't tell a cardiothoracic surgeon what information they need to operate.

But I'm very familiar with an old standby in the health policy world and the popular media: that high-tech imaging, like CT scans, has contributed to runaway growth in the cost of American healthcare.

Advanced scans cost much more than older techniques, reveal "incidentalomas" that may cause more harm than good, and create a profit motive to drive their own use unnecessarily. I have no doubt that this is true much of the time. But reducing the issue down to one axiom is deceptive and simplistic.

It's not enough to ask what the costs, benefits, and harms of an imaging study will be. We also need to understand what we're comparing it to. A CT or an MRI will always be more expensive than an X-ray, and if we can get the same information from the latter, the more advanced images are indeed wasteful. But compared to catheterization, exploratory surgery—or worse, misdiagnosis—advanced imaging is a steal. It's cheaper and often less harmful than the more invasive alternatives.

The crucial question is who should undergo imaging. If our patient were likely to have a blockage and need catheterization anyway, it wouldn't make sense to start with CTA. But since her "pre-test probability" of a blockage was low, CTA could've averted a catheterization. This also doesn't mean hospitals should go on imaging technology shopping sprees in order to save our system money.

They are huge upfront investments, carrying perverse incentives to churn patients through in order to break even on the initial cost. And we already have far more of these devices than our peers in the developed world. We could probably make do with fewer.

Of course, this is probably not why the surgeons didn't trust CTA. Their job is to operate safely and proficiently, not to police our use of advanced imaging, and they had no financial incentive to request catheterization. My guess is that when the stakes are as high as when opening someone's chest, they tend to trust what they know for certain to work. But preferences like these change over time.

Our patient's angiography showed beautiful, intact coronary arteries. Her surgeons will probably go with the less invasive surgical approach, because they have no blockages to bypass. This is great news for her and her family. It would be even greater news if our policymakers and pundits took note of her story, and adopted a more nuanced approach to medical imaging. Eventually the surgeons will come around too. The only dogma compatible with the realities of healthcare is: if it sounds too simple to be true, it probably is. High-cost and high-tech, in the right patients, can also be high-value.

—Karan Chhabra. "Actually,
High-Tech Imaging Can Be High-Value Medicine."
The Health Care Blog (www.thehealthcareblog.com)
and Costs of Care, 2014 (www.costsofcare.org)

CHALLENGES

There are many substantial obstacles to the definition of healthcare value. These challenges are not insurmountable, and we present them here as the beginning of the conversation (see also Chapter 10). Much of our discussion throughout this book will focus on the way forward for clinicians and healthcare systems.

Undefined measurements

The first step to improving quality is measurement. And yet cost data in healthcare remains frustratingly opaque.[50] American businessman, engineer, and former head of Intel, Andy Grove has likened the current situation in healthcare to the plight of the automobile consumer of the 1950s.[51] "In the early 1950s, it was nearly impossible to know the value of an automobile," he wrote.[51] "They had prices, yes, but these would differ radically from dealer to dealer, the customer a pawn in the hands of the seller." Those buying a car had no way to know the true quality of the vehicle, nor how much it is really worth.

This all changed in 1958, with a Congressional bill that introduced the "window sticker." Soon all vehicles sold in the United States included a manufacturer's suggested retail price along with clear and meaningful quality metrics such as the car's fuel economy.[51] This revolutionized the process of purchasing a car and "made automobile pricing rational and understandable."[51] There is still no "window sticker" for healthcare pricing or costs. As many have previously commented, "consumers often know more about the pros, cons, and costs of televisions, cars, and appliances than they do about healthcare interventions."[52]

Cost transparency is a necessary early step toward measuring healthcare value; however, it does not solve the entire problem. Even if we have open access to costs, there will still be plenty of debate about how best to define the "costs" and "outcomes" in the value equation.[53] As discussed in Chapter 3, there are major fundamental differences between healthcare prices, costs, and reimbursements. Furthermore, since for healthcare systems value should include entire populations and episodes of care, there will need to be some consensus on which downstream costs and benefits should be included in value analyses.[53] And how should one deal with opportunity costs? These are among many questions that will need to be adequately answered.

Chapters 10, 15, and 16 further explore issues with accurately measuring and defining quality and costs.

Insufficient evidence-base

The delivery of high-value care depends on the appropriate and efficient execution of evidence-based care. But the problem is that we lack reliable data for the vast majority of real-world clinical decisions. Even when there is adequate guidance from randomized controlled trials, it takes an average of 17 years for this evidence to be incorporated into practice ("the lifetime of a cicada").[43,54]

Not only is slow adoption an issue, the guidelines themselves are based on trials with extensive inclusion and exclusion criteria that may not be generalizable to the heterogeneous population that a clinician actually sees in practice.[55] Despite an astronomically increasing medical knowledgebase, the vast majority of clinical decision-making remains unchartered.

The many challenges notwithstanding, the delivery of high-value care—in essence, aiming to make good on the promises of the triple aim—is a noble task that warrants the dedication of clinicians and healthcare systems united in overcoming these obstacles. The goal is deceptively simple: provision of the best quality care for patients delivered efficiently, safely, consistently, and at lower costs for both individuals and our nation.

KEY POINTS:

- The triple aim includes the interdependent goals of improving the experience of care, improving the health of populations, and reducing the per capita costs of healthcare.
- A simple definition of value in healthcare is quality divided by costs, or, more specifically, health outcomes achieved per dollar spent. However, there are currently substantial challenges in appropriately defining and measuring these variables.
- True improvements in value are dependent on either measurable improvement in outcomes measures (morbidity, mortality) and/or reductions in total costs of care. However, process measures and intermediate outcomes remain important as actionable items, particularly for local efforts.
- A more-than-decades-long progression in QI has led to an emphasis on measuring and improving healthcare value.

References:

1. Deyo RA, Mirza SK, Martin BI. Back pain prevalence and visit rates: estimates from U.S. national surveys, 2002. *Spine.* 2006;31(23):2724-2727.
2. Martin BI, Deyo RA, Mirza SK, et al. Expenditures and health status among adults with back and neck problems. *JAMA.* 2008;299(6):656-664.
3. Katz JN. Lumbar disc disorders and low-back pain: socioeconomic factors and consequences. *J Bone Joint Surg Am.* 2006;88(suppl 2):21-24.
4. Chou R, Qaseem A, Owens DK, Shekelle P, Clinical Guidelines Committee of the American College of Physicians. Diagnostic imaging for low back pain: advice for high-value health care from the American College of Physicians. *Ann Intern Med.* 2011;154(3):181-189.
5. Boden SD, Davis DO, Dina TS, Patronas NJ, Wiesel SW. Abnormal magnetic-resonance scans of the lumbar spine in asymptomatic subjects. A prospective investigation. *J Bone Joint Surg Am.* 1990;72(3):403-408.
6. Chou R, Qaseem A, Snow V, et al. Diagnosis and treatment of low back pain: a joint clinical practice guideline from the American College of Physicians and the American Pain Society. *Ann Intern Med.* 2007;147(7):478-491.
7. Davis PC, Wippold FJ II, Brunberg JA, et al. ACR appropriateness criteria on low back pain. *J Am Coll Radiol.* 2009;6(6):401-407.
8. Di Iorio D, Henley E, Doughty A. A survey of primary care physician practice patterns and adherence to acute low back problem guidelines. *Arch Fam Med.* 2000;9(10):1015-1021.
9. Srinivas SV, Deyo RA, Berger ZD. Application of "less is more" to low back pain. *Arch Intern Med.* 2012;172(13):1016-1020.
10. Deyo RA. Cascade effects of medical technology. *Annu Rev Public Health.* 2002;23:23-44.
11. Kendrick D, Fielding K, Bentley E, Kerslake R, Miller P, Pringle M. Radiography of the lumbar spine in primary care patients with low back pain: randomised controlled trial. *BMJ.* 2001; 322(7283):400-405.
12. Jarvik JG, Hollingworth W, Martin B, et al. Rapid magnetic resonance imaging vs radiographs for patients with low back pain: a randomized controlled trial. *JAMA.* 2003;289(21):2810-2818.
13. Verrilli D, Welch HG. The impact of diagnostic testing on therapeutic interventions. *JAMA.* 1996;275(15):1189-1191.

14. Rosenbaum L. The whole ball game—overcoming the blind spots in health care reform. *N Engl J Med*. 2013;368(10):959-962.

15. Porter ME. What is value in health care? *N Engl J Med*. 2010;363(26):2477-2481.

16. Eddy DM. Clinical decision making: from theory to practice. Connecting value and costs. Whom do we ask, and what do we ask them? *JAMA*. 1990;264(13):1737-1739.

17. Holden DJ, Harris R, Porterfield DS, et al. *Enhancing the Use and Quality of Colorectal Cancer Screening*. Rockville, MD: Agency for Healthcare Research and Quality; 2010. http://www.ncbi. nlm.nih.gov/books/NBK44526. Accessed September 30, 2013.

18. Kuppermann M, Pena S, Bishop JT, et al. Effect of enhanced information, values clarification, and removal of financial barriers on use of prenatal genetic testing: a randomized clinical trial. *JAMA*. 2014;312(12):1210-1217.

19. Carman KL, Maurer M, Yegian JM, et al. Evidence that consumers are skeptical about evidence-based health care. *Health Aff*. 2010;29(7):1400-1406.

20. Gill L. Risky prescription drug practices are on the rise in a grim economy. *ConsumerReports.org*. http://news.consumerreports.org/health/2011/09/risky-prescription-drug-practices-are-on-the-rise-in-a-grim-economy.html. Accessed November 15, 2012.

21. Moriates C, Shah NT, Arora VM. First, do no (financial) harm. *JAMA*. 2013;310(6):577-578.

22. Himmelstein DU, Warren E, Thorne D, Woolhandler S. MarketWatch: illness and injury as contributors to bankruptcy. *Health Aff*. 2005; Supplemental Web Exclusives:W5-63-W5-73.

23. Schoen C, Collins SR, Kriss JL, Doty MM. How many are underinsured? Trends among U.S. adults, 2003 and 2007. *Health Aff*. 2008;27(4):w298-w309.

24. Lee TH. The Word That Shall Not Be Spoken. *N Engl J Med*. 2013;369(19):1777-1779.

25. Hibbard JH, Greene J. What the evidence shows about patient activation: better health outcomes and care experiences; fewer data on costs. *Health Aff*. 2013;32(2):207-214.

26. Hibbard JH, Greene J, Overton V. Patients with lower activation associated with higher costs; delivery systems should know their patients' "scores." *Health Aff*. 2013;32(2):216-222.

27. Graham JD, Potyk D, Raimi E. Hospitalists' awareness of patient charges associated with inpatient care. *J Hosp Med*. 2010;5(5):295-297.

28. Berwick DM, Nolan TW, Whittington J. The triple aim: care, health, and cost. *Health Aff*. 2008;27(3):759-769.

29. Lee TH. Putting the value framework to work. *N Engl J Med*. 2010;363(26):2481-2483.

30. Rickard CM, Webster J, Wallis MC, et al. Routine versus clinically indicated replacement of peripheral intravenous catheters: a randomised controlled equivalence trial. *Lancet*. 2012;380 (9847):1066-1074.

31. Webster J, Osborne S, Rickard C, Hall J. Clinically-indicated replacement versus routine replacement of peripheral venous catheters. In: The Cochrane Collaboration, Webster J, eds. *Cochrane Database of Systematic Reviews*. Chichester, UK: John Wiley & Sons, Ltd; 2010. http://hospital-medicine.jwatch.org/cgi/content/full/2010/524/2. Accessed February 6, 2013.

32. Webster J, Clarke S, Paterson D, et al. Routine care of peripheral intravenous catheters versus clinically indicated replacement: randomised controlled trial. *BMJ*. 2008;337:a339.

33. Volpp KG, Loewenstein G, Asch DA. Assessing value in health care programs. *JAMA*. 2012;307(20):2153-2154.

34. Brook RH, McGlynn EA, Shekelle PG. Defining and measuring quality of care: a perspective from US researchers. *Int J Qual Health Care*. 2000;12(4):281-295.

35. Mant J. Process versus outcome indicators in the assessment of quality of health care. *Int J Qual Health Care*. 2001;13(6):475-480.

36. Kaplan RS, Porter ME. How to solve the cost crisis in health care. *Harv Bus Rev*. 2011;89(9):46-52, 54, 56-61 passim.

37. Rauh SS, Wadsworth EB, Weeks WB, Weinstein JN. The savings illusion—why clinical quality improvement fails to deliver bottom-line results. *N Engl J Med*. 2011;365(26):e48.

38. Zilberberg MD, Shorr AF. Effect of a restrictive transfusion strategy on transfusion-attributable severe acute complications and costs in the US ICUs: a model simulation. *BMC Health Serv Res*. 2007;7:138.

39. Roberts RR, Frutos PW, Ciavarella GG, et al. Distribution of variable vs fixed costs of hospital care. *JAMA*. 1999;281(7):644-649.

40. Dychter SS, Gold DA, Carson D, Haller M. Intravenous therapy: a review of complications and economic considerations of peripheral access. *J Infus Nurs*. 2012;35(2):84-91.

41. Kaplan RS, Anderson SR. Time-driven activity-based costing. *Harv Bus Rev*. 2004. http://hbr.org/2004/11/time-driven-activity-based-costing/ar/1. Accessed September 4, 2013.

42. Institute of Medicine. *To Err Is Human: Building a Safer Health System*. Washington, DC: National Academies Press; 1999.

43. Institute of Medicine. *Crossing the Quality Chasm a New Health System for the 21st Century*. Washington, DC: National Academy Press; 2001.

44. Wachter RM. *Understanding Patient Safety*. 2nd ed. New York, NY: McGraw Hill Medical; 2012.

45. Institute of Medicine. Committee on the Learning Health Care System in America. *Best Care at Lower Cost: The Path to Continuously Learning Health Care in America*. Washington, DC: National Academies Press; 2012.

46. Pronovost PJ, Wachter RM. Progress in patient safety: a glass fuller than it seems. *Am J Med. Qual*. 2014;29(2):165-169.

47. Berwick DM. The moral test. Institute for Healthcare Improvement 23rd Annual National Forum. 2011. http://www.ihi.org/knowledge/Pages/Presentations/TheMoralTestBerwickForum2011Keynote.aspx. Accessed November 15, 2012.

48. Levinson DR. *Adverse Events in Hospitals: National Incidence Among Medicare Beneficiaries*. Washington, DC: US Department of Health and Human Services, Office of the Inspector General; 2010.

49. Berwick DM, Hackbarth AD. Eliminating waste in US health care. *JAMA*. 2012;307(14):1513.

50. United States Government Accountability Office. *Health Care Price Transparency—Meaningful Price Information Is Difficult for Consumers to Obtain prior to Receiving Care*. Washington, DC: United States Government Accountability Office; 2011:43.

51. Grove A. Peeling away health care's sticker shock. *Wired*. 2012. http://www.wired.com/business/2012/10/mf-health-care-transparency/. Accessed November 15, 2012.

52. Owens DK, Qaseem A, Chou R, Shekelle P. High-value, cost-conscious health care: concepts for clinicians to evaluate the benefits, harms, and costs of medical interventions. *Ann Intern Med*. 2011;154(3):174-180.

53. Gusmano MK, Callahan D. "Value for money": use with care. *Ann Intern Med*. 2011;154(3):207-208.

54. Casey DE Jr. Why don't physicians (and patients) consistently follow clinical practice guidelines?: Comment on "worsening trends in the management and treatment of back pain". *JAMA Intern Med*. 2013;173(17):1581-1583.

55. Goldberger JJ, Buxton AE. Personalized medicine vs guideline-based medicine. *JAMA*. 2013;309(24):2559-2560.

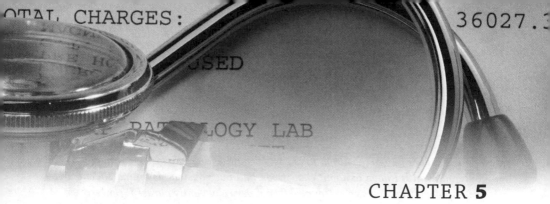

CHAPTER **5**

A Changing Landscape:
Cost Consciousness and Value
in Healthcare Delivery

*H*e winced in a way that made me feel his discomfort. It wasn't overly dramatic. It was the response of a man trying to put on a brave face and hide his pain, but—as I gently laid my hands on his belly—failing against his best efforts. This man had real abdominal pain, the kind that is impossible to not immediately empathize with. I got concerned.

"How long has this been going on?" I asked, while my mind began to immediately tick through a differential diagnosis.

"Well it probably started a year ago, but got really bad about four months ago," this otherwise healthy-appearing, 30-something-year-old man said.

We were in a small curtained-off area in the hectic Emergency Department at San Francisco General Hospital. I was an internal medicine resident in my last year of training. I started to wonder what in the world would possibly cause somebody to wait many months with severe abdominal pain and rectal bleeding before coming to see a doctor.

I asked a few more questions, verifying that he was indeed having bright red blood with his bowel movements, had lost at least 10 pounds over the last few months, and has dealt with nausea and debilitating abdominal pain ever since the end of last year.

So, I pulled out one of my most tried-and-true questions that I had picked up during residency:

"What made you come to the hospital today as opposed to yesterday or last week?" The answer should have surprised me.

"Well, I didn't want to see a doctor because I couldn't pay for it. I had to wait until my benefits kicked in so that I had insurance."

The Emergency Department had already put him through the CT scanner prior to calling me to admit him to the hospital, to ensure that he "didn't have something really bad going on," which I have to admit that if you had put your hands on his abdomen you would probably think was a reasonable (if not very eloquently phrased) concern.

The CT scan showed inflammation of his colon in a pattern that the radiologist said was very likely Crohn's disease.

His lab tests returned with severe anemia (hemoglobin of less than seven) and an undetectable iron level, revealing that the bleeding had been going on for a long time. I told him that I thought he needed a blood transfusion and a colonoscopy procedure in the morning by one of our gastroenterologists.

Then he asked me one of my most feared questions:

"But how much will that all cost and will my insurance pay for it?"
"I wish that I could answer that for you, but I really don't know."

Now, the thing is that I had actually spent more than the past year working on cost awareness for residents and looking into issues related to costs of care, and even I couldn't answer this question in a straightforward and truthful manner. This man needed these things done and costs be damned. Sure, but let's be honest, his concern is very real.

(Christopher Moriates, Costsofcare.org, May, 2012)

It has been well established that in general both patients and physicians do not know how much medical interventions cost their patients or the medical system.[1-5] Patients often experience "sticker shock" at the time they obtain a bill weeks after having received some form of healthcare. Comedian Julian McCullough explained this dreadful situation on an episode of National Public Radio's "This American Life"[6]: "I found out [about the cost of my hospitalization] when I got a bill in the mail for $45,000—in the mail, with the other mail, like it was just more mail. But it was a bill for $45,000—in a white envelope, like all the other envelopes. That should not come in a white envelope—that should come in a black envelope with a skull-and-crossbones on it, and when you open it a picture of your hopes and dreams falls out and burst into flames, because now you owe the hospital $45,000."

This chapter introduces how the landscape of cost consciousness in healthcare is rapidly changing, for both clinicians and the public. Despite the burgeoning attention paid to "out-of-control" healthcare costs recently, this is not a new problem. Unaffordable healthcare—on both national and individual levels—is like a cancer that developed decades ago and without adequate treatment has inexorably festered, grown, and metastasized to affect other economic sectors of our society.

HEALTHCARE COSTS BECOME A NATIONAL CRISIS

Some physicians and ethicists may warn that the separation of medical care and costs is an important, necessary aspect of the medical profession, ensuring a firewall between clinicians' medical decisions and their financial incentives (see Chapter 6). However, this separation is actually relatively new to the profession of medicine. As previously discussed, prior to the rise of medical insurance, basically all medical care was paid for by out-of-pocket cash payments and/or by bartering (see Chapter 2).[7] Therefore physicians and patients were often acutely aware of all the costs associated with their medical care and delivery. Even as late as the 1960s, about 50% of healthcare costs in the United States were paid out-of-pocket.[8]

As third-party insurance grew to dominate the market, healthcare costs became less transparent and more difficult for individuals to cover. In 1965, it was recognized that healthcare costs had begun to pose a menacing threat to Americans' wallets. As he signed Medicare into law, President Lyndon B. Johnson proclaimed: "No longer will illness crush and destroy the savings that [older Americans] have so carefully put away over a lifetime so that they might enjoy dignity in their later years."[9] As previously discussed in this book, Medicare has played a critical role in providing healthcare coverage for the elderly, but it has not necessarily fulfilled its promise to avoid damaging personal expenses for patients and their families, particularly during the last few years of life.[9,10]

By 1969, President Nixon declared that healthcare costs were a crisis.[11] At this time, healthcare represented an "unsustainable" 7.5% of the gross domestic product (GDP). Over the past 45 years, the crisis has not been averted; healthcare spending per capita has relentlessly increased each year since.[12]

Why has this happened?

There are many driving factors that have contributed to this current situation. As discussed in the preceding chapters, inflated and irrational medical pricing, lack of cost transparency, clinical inefficiencies, and inappropriate overuse have all played important roles.

"The tragedy of the commons"

There is also a broader behavioral science perspective that may best illustrate our situation. In a 1968 article in "*Science*," biology Professor Garrett Hardin described what he referred to as "the tragedy of the commons."[13] He noted that much like adults playing a game of "Tic-Tac-Toe," this dilemma did not have a "technical solution." He portrayed an open pasture shared by a group of cattle herdsmen. In this scenario, naturally each herdsman will want to keep as many cattle as possible. This will likely work out fine for centuries since conditions such as wars and disease keep the numbers of both men and cattle well below the carrying capacity of the land.

However, social stability is reached one day and "the inherent logic of the commons remorselessly generates tragedy." The reason is that each herdsman rationally seeks to maximize his own gain. They sense that adding a few more cattle to their herd will directly benefit themselves. On the other hand, a few more cattle will have only a minimal effect on the overall general welfare of the group. In other words, all will share the incremental cost on the land of adding another animal. Of course, as each herdsman behaves rationally in this way, eventually the meadow will become overgrazed resulting in catastrophe that will affect all. Hardin concludes: "Each man is locked into a system that compels him to increase his herd without limit—in a world that is limited."[13]

"Ruin," warns Hardin, "is the destination toward which all men rush, each pursuing his own best interest in a society that believes in the freedom of the commons. Freedom in a commons brings ruin to all."[13]

Much like Hardin's grazing area, medical resources are also finite. And many patients and clinicians have doubtlessly thought, "Well, what's one more MRI, even if it might not be necessary?" Over decades, this behavior has eaten away at medical resources, and now the toll is being paid across various sectors of society.

In 1975, Dr Howard Hiatt (then Dean of the Harvard School of Public Health) famously repurposed the "tragedy of the commons" for healthcare, calling on physicians to collaborate with other experts and the public in order to protect the "medical commons."[14] However, "not only have we failed to rise to his challenge," University of California, San Francisco (UCSF) Professor Dr. Molly Cooke noted in 2010,[15] "but our overconsumption and waste are now compromising our ability to address other pressing social needs and national priorities."

Story From the Frontlines—"How Much Will My MRI Cost?"

Approximately one year ago, I developed a phantom pain in my left eye that no doctor—whether primary care physician, neuro-opthalmalogist, or even neurologist—seemed to be able to diagnose. It was difficult enough to describe the pain, let alone repeatedly be told there was nothing visible creating it; the root cause did not seem to exist anywhere tangible that could lead to a potential diagnosis. I was eventually given a referral by a neurologist to get an MRI, both of the orbital areas of the cranium and of the brain.

As a graduate student on a student health insurance policy, I double-checked my insurance coverage to make sure that I would have enough money for this procedure. MRIs are notoriously not inexpensive. The result was that for every referred procedure there would be a maximum of $2,000 covered, leaving me to pay for the rest. I initially looked online to find some sort of general idea for the pricing of MRIs. The hospital where I was to have the procedure did not list pricing online. I had to look elsewhere, and eventually located a website that provided an average cost for MRIs of various kinds based on a handful of hospital submission from the Boston area, my hospital not included. The website reported costs of approximately $1,000 to $2,500 per MRI of the brain and orbits.

With this in mind, I called my hospital's main helpline and inquired and inquired about where I could find the price per MRI for this particular hospital. I was told they did not give out such information, but was referred to the radiology department, who told me that they were unaware of the pricing of procedures. Eventually I found out that not even the billing department at this hospital would give it pricing information. When I had called radiology, I inquired whether my insurance amount would suffice and was told that I "should be fine." In one last attempt, I called back and asked whether anyone in the hospital could just take a stab at the price of my MRI—I was bluntly told "No." And so in December of last year, I went in the day before leaving for Christmas break and underwent the two ordered MRI procedures.

When I returned for spring semester approximately one month later, I received a bill in the mail for more than $6,000. The total for the two MRIs exceeded $10,000. Luckily, the insurance covered each MRI as separate referrals and paid $4,000, instead of $2,000. But I was left then to deal with the remains of this $10,000+ procedure.

I consider myself a bright person, and I even have insurance, but when there is no possible way to determine that a procedure is going to end up costing $10,000, how could I have made an informed decision?

—Ingrid Stobbe. "How Much Will My MRI Cost?" Costs of Care, 2010.
(www.costsofcare.org)

PROGRESS IN "FITS AND STARTS"

Despite election cycles in the early 1970s, 1980s, and 1990s that included public mandates to make healthcare more affordable, progress has occurred in fits and starts. As Drs Andrew Auerbach and Robert M. Wachter from UCSF have put it: "Over the last 30 years, rounds of therapeutic treatments with cost consciousness and cost containment have been administered to the healthcare industry, with generally disappointing clinical response."[16]

Starting back with the Great Depression, more and more people could not afford medical services. This reality led President Franklin D. Roosevelt to propose publicly funded healthcare programs. However, he was met with severe opposition from the medical profession, ultimately forcing him to remove these provisions from the Social Security Act of 1935.[17] Many subsequent policy efforts to reform healthcare have also met staunch opposition by the medical profession. Broadly, President Roosevelt fought claims against "socialism," President Johnson against outcries of "entitlement," and President Clinton against vocal arguments in favor of "private markets." All of these attempts largely suffered from a lack of meaningful physician engagement. By contrast, President Obama's Affordable Care Act was bolstered by the physician-led Doctors for America, and ultimately was endorsed by the American Medical Association.[18,19] For the first time in US history, most major physician organizations were vocally and formally supportive of policy changes to provide more access to affordable healthcare.

THE CURRENT LANDSCAPE OF COST CONSCIOUSNESS AND VALUE

Clinician-led efforts to address healthcare costs

Over the years, individual clinicians have attempted many times in a myriad of ways to implement their own efforts to address healthcare costs. One often-tried method has been clinician-led educational programs. The first published effort to educate medical trainees about the costs of care was undertaken in 1975,[20] with subsequent efforts transiently appearing during the managed care debate of the early 1990s and other eras of attempted healthcare reform.[21,22] To date, the results of even the most creative efforts have been mixed and conspicuously local. In 1984, Dr Steven Schroeder and colleagues at UCSF accurately predicted the failure of physician education as a stand-alone cost containment strategy.[23] In the 1970s and 1980s, Dr Jerry Avorn at Harvard and others attempted having trained individuals, often clinical pharmacists, provide physicians with information about appropriate prescribing and diagnostic testing.[24,25] This resulted in very modest improvements in prescribing patterns.[25] Chapter 11 includes a full discussion of healthcare value education, including emerging tools and strategies.

Other clinician efforts have focused specifically on lab testing. In the 1970s, some administrators tried to bluntly ration lab tests by assigning resident physicians a finite number of "coupons" that could be redeemed for individual lab tests. The problems with this strategy are obvious. And residents predictably displayed their uncanny ability to work around any system that impedes them getting their work done or taking care of their patients: Counterfeit coupons "mysteriously" appeared on the wards and the program was quickly undercut. Some tried educational-driven efforts directed at lab utilization, particularly during the 1980s and 1990s, but effects quickly dissipated once the education was stopped.[26,27] More recently there seems to be a resurgence in these types of efforts. Some education programs coupled with targeted feedback have shown promising results in successfully decreasing lab utilization among residents.[26,28,29] One memorably titled paper by a surgical resident referred to the daily lab practices of "surgical vampires," and demonstrated impressive results with a simple educational and feedback program.[28] In addition, systems efforts to use technology for providing costs, giving trainee-specific feedback on utilization, or embedding value-based decision-support have recently emerged.[30-32] Of course, only time will tell whether any of these renewed efforts will have any staying power, or if they too will become yet another footnote in the long history of attempts.

Key influencers in the clinical professions arena

Although many of the recent educational efforts are similar to those tried in the past, it is possible that the overall environment that they are being introduced in has changed. A notable recent development is the number of influential professional organizations that have put forth substantial efforts to address stewardship, overutilization, and healthcare costs. These efforts are remarkable because they have been generated by the healthcare professional organizations themselves, rather than prompted directly by governmental or regulatory mechanisms. It is very possible that with these different inputs, clinicians have now become more primed to care about healthcare costs and resources.

A watershed moment for this movement was the widely endorsed 2002 release of the "Physician Charter on Medical Professionalism in the New Millennium," by the ABIM Foundation which called for minimizing "overuse of healthcare resources."[33] The American College of Physicians (ACP) subsequently added "parsimonious care" as an ethical responsibility to their sixth edition of the ACP Ethics Manual.[34] The ACP's "positions on efficiency, parsimony, and cost-effectiveness constitute an important shift, if not in ethics then in emphasis," stated Dr Ezekiel Emanuel.[35] This shifting ethical landscape will be studied in much more detail in Chapter 6.

Following the ABIM Foundation-led physician charter on professionalism, the Foundation, under the leadership of Dr Christine Cassel, launched the "*Choosing Wisely*" campaign in 2011. Choosing Wisely aims to promote conversations between physicians and patients by helping patients choose care that is:

- Supported by evidence
- Not duplicative of other tests or procedures already received
- Free from harm
- Truly necessary[36]

Choosing Wisely asks national organizations representing medical specialists to identify five tests or procedures commonly used in their field, whose necessity should be questioned and discussed. As of 2013, they had more than 50 organizations release at least one "top five" list for the campaign (available at www.choosingwisely.org). The concept of these "top five" lists was originally conceived by the National Physicians Alliance, and simultaneously by a 2010 editorial written by University of Texas physician-ethicist Dr Howard Brody in the *New England Journal of Medicine*.[37,38] The "top five" strategy was then piloted with the creation of three lists for internal medicine, family medicine, and pediatrics (Table 5-1).[37] Although the focus of these lists is on unnecessary use, there are, of

Table 5-1 Top five lists in primary care

Family Medicine	Internal Medicine	Pediatrics
1. Do not do imaging for low back pain within the first 6 weeks unless "red flags" are present.	1. Do not do imaging for low back pain within the first 6 weeks unless "red flags" are present.	1. Do not prescribe antibiotics for pharyngitis unless the patient tests positive for streptococcus.
2. Do not routinely prescribe antibiotics for acute mild to moderate sinusitis unless symptoms (which must include purulent nasal secretions AND maxillary pain or facial or dental tenderness to percussion) last for 7 or more days OR symptoms worsen after initial clinical improvement.	2. Do not obtain blood chemistry panels (eg, basic metabolic panel) or urinalysis for screening in asymptomatic, healthy adults.	2. Do not obtain diagnostic images for minor head injuries without loss of consciousness or other risk factors.
3. Do not order annual ECGs or any other cardiac screening for asymptomatic, low-risk patients.	3. Do not order annual ECGs or any other cardiac screening for asymptomatic, low-risk patients.	3. Do not refer otitis media with effusion (OME) early in the course of the problem.
4. Do not perform Pap tests on patients younger than 21 years or in women status post hysterectomy for benign disease.	4. Use only generic statins when initiating lipid-lowering drug therapy.	4. Advise patients not to use cough and cold medications.
5. Do not use DEXA screening for osteoporosis in women under age 65 years or men under 70 years with no risk factors.	5. Do not use DEXA screening for osteoporosis in women under age 65 years or men under 70 years with no risk factors.	5. Use inhaled corticosteroids to control asthma appropriately.

Source: Data from The "Top 5" lists in primary care: Meeting the responsibility of professionalism. *Arch Intern Med.* 2011;171(15):1385.

course, inherent cost implications. The potential savings from enacting just these first three primary care "top five" lists could top $5 billion, although notably the lion share of these savings would be from prescribing generic instead of brand name statins.[39]

Choosing Wisely is a campaign aimed at both healthcare professionals and patients. In order to translate some of these recommendations directly to patients, the ABIM Foundation has teamed up with *Consumer Reports* to provide and disseminate patient-friendly materials about appropriate care recommendations.[40] In fact, one day on my doorstep landed a flyer from *Consumer Reports* sent to patients with the headline "Imaging tests for lower-back pain: You probably do not need an x-ray, CT scan, or MRI." The pamphlet proceeded to explain in clear language that these imaging tests "do not help you feel better faster," "have risks," and "are expensive." It provided guidance on when imaging tests "are a good idea" and gave advice on how to treat common low back pain. While it is easy to identify radiological tests as part of the problem, it is important to note that many radiologists are committed to improved stewardship of resources. For example, prior to the launch of Choosing Wisely, the American College of Radiology (ACR) had released "appropriateness criteria" for imaging in many different situations, including low back pain, to help guide clinicians to avoid ordering unnecessary and wasteful radiological imaging.[41]

The Choosing Wisely campaign has gained considerable traction and is even now considered "an understood shorthand" among medical professionals.[42] Part of the initial successes of Choosing Wisely are due to the fact that the framing of the initiative was carefully calculated, and thus "successfully avoided the caricatures of 'rationing' or 'death panels,' reactions that doomed prior efforts to engage all stakeholders in a reasoned national dialogue about costs and value."[16] Another reason for the success is the use of trusted medical specialty societies who directly interface with their constituent physician members. As executive vice president and chief operating officer of the ABIM Foundation Daniel Wolfson stated, "There's incredible leadership being shown by the specialty societies in addressing appropriate care and waste, and a willingness to partner with consumers and patients to talk about these issues."[43]

The ACP has also contributed remarkable leadership in the domain of high-value care. They have led a broad program that aims to help "physicians to provide the best possible care to their patients, (while) simultaneously reducing unnecessary costs to the healthcare system."[44] The ACP has developed clinical recommendations, physician resources, curricula and public policy recommendations, as well as patient resources to help them understand the benefits, harms, and costs of tests and treatments of common clinical issues. The ACP guidelines and clinical recommendations have created an important evidence-based backbone for many other initiatives and targets, such as efforts to decrease imaging in low back pain, inappropriate prostate cancer screening, and upper endoscopy in gastroesophageal reflux disease. The ACP High-Value Care Curriculum for internal medicine residents will be discussed in detail in Chapter 11.

The Institute of Medicine (IOM) is an independent, nonprofit organization tasked with providing "unbiased and authoritative advice to decision makers and the public."[45] In 2010, the IOM convened a "Roundtable on Value and Science-Driven Care," and has subsequently created a "Value Incentives Learning Collaborative."[46,47] This work has led to important insights, including the widely referenced estimates of approximately $750 billion of annual waste in healthcare. The IOM also released an influential report in 2012 entitled "Best Care at Lower Cost."[48] This report provided a compelling argument for the need to radically transform healthcare to provide "continuously learning" systems, and outlined a number of emerging tools and strategies to accomplish this goal.[48]

Costs of Care, Inc. is a nonprofit directed by the three authors of this book with a mission to "empower patients and their caregivers to deflate medical bills."[49] Founded in 2009 by Dr Neel Shah, Costs of Care has held an annual essay contest each year since that time, crowdsourcing hundreds of anecdotes from all over the country that illustrate opportunities to improve the value of care. These stories have provided important insights and have shone a light on many defects currently in the system. They are also a key feature highlighted throughout this book and have been used to provide necessary clinical detail to influential policy reports.[48] Costs of Care has contributed to medical education through a partnership with the ABIM Foundation. The "Teaching Value" Project convenes educators and trainees on a Web-based platform and uses video education modules to teach clinicians why, when, and how to "choose wisely" (see Chapter 11).[50]

WILL IT WORK THIS TIME?

With such a long history of failed attempts at cost containment and improving healthcare value, why would this time be any different?

Well, for starters it seems that unlike in the past, this time all of the stakeholders—not just the payers or employers—are aligned in addressing healthcare costs. The need to decrease healthcare costs and pay clinicians for value rather than volume has become one of the very few platforms that both political parties in the United States have agreed on in 2013. Along with political willpower, there is also a recent increased awareness and sea change in public opinion about healthcare costs and unnecessary care. The lay press, including multiple influential *New York Times* articles, has begun to illustrate to the public the harms of overtreatment and has also frankly discussed healthcare costs.[51-53] Some of these articles, such as one (part of physician-journalist Elizabeth Rosenthal's "Paying Till it Hurts" series) that reported on patients being billed upwards of $500 for a single stitch placed in an emergency department[53], generated significant public outrage and attention.

In addition, clinicians increasingly see controlling costs as part of their jobs.[54,55] Some, including the authors of this book, have argued that the damages done to patients by healthcare costs are substantial, and thus clinicians now have a responsibility to consider "out-of-pocket costs as side-effects" or the "financial toxicity" of their interventions.[56-58] In 2013, we called for the well-established mantra of "first, do no harm" to be reconceptualized for this era of unsustainable healthcare spending as "first, do (financial) harm."[57] Despite these advancements, many physicians are still quick to point the "major responsibility" for healthcare costs at other stakeholders including the insurance industry and malpractice lawyers.[54] In response, some have taken the profession to task for lacking the "all-hands-on-deck" mentality required by the current situation,[59] but the fact is that 93% of physicians recognize that they have at least "some responsibility" in controlling health costs, even if they may be unsure how best to do that (Figure 5-1).[54]

Figure 5-1. Degree of agreement/disagreement among physicians regarding their role in containing healthcare. (Data from Tilburt JC, Wynia MK, Sheeler RD, et al. Views of US physicians about controlling health care costs. *JAMA*. 2013;310(4):380-388.)

Lastly, the implementation of the Affordable Care Act (ACA) reinforces many efforts aimed at moving toward providing "value" and will give some of the measures administrative "teeth." On a high level, the ACA creates new structures to facilitate and promote cost reductions and puts in place incentives for both healthcare systems and individual clinicians to improve the value of care that they provide (see Chapter 15).

THE WAY FORWARD

Part III of this book will largely focus on "solutions," particularly concentrated on distinct strategies for clinicians on the frontlines, but we can introduce some of the overarching concepts here. The "tragedy of the commons" is not unique to healthcare. Much like the growing momentum of the largely youth-driven—but structurally and governmentally supported—environmentalism movement, addressing healthcare costs will take countless marginally incremental efforts from all involved. Sure, turning off your water while you brush your teeth is an infinitesimally small drop in the bucket to preserving overall water resources, but turning off the tap can save up to 20 to 30 gallons of water per person per week. Multiply that by entire communities and you start making a real difference.

Just like the "Green" movement, the need to address healthcare resources has become an imperative of our time. It is particularly inspiring that the environmental movement of the late 1960s was led by college students. We have observed that the new value movement in healthcare is largely driven by the enthusiasm of trainees. There are many foundational steps including education, price transparency, and systems changes that need to firmly be in place, and there is clearly no magic bullet here. It will take the sustained efforts of clinicians, patients, healthcare systems, and the government to really affect change. However, also like environmentalism, incredible gains can be made in shifting culture, changing social norms, and pitching-in with an "all-hands-on-deck" mentality.

Further drawing from the environmental movement, Drs Donald Berwick and Andrew Hackbarth have adopted a "wedges" model—originally created as a strategy to keep atmospheric carbon dioxide within a sustainable range[60]—for reducing spending in US healthcare (Figure 5-2).[61] The solid black line represents a "business as usual" projection for healthcare spending, showing the familiar astronomical growth exceeding increases in GDP, and plotting the road to ruin. But they also present six "wedges," each representing an area of waste that could potentially be eliminated over time. Together these different strategies each contribute to closing the gap.

So, in summary, why are we so optimistic that this time the drive toward healthcare value and cost-consciousness will stick? For the first time in our history, it seems like the wills of the medical, policy, and public spheres have

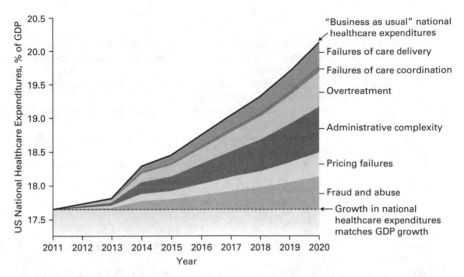

Figure 5-2. Wedges model for US healthcare, with theoretical spending reduction targets for six categories of waste. (Reproduced, with permission, from Berwick DM, Hackbarth AD. Eliminating waste in US health care. *JAMA*. 2012;307(14):1513. Copyright © 2012 American Medical Association. All rights reserved.)

aligned in the same broad direction. There are still many disagreements regarding the details, the mechanisms, and strategies to achieve these goals. Some of these are based on deeply held philosophical or ideological constructs. While not everyone may agree on the exact best way to get to the moon, at least now it seems everyone has looked up to the sky and settled on where the target lies.

KEY POINTS:

- Rising healthcare costs have been identified as a problem on both a national and an individual level for many decades; however, costs have continued to rise unabated.
- The lack of medical professional engagement helped doom numerous prior health reform efforts, but major physician organizations officially endorsed the Affordable Care Act of 2010, which helped lead to its passage.
- Numerous medical professional societies have recently put forth substantial independent efforts to curb healthcare costs and provide high-value care. The ABIM Foundation's "Choosing Wisely" campaign, the ACP "High-Value Care" initiatives, and the ABIM Foundation-Costs of Care "Teaching Value Project" have created momentum in this era of renewed enthusiasm for improved healthcare value.

References:

1. Ferraro M. Medicine's big mystery, what does treatment cost? *Bloomberg*. http://www.bloomberg.com/news/2011-07-12/medicine-s-big-mystery-what-does-treatment-cost-mimi-ferraro.html. Accessed November 15, 2012.
2. Allan GM, Lexchin J. Physician awareness of diagnostic and nondrug therapeutic costs: a systematic review. *Int J Technol Assess Health Care* 2008;24(2):158-165.
3. Graham JD, Potyk D, Raimi E. Hospitalists' awareness of patient charges associated with inpatient care. *J Hosp Med*. 2010;5(5):295-297.
4. Rosenthal JA, Lu X, Cram P. Availability of consumer prices from US hospitals for a common surgical procedure. *JAMA Intern Med*. 2013:1-6.
5. United States Government Accountability Office. *Health Care Price Transparency—Meaningful Price Information Is Difficult for Consumers to Obtain Prior to Receiving Care*. Washington, DC: United States Government Accountability Office; 2011:43.
6. A House Divided. *This American Life*. http://www.thisamericanlife.org/radio-archives/episode/439/a-house-divided?act=2#play. Accessed December 14, 2013.
7. Starr P. *The Social Transformation of American Medicine*. New York, NY: Basic Books; 1982.
8. Bodenheimer T, Grumbach K. *Understanding Health Policy: A Clinical Approach*. 6th ed. New York, NY: McGraw-Hill Medical; 2012.
9. Baicker K, Levy H. The insurance value of medicare. *N Engl J Med*. 2012;367(19):1773-1775.
10. Kelley AS, McGarry K, Fahle S, Marshall SM, Du Q, Skinner JS. Out-of-pocket spending in the last five years of life. *J Gen Intern Med*. 2013;28(2):304-309.
11. Nixon R. Remarks at a briefing on the nation's health system. 1969. http://www.presidency.ucsb.edu/ws/?pid=2121. Accessed April 9, 2013.
12. Centers for Medicare & Medicaid Services, Office of the Actuary. National health expenditures. 2013. http://www.cms.gov/Research-Statistics-Data-and-Systems/Statistics-Trends-and-Reports/NationalHealthExpendData/NationalHealthAccountsHistorical.html. Accessed July 14, 2013.
13. Hardin G. The tragedy of the commons. *Science*. 1968;162(3859):1243-1248.
14. Hiatt HH. Protecting the medical commons: who is responsible? *N Engl J Med*. 1975;293(5):235-241.
15. Cooke M. Cost consciousness in patient care—what is medical education's responsibility? *N Engl J Med*. 2010;362(14):1253-1255.
16. Auerbach AD, Wachter RM. Focusing on value: this time is different. *J Hosp Med*. 2013;8(9):543-544.
17. Patel K, Rushefsky ME. *Health Care Politics And Policy in America*. 3rd ed. Armonk, NY: M.E.Sharpe; 2006.
18. Doctors for America. http://www.drsforamerica.org/. Accessed December 14, 2013.
19. Maves MD. American Medical Association letter to Senator Harry Reid. 2009. http://www.ama-assn.org/resources/doc/washington/hsr-ama-reid-hr3590.pdf. Accessed December 13, 2013.
20. Lyle CB Jr, Bianchi RF, Harris JH, Wood ZL. Teaching cost containment to house officers at Charlotte Memorial Hospital. *J Med Educ*. 1979;54(11):856-862.
21. Sabin JE. How to teach residents about ethical managed care—even if the mention of "managed care" makes your blood boil. *Harv Rev Psychiatry*. 1999;7(1):64-67.
22. Sabin JE. A credo for ethical managed care in mental health practice. *Hosp Community Psychiatry*. 1994;45(9):859-860, 869.
23. Schroeder SA, Myers LP, McPhee SJ, et al. The failure of physician education as a cost containment strategy. Report of a prospective controlled trial at a university hospital. *JAMA*. 1984;252(2):225-230.
24. Avorn J, Chen M, Hartley R. Scientific versus commercial sources of influence on the prescribing behavior of physicians. *Am J Med*. 1982;73(1):4-8.
25. Oxman AD, Thomson MA, Davis DA, Haynes RB. No magic bullets: a systematic review of 102 trials of interventions to improve professional practice. *CMAJ*. 1995;153(10):1423-1431.

26. May TA, Clancy M, Critchfield J, et al. Reducing unnecessary inpatient laboratory testing in a teaching hospital. *Am J Clin Pathol*. 2006;126(2):200-206.
27. Wong ET, McCarron MM, Shaw ST Jr. Ordering of laboratory tests in a teaching hospital: can it be improved? *JAMA*. 1983;249(22):3076-3080.
28. Stuebing EA, Miner TJ. Surgical vampires and rising health care expenditure: reducing the cost of daily phlebotomy. *Arch Surg*. 2011;146(5):524-527.
29. Han SJ, Saigal R, Rolston JD, et al. Targeted reduction in neurosurgical laboratory utilization: resident-led effort at a single academic institution. *J Neurosurg*. 2014;120(1):173-177.
30. Dine CJ, Miller J, Fuld A, Bellini LM, Iwashyna TJ. Educating physicians-in-training about resource utilization and their own outcomes of care in the inpatient setting. *J Grad Med Educ*. 2010;2(2):175-180.
31. Bates DW, Kuperman GJ, Jha A, et al. Does the computerized display of charges affect inpatient ancillary test utilization? *Arch Intern Med*. 1997;157(21):2501-2508.
32. Feldman LS, Shihab HM, Thiemann D, et al. Impact of providing fee data on laboratory test ordering: a controlled clinical trial. *JAMA Intern Med*. 2013;173(10):903-908.
33. ABIM Foundation, American College of Physicians-American Society of Internal Medicine, European Federation of Internal Medicine. Medical professionalism in the new millennium: a physician charter. *Ann Intern Med*. 2002;136(3):243-246.
34. Snyder L. American College of Physicians Ethics Manual. 6th ed. *Ann Intern Med*. 2012;156(1, pt 2):73-104.
35. Emanuel EJ. Review of the American College of Physicians Ethics Manual, 6th ed. *Ann Intern Med*. 2012;156(1, pt 1):56-57.
36. Choosing Wisely. An Initiative of the ABIM Foundation. http://www.choosingwisely.org/. Accessed October 7, 2013.
37. The Good Stewardship Working Group. The "Top 5" lists in primary care: meeting the responsibility of professionalism. *Arch Intern Med*. 2011;171(15):1385.
38. Brody H. From an ethics of rationing to an ethics of waste avoidance. *N Engl J Med*. 2012;366(21):1949-1951.
39. Kale MS, Bishop TF, Federman AD, Keyhani S. "Top 5" lists top $5 billion. *Arch Intern Med*. 2011;171(20):1856-1858.
40. Consumer Reports. Consumer health choices. http://consumerhealthchoices.org/. Accessed July 7, 2013.
41. Davis PC, Wippold FJ II, Brunberg JA, et al. ACR appropriateness criteria on low back pain. *J Am Coll Radiol*. 2009;6(6):401-407.
42. McKinney M. At the heart of quality. *Modern Healthcare*. 2013. http://www.modernhealthcare.com/article/20131102/MAGAZINE/311029983. Accessed December 14, 2013.
43. Bebinger M. You May Not Need That Test, But Will You Still Get It? CommonHealth. 2013. http://commonhealth.wbur.org/2013/02/you-may-not-need-this-test-but-will-you-still-get-it. Accessed December 16, 2013.
44. American College of Physicians. High value cost conscious care. http://hvc.acponline.org/. Accessed October 7, 2013.
45. About the IOM—Institute of Medicine. http://www.iom.edu/About-IOM.aspx. Accessed December 15, 2013.
46. Institute of Medicine. Roundtable on value & science-driven health care. *Value in Health Care Accounting for Cost, Quality, Safety, Outcomes, and Innovation: Workshop Summary*. Washington, DC: National Academies Press; 2010. http://site.ebrary.com/id/10395837. Accessed November 15, 2012.
47. Institute of Medicine. Value Incentives Learning Collaborative. http://iom.edu/Activities/Quality/VSRT/2013-FEB-19.aspx. Accessed December 14, 2013.
48. Institute of Medicine. *Best Care at Lower Cost: The Path to Continuously Learning Health Care in America*. Washington, DC: National Academies Press; 2012.
49. Costs of Care. http://www.costsofcare.org/. Accessed December 14, 2013.

50. Costs of Care, ABIM Foundation. Teaching value project. http://www.teachingvalue.org/. Accessed August 4, 2013.
51. Parker-Pope T. Overtreatment is taking a harmful toll. *Well blog, The New York Times*. http://well.blogs.nytimes.com/2012/08/27/overtreatment-is-taking-a-harmful-toll/. Accessed November 15, 2012.
52. Konrad W. Some heart disease screens may be unnecessary. *The New York Times*. http://www.nytimes.com/2011/06/11/health/11consumer.html. Published June 10, 2011. Accessed November 15, 2012.
53. Rosenthal E. As hospital prices soar, a stitch tops $500. *The New York Times*. http://www.nytimes.com/2013/12/03/health/as-hospital-costs-soar-single-stitch-tops-500.html. Published December 2, 2013. Accessed December 14, 2013.
54. Tilburt JC, Wynia MK, Sheeler RD, et al. Views of US physicians about controlling health care costs. *JAMA*. 2013;310(4):380-388.
55. Farkas C, van Biesen T. *The New Cost-Conscious Doctor: Changing America's Healthcare Landscape*. Boston, MA: Bain and Company; 2011.
56. Ubel PA, Abernethy AP, Zafar SY. Full disclosure—out-of-pocket costs as side effects. *N Engl J Med*. 2013;369(16):1484-1486.
57. Moriates C, Shah NT, Arora VM. First, do no (financial) harm. *JAMA*. 2013;310(6):577-578.
58. Zafar SY, Abernethy AP. Financial toxicity, Part I: a new name for a growing problem. *Oncol Williston Park N*. 2013;27(2):80-81, 149.
59. Emanuel EJ, Steinmetz A. Will physicians lead on controlling health care costs? *JAMA*. 2013;310(4):374-375.
60. Pacala S, Socolow R. Stabilization wedges: solving the climate problem for the next 50 years with current technologies. *Science*. 2004;305(5686):968-972.
61. Berwick DM, Hackbarth AD. Eliminating waste in US health care. *JAMA*. 2012;307(14):1513.

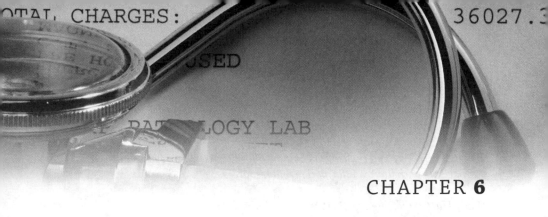

CHAPTER 6

Ethics of Cost Conscious Care

*M*ichael is 12 years old. "Not hungry?" I ask when I enter the room, eyeing the plate. He doesn't answer my question, but instead remarks with a lopsided grin, "You look funny." I look sideways at [my reflection in] the mirror and see a yellow-gowned creature fumbling around. Michael is right. I do look strange, but these precautions are necessary because he is undergoing chemotherapy for metastatic Ewing's sarcoma. He was diagnosed 3 months after he first saw his physician for leg pain. At the time, his pediatrician told him that he was having growing pains, and instructed Michael to call back if the pain worsened. Surprisingly, Michael's pain went away after the visit. However, some weeks later, his pain returned with a new, burning intensity. Concerned, Michael's mother made another appointment with their pediatrician. This time, the pediatrician attributed Michael's pain to a sports injury and advised him to, "Ice the leg, take some Tylenol and call back if the pain persists." While Michael felt somewhat better, a few weeks later when the pain began awakening him from sleep, Michael's mother took him to the emergency room. The doctors ordered an x-ray of his leg, which showed "onion-skinning" lesions on his bone, a classic finding in Ewing's sarcoma. A subsequent CT scan showed that the tumor had metastasized to his lungs.

In medical school, we are taught cost-effective care. On a population basis, x-raying every child with leg pain is not cost-effective. But on an individual basis, which parent given the choice would forego an x-ray even if the likelihood of their child having a tumor were small? Most children with leg pain do not have tumor, but what if he or she is in the minority? And even with the most rigorous of algorithms, some patients may have atypical presentations, and we may still miss the diagnosis. Michael's mother blames herself. She believes that if had she pushed more aggressively for an x-ray early on, the tumor might have been discovered sooner.

In medicine, a perpetual struggle exists between preventing the most serious outcomes while not incurring too much costly, unnecessary testing. On my pediatrics rotation, one of my attending physicians taught me that the most important test was the "pillow-test." In short, would I be able to fall asleep that night knowing that I had done everything that I could have for my patient? If I had been Michael's pediatrician, would I have *passed the "pillow-test?" Encounters with patients like Michael leave us wondering if cost-effective care for the population is at odds with delivering the best care for individuals. We can never "do everything possible" for a patient; we can only do our best—which is to order tests and services thoughtfully guided by outcomes from clinical trials. Ultimately the joy and challenge of being a physician is "doing everything possible" for our patients with limited information and resources.*

(Lissy Hu, Costsofcare.org, 2010)

Considering costs while caring for patients can seem ethically murky, particularly when delivering cost-effective care is at odds with the desire to "do everything possible." While most acknowledge that cost consideration is necessary, there is tremendous debate over whose responsibility this is. In 2014, Harvard neurologist Dr Martin Samuels was quoted in the *New York Times*, stating:

> There should be forces in society who should be concerned about the budget, about how many MRIs we do, but they should not be functioning simultaneously as doctors.[1]

But if not doctors and other clinicians, then who? Certainly patients, policymakers, and administrators of payer and provider organizations must all play a role as well. However, as we have discussed, much of healthcare is left to the clinician's discretion. Without defining an ethically coherent way for clinicians to consider cost, achieving the goal of the best possible care at the lowest possible cost may not be feasible.

Dr Samuels and others perceive an insurmountable tension between doing what is best for the individual patient (beneficence) and what is best for society as a whole (justice).[2] Every day in intensive care units around the country, patients at the very end of their lives may benefit from exorbitantly expensive care that nonetheless comes at high societal cost. Every day, clinicians struggle with tough decisions about the "right" level of care to provide. The need to also respect patient autonomy adds to the challenge. Occasionally patients may request expensive care that strains societal budgets without offering much benefit.[3] For example, proton beam therapy is a much more expensive way to treat prostate cancer than other forms of radiation therapy. Yet despite any evidence that proton beam therapy is any better than x-ray radiation therapy, it continues to be requested and used all the time.[4,5]

Lissy Hu, who wrote the anecdote above when she was a medical student, is not alone in her concerns about passing the "pillow test." A large survey of American physicians revealed that 54% of physicians agree "cost to society is important in my decisions to use or not to use an intervention," yet 78% felt that: "I should be solely devoted to the best interests of my individual patients, even if it is expensive," and 85% disagreed that they should sometimes deny services to patients because "those resources should go to other patients who need them more."[6]

To understand how we might deal with the tensions that clinicians face every day, this chapter reviews how the main principles of medical ethics can be applied to value-based care, how these principles are integrated into professional guidelines, and how we might reconcile concerns about "rationing" with a necessary path forward.

MAIN PRINCIPLES OF CLINICAL MEDICAL ETHICS

Medical ethics is not just about right and wrong—if only things were that easy. It is a rigorous academic discipline combining philosophy, history, sociology, and (in some cases) theology, which helps clinicians navigate the complex moral choices that are increasingly common in the modern era of medical practice. The basic principles of medical ethics are not new. In fact, they have been debated and refined by many societies over many centuries—the Hippocratic Oath dates to the 5th century BC. In the modern era of Western medicine, these principles have been consolidated into four, widely accepted "values": autonomy, beneficence, nonmaleficence, and justice.[7]

The values themselves (described below) are relatively straightforward. It is the application of these values to practice that is challenging and where disagreement more commonly lies. As a result, the basic values of medical ethics guide clinical decision making but they do not automatically dictate the right or wrong answer. As we will discuss, in some cases, particularly with regard to providing value-based care, these principles can appear to contradict each other. The balance of these principles is often embedded in a clinician or institution or culture's "normative assumptions." Nonetheless, the four values provide a framework from which clinicians can argue for what the right balance should be.

1. *Respect for autonomy.* The patient has the right to refuse or choose their treatment. The respect for autonomy is sometimes viewed in contrast to a more traditional "paternalistic" manner of clinical practice, where the clinician knows best and makes decisions on the patient's behalf. Respect for autonomy also underlies recent efforts to empower patients to make more informed and assertive decisions about their healthcare (see Chapter 12).

2. *Beneficence.* A clinician should act in the best interest of the patient. While this may appear to be easy for most clinicians, it is important to recognize that there are significant "agency" problems in the clinician-patient relationship, as we discussed in Chapter 3. Although clinicians are expected to act in the best interest of their patients, patients do not often have complete information about the value of care they are receiving.

3. *Nonmaleficence.* "First, do no harm" is the famous credo of nonmaleficence and underscores the need to avoid tests or treatments that could be harmful. In addition to "medical harm," patients may also face "financial harm" due to the high cost of their healthcare and treatments.[8,9]

4. *Justice*. This value concerns the fair and equitable distribution of limited health resources, as well as the ultimate decision of who gets what care. While the moral obligation to care for patients in a just manner appears straightforward, justice can often seem abstract and challenging to operationalize at the point-of-care.

The need for clinicians to take responsibility for the just distribution of healthcare resources is well-illustrated by a classic dilemma known as the "tragedy of the commons" (see Chapter 5) applied to healthcare resources.[10] As former Harvard School of Public Health Dean, Howard Hiatt, highlighted, healthcare is no different than any other scarce resource, such as land or the environment. It is true that clinicians are primarily responsible for the care of the patient in front of them. But if every clinician only acted in the interest of their own patients, the ultimate outcome will not necessarily be fair and might cause the depletion of important common resources. Through this depletion, all patients end up being worse off. Therefore, justice is an effort to protect the "commons," to ensure sustainability of the healthcare system's resources for the future.

AN ETHICAL BASIS FOR CONSIDERING VALUE

In considering whether clinicians should order a test, the decision is relatively easy when the test is both affordable for the patient (beneficence) and cost-effective for society (justice). There are many examples of this type of win-win care, such as the use of generic drugs, vaccination programs, and prenatal screening during pregnancy. Similarly, if it is clear the test is both unaffordable and potentially more harmful than beneficial to patients, and also not cost-effective for society, then the test should not be ordered. Ordering a mammogram for an 85-year-old diabetic woman with kidney failure would be one such example (see Chapter 14).

The decisions are much more challenging when the patient and societal interests are not congruent (Figure 6-1). Ethicist Robert Veatch highlights this challenge well:

> The ethics of the Hippocratic physician makes yes or no decisions on the basis of benefit to a single individual without taking into account what economists call alternative costs.... If physicians are asked to reject such care for their patients in order to serve society, they must abandon their Hippocratic commitment.[11]

Some have expressed skepticism that this challenge can be navigated in an ethically coherent way. In a recent Massachusetts Medical Society lecture, Dr Martin Samuels stated, "The important question is which master do we serve? ... Simultaneously considering the interests of society and the individual patient represents an irresolvable conflict of interest...."

He has gone on to say in other sources that doctors who consider costs will ultimately lose their public trust and he advocates for a complete separation between those who provide medical care and those who consider healthcare costs.

One counter to these traditional views is that it is not the case that doing more for a patient automatically leads to better care. As we highlight throughout this

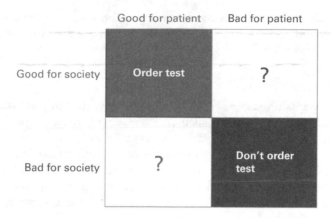

Figure 6-1. Ethical motivation for considering costs.

book, overuse of medicine can be just as harmful as underuse in medicine. Moreover, although doing everything possible for our patients is an aspirational goal, it is rarely practically feasible. Dr Molly Cooke from the University of California, San Francisco has pointed out that we actually make implicit value-based medical decisions every day, such as how best to triage scarce resources like intensive care unit beds.[12] Such decisions are not based on the well-being of the single patient in front of us, but on the well-being of many patients that we also feel responsible for in tandem. The fact that these value-based decisions are currently "below board" is problematic because there is very little transparency about how they are made. The last thing anyone wants are clinicians who are making "rogue rationing decisions" at the bedside without a clear, explicit, and widely agreed-upon process.[13]

With this grounding, we might then develop specific case examples of when societal and individual interests are in conflict in order to come up with strategies for how to navigate the tension. In many cases it might be reasonable for a clinician to put the patient's interests in front of those of society. From a societal perspective, screening all 50-year-olds with a colonoscopy makes sense. For a given individual patient this may be very expensive, particularly if there is a false positive. In other cases, it might be necessary for a delivery system to make hard choices to avoid a tragedy of the commons. In these cases, it may help clinicians to establish transparent rules for withholding services, along with processes for appeal and oversight.[13,14]

Beneficence and nonmaleficence

Stewardship is consistent with beneficence and nonmaleficence because inappropriate care and overuse can harm patients both physically and financially.[8] For example, a patient who receives an unnecessary CT scan would be subject to harm not only due to exposure to radiation and contrast, but also due to subsequent costly and potentially harmful workups from the discovery of incidental findings.

Justice

Effective stewardship ensures that healthcare services and resources are not wasted so that they remain available to those who need those service and resources most.[10] This is particularly important in areas where treatments are already scarce, such as supply of vaccines for certain conditions. The Association of American Medical Colleges President Darrel Kirsch has pointed out that despite a professional obligation, "Considerations of justice, especially when viewed in the context of society as a whole, seem underemphasized relative to the other fundamental ethical principles of medicine."[15]

Respect for autonomy

There are times at which stewardship is at odds with respect for a patient's autonomy. This is most likely to occur when patients ask to receive medical care that is unnecessary or not indicated. To resolve this conflict, physicians and other healthcare professionals need to listen to patients and the rationale for the request. Effective communication and education can keep an open dialogue to promote informed and shared decision making between patients and physicians. When the situation cannot be resolved, it is important for physicians to acknowledge that patient autonomy is not limitless, and they should not consider a patient request that would result in greater harm than good to the patient.[3]

Story From the Frontlines: "A Question of Worth"

As an OB/GYN resident, I tried to reconcile quality and cost of care every day. This is the story of one patient who cost the system a lot of money, but I don't know to this day if it was too much.

Cheryl (name changed) had HIV, a history of cervical cancer, and 3 kids. At age 35, she had been cured from cervical cancer after surgery and radiation therapy. However, due to treatment-related fistulas, she had been in and out of the hospital for most of the year. I was taking call for the gynecology service the last time her family brought her in, delirious and with black, sticky stool oozing from an opening in her unhealed abdominal incision.

She needed wound care and close monitoring in the intensive care unit (ICU). I paged the ICU team.

The ICU fellow came promptly, and briskly refused to accept her to his unit. "She is a poor use of scarce resources," he stated matter-of-factly. "Further treatment is futile." Without missing a beat, I looked him in the eye and countered, "What if this was your sister? Your mom?" He relented begrudgingly, but added, "This is why healthcare is so expensive in this country. You surgeons don't know when to let go."

Thanking him for accepting my patient, I went back to Cheryl to clean up her wound. She grabbed my arm and whispered, "Dr. Wu, I'm scared. Don't leave." I assured her that we would do everything we could to get her back to her kids. After all, her cancer was gone and her HIV viral load was undetectable. We couldn't quit now. Two days later, Cheryl was leaving her room to sneak a cigarette. One day after that, she was found dead in her hospital bed by a nurse checking vital signs. Cheryl had quietly passed away in her sleep from a massive gastrointestinal bleed.

Had I gotten too attached and lost sight of the big picture, as the ICU fellow purported? Who deserved that last ICU bed that night? Someone who would have only cost taxpayers $10,000, $100,000, or $1,000,000 during her stay? Would it have mattered to the hypothetical taxpayer that Cheryl had lost her professional job and employer-based insurance due to her long treatment, then lost her home, then spent down her income and thus qualified for Medicaid? Was it my responsibility to be considering resource allocation while my patient was critically ill? Besides, the ICU fellow abandoned his cost-conscious argument quite quickly at the mere suggestion that he would do otherwise for his family member.

I had worked in the private, public, and not-for-profit sectors prior to going to medical school. I had pondered the roles of corporations, governments, and single-issue foundations in shaping our healthcare system. I knew about the slippery politics, limited data, legal pressures, and economic realities. Yet, time and time again when my patients come into the emergency room or are lying on the operating table or get better or worse after some intervention, I struggle to see the forest for the trees.

On some level, I don't think my patients want me to be thinking about the sustainability of the healthcare system when I'm counseling them about their options. They want to know that I am their unwavering advocate. Their interests are my top priority in that fiduciary relationship. If I suggested more or less, it would only be watching out for them, not for the general public.

Yet, my experience tells me that providers, the people who oversee these cherished doctor-patient interactions, must play a principal role in revamping this overwrought and overpriced healthcare structure that does not produce the quality and safety outcomes any moral society would demand. Doctors wrestle with the nuances and inefficiencies of the institution every day. Medicine is not mathematics, but it is prudent to inject a measure of cost-awareness into our diagnostic work-ups, treatment algorithms and clinical trials. It may seem distasteful to knowingly put a monetary value on life, but we already do that calculation with each clinical decision we make. Higher quality can be affordable and accessible.

So for now, I continue to navigate that difficult space between being a good doctor and a conscientious citizen. I will see many more patients like Cheryl in my career. They will always be pushing me to do better.

—Eijean Wu. "A Question of Worth." Costs of Care, 2012.
(www.costsofcare.org)

FEAR OF RATIONING

Ultimately, hedging regarding the need to steward resources is often attributable to concerns regarding rationing of care. Discussions surrounding high-value care can be easily politicized, particularly at the end of life.[16] This controversy is not new and in part led to the failure of healthcare reform in the 1980s and 1990s, as discussed in Chapter 5. This concern also emerged in the 2009 debate about the impending healthcare reform law when former Governor and Vice Presidential candidate Sarah Palin alleged that the Affordable Care Act would lead to the formation of "death panels," or bureaucratic groups that would deny healthcare. Although this claim was clearly refuted, numerous sources credit this phrase as almost derailing the healthcare reform effort.[17] For example, University of Chicago Professor Harold Pollack has warned that given the "anxieties captured in the crystalline phrase 'death panel,' I would not commence a national cost-control discussion within the frightening and divisive arena of end-of-life care."[18]

One reason the term "rationing" is not viewed favorably by Americans is the connotation of wartime America, in which food, gasoline, and other goods have been "rationed."[19] Moreover, the fear of rationing in healthcare overlooks the actual reality that American healthcare is already rationed on many levels. Many economic experts agree that healthcare in the United States is not a limitless resource, and therefore is already rationed.

As David Leonhardt argued in the *New York Times* in "Health Care Rationing Rhetoric Overlooks Reality" in June 2009,[20] "The choice isn't between rationing and not rationing. It's between rationing well and rationing badly. Given that the United States devotes far more of its economy to health care than other rich countries, and gets worse results by many measures, it's hard to argue that we are now rationing very rationally."

Types of rationing in healthcare

There are several levels at which healthcare resources might be rationed. Operationally, this means that rationing of healthcare services can either occur primarily at the bedside through individual clinical decisions, or more broadly at the level of the healthcare system.

Bedside rationing

First, care could be rationed by ability to pay for healthcare. When rationing by ability to pay for healthcare, patients who are either unable or not willing to pay for certain services are unable to receive certain costly treatments. This type of rationing is especially common with high copayments for medications or health-care services that are passed along to patients by insurers. In addition, premiums for health insurance may also be too high for patients to afford healthcare insurance, and therefore affects their access to care.

An increasingly common mechanism to incentivize rational use of healthcare resources at the point of clinical decision is through reimbursement designs that utilize fixed or global payments (see Chapter 15). These forms of reimbursement place the impetus on clinicians to provide care with a discrete budget. An alternate and sometimes complementary mechanism of rationing uses clinician "gatekeepers" to restrict use of certain services. Typically gatekeepers are primary care clinicians in health maintenance organizations (HMOs) that must provide referrals for subspecialty care or certain types of advanced testing.

Rationing at the system level

Care is also often rationed through insurance coverage, including who is covered and what they are covered for (Chapter 2). This is a common tool used by healthcare insurers to keep costs down. For example, Medicare decided which tests and technologies will be covered and therefore available to its beneficiaries. The United Network for Organ Sharing also utilizes this technique to prioritize which recipients should receive organ transplant.[21] One criticism of this type of rationing is that it does limit the autonomy of the individual clinician in choosing healthcare services for their patients to a specific list of "covered services."

Rationing versus rational decision making

The term "rationing" has been coopted by politicians and is often understood to be synonymous with withholding necessary care. Efforts to improve value of care are often confused with rationing by the public and policymakers, making it harder to improve care.[22]

In recognition of this, the American College of Physicians (ACP) Health and Public Policy Committee tackled the polarized notion of "rationing" by issuing a policy paper titled "How Can Our Nation Conserve and Distribute Health Care Resources Effectively?"[23] The policy paper makes a clear distinction between "rationing" and "rational decision making" through the following:

> Achieving a national consensus on how best to use health care resources effectively, efficiently, and rationally should distinguish between medical rationing, in which decision makers determine which scarce medical resources are provided and who receives them, and rational decision making, by which judicious choices are made among clinically effective alternatives. Rationing can result in denial of care, whereas choosing among clinically effective alternatives focuses on using medical evidence to provide appropriate and effective care to create better health outcomes.[23]

Other healthcare leaders have assured "recent calls for waste avoidance and parsimonious care are not just a clever way to help physicians ration healthcare," pointing out the difference between the "ethics of rationing" and the "ethics of parsimonious care."[24] Rationing refers to not providing treatments that may have a net clinical benefit, whereas rational (or parsimonious) care means "delivering appropriate healthcare that fits the needs and circumstances of patients and that actively avoids wasteful care—care that does not benefit patients."[24] Rationing is often important in circumstances of resource scarcity, and relies on the principles of distributive justice. Parsimonious care is about doing no harm and providing beneficence for patients.[24,25]

RELEVANT PROFESSIONAL ETHICAL GUIDELINES FOR CLINICIANS

In recent years, the ethical obligations to deliver value-based care have been viewed as a matter of professionalism. Several professional guidelines make a clear case for how clinicians can act as effective stewards of healthcare resources (Table 6-1).

In a landmark professionalism charter,[26] The American Board of Internal Medicine, American College of Physicians Foundation, and the European Federation of Internal Medicine included a commitment to a just distribution of finite resources, highlighting the importance of individual physicians applying the ethical principle of justice while also meeting the needs of individual patients. Likewise, the sixth edition of the *ACP Ethics Manual* asserts that individual physicians are responsible for practicing "effective and efficient healthcare and to use healthcare resources responsibly" when diagnosing and treating patients.[27]

Table 6-1 Professional group ethical guidelines or position on high-value care

Professional Group and Source	Ethical Guideline or Position on High-Value Care
American Board of Internal Medicine Professionalism Charter	"While meeting the needs of individual patients, physicians are required to provide healthcare that is based on the wise and cost-effective management of limited clinical resources. They should be committed to working with other physicians, hospitals, and payers to develop guidelines for cost-effective care. The physician's professional responsibility for appropriate allocation of resources requires scrupulous avoidance of superfluous tests and procedures. The provision of unnecessary services not only exposes one's patients to avoidable harm and expense but also diminishes the resources available for others."
American College of Physicians Ethics Manual, Sixth Edition	"Physicians have a responsibility to practice effective and efficient healthcare and to use healthcare resources responsibly. Parsimonious care that utilizes the most efficient means to effectively diagnose a condition and treat a patient respects the need to use resources wisely and to help ensure that resources are equitably available."
American Medical Association Code of Medical Ethics, Opinion 8.054, "Financial Incentives and the Practice of Medicine"	"[Physicians] first duty must be to the individual patient. This obligation must override consideration of the reimbursement mechanism.... Physicians should ... advocate for incentives that promote efficient practice, but are not designed to realize cost savings beyond those attainable through efficiency. As a counterbalance to the focus on utilization reduction, physicians should also advocate for incentives based on the quality of care and patient satisfaction."[15] It is worth noting that the AMA specifically notes in a separate policy statement that it "strongly opposes, and will take appropriate action necessary to restrict, third-party cost-containment strategies that jeopardize patient health and the quality of care"
American College of Emergency Physicians Stewardship of Finite Resources	"In day-to-day clinical decision making, the emergency physician has dual responsibilities to patients and society to employ prudent stewardship, namely, the responsible use of available healthcare resources. To ensure the protection of an individual patient's interests under the constraints of limited resources, ACEP endorses the following: (1) the best medical interest of the patient should be foremost in any clinical decision-making process; (2) criteria for appropriate use of finite resources should include (a) urgency of the patient's medical condition; (b) likelihood, magnitude, and duration of medical benefit to the patient; (c) burdens and costs of care to the patient; and (d) cost to society; and (3) emergency physicians should not allocate healthcare resources on the basis of a patient's ability to pay, contribution to society, past use of resources, or responsibility for their medical condition."

In contrast, the American Medical Association (AMA) Code of Medical Ethics espouses an approach that is more focused on the individual patient. The AMA code clearly outlines that physicians' "first duty" is to the individual patient.[28]

The American College of Emergency Physicians (ACEP) in their Stewardship of Finite Resources document emphasizes the dilemma faced every day by emergency physicians on the frontlines of care, and affirms that the best interest of the patient should be "foremost" in any medical decision-making process.[29] These guidelines also specify criteria for appropriate use of finite resources, such as urgency of the medical condition, likelihood of medical benefit to patient, and the costs to both the patient and to society. ACEP advises emergency physicians to avoid allocating healthcare resources based on any patient factors, including ability to pay or contribution to society.

CONCLUSION

There may remain controversy in how to best incorporate cost considerations into individual clinician decision making, but it appears clear that achieving the goal of providing the best care at lower costs for patients is dependent on clinicians resolving these ethical tensions. There are many opportunities where the best interests of individual patients and society align, and these easy targets should be sought. But clinicians must also begin to navigate the rougher waters of clashing ethical principles. Clinicians do this regularly around similarly challenging topics including the withdrawal of life-sustaining support or determining a patient's capacity to make specific medical decisions. A growing number of ethical guidelines, professional charters, and other representative bodies have identified the professional duty of clinicians to address unnecessary care and to use healthcare resources responsibly.

It is a massive responsibility. But one that fits well in the duty of a healthcare professional.

KEY POINTS:

- Ethics of cost-conscious care can be defined by decisions that balance the four main principles of medical ethics: Respect for patient autonomy, beneficence, non-maleficence, and justice.
- Several professional physician societies and organizations have highlighted stewardship of healthcare resources as an ethical responsibility of physicians.
- Despite a strong fear of rationing healthcare in the United States, American healthcare is currently rationed through several different ways. However, given the high costs of healthcare, critics argue we are not rationing healthcare in the most fair or effective manner.

References:

1. Pollack A. Cost of treatment may influence doctors. *New York Times*. http://www.nytimes.com/2014/04/18/business/treatment-cost-could-influence-doctors-advice.html?_r=2. Accessed May 6, 2014.
2. Fuchs VR. The doctor's dilemma—what is "appropriate" care? *N Engl J Med*. 2011;365(7): 585-587.
3. D'Souza R. Caesarean section on maternal request for non-medical reasons: putting the UK National Institute of Health and Clinical Excellence guidelines in perspective. *Best Pract Res Clin Obstet Gynaecol*. 2012.
4. Sugerman D, Livingston EH. Proton beam therapy for prostate cancer. *JAMA*. 2014;311(14): 1462-1462.
5. Sheets NC, Goldin GH, Meyer A, et al. Intensity-modulated radiation therapy, proton therapy, or conformal radiation therapy and morbidity and disease control in localized prostate cancer. *JAMA*. 2012;307(15):1611-1620.
6. Tilburt JC, Wynia MK, Sheeler RD, et al. Views of us physicians about controlling health care costs. *JAMA*. 2013;310(4):380-388.
7. Gillon R. Medical ethics: four principles plus attention to scope. *BMJ*. 1994;309(6948):184-188.
8. Moriates C, Shah NT, Arora VM. First, do no (financial) harm. *JAMA*. 2013;310(6):577-578.
9. Ubel PA, Abernethy AP, Zafar SY. Full disclosure—out-of-pocket costs as side effects. *N Engl J Med*. 2013;369(16):1484-1486.
10. Hiatt HH. Protecting the medical commons: who is responsible? *N Engl J Med*. 1975;293(5): 235-241.
11. Rosenbaum L, Lamas D. Cents and sensitivity—teaching physicians to think about costs. *N Engl J Med*. 2012;367(2):99-101.
12. Cooke M. Cost consciousness in patient care—what is medical education's responsibility? *N Engl J Med*. 2010;362(14):1253-1255.
13. Pearson SD. Caring and cost: the challenge for physician advocacy. *Ann Intern Med*. 2000;133(2):148-153.
14. Shah NT. A role for physicians: an observation on cost containment. *Am J Prev Med*. 2013; 44(1, suppl 1):S19-S21.
15. Kirch DG, Vernon DJ. The ethical foundation of American medicine: in search of social justice. *JAMA*. 2009;301(14):1482-1484.
16. Bloche MG. Beyond the "R Word"? Medicine's new frugality. *N Engl J Med*. 2012;366(21): 1951-1953.
17. Scherer M. The White House scrambles to tame the news cyclone. *Time*. http://content.time.com/time/magazine/article/0,9171,1969723,00.html. Accessed April 14, 2014.
18. Pollack H. It's not just the money: cost control in cancer care (guest opinion). *Kais Health News*. http://www.kaiserhealthnews.org/Columns/2011/July/071511pollack.aspx.
19. Health Care Rationing Is Nothing New [Excerpt]. http://www.scientificamerican.com/article/health-care-rationing is/. Accessed April 14, 2014.
20. Leonhardt D. Health care rationing rhetoric overlooks reality. *The New York Times*. http://www.nytimes.com/2009/06/17/business/economy/17leonhardt.html. Published June 17, 2009. Accessed April 14, 2014.
21. Vladeck BC, Florman S, Cooper J. Rationing livers: the persistence of geographic inequity in organ allocation. *Virtual Mentor VM*. 2012;14(3):245-249.
22. Lee TH. Improving value is improving health care, not rationing. *JAMA Intern Med*. 2014;174(6):847-848.
23. American College of Physicians. *How Can Our Nation Conserve and Distribute Healthcare Resources Effectively and Efficiently?* Philadelphia, PA: American College of Physicians; 2011.
24. Tilburt JC, Cassel CK. Why the ethics of parsimonious medicine is not the ethics of rationing. *JAMA*. 2013;309(8):773-774.

25. Brody H. From an ethics of rationing to an ethics of waste avoidance. *N Engl J Med*. 2012;366(21):1949-1951.
26. ABIM Foundation, American College of Physicians-American Society of Internal Medicine, European Federation of Internal Medicine. Medical professionalism in the new millennium: a physician charter. *Ann Intern Med*. 2002;136(3):243-246.
27. Snyder L. American College of Physicians Ethics Manual: sixth edition. *Ann Intern Med*. 2012;156(1, pt 2):73-104.
28. American Medical Association. Opin 8054—Financ Incent Pract Med. http://www.ama-assn.org//ama/pub/physician-resources/medical-ethics/code-medical-ethics/opinion8054.page.
29. Emergency Physician Stewardship of Finite Resources. *Am Coll Emerg Physicians*. http://www.acep.org/Clinical---Practice-Management/Emergency-Physician-Stewardship-of-Finite-Resources/.

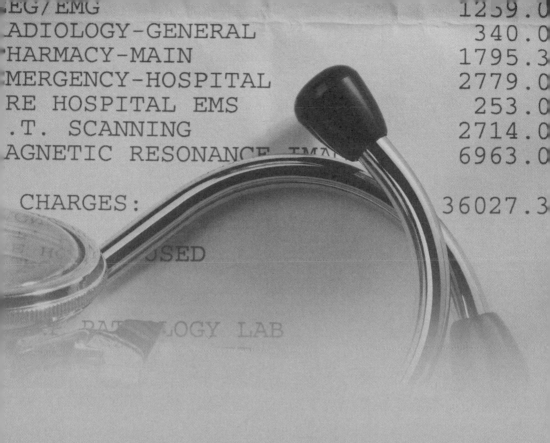

```
EG/EMG                              1259.0
ADIOLOGY-GENERAL                     340.0
HARMACY-MAIN                        1795.3
MERGENCY-HOSPITAL                   2779.0
RE HOSPITAL EMS                      253.0
.T. SCANNING                        2714.0
AGNETIC RESONANCE IMA               6963.0

   CHARGES:                        36027.3

        USED

    PATHOLOGY LAB
```

PART II

Causes of Waste

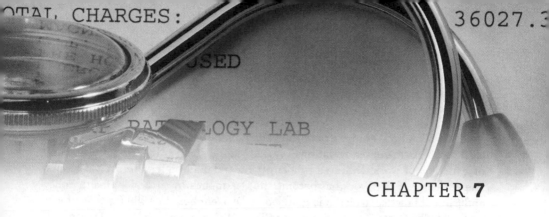

CHAPTER **7**

The Importance of Zip Codes and Genetic Codes: Variation in Resource Utilization

James is an 11-year-old boy who has had a persistent dry cough and sore throat for the past 3 weeks. Overall he feels fine but just cannot seem to shake this nagging cough. He has had three separate sore throats this winter. His mother is a bit concerned because her older son did not seem to get as many colds while he was in elementary school. She takes him to the pediatrician to get "checked out." The pediatrician examines the young boy and reassures her that overall he is healthy and doing okay, but that due to three episodes of a sore throat, he recommends that James get a tonsillectomy.

Tonsillectomies are the most common procedures performed in children under general anesthesia, and have been so for nearly a century.[1] A 1938 report by a British surgeon named J Alison Glover to the Royal Academy of Medicine in the United Kingdom showed a threefold difference in tonsillectomy procedure rates across communities cared for by clinicians in Oxford and Cambridge.[2] Around the same time, a study of typical 11-year-old children in New York City found 93.5% of them either had already had a tonsillectomy or were recommended to have the procedure when sequentially evaluated by study physicians.[1] In contrast, if you were an 11-year-old in some other parts of the country in the 1930s, it was unlikely that anyone ever recommended your tonsils be removed. Who actually benefits from tonsillectomies has been a point of contention for decades, with very little consensus.[1]

The rates of many medical and surgical procedures vary impressively between areas in the United States—no matter how big or small you define the area. Much of this variation has not been linked to better outcomes. In fact, there is no consistent correlation between more healthcare utilization and measures of quality for various diseases.[3]

HOW THE DARTMOUTH ATLAS CHANGED THE HEALTHCARE POLICY WORLD

In 1973, Dr John Wennberg published a landmark article in *Science* that revealed the degree of small area variations in healthcare delivery.[4] This formed the basis of a lifetime of work dedicated to identifying and defining healthcare variations. The epicenter of this work has become the Dartmouth Institute for Health Policy and Clinical Practice, which was founded by Dr Wennberg in 1988 (at that time it was called The Center for the Evaluative Clinical Sciences located within Dartmouth Medical School). Since the 1980s, experts at the Dartmouth Institute for Health Policy have used administrative data, primarily Medicare claims, to show significant variation in both spending and quality of medical care across geographic regions in the United States, notably finding no consistent correlation between the two.[5]

The most iconic contribution of this work was the development of the *Dartmouth Atlas of Health Care* (available at http://www.dartmouthatlas.org), which was first published in 1996 and has since documented in colorful detail the large variations in the delivery of many health services across the country (Figure 7-1). The

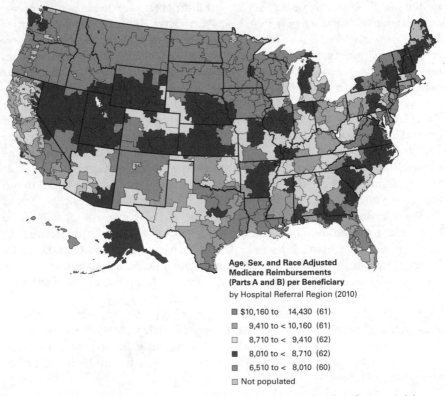

**Age, Sex, and Race Adjusted
Medicare Reimbursements
(Parts A and B) per Beneficiary**
by Hospital Referral Region (2010)

■	$10,160 to 14,430 (61)
■	9,410 to < 10,160 (61)
□	8,710 to < 9,410 (62)
■	8,010 to < 8,710 (62)
■	6,510 to < 8,010 (60)
▢	Not populated

Figure 7-1. Dartmouth atlas of healthcare. (Reproduced, with permission, from Dartmouth Atlas; www.dartmouthatlas.org.)

current atlas is available in both report and interactive formats and includes national data on a number of different metrics, filterable by region, hospital, or topic.

Dr Wennberg summarizes the overall results of years of research from the Dartmouth group thusly, "We have a system that essentially the amount of care that you get depends on where you live, the capacity of the local system, how many doctors per capita there are, how many beds per capita there are. That's what determines the frequency with which you are hospitalized, the frequency with which you visit doctors, how many days you spend in intensive care units, and how many imaging exams you get."[6]

This realization has dramatically changed the healthcare policy discussion in the United States. A 2013 Institute of Medicine (IOM) report that was commissioned to evaluate geographic variation in healthcare spending and growth, and to make recommendations for potential changes in Medicare payment systems under the Affordable Care Act (ACA), found that "Geographic variation in spending and utilization is real, and not an artifact reflecting random noise; it persists across geographic units and healthcare services over time."[3]

VARIATION ACROSS THE UNITED STATES

A 2009 *New Yorker* article by Dr Atul Gawande told a remarkable story that made McAllen, Texas—a self-proclaimed Square Dance Capital of the World—into an infamous Ground Zero for unwarranted Medicare spending.[7] As Dr Gawande tells it, "McAllen, Texas, the most expensive town in the most expensive country for healthcare in the world, seemed a good place to look for some answers."[7]

McAllen had lower than average cardiovascular-disease rates, asthma, HIV, infant mortality, and injury, yet this town spent $15,000 per Medicare enrollee in 2006—twice the national average, and twice as much as nearby El Paso, which had similar demographics. Quality of care was not measurably better in McAllen compared to elsewhere; in fact, the largest hospitals in McAllen performed worse than average on 23 of 25 Medicare quality metrics.

Why were costs so high? In the article, physicians from McAllen sit down over dinner with Dr Gawande and list possible explanations including concerns regarding malpractice. But then a general surgeon—in perhaps classic surgeon fashion—cuts through with a no-nonsense, "Come on, we all know these arguments are bullshit. There is overutilization here, pure and simple." Doctors were performing extra tests, services, and procedures and the associated bills were racking up the charges. This suspicion was verified by the data that Dr Gawande and others explored.[7]

The "Cost Conundrum" magazine article helped healthcare variation statistics spring to life, inciting a renewed fervor for investigating healthcare costs. It has essentially become a call-to-arms, and was even required reading in the Obama White House.

Table 7-1 "Acceptable" and "unacceptable" sources of variation

Source of Variation	Definition	Examples
"Acceptable" (or "warranted")	Variation that is driven by genuine health needs or real area-level differences in demographics and/or costs. This variation is beyond the control of both providers and patients	• Aspects of health status or population demographics • Area-level differences in wage, rent, and other overhead costs
"Unacceptable" (or "unwarranted")	Variation that cannot be explained by variation in patient illness or patient preferences	• Aspects of system inefficiencies • Overuse of low-value services • Unnecessary service duplication

Sources: Data from Wennberg JE. *BMJ.* 2011; Wennberg JE. *BMJ.* 2002.

Sources of variation

One of the fundamental keys behind understanding geographic variation is differentiating "acceptable" and "unacceptable" sources of variation—sometimes more delicately referred to as "warranted" and "unwarranted" variation (Table 7-1).

"Acceptable" (or "warranted") sources of variation include aspects of health status or population demographics. This variation is expected in an efficient health system since it is driven by genuine health needs. Area-level differences in wage, rent, and other overhead costs are also considered "acceptable" sources of variation since they are beyond the control of both providers and patients.

"Unacceptable" (or "unwarranted") sources of variation include aspects of system inefficiencies, such as overuse of low-value services and unnecessary service duplication. This variation cannot be explained by differences in patient illness or patient preferences.

As with nearly all things, grey areas abound. For example, some demographic factors, such as race, represent a mix of acceptable and unacceptable sources of variation, as discussed further below.

For the sake of investigating variations, all clinical care can be grouped roughly into three categories (Table 7-2)[8,9]:

1. *Effective care* refers to interventions that provide clear net benefit (the benefits far outweigh the risks). The goal should be to provide 100% of eligible patients with appropriate effective care. Unwarranted variation in effective care results in "underuse." For example, angiotensin-converter enzyme (ACE) inhibitor medications have been shown to improve mortality for patients with congestive heart failure (CHF), yet there

Table 7-2 **Effective, preference-sensitive, and supply-sensitive care**

Categories of Clinical Care	Definition	Example
Effective	Interventions that provide clear net benefit (the benefits far outweigh the risks)	• β-Blockers for patients that had heart attacks • Screening diabetics for early signs of retinal disease • Pneumococcal vaccinations for unvaccinated patients with pneumonia
Preference-sensitive	Situations when more than one generally accepted treatment option is available and thus choice should depend on patient preferences	• Prostate cancer screening • Early prostate cancer treatments • Mastectomy versus lumpectomy for early-stage breast cancer • Knee or hip replacement for arthritis
Supply-sensitive	Activities for which the frequency of use relates to the capacity of the local healthcare system	• Frequency of follow-up clinic visits for chronic illness • Intensity of care (number of hospital days, ICU days, etc) in the last 6 months of life

Sources: Data from Wennberg JE. *BMJ.* 2011; Wennberg JE. *BMJ.* 2002.

are many patients with CHF (without a contraindication to ACE inhibitors) who are not prescribed these potentially life-saving medications.[10,11] Some causes of underuse of effective care include lack of clinician knowledge, discontinuity of care, and absence of systems that would facilitate the appropriate use of these services.

2. *Preference-sensitive care* is defined as situations when more than one generally accepted treatment option is available and thus choice should depend on patient preferences. The correct rate of treatment in this category should depend on informed patient choice; however, treatment rates can vary considerably due to differences in professional opinion. Treatment decisions that do not match patient preferences are often considered "misuse." Examples of preference-sensitive conditions include joint arthritis and early-stage prostate cancer. Each of these conditions has more than one legitimate treatment option with considerable trade-offs between benefits and risks to the patient. Therefore, the treatment plan for any given patient should be personalized based on their own preferences and goals. An important limitation to appropriate preference-sensitive care is that clinicians oftentimes do not properly inform patients about possible options and alternatives, making it impossible for them to make educated decisions.[12]

3. *Supply-sensitive care* involves activities for which the frequency of use relates to the capacity of the local healthcare system. This includes doctor visits, diagnostic tests, and hospital admissions. Healthcare in this category is usually deemed as "overuse." Consider seeing a patient in clinic with inadequately controlled diabetes. When do you have them come back for a follow-up appointment? Two weeks? Six weeks? Six months? Probably depends largely on how many open clinic appointment slots you have. Do you send them to a diabetes specialist? Once again, depends at least partly on how many diabetes specialists there are in your area and how easy it may be to get your patient an appointment. These are often seemingly simple, small decisions that clinicians make every day, but that over the aggregate have gigantic implications for resource utilization. The principle here is that studies show the most important determinant of supply-sensitive care is the local supply of hospital beds, clinicians, specialists, MRI machines, and other resources.[13] "Variations in supply-sensitive care," explains Dr Wennberg,[8] "are perplexing because medical theory and medical evidence play virtually no role in determining the relative frequency of their use among defined populations." Where there is greater capacity, more care is delivered, whether or not it is actually needed. Public health researcher Milton Roemer described this phenomenon first in 1959, succinctly stating "A built [hospital] bed is a filled bed."[14] This has since been termed "Roemer's law."

It is worth noting that it is possible for some care to overlap with more than one category. Consider a patient that wants to get an orthopedic surgical procedure for their knee instead of continuing to try physical therapy and/or anti-inflammatory medications (a preference-sensitive decision). If this patient also happens to live in an area that has abundant orthopedic physicians that stand to gain by doing business, then the patient is much more likely to be readily referred to a surgeon, get an appointment and schedule an operation (a supply-sensitive situation).

Unwarranted variation

There are many well-known clinical examples of unexplained or "unwarranted" variation including knee surgery,[15] cardiac stenting,[16] and cesarean sections.[17] In fact, there is impressive variation across profiles of the most common surgical procedures (Figure 7-2).[18] The likelihood that a patient receives one of these procedures may depend more on where she gets care than on how sick she may be or how much she might need the procedure. For example, the cesarean delivery rate varies 10-fold by institution in the United States, even after correcting for clinical case-mix.[19] This variation has tremendous impact on the delivery system. Childbirth is the most common hospitalized condition in the country and cesarean sections are the most common major surgery performed on Americans. The evidence is teeming with other examples: Screening tests have been shown to have large variation, with the likelihood of undergoing an inappropriate colonoscopy depending on where the patient lives and what physician he sees.[20] In some areas vascular surgeons are

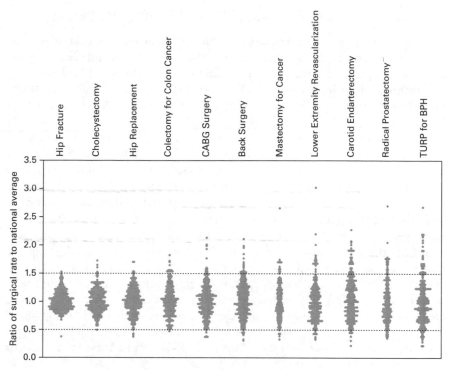

Figure 7-2. Variation profiles of common surgical procedures. (Reproduced, with permission, from Dartmouth Atlas; www.dartmouthatlas.org.)

aggressive about vascular care provided to patients in the year before a major amputation, but there is little evidence that higher regional spending is associated with lower amputation rates.[21,22] So, these patients may be going through many procedures, spending a lot of money, and then losing their leg anyways.

Another critical area for variation in care is at the end-of-life. Although most patients with serious illness say that they would prefer to die at home, the majority of them actually die in the hospital receiving aggressive therapies that don't match their preferences.[23,24] Even US hospitals with strong reputations for clinical care tend to provide incredible variability in the "intensity" of care for patients during the last 6 months of life.[25] Days in the hospital per patient range from about 9 to 27; Intensive Care Unit (ICU) days from 1.5 to 9.5; and number of physician visits from 18 to 76.[25] This "aggressive" care diminishes the quality of life for patients in their final weeks or days,[26,27] and too often presents serious financial strain for the patient and their families.[28] Where you live and which hospital you go to seems to matter more than your own personal preferences when it comes to the likelihood that you will die in an ICU hooked up to a breathing machine and receiving aggressive care.[23,24,29]

WHY IS THERE SO MUCH VARIATION IN HEALTHCARE DELIVERY

Medicare spending per beneficiary is 52% higher in regions that spend the most money compared to those that spend the least.[30] After adjusting for many sources of "acceptable" variation, including demographics and health status, the difference is still a gaping 33% between these regions.[30] These variations persist over time: regions that were high- or low-cost in 1992 remained so in 2010.[3,31]

Although much of the discussion on variation has focused largely on "geographic regions," differences in healthcare resource utilization can be traced down to the level of individual clinicians making individual healthcare decisions.[3] This makes sense since ultimately clinicians decide which services and treatments to provide. It is not "regions" or "institutions" that write orders, but rather clinicians that actually put the pen to paper (or type in a computerized provider order entry system). Thus, differences in provider practice patterns can explain a substantial portion of geographic variation.[32-34] Physicians in high-spending regions request shorter follow-up periods, see patients in the office more frequently, and are more likely to recommend discretionary interventions and screening tests of unproven benefit.[33] But physicians in both high-spending and low-spending areas have been found to be equally likely to recommend guideline-supported interventions.[33] Over the past decade, the appropriate use of effective care (as measured by "underuse quality indicators") has improved, but overuse remains a largely unaddressed problem.[35]

As discussed throughout this book, there are many different reasons that clinicians may over-order tests, provide unnecessary treatments, or perform inappropriate procedures. Omnipresent local "culture" plays a prominent role in driving healthcare variation. Many clinicians are also quick to blame fear of malpractice. Although an association between malpractice premiums and Medicare spending has been demonstrated, particularly for diagnostic imaging, it is unknown how much malpractice causally drives utilization or pricing.[36] And despite the fact that malpractice designs (with regard to both premiums and damage caps) vary regionally, malpractice appears to contribute relatively little to overall costs.[37] Furthermore, tort reforms have not alleviated clinicians' fears of lawsuits (see Chapter 10).[38]

Inappropriate resource utilization of preference-sensitive treatment decisions also contributes to healthcare waste. These decisions may be colored by the fact that patients are often not properly informed by their clinicians about possible treatment options and alternatives.[12] Only about 10% of patients that received elective cardiac stents reported that they were presented with other options to seriously consider. Although 77% said they talked to their doctors about the reasons to get a stent, few (19%) said that they talked about any potential cons to cardiac stenting. And only 16% said they were asked about their treatment preferences.[12] Evidence demonstrates that patients who receive specific, unbiased information about treatment options often end up receiving lower-intensity services and incur lower healthcare costs for preference-sensitive conditions.[39,40] Shared decision making will be explored further in Chapter 12.

On the supply-sensitive side, the medical world has worked not by the basic economic mechanisms of "supply and demand," but rather by a "if you build it, they will come" mentality. The more MRI machines available, the more images done. The more hospital beds, the more patients are hospitalized. This can sometimes be propelled by a hospital "arms race" that builds an MRI in order to compete, but then once the MRI is built, it needs to be used to pay for itself.

Part of the overarching issue with supply-sensitive care includes that services are too often not "built" where they are needed. Between 1993 and 2004, 301 new cardiac surgery programs opened despite a decreasing overall demand for cardiac bypass surgery.[41] Nearly half of these new programs opened in communities that already had access to cardiac surgery. Overall, travel time to the nearest cardiac surgery program changed little, suggesting that these programs really did not improve geographic access.[41] Even worse, since mortality rates are inversely related to cardiac surgery volume,[42,43] an unintended consequence of adding more cardiac surgery programs where they are not needed is that patients are siphoned away from higher-volume medical centers—a side effect that could actually increase mortality across programs.[44]

Is the reason for variation in costs due to utilization or pricing?

The quick answer to the question is: probably both.

Variations in Medicare spending are largely attributable to differences in acute care and post-acute care services. If this source of variation were eliminated, total Medicare spending variation would drop by 89%.[3] This is mostly driven by the large regional differences in rates of admission and readmission,[45] and average lengths of stay.[46] Also, while a patient is in the hospital, the efficiencies of nursing staffing, tests, procedures and drugs differ widely.[47]

But pricing has a role in healthcare cost variation as well. In fact, in the commercial insurance market, the IOM found that regional differences in price markups are the prime influencers on geographical variation in spending, rather than utilization of healthcare services.[3,48] Some price variation is due to real differences in the local prices of overhead costs, which are beyond a provider's control. But there is also significant price variation related to the margin above the cost of inputs that a payer or provider chooses to set or negotiate.[49] This is not the case for Medicare, which basically sets a take-it-or-leave-it price for services, and therefore the differences in spending are driven by utilization not pricing.[50] The "Story From the Frontlines" case story included here concerns price variation, whereas the *Dartmouth Atlas* has primarily focused on Medicare utilization.

Story From the Frontlines—"Pricing Variation: The Case of the $517 Chest X-Ray"

So the story goes like this. A patient of mine needed a chest x-ray. He does not have health insurance, so rather than just give him a requisition and send him to the local hospital, I decided to do a little calling around on his behalf to find out what the damage would be ...

Vendor #1: A well-known local hospital

I called up the radiology department and asked them how much a PA and Lateral Chest X-ray would cost. "I don't know—we don't have that information," I was told by the clerk. The radiologist gave me the same answer. They both said I should just send the patient over and he would find out the cost when he received the bill.

That seemed a little dumb. Since when do we go into stores and buy things without knowing the price?

So after four additional phone calls and about two hours, my assistant and I finally reached Bob who is in charge of uninsured patient billing. He was able to tell me the price: $517.

For a PA and Lateral Chest x-ray.

For cash paying patients who pay at the time of service and know to ask for the "20-20" discount by name, the price ends up being reduced to $310.20. But you have to know the secret code word.

Time to receive report in my office: 2–3 days.

Quality: Good

Vendor #2: Free-Standing Private Radiology Office

I called up and the receptionist answered on the first ring. I asked how much for a PA and Lateral Chest x-ray.

An immediate answer: $73.

Time to receive report in my office: 1 hour.

Quality: Just as Good

So my question is this: how can the hospital be charging 4.25 times as much (or seven times as much without the secret code word) as the place down the street to cash-paying patients, for the same product and actually inferior response time?

—Paul Abramson. "The Case of the $517 Chest X-Ray."
Costs of Care, 2012. (www.costsofcare.org)

VARIATION IS AN IMPORTANT AREA OF HEALTHCARE WASTE AND INAPPROPRIATE CARE

It seems clear that variation is an important—and perhaps generally fixable—source of healthcare waste and inappropriate care. As discussed in Chapter 1, one key area of healthcare waste is overtesting. To this point, substantial differences in diagnostic practices that are unlikely to be related to patient characteristics have been shown across the United States. In one large study, patients that moved from regions in the lowest quintile of medical care intensity to a higher quintile received more laboratory testing, imaging, and diagnoses than those who moved to regions in the lowest quintile.[51] In another example of misuse and overuse, the quality of medication prescribing for the elderly varies substantially across the United States, with lower-quality prescription patterns intuitively associated with more adverse drug events, which in turn require additional expenses to treat.[52] Thus is created a vicious cycle of increasing harm and costs.

If practices of the lowest-cost, highest-quality regions were adopted nationwide, then Medicare spending would immediately drop by as much as 29%.[8] But placing healthcare costs aside, is it better as a patient to live in an area that spends more on healthcare? Well, much like in McAllen, not necessarily. Medicare beneficiaries who live in higher spending regions often do not get better-quality care than those in lower-spending regions.[53] Patients with hip fractures, heart attacks, and colon cancer got more tests, more procedures, more visits with specialists, and more hospitalizations if they lived in higher-spending regions. But not only did they not have better outcomes, in many instances they seemed to do worse.[29]

In summary, patients who live in regions with very intensive care, like Miami or Los Angeles, do not live as long and seem to have worse quality of life than similar patients with the same conditions who live in areas with more conservative practice patterns.[29] The more money that Medicare spends per person in a given state, the lower that state's quality of care tends to rank.[54] And despite a prevailing spirit that "more is better," patients receiving more medical care are actually less satisfied about their healthcare.[29]

There are many examples to illustrate instances where more care is not better. In 1998 a trial was published investigating home monitoring for pregnant women at risk for preterm labor.[55] These women were randomized to receive education and have one of the following: weekly contact with a nurse, daily contact with a nurse, or daily contact with a nurse and home monitoring of uterine activity. Surely, more care in the form of daily nursing visits and uterine monitoring would help, right?

Nope. There were no differences among the groups in outcomes, including the timing of birth. Instead, daily contact with a nurse increased the number of unscheduled visits to obstetricians, resulting in more trips to the doctor's office but no benefit to having gone there.[55] Even more concerning, women that had more monitoring received more tocolytic drugs (medications used to suppress premature labor), without any measurable benefits.[55]

In other cases more medical care does not only increase utilization and costs without benefit, but actually leads to harm.[56-58] Medical care may cause harm by generating more diagnoses and/or more treatment, which in turn generates "more to do" and ultimately can lead to more worry and disability, unnecessary treatments, mistakes, and adverse events (Figure 7-3).[58]

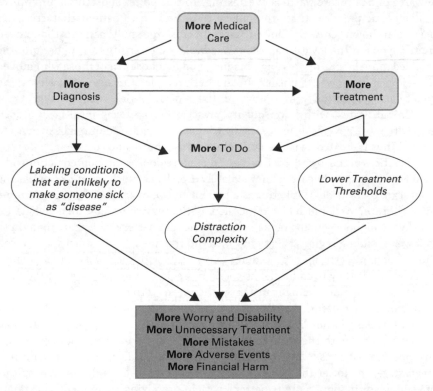

Figure 7-3. Pathways by which more medical care may lead to harm. (Adapted, with permission, from Fisher ES, Welch HG. Avoiding the unintended consequences of growth in medical care: How might more be worse? *JAMA*. 1999;281(5):446-453. Copyright © 1999 American Medical Association. All rights reserved.)

In one dramatic example of overtesting leading to unsuspected harm, a 27-year-old man presented to his primary care provider complaining of chronic diarrhea and occasional scant bright red blood following bowel movements.[59] He did not have any other concerning symptoms and his history revealed that this was almost certainly due to benign irritable bowel syndrome and associated hemorrhoids. However, he underwent an unnecessary diagnostic colonoscopy anyways. The colonoscopy reportedly "looked normal" except for a very small "benign-appearing" growth in his rectum. To be thorough, the gastroenterologist decided to biopsy this lesion. Shockingly, the pathology report returned as "high-grade B-cell lymphoma," a serious malignancy. The patient did not have any other concerning findings to suggest lymphoma but due to this finding he was hospitalized and underwent an "expedited work-up" that included multiple invasive tests. Ultimately, the pathology turned out to be incorrect and instead represented a normal fragmented germinal center (an area where normal B cells [a subset of disease-fighting white blood cells in the body] gather during a normal immune response) rather than a menacing cancer. This patient suffered from significant physical discomfort due to the multiple subsequent invasive testing, as well as unthinkable psychological distress resulting from the presumed potentially life-threatening cancer.

Patients that have false positive tests, such as for breast cancer or HIV on routine screening, may have profound psychological impacts that can persist for years.[60,61] For the population overall, more care has led to greater levels of worry, pain, and restricted activity days, with no gains in functional status.[58,62]

Dr H. Gilbert Welch, another Dartmouth investigator, has studied extensively how our cancer screening, and thresholds for blood pressure and other disease states have led to arbitrary overtreatment.[63-68] Despite an overwhelming "enthusiasm for cancer screening" in the United States,[69] it is well established that testing can commonly produce harms including false-positive test results, further testing, and unnecessary invasive procedures (also see Chapter 14).[63,64,69,70] "Overdiagnosis" in cancer occurs when tumors are detected that, if left unattended, would not become clinically apparent or cause death.[63,71] These actually occur commonly in diagnoses of breast, lung, prostate, and thyroid cancer.[71] In March 2012, the National Cancer Institute convened a meeting to evaluate the problem of overdiagnosis in cancer, concluding: "Physicians, patients, and the general public must recognize that overdiagnosis is common and occurs more frequently with cancer screening."[71] They even recommended renaming many conditions to avoid the word "cancer"—reserving the charged term only for "describing lesions with a reasonable likelihood of lethal progression if left untreated."[71]

VARIATION REVEALS IMPORTANT RACIAL DISPARITIES AND HEALTH INEQUITIES

It is not only where you live that matters, but also, unfortunately, who you are. Hospitals that disproportionately serve black patients have higher risk-adjusted mortality after a heart attack (acute myocardial infarction).[72] The rate of leg amputation is four times greater in black versus white patients, and black patients are less likely to receive recommended diabetes care.[73] They also are more likely to have diabetes in the first place: compared to non-Hispanic white adults, the risk is 77% higher among black patients, and 66% higher among Hispanics.[74] Ethnic minorities consistently receive less preventative care, undergo fewer procedures, and are seen by fewer specialists.[75] According to a 2002 study by the Institute of Medicine,[75] these differences cannot be accounted for by insurance status, household income, education, or age. Unfortunately, some of these disparities may be bluntly due to bias or racism.[76-78] However, it is also true that ethnic minorities disproportionately live in areas that have low-quality hospitals and providers, which may explain a large portion of the observed disparities in care.[79] In fact, overall variation between providers in the quality of care for some conditions clearly exceeds the racial gap in treatment.[73,80] Therefore, unequal healthcare for minorities is likely due to a combination of where they live and providers' biases—unconscious or not.

But the overarching problem remains differences in quality of care across regions, regardless of the underlying motivations. Reducing disparities in quality of care across regions "would play a major role in improving the healthcare received by all Americans and by minority Americans in particular."[80] In an equitable healthcare system, variations in underuse, misuse, and overuse would be eliminated.

KEY POINTS:

- Healthcare spending and utilization varies widely across regions in the United States—no matter how large or small these regions are defined, down to the level of individual clinicians.
- "Acceptable" variation results from genuine health needs due to aspects of health status or population demographics. "Unacceptable" sources of variation include aspects of system inefficiencies, such as overuse of low-value services and unnecessary service duplication.
- More medical care and higher healthcare spending is *not* associated with better outcomes, and in some conditions may result in inferior or undesirable results.
- Unequal healthcare for minorities is likely due to a combination of providers' biases and disproportionately living in areas with low-quality healthcare.
- Variation is an important and perhaps largely fixable source of healthcare waste, harm, and inappropriate care.
- An equitable healthcare system would not have significant variations in underuse, misuse, and overuse, for any reason.

References:

1. Goodman DC, Challener GJ. Tonsillectomy: a procedure in search of evidence. *J Pediatr*. 2012;160(5):716-718.
2. Glover JA. The incidence of tonsillectomy in school children. *Proc R Soc Med*. 1938;31(10):1219-1236.
3. Institute of Medicine. Variation in health care spending: target decision making, not geography. http://www.iom.edu/Reports/2013/Variation-in-Health-Care-Spending-Target-Decision-Making-Not-Geography.aspx. Accessed November 11, 2013.
4. Wennberg JE, Gittelsohn A. Small area variations in health care delivery. *Science*. 1973;182(4117): 1102-1108.
5. The Dartmouth Institute—History. http://tdi.dartmouth.edu/about/history. Accessed November 14, 2013.
6. Dr Jack Wennberg. The Dartmouth Institute for Health Policy and Clinical Practice: Q&A with Dr Jack Wennberg. 2008. http://www.dartmouthatlas.org/downloads/press/Wennberg_interviews_DartMed.pdf. Accessed November 15, 2013.
7. Gawande A. The cost conundrum. *New Yorker*. 2009. http://www.newyorker.com/reporting/2009/06/01/090601fa_fact_gawande?currentPage=all. Accessed November 15, 2012.
8. Wennberg JE. Unwarranted variations in healthcare delivery: implications for academic medical centres. *BMJ*. 2002;325(7370):961-964.
9. Wennberg JE. Time to tackle unwarranted variations in practice. *BMJ*. 2011;342(3): d1513-d1513.
10. Masoudi FA, Rathore SS, Wang Y, et al. National patterns of use and effectiveness of angiotensin-converting enzyme inhibitors in older patients with heart failure and left ventricular systolic dysfunction. *Circulation*. 2004;110(6):724-731.
11. Hlatky MA. Underuse of evidence-based therapies. *Circulation*. 2004;110(6):644-645.
12. Fowler FJ, Gallagher PM, Bynum JPW, Barry MJ, Lucas FL, Skinner JS. Decision-making process reported by medicare patients who had coronary artery stenting or surgery for prostate cancer. *J Gen Intern Med*. 2012;27(8):911-916.
13. Fisher ES, Wennberg JE. Health care quality, geographic variations, and the challenge of supply-sensitive care. *Perspect Biol Med*. 2003;46(1):69-79.
14. Shain M, Roemer MI. Hospital costs relate to the supply of beds. *Mod Hosp*. 1959;92(4):71-73 passim.
15. Fisher ES, Bell J-E, Tomek IM, Esty AR, Goodman DC. Trends and regional variation in hip, knee, and shoulder replacement. The Dartmouth Institute for Health Policy and Clinical Practice; 2010. http://www.dartmouthatlas.org/downloads/reports/Joint_Replacement_0410.pdf. Accessed July 10, 2013.
16. Matlock DD, Groeneveld PW, Sidney S, et al. Geographic variation in cardiovascular procedure use among medicare fee-for-service vs medicare advantage beneficiaries. *JAMA*. 2013;310(2):155-162.
17. Baicker K, Buckles KS, Chandra A. Geographic variation in the appropriate use of cesarean delivery. *Health Aff (Millwood)*. 2006;25(5):w355-w367.
18. Birkmeyer JD, Sharp SM, Finlayson SR, Fisher ES, Wennberg JE. Variation profiles of common surgical procedures. *Surgery*. 1998;124(5):917-923.
19. Kozhimannil KB, Law MR, Virnig BA. Cesarean delivery rates vary tenfold among US hospitals; reducing variation may address quality and cost issues. *Health Aff (Millwood)*. 2013;32(3):527-535.
20. Sheffield KM, Han Y, Kuo YF, Riall TS, Goodwin JS. Potentially inappropriate screening colonoscopy in medicare patients: variation by physician and geographic region. *JAMA Intern Med*. 2013;173(7):542-550.
21. Goodney PP, Travis LL, Nallamothu BK, et al. Variation in the use of lower extremity vascular procedures for critical limb ischemia. *Circ Cardiovasc Qual Outcomes*. 2012;5(1):94-102.
22. Goodney PP, Travis LL, Brooke BS, et al. Relationship between regional spending on vascular care and amputation rate. *JAMA Surg*. 2014;149(1):34-42.

23. Pritchard RS, Fisher ES, Teno JM, et al. Influence of patient preferences and local health system characteristics on the place of death. SUPPORT Investigators. Study to understand prognoses and preferences for risks and outcomes of treatment. *J Am Geriatr Soc*. 1998;46(10):1242-1250.

24. Barnato AE, Herndon MB, Anthony DL, et al. Are regional variations in end-of-life care intensity explained by patient preferences? A study of the US Medicare population. *Med Care*. 2007;45(5):386-393.

25. Wennberg JE, Fischer ES, Stukel TA, Skinner JS, Sharp SM, Bronner KK. Use of hospitals, physician visits, and hospice care during last six months of life among cohorts loyal to highly respected hospitals in the United States. *BMJ*. 2004;328(7440):607-610.

26. Mack JW, Weeks JC, Wright AA, Block SD, Prigerson HG. End-of-life discussions, goal attainment, and distress at the end of life: predictors and outcomes of receipt of care consistent with preferences. *J Clin Oncol*. 2010;28(7):1203-1208.

27. Harrington SE, Smith TJ. The role of chemotherapy at the end of life: "when is enough, enough?" *JAMA*. 2008;299(22):2667-2678.

28. Kelley AS, McGarry K, Fahle S, Marshall SM, Du Q, Skinner JS. Out-of-pocket spending in the last five years of life. *J Gen Intern Med*. 2013;28(2):304-309.

29. Fishel ES, Wennberg DE, Stukel TA, Gottlieb DJ, Lucas FL, Pinder EL. The implications of regional variations in Medicare spending. Part 2: health outcomes and satisfaction with care. *Ann Intern Med*. 2003;138(4):288-298.

30. Zuckerman S, Waidmann T, Berenson R, Hadley J. Clarifying sources of geographic differences in Medicare spending. *N Engl J Med*. 2010;363(1):54-62.

31. Acumen LLC. *IOM Study of Geographic Variation: Growth Analysis*. Washington, DC: Institute of Medicine; 2013.

32. Baicker K, Chandra A. Medicare spending, the physician workforce, and beneficiaries' quality of care. *Health Aff (Millwood)*. 2004;Suppl Web Exclusives W4:184-197.

33. Sirovich B, Gallagher PM, Wennberg DE, Fisher ES. Discretionary decision making by primary care physicians and the cost of U.S. health care. *Health Aff*. 2008;27(3):813-823.

34. Sirovich BE, Gottlieb DJ, Welch HG, Fisher ES. Variation in the tendency of primary care physicians to intervene. *Arch Intern Med*. 2005;165(19):2252-2256.

35. Kale MS, Bishop TF, Federman AD, Keyhani S. Trends in the overuse of ambulatory health care services in the united states. *JAMA Intern Med*. 2013;173(2):142-148.

36. Baicker K, Fisher ES, Chandra A. Malpractice liability costs and the practice of medicine in the Medicare program. *Health Aff*. 2007;26(3):841-852.

37. Mello MM, Chandra A, Gawande AA, Studdert DM. National costs of the medical liability system. *Health Aff (Millwood)*. 2010;29(9):1569-1577.

38. Carrier ER, Reschovsky JD, Mello MM, Mayrell RC, Katz D. Physicians' fears of malpractice lawsuits are not assuaged by tort reforms. *Health Aff*. 2010;29(9):1585-1592.

39. Stacey D, Bennett CL, Barry MJ, et al. Decision aids for people facing health treatment or screening decisions. *Cochrane Database Syst Rev*. 2011;(10):CD001431.

40. Veroff D, Marr A, Wennberg DE. Enhanced support for shared decision making reduced costs of care for patients with preference-sensitive conditions. *Health Aff (Millwood)*. 2013;32(2):285-293.

41. Lucas FL, Siewers A, Goodman DC, Wang D, Wennberg DE. New cardiac surgery programs established from 1993 to 2004 led to little increased access, substantial duplication of services. *Health Aff (Millwood)*. 2011;30(8):1569-1574.

42. Birkmeyer JD, Siewers AE, Finlayson EVA, et al. Hospital volume and surgical mortality in the United States. *N Engl J Med*. 2002;346(15):1128-1137.

43. Peterson ED, Coombs LP, DeLong ER, Haan CK, Ferguson TB. Procedural volume as a marker of quality for CABG surgery. *JAMA*. 2004;291(2):195-201.

44. Wilson CT, Fisher ES, Welch HG, Siewers AE, Lucas FL. U.S. trends in CABG hospital volume: the effect of adding cardiac surgery programs. *Health Aff*. 2007;26(1):162-168.

45. Fisher ES, Wennberg JE, Stukel TA, Sharp SM. Hospital Readmission Rates for Cohorts of Medicare Beneficiaries in Boston and New Haven. *N Engl J Med*. 1994;331(15):989-995.

46. Yuan Z, Cooper GS, Einstadter D, Cebul RD, Rimm AA. The association between hospital type and mortality and length of stay: a study of 16.9 million hospitalized Medicare beneficiaries. *Med Care*. 2000;38(2):231-245.
47. Franzini L, Mikhail OI, Skinner JS. McAllen and El Paso revisited: Medicare variations not always reflected in the under-sixty-five population. *Health Aff*. 2010;29(12):2302-2309.
48. Donohue JM, Morden NE, Gellad WF, et al. Sources of regional variation in Medicare Part D drug spending. *N Engl J Med*. 2012;366(6):530-538.
49. Geographic Variation in Medicare per Capita Spending. RWJF. http://www.rwjf.org/en/research-publications/find-rwjf-research/2004/07/geographic-variation-in-medicare-per-capita-spending.html. Accessed November 22, 2013.
50. Gottlieb DJ, Zhou W, Song Y, Andrews KG, Skinner JS, Sutherland JM. Prices don't drive regional Medicare spending variations. *Health Aff*. 2010;29(3):537-543.
51. Song Y, Skinner J, Bynum J, Sutherland J, Wennberg JE, Fisher ES. Regional variations in diagnostic practices. *N Engl J Med*. 2010;363(1):45-53.
52. Zhang Y, Baicker K, Newhouse JP. Geographic variation in the quality of prescribing. *N Engl J Med*. 2010;363(21):1985-1988.
53. Fisher ES, Wennberg DE, Stukel TA, Gottlieb DJ, Lucas FL, Pinder EL. The implications of regional variations in Medicare spending. Part 1: the content, quality, and accessibility of care. *Ann Intern Med*. 2003;138(4):273-287.
54. Baicker K, Chandra A. Medicare spending, the physician workforce, and beneficiaries' quality of care. *Health Aff*. 2004;Suppl Web Exclusives:W4-184-W4-197.
55. Dyson DC, Danbe KH, Bamber JA, et al. Monitoring women at risk for preterm labor. *N Engl J Med*. 1998;338(1):15-19.
56. Caverly TJ, Combs BP, Moriates C, Shah N, Grady D. Too much medicine happens too often: the teachable moment and a call for manuscripts from clinical trainees. *JAMA Intern Med*. 2014;174(1):8-9.
57. Grady D, Redberg RF. Less is more: how less health care can result in better health. *Arch Intern Med*. 2010;170(9):749-750.
58. Fisher ES, Welch HG. Avoiding the unintended consequences of growth in medical care: how might more be worse? *JAMA*. 1999;281(5):446-453.
59. Sheu L, Gottenborg E. False-positive results from a diagnostic colonoscopy: a teachable moment. *JAMA Intern Med*. 2014;174(5):665-666.
60. Bond M, Pavey T, Welch K, et al. Psychological consequences of false-positive screening mammograms in the UK. *Evid Based Med*. 2013;18(2):54-61.
61. Bhattacharya R, Barton S, Catalan J. When good news is bad news: psychological impact of false positive diagnosis of HIV. *AIDS Care*. 2008;20(5):560-564.
62. Newhouse JP, Group RCIE. *Free for All?: Lessons from the Rand Health Insurance Experiment.* Cambridge, MA: Harvard University Press;1993.
63. Welch HG, Black WC. Overdiagnosis in cancer. *J Natl Cancer Inst*. 2010;102(9):605-613.
64. Welch HG, Albertsen PC. Prostate cancer diagnosis and treatment after the introduction of prostate-specific antigen screening: 1986–2005. *J Natl Cancer Inst*. 2009;101(19):1325-1329.
65. Bleyer A, Welch HG. Effect of screening mammography on breast cancer incidence. *N Engl J Med*. 2013;368(7):679.
66. Taylor BC, Wilt TJ, Welch HG. Impact of diastolic and systolic blood pressure on mortality: implications for the definition of "normal." *J Gen Intern Med*. 2011;26(7):685-690.
67. Welch HG. Overdiagnosis as a flaw in health care. *The New York Times*, February 27, 2012. http://www.nytimes.com/2012/02/28/opinion/overdiagnosis-as-a-flaw-in-health-care.html. Accessed November 29, 2013.
68. Woloshin S, Schwartz LM, Kerin K, Welch HG. Estimating the impact of adding C-reactive protein as a criterion for lipid lowering treatment in the United States. *J Gen Intern Med*. 2007;22(2):197-204.

69. Schwartz LM, Woloshin S, Fowler FJ Jr, Welch HG. Enthusiasm for cancer screening in the United States. *JAMA*. 2004;291(1):71-78.

70. Welch HG, Frankel BA. Likelihood that a woman with screen-detected breast cancer has had her "life saved" by that screening. *Arch Intern Med*. 2011;171(22):2043-2046.

71. Esserman LJ, Thompson IM, Reid B. Overdiagnosis and overtreatment in cancer: an opportunity for improvement. *JAMA*. 2013;310(8):797-798.

72. Skinner J, Chandra A, Staiger D, Lee J, McClellan M. Mortality after acute myocardial infarction in hospitals that disproportionately treat black patients. *Circulation*. 2005;112(17):2634-2641.

73. Bynum JPW, Fisher ES, Song Y, Skinner J, Chandra A. Measuring racial disparities in the quality of ambulatory diabetes care: *Med Care*. 2010;48(12):1057-1063.

74. CDC - 2011 National Estimates - 2011 National Diabetes Fact Sheet - Publications - Diabetes DDT. http://www.cdc.gov/diabetes/pubs/estimates11.htm. Accessed December 4, 2013.

75. Institute of Medicine. *Unequal Treatment: Confronting Racial and Ethnic Disparities in Health Care*; 2002. http://www.iom.edu/Reports/2002/Unequal-Treatment-Confronting-Racial-and-Ethnic-Disparities-in-Health-Care.aspx. Accessed November 29, 2013.

76. Schulman KA, Berlin JA, Harless W, et al. The effect of race and sex on physicians' recommendations for cardiac catheterization. *N Engl J Med*. 1999;340(8):618-626.

77. Peek ME, Odoms-Young A, Quinn MT, Gorawara-Bhat R, Wilson SC, Chin MH. Racism in healthcare: its relationship to shared decision-making and health disparities: a response to Bradby. *Soc Sci Med*. 2010;71(1):13-17.

78. Van Ryn M, Fu SS. Paved with good intentions: do public health and human service providers contribute to racial/ethnic disparities in health? *Am J Public Health*. 2003;93(2):248-255.

79. Hasnain-Wynia R, Baker DW, Nerenz D, et al. Disparities in health care are driven by where minority patients seek care: examination of the hospital quality alliance measures. *Arch Intern Med*. 2007;167(12):1233-1239.

80. Baicker K, Skinner J, Chandra A. Geographic variation in health care and the problem of measuring racial disparities. *Perspect Biol Med*. 2005;48(1):S42-S53.

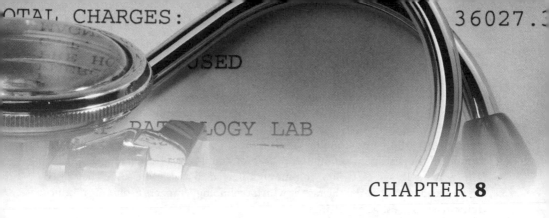

CHAPTER **8**

Stents, Robots, and the Role of Technology Diffusion

*A*s Mr Wolfman stepped out of the cold into Philadelphia's bustling 30th Street train station, a billboard near the entryway caught his attention. The blurred image of an athletic bicyclist filled the background while a bold-faced statement proclaimed, "THE WIND IN YOUR FACE IS WORTH PROTON THERAPY." Similar ads adorned the walls between the ticket counter and the waiting area. One showed a man and woman gleaming over a candle-lit dinner. Another, his favorite, showed an ecstatic pair of octogenarians dancing the night away. "SATURDAY NIGHT JITTERBUG IS WORTH PROTON THERAPY."

Mr Wolfman's mind wandered to the recent news special he saw on TV. Not too long ago, just a few miles away, a futuristic $150 million proton therapy center opened. The special said the new facility spanned the length of a football field and contained some of the most sophisticated medical technology ever created. To destroy cancer cells at the microscopic level, they assembled more than 200 tons of superconducting magnets and computer-guided subatomic particle accelerators.

Neither the news special nor the billboards at 30th Street Station mentioned whether all that equipment was truly necessary. They did not mention that each treatment with proton therapy is somewhere between two and six times as expensive as the alternative form of radiation. They did not mention that in many cases there is no evidence that proton beams work better than previously available, less expensive methods.

So Mr Wolfman chuckled to himself. The jitterbugging octogenarians reminded him of his own mother and father. As he stepped off the platform to board his train he marveled, "It's amazing what modern medicine can do."

We expect new technologies to be more expensive than their older counterparts. Of course the iPhone 6 is more expensive than the iPhone 5. It is faster. It has a better camera. It *performs* better. What we *do not* expect is to pay more money for iPhone 5-level performance year after year. This is because in almost every industry, technology that improves performance renders older technology less expensive. In 1965, Intel founder Gordon Moore observed that every 2 years the number of transistors in a computer processor doubles and the cost of computing falls by half.[1] This observation, commonly referred to as "Moore's law," has since been extended to describe the rate at which technology impacts economic productivity in a broad range of settings.

Healthcare, as an industry, appears to be an exception to Moore's law. Rather than falling, the costs of healthcare are rapidly rising. Meanwhile, the performance of our healthcare system has improved at a much slower pace. Consider life expectancy as one measure of health-system performance. Over the last 50 years, the average US life expectancy has risen by 14%, from 69 to 79 years old. Meanwhile, the fraction of total spending in the United States that is devoted to healthcare has risen from 5% of GDP to 18% of GDP—an overall 360% increase. Certainly the 10 extra years of life we have gained make us better off today than 50 years ago. But it also seems very possible that we might have achieved the same result for less money. In fact, if healthcare obeyed Moore's law, we would expect that at current healthcare spending levels we should be living well to the ripe old age of 69 times 360%—about 250 years old!

There is widespread consensus that our return on investment for new healthcare technologies ought to be better. The question (for which there is no obvious answer) is how much better? Expecting to live beyond age 250 may be asking too much. In healthcare we appear to be more willing to pay for limited performance compared to other industries where there is less at stake. Additionally, for any given medical condition in the modern era we have many different options to choose from and relatively little information available about the value of each option (see Chapters 3 and 4). Even when some value information is available, creating a payment system that rewards value is not straightforward (see Chapter 15). Dartmouth economist Jonathan Skinner explains the limitations of our current payment system bluntly, claiming health insurance is currently designed to "[pay] for any treatment that doesn't obviously harm the patient, regardless of how effective it is."[2]

This payment system creates strong commercial incentives to deploy expensive technologies before we really know how well they work. Once a hospital builds a facility like a $150 million proton therapy center, they have every reason to use it as much as possible. Unsurprisingly, hospitals around the United States are "loading up" on proton beam accelerators at an astonishing rate (Figure 8-1). In the last 5 years alone, the number of proton therapy centers in the United States has doubled even though the benefits remain largely unproven.[3,4]

Until recently hospitals were also purchasing the DaVinci surgical robot—a technology with similarly unproven benefits—with equal fervor. But then something interesting happened. After being named one of the "fastest growing"

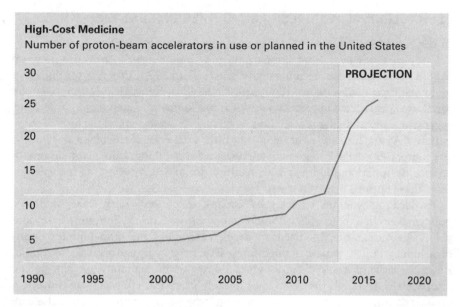

High-Cost Medicine
Number of proton-beam accelerators in use or planned in the United States

Figure 8-1. Number of proton-beam accelerators in use or planned in the United States. (Republished with permission of MIT Technology Review. From Skinner J. The costly paradox of health care technology. *MIT Tech Rev.* September 5, 2013. http://www.technologyreview.com/news/518876/the-costly-paradox-of-health-care-technology/. Permission conveyed through Copyright Clearance Center, Inc.)

companies of 2012 by *Fortune* magazine, Intuitive Surgical (the makers of DaVinci robots), saw its sales slump significantly during the summer of 2014, largely due to widespread concerns about cost efficiency.[5,6] Then more examples emerged of low-value technology getting scuttled in favor of cost-effective alternatives. During the fall of 2014, even as three new proton therapy centers were opening in other parts of the country, Indiana University announced that it would be closing its proton therapy center because insurers were refusing to pay for it.[7] Many believe that these signs of wariness may be harbingers for the new era of value-based care. Certainly, as payers, purchasers, and patients continue to demand a better care at lower cost, frontline clinicians will be increasingly responsible for thoughtfully evaluating new technologies.

To meet this challenge we need to understand the return on investment of new technology more deeply. We need to know how much of our skyrocketing healthcare spending can be attributed to new technologies, as opposed to rising prices, the growing population, or any other cause. We need to know how to assess whether specific technologies are actually worth it, and have a reliable way of determining what "worth it" even means. In this chapter, we review some of the ways that economists have aimed to address these challenges as well as how clinicians might use these insights to provide our patients with better care.

TECHNOLOGICAL PROGRESS AS A DRIVER OF COST GROWTH

In the early 1960s, before Medicare was even officially launched, a contentious debate broke out over what the nation's new public health insurance program should pay for and what it should not (Chapter 2). In 1972, after nearly a decade of highly politicized disagreement, Congress passed landmark legislation to extend Medicare coverage to all patients with failing kidneys.[8] Around the same time, several new technologies made it possible to significantly extend the lives of these patients. As machines were developed to filter waste out of the blood stream, the first outpatient dialysis centers opened their doors.[9] Soon, transplant surgery to replace dysfunctional kidneys with healthy donor kidneys became increasingly safe. These options were not cheap.

In deciding whether to extend Medicare to patients with failing kidneys, policymakers had to grapple with uncomfortable questions about how to reasonably value human life. The decision largely turned on the compelling testimony of a kidney-failure patient named Shep Glazer who argued that thousands of American citizens would die if Congress did not act immediately to make dialysis affordable.[10] Although the law was ultimately passed, there was little consensus on how to address these challenges moving forward and there remains little consensus to this day.[11] Nonetheless, the debate itself has made it very clear that medical innovation has a flipside. Richard Rettig, a RAND senior scientist who studied the policy implications of the decision to cover end-stage kidney disease, warned about an "inevitably sharper conflict that looms ahead between two societal goals: moderating the growth of medical expenditures and maintaining a world-class capacity to innovate in medicine."[12]

In the late 1970s, two health policy professors from Brandeis University—Stuart Altman and Stanley Wallack—summarized the available evidence and helped popularize the view that technology was the "culprit" behind rising health costs.[13] Proving this to the satisfaction of many economists took more research however. The first task was formally defining what "technological progress" means. The United States Congressional Budget Office (CBO) includes all "changes in clinical practice that enhance the ability of providers to diagnose, treat, or prevent health problems."[14] These advances can take several forms, ranging from novel drugs and devices to new applications of existing technologies. Given the expansiveness of this definition, adding up the effects of each individual change in clinical practice is highly cumbersome. Instead, some economists have aimed to estimate the impact of technology on healthcare costs indirectly, by first adding up other contributing factors and then seeing what is left over.

In 1992, Harvard economist Joseph Newhouse used one of the most famous examples of this approach.[15] In order to isolate the impact of technology alone, he first estimated the contribution of an aging of the population, rising per capita incomes, and changes in the distribution of health insurance. He additionally factored in administrative costs, *"defensive medicine"* (clinicians utilizing technology

Table 8-1 **Estimated contributions of selected factors to growth in real healthcare spending per capita, 1940 to 1990 (percent)**

	Smith, Heffler, and Freedland (2000)	Cutler (1995)	Newhouse (1992)
Aging in the population	2	2	2[a]
Changes in third-party payment	10	13	10[b]
Personal income growth	11–18	5	<23
Prices in the healthcare sector	11–22	19	*
Administrative costs	3–10	13	*
Defensive medicine and supplier-induced demand	0	*	0
Technology-related changes in medical practice	38–62	49	>65

Sources: Congressional Budget Office based on Sheila D. Smith, Stephen K. Heffler, Mark S. Freeland. "The Impact of Technological Change on Health Care Cost Increases: An Evaluation of the Literature" (working paper, 2000); David M. Cutler, "Technology, Health Costs, and the NIH" (paper prepared for the National Institutes of Health Economics Roundtable on Biomedical Research, September 1995); and Joseph P. Newhouse. Medical care costs: how much welfare loss? *J Eco Perspect.* Summer 1992;6(3):3-22. http://www.cbo.gov/sites/default/files/cbofiles/ftpdocs/89xx/doc8947/01-31-techhealth.pdf
Notes: Amounts in the table represent the estimated percentage share of long-term growth that each factor accounts for.
< = less than; > = greater than; * = not estimated.
[a]Represents data for 1950 to 1987.
[b]Represents data for 1950 to 1980.

to reduce malpractice liability), "physician-induced" demand (clinicians utilizing technology to make more money), and even the costs of caring for the terminally ill during the last year of their life. Surprisingly, he and others have consistently found that, collectively, changes in these factors over time explain only a fraction of the real growth in healthcare costs (Table 8-1).

Instead, Newhouse concluded that the unmeasured factor contributing to cost growth must be "the march of science and the increased capabilities of medicine"—in other words, the introduction of new technology itself! Using this method, Newhouse and other economists have estimated that up to 70% of medical spending growth over the last half-century may be due to cost-increasing advances in medical technology.[16]

Understanding the net benefits of technology

For decades, these cost increases have portended trouble by straining budgets. As a result, healthcare cost growth is seldom seen in positive light. Then, in the early 2000s a Harvard economist named David Cutler began upending conventional wisdom. He argued that although there is clearly waste in the system, much of our increased spending on healthcare over time has in fact been worth it.[17] While Newhouse primarily focused on estimating the costs of technology, Cutler focused on the benefits.

Consider how we used to manage heart attacks. In 1955 when President Dwight Eisenhower had a heart attack, his physicians recommended top-of-the-line medical care: one month of bed rest.[18] Needless to say, this treatment was not very expensive. It was not very effective either. Today treating a heart attack with prolonged bed rest would be considered dangerous and grounds for medical malpractice. This is because since 1955 our treatments options have expanded enormously. Although these options have also made treating heart attacks more expensive, people who have heart attacks in the 21st century are unquestionably better off than those in the mid-20th century.

A heart attack patient today is likely to receive a number of intensive therapies, starting with an array of medicines: β-blockers to reduce the work effort of the heart (introduced in the 1970s), thrombolytics to dissolve any existing blood clots (introduced in the 1970s and 1980s), and drugs such as aspirin and heparin to thin the blood and prevent future clotting (first used for heart attack treatment in the 1980s).[19,20] Surgical treatments have also become much more common. Coronary artery bypass—an "open heart" surgery that requires dividing the breast bone—was introduced in the late 1960s. Shortly afterwards, a "minimally invasive" procedure called percutaneous angioplasty made it possible to reopen blocked arteries without a large and painful incision in the chest. Before long, angioplasty would replace bypass surgery in the majority of cases. In the 1990s an additional procedure was added when angioplasty became paired with "bare metal" and then "drug-eluting" stents (wire mesh scaffolding designed to help keep arteries open). Although these stents are very expensive, they are also very effective and by the late 1990s they were used in over 84% of angioplasty cases.[21]

To compare the costs and benefits of these changes, Cutler and fellow economist Mark McClellan examined Medicare data over a 14-year period.[22] In 1984, $3 billion was spent in total on heart attacks annually. By 1998 this number became $5 billion, even though the total number of heart attacks in the United States actually declined due to improvements in blood pressure, cholesterol, smoking, and other preventive measures. Cutler and McClellan attributed the increased total spending to an increase in the average amount spent per case, calculated to be nearly $10,000 after adjusting for inflation.[23] They also showed that this difference was mostly driven by the increased use of technology-enabled surgery rather than increased prices. In 1984 nearly 90% of heart attacks were still being managed with medicine only; by 1998, more than half of heart attacks patients received surgical treatment.[24]

Cutler and McClellan then used social security records to determine how length of survival after a heart attack changed over this time period. In 1984 life expectancy after a heart attack was approximately 5 years on average, whereas by 1998 it had risen to 6 years.[22] One interpretation of this information is that although we spent $10,000 more per person with a heart attack in 1998, this spending appeared to help them gain one year of life. Compared to many other things we spend money on this appears to be an incredibly great deal (just a few days in the hospital can easily cost $10,000). Cutler and McClellan conservatively estimated that the benefits to society of that 1 year of gained life is worth $70,000 per heart attack patient (this number is on par with other estimates, as we will discuss in the next section of this chapter).[22] At a cost of $10,000 per patient, they concluded that society receives a net benefit of $60,000 per patient we treat for a heart attack.

Dr Cutler and others have similarly examined a variety of other key conditions as well, including advances in the treatment of hypertension, low-birthweight infants, and breast cancer (Table 8-2). The costs increases of caring for low-birthweight infants are particularly dramatic. Due to advances in neonatal intensive care, spending per patient increased by $40,000 between 1950 and 1990.[25] Nonetheless, Cutler and fellow economist Ellen Meara assert that this investment was even more valuable that our investment in heart attacks because they caused infant mortality rates to plummet. The improved survival translated to an average of 12 years of life expectancy gained per patient, worth $240,000 to

Table 8-2   Summary of research on the value of medical technology changes

Condition	Years	Change in Treatment Costs	Outcome		
			Change	Value	Net Benefit
Heart Attack	1984–1998	$10,000	1-year increase in life expectancy	$70,000	$60,000
Low-birthweight infants	1950–1990	$40,000	12-year increase in life-expectancy	$240,000	$200,000
Breast Cancer	1985–1996	$20,000	4-month increase in life expectancy	$20,000	$0
Hypertension	1959–2000	$520	6-month increase in life expectancy, discounted over an average lifespan	$5,117	$4,597

Sources: Data from http://content.healthaffairs.org/content/20/5/11/T2.expansion.html and http://content.healthaffairs.org/content/26/1/97.long.

society ($200,000 net benefit). While most heart attack survivors do not work, all of the life years gained for low-birthweight infants are economically productive. University of Chicago economist David Meltzer has shown that for younger patients in particular, considering economic productivity and other future costs alongside survival can significantly increase the perceived cost-effectiveness of healthcare interventions.[26]

The limitations of considering averages

The type of analysis spearheaded by Cutler and his colleagues where costs and benefits are quantified, summed, and compared head-to-head, is referred to as "cost-benefit analysis." While many technologies have netted positive benefits over the long-term when viewed this way, it does not necessarily mean that these technologies are always used appropriately. In Chapter 1, we pointed out the gulf between the United States and our peer countries comparing our return on investment in healthcare (see Figure 1-6). Clearly, there is massive waste. How do we reconcile Cutler's finding that much of the increased healthcare spending over time has been worth it with the notion that the United States could be getting more bang for its buck?

One explanation is that for every single technology that has been net beneficial over time, there are other technologies where the costs outweigh the benefits. On average, technology has yielded great net benefits for treatment of low-birthweight infants after they are born. By contrast, on average, technology has generated great waste in the way many pregnant women are managed before their infants are born. In the early 1970s, a few hospitals introduced fetal telemetry—the ability to monitor the heart beats of babies in utero in real time—in order to better predict which babies were distressed and needed to be quickly delivered by C-section. Within a few years, this technology became the standard of care and was used by nearly every hospital in the country, despite no evidence that newborn babies were better off.[27] In fact, the only thing fetal telemetry appeared to do reliably was markedly increase the national C-section rate from just 5% of births in the early 1970s to 32% of births in 2014.[28] Despite a lack of any apparent benefits, fetal telemetry continues in wide use today and is a significant contributor to the $5 billion price tag of avoidable C-sections.[29]

A second, more nuanced, explanation to reconcile the net benefits of technology with health system waste is that although many technologies are worth it some of the time, few technologies are worth it all the time. Take coronary stents for example. Cutler and McClellan showed that, on average, advances in cardiac care—particularly the increased use of stents over the last 20 years—have yielded benefits that far outweigh the increased costs. Still, to see these benefits we have to focus on improvements in care to the *average* patient over an extended time horizon. By contrast, studies of geographic variation in care (see Chapter 7), aim to determine the value of care for the *marginal* patient during a fixed snapshot in time (by "marginal patient" we are referring to a nonaverage patient for whom the technology is wasteful because they are different from the average patient in an important way). Washington University cardiologist Dr Amit Amin and his colleagues found that between 2004 and 2010 the use of drug eluting stents varied between 2% and 100% among physicians.[30] Incredibly, this tremendous variation was only modestly correlated with patient risk. Dr Amin's study and other examinations of geographic variation in healthcare, support the estimate that much of healthcare spending is unnecessary *on the margin*, even while increases in spending *on average* may be worthwhile.

In addition to these distinctions, only focusing on average net benefits has a pragmatic limitation. At the end of the day, staggering up front costs can make achieving downstream benefits unfeasible, regardless of the average value. For both public and commercial payers, treatment of heart attacks and low birthweight infants are usually affordable at the point-of-care and also happen to be good investments. However, many valuable treatments may overextend our ability to pay. Sofosbuvir (trade name Sovaldi, Gilead Sciences Inc.) is a relatively new medication that can achieve near universal cure rates for hepatitis C at tremendous benefit to society. However, due to its $84,000 sticker price for a full course of treatment, the amount of money it would cost for the state of Oregon to provide Sofosbuvir to its Medicaid population is almost equal to the amount Oregon Medicaid spends for all other prescription drugs combined.[31] Even then, at the time of this writing, Oregon Medicaid and other payers are considering ways to provide coverage for Sofosbuvir. But what about a technology that costs one million dollars up front and yields one million and one dollars of societal benefit? How do we know where to draw the line?

MEASURING VALUE TO SOCIETY

While cost-benefit analysis provides an excellent way to consider the value of care on average, *cost-effectiveness analysis* (CEA) provides a way of also measuring the value of care at the margin, where most of the waste occurs.[32] Instead of asking how the average costs compare to the average benefits for a single type of technological progress, CEA provides a way of comparing different technologies or applications of technologies (eg, comparing the same technology across different disease states). Costs are usually, but not always, considered from the societal perspective, as opposed to the hospital or patient perspective (see Chapter 3). Unlike cost-benefit analysis where both costs and benefits must be expressed as dollars, in CEA the benefits or "effects" can be expressed in any unit. As a result, effects may include clinical outcomes, patient experience, or both.

CEA expresses the incremental costs and benefits as a ratio, known as the *incremental cost-effectiveness ratio* (ICER):

$$\text{ICER} = \frac{(C_1 - C_2)}{(E_1 - E_2)}$$

where C_1 and E_1 represent the cost and effect of the technology being evaluated and C_2 and E_2 represent the same for a reference scenario (either a different technology or a different application of the same technology).[33] The ratio of "incremental" difference between costs and effects can often be held up against a standard threshold value that is deemed acceptable (more on that in a moment). This makes the ICER particularly useful for considering where to draw the line for the hypothetical technology that costs one million dollars up front and yields one million and one dollars of societal benefit.

Let us break down the ICER one component at a time. Taking the societal perspective, the numerator of this ratio must take into account all of the relevant types of cost that are accrued, including direct costs to society (costs of delivering care) as well as the indirect or "opportunity" costs (such as foregone wages or other loss of economic productivity from being admitted to the hospital). Depending on the analysis, direct costs may include only the variable costs of delivering a service (materials and staff) or may also include the fixed costs (infrastructure and installed capacity)—see Chapter 4.

A common consideration is how detailed the cost accounting needs to be. Consider the lifetime societal costs of providing adolescent women with the human papilloma virus (HPV) vaccine.[34] Relevant costs include the administration of the vaccine itself, but must also include the costs of medical staff, equipment and facilities to screen, diagnose, and treat HPV and its sequelae. Additional costs borne by the patient (such as time and transportation to the facility) might also be included. Two common reasons to exclude costs from the accounting are if the costs of a particular item are negligibly small in comparison to other items (ie, the band aid used to cover the injection site), or if the item that is being costed is unlikely to change the outcome of interest (the costs of building a pediatric or gynecology office would exist with or without the vaccine). All other items must be fully accounted for.

Figuring out *which* costs to include is only one aspect of determining accurate costs. It is equally important to note *when* the cost is being accrued. For historical costs, the same item will cost different amounts at different times—it is not fair to compare the cost of robotic surgery in 2015 to the cost of robotic surgery in 2009. To solve this problem, costs are usually converted from "nominal" dollars (historical monetary value) to "real" dollars (adjusting for price inflation). In the United States, this adjustment is based on the consumer price index, which is a measurement provided by the Bureau of Labor Statistics of how the prices of a standard list of consumer goods change over time.[35]

Intervals of time also matter. Costs that are considered over time intervals that extend into the future are usually "discounted" to reflect the time-value of money (the fact that money available today is worth more to most people than money available in the future). Because some people are more willing to wait for future money than others, this discount rate is subjective and can vary. Although many health economists conservatively use a rate of 3% annually, rates of up to 10% annually have also been used.[36] Generally, more impoverished institutions or societies will use higher discount rates.

While the numerator of the ICER ratio requires careful accounting, it is relatively easy to develop a comprehensive picture of costs because there are clear criteria for inclusion and exclusion. Determining what should go into the denominator of the ICER ratio is much less straightforward. The "effects" of the technology can include any change in health status. Ideally, the effects of interest would include clinical patient outcomes, as well as an understanding of patient risk and experience. Combining these different dimensions of care into a single metric requires a fair amount of inference. Moreover, there are no clear criteria for what to include and exclude.

The simplest way to measure the effect of a technology on health status is to use natural measures such as a discrete number of lives saved. The challenge with looking at discrete events such as lives is that they are often "all or none," resulting in great loss of information. For example, if we only account for being either dead or alive, we are missing information about the quality of life. Natural effect measures that provide a little more information might include the number of complications avoided or symptom-free days. However these too are limited by only considering one dimension of care at a time.

Estimating quality of life

To better evaluate the effects of new technologies, several economists in the late 1960s and early 1970s suggested the idea of substituting single, discrete health outcome measures with a more comprehensive index. In 1977, Harvard economist Richard Zeckhauser coined the term *quality-adjusted life year* (QALY) to describe the idea of using length of life as a continuous measure of health that could then be adjusted for other indices of health status.[37] Both the idea and terminology stuck. Shortly thereafter the United States Congressional Office of Technology Assessment began using QALYs preferentially in assessing the value of new healthcare technologies.[38] Today, QALYs are a standard measure used to estimate the effects of technologies and social policies by governments and other appraising bodies around the world.

The QALY is conceptually based on "multi-attribute utility theory," in which "utility" (a theoretical construct of well-being) is a function of a number of independent, proportionally weighted inputs (mobility, pain, etc).[39] For this reason, a CEA that uses QALYs is sometimes referred to as a "cost-utility analysis." Typically,

QALYs range continuously from zero to one, where one represents one year of perfect quality life and zero represents the state of being dead.[40] Less than perfect health status (such as living with blindness or some other disability) is assigned a value less than one and more than zero. In the rare case of a condition that is considered worse than death (eg, a patient on a ventilator who did not wish to be intubated), the QALY can be assigned a negative value.

As you might imagine, the leap of faith in using QALYs stems from how the disabled or ill state is assigned a numerical value. Several estimation techniques are used (Table 8-3). A European network of researchers known as the EuroQol Group has developed a widely used, standardized questionnaire called the EQ-5D that has been validated for use in a number of chronic conditions.[41] This very brief questionnaire asks patients to indicate their health status by ticking the statement that best corresponds to them across five health dimensions—mobility, self-care, performance of "usual" activities including work and leisure, pain/discomfort, and anxiety/depression. Patients are additionally presented with a 20-cm vertically oriented "visual analog scale" resembling a ruler, with end-points labeled "the best health you can imagine" on top and "the worse health you can imagine" on the bottom. Patients self-rate their overall health by placing an "X" along the scale. The placement of the "X" corresponds with a score that is incorporated with their questionnaire responses to determine quality of life.

Other estimation techniques present patients with theoretical trade-offs that they must choose between. In the time-trade-off method, patients are typically

Table 8-3 Utility estimation methods

Utility Estimation Method	Description	Example
Questionnaire	Choose from descriptive options	Are you in pain once per month, once per week, or once per day?
Visual analog scale	Choose placement on visual scale	On a scale from 1 to 10 where 10 is the most pain you have ever had, circle the number that corresponds to your pain level.
Time-trade-off	Choose between a good state of health for shorter time and poor state of health for longer time	Would you prefer to live 10 more years with chronic pain or 8 years pain free?
Standard gamble	Choose between poor state of health and taking a risk between perfect health and worse health/death	Would you prefer 10 years of chronic pain or gamble between 90% chance of 10 pain free years and 10% chance of death?

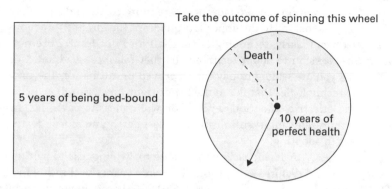

Figure 8-2. Examples of the standard gamble method.

asked to choose between living for a certain amount of time with a disability or illness and living for a shorter amount of time in a perfect state of health.[42] (For example, would you rather live for 15 more years with blindness or 10 more years with perfect sight?) Another type of trade-off estimation is called the "standard gamble." Here the patient is asked to choose either remaining disabled or ill for some period of time or taking a risk on a medical intervention that has some known probability of either restoring perfect health or making them much worse off (Figure 8-2).[43]

Like any estimate, these scores are imperfect. Sometimes a discrete effect measure may be preferable to a QALY, particularly if precision is more important that comprehensiveness. A major limitation of using QALYs is that different estimation methods may yield different utility scores for the same patient.[44] Moreover, patients with different baseline health states may value care differently—those who are young and healthy (and therefore have more QALYs readily available to them) may undervalue healthcare whereas those who are older and frailer may overvalue healthcare. For the healthy in particular, there is likely to be a "ceiling effect" in which at high levels of utility, incremental differences are more difficult to observe. As a result, QALY estimates are likely to vary by the population of interest and may be fundamentally less accurate for populations that are healthier.

Considering willingness to pay

No matter which costs go into the numerator and which effects are included in the denominator, the ICER provides a common means of interpretation. A four-quadrant graph of the ICER is often used to help visualize whether the technology being evaluated should ultimately be adopted (Figure 8-3). By convention, incremental cost is represented on the y-axis and incremental effect (QALYs) are represented on the x-axis. Technologies that fall in the upper-right quadrant (by convention called quadrant 1) are more costly and also more effective. Technologies that fall in the upper-left quadrant (quadrant 2) are more costly and less effective. Clearly, technologies that fall into quadrant 2 are not worth adopting. The decision to adopt technologies that fall into quadrant 1 depends on how much you are willing to pay for improved performance. The same logic holds for the technologies that fall in the lower-right (quadrant 3), which are less costly and less effective (adoption depends on willingness to pay). The lower-left (quadrant 4) represents interventions that are less costly and more effective, thus are always worth adopting.

Much like the QALY itself, assigning a value to "willingness to pay" is inherently subjective and requires estimation. For many years the threshold value for one QALY in the United States was set at $50,000, based somewhat arbitrarily

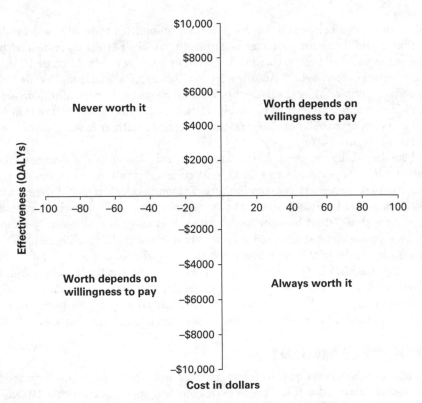

Figure 8-3. Four-quadrant graph of incremental cost effectiveness ratios (ICERs).

on the amount it purportedly cost Medicare to maintain one QALY for a dialysis patient.[45] This figure was later updated due to what was felt to be gross underestimation of the Medicare program's costs. Just accounting for inflation alone, the price per QALY based on the dialysis standard was $82,000 in 2002 US dollars.[46] By convention, the acceptable cost per QALY was subsequently set between $50,000 and $100,000 as a "rule of thumb," based partly on adjustments to the dialysis standard and partly on a survey of health economists' opinions.[47]

Since then, there have been many efforts to estimate societal willingness to pay using more rigorous methods, including direct estimations and natural experiments. Interestingly, many of the direct estimates have fallen in the same range as the arbitrary dialysis standard. "Contingent valuation" studies estimate willingness to pay by presenting patients with hypothetical scenarios to choose from. Unsurprisingly, contingent valuation suffers from the same limitations as the similar methods used to estimate QALYs. Instead, "revealed preference" studies use natural experiments to infer the value of life from actual behaviors undertaken by members of society that influence their risk of death. Examples include multiplying the amount paid for a smoke detector by the risk of fire, multiplying the amount needed to compensate a construction worker to work on a high-rise building by the risk of a fall, and so on. Notably, a systematic review of willingness to pay estimates using revealed preference found that in some cases—particularly with regard to occupational risks—willingness to pay may be significantly higher than the $100,000 rule of thumb cut-off.[45] For this reason, some have suggested that willingness to pay thresholds are likely to rise in the future, particularly in segments of society where there is upward socioeconomic mobility and people require more compensation to assume risk.[46]

Given the considerable uncertainty in estimating cost-effectiveness, a number of methods have emerged to lend confidence to decisions regarding technology adoption. One way to manage the uncertainty is to perform a "sensitivity analysis" to see if any conclusions change when individual inputs to the ICER are varied, either one at a time, or in groups. Another method assigns a probability distribution representing the uncertainty to each input estimate, and simulates the range of expected outputs. Using both methods, a range of outputs that fall more in quadrant 2 (more costly, less effective) would inspire less confidence, whereas a range of outputs that fall more in quadrant 1 (less costly, more effective) would inspire more confidence.

Alternatively, the expected cost-effectiveness can be examined with respect to different willingness to pay thresholds using a *"cost-effectiveness acceptability curve"* or CEAC. Increasingly common in CEA research, the CEAC provides an estimate of the proportion of the sampling distribution of costs and effects that lie below various willingness to pay amounts.[48] The probability of a cost-effective result is plotted on the y-axis and the willingness to pay level is plotted on the x-axis. It is easiest to see how this works with an example—Figure 8-4 shows a CEAC that examines three strategies for managing early pregnancy failure.

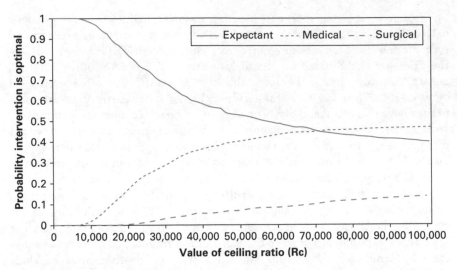

Figure 8-4. Cost-effectiveness acceptability curve. (Reproduced, with permission, from Petrou S, Trinder J, Brocklehurst P, Smith L. Economic evaluation of alternative management methods of first-trimester miscarriage based on results from the MIST trial. *Int J Obstet Gynaecol.* 2006;113(8):879-889.)

About one in five women who learn they are pregnant experience a miscarriage within the first few months. Although this is an incredibly common problem, at the beginning of the 19th century, miscarriage could place a woman's life at risk. A small percentage of the failed pregnancies would become retained, leading to massive hemorrhage and sepsis. Before there were blood banks and antibiotics, the safest course of action was often to evacuate the uterus using a newly developed surgical procedure known as dilation and curettage. Over nearly two centuries this surgery became cemented as the standard of care, even after blood banks, antibiotics, and other forms of medical treatment were invented.

In the modern era, most patients and their clinicians (almost 90% in the United States) still immediately opt for a version of the traditional surgery. Nonetheless, many patients can instead be given inexpensive medicines to help expel the failed pregnancy (over 85% success rate), or simply be watched at minimal cost to society (greater than 50% success rate). If needed, those who do not pass the pregnancy with medicine or after a short period of waiting, can then go on to have surgery at minimal risk.

Based on the "miscarriage treatment" or MIST trial, Figure 8-4 shows the calculated CEAC for these three strategies at different willingness to pay levels (measured in the old United Kingdom currency of pounds sterling) to avoid a gynecological infection.[49] At the estimated £10,000 willingness to pay to avoid one infection (called the "ceiling ratio" in this paper), there is a 98% probability that waiting or "expectant" management is the optimal strategy and only a 2%

probability that surgery is the optimal strategy. It is not until you are willing to pay £70,000 to avoid one infection that medical management dominates expectant management. Impressively, there is no plausible scenario where up front surgical treatment on nearly every patient is the most cost-effective strategy. Nearly 10 years after this paper was published, up front surgical treatment continues to be the most commonly used treatment in the majority of patients in the United States. It is unclear if this gap between evidence and practice is due to true patient preferences, lack of shared decision making (Chapter 12), other health system pressures (Chapter 10), or some combination. Nonetheless, it leaves an open question: once we know that a technology or treatment strategy is high- or low-value, what is our role in translating this knowledge into good care?

Story From the Frontlines—"A Diet of Limitless Technology"

Most physicians recall the medical school ritual of unboxing our first stethoscope. From the first physical diagnosis course, we were all solemnly instructed as to the importance of the physical examination in the diagnosis and of management of illness. Given that perhaps the most notable use of the stethoscope is cardiac auscultation, it would seem that this should hold particularly true for cardiology.

And yet, on moving from classroom to bedside, most of us soon discover that the heart murmur does not hold the cherished place that our teachers implied. Reviewing charts on the typical telemetry floor, one will find a surprising number of cardiac auscultations that produce "no murmurs, rubs, or gallops." On the unusual occasion when a finding is produced, the physician-in-training quickly becomes accustomed to the words "order an echo." Clearly, this is not the most cost-effective tactic. Few of us realize that it is also a limiting one.

I discovered this during my final year of residency, when I had the good fortune to spend six weeks on the medical ward at a hospital in East Africa. Though the physicians, nurses, and supporting staff there were uniformly wonderful, they—we—had few resources. There was basic laboratory equipment but for most of my tenure there we lacked the reagents to run a basic metabolic panel. The turnaround for an electrocardiogram was measured in days. And even when the CT scanner was working, few patients could afford the exam. Cost-effective diagnosis was not an option—it was the only option.

I soon discovered that the problem was not that I lacked the skills, for I could indeed recognize many of the signs of disease. Rather, weaned on a diet of limitless technology, I lacked the confidence to believe in my findings without digital confirmation. And so, fighting years of bad habits, I had to slowly learn to trust my physical exam skills. In a young boy with atrial fibrillation and heart failure, I searched for the opening snap of mitral stenosis. In a gentleman with probable myocardial infarction and no possibility of revascularization, I listened carefully for mechanical complications. In a young woman with tuberculosis and a pericardial rub, I observed my first Kussmaul sign. For a physician trained in the West, it was a difficult but enlightening process, but eventually I realized: I could diagnose without testing. I could treat without hedging. I did not need an echocardiogram to manage heart failure, an angiogram to treat ischemia, or a CT scan to diagnose a stroke. Ears, hands, and a brain were often enough.

Since then, as an internist and a cardiology fellow, I have performed my fair share of echocardiograms, angiograms, stress tests, and other studies. I like to believe that most of them were indicated. But when I hold a probe or a cathether, I always try to remember: this is a tool. It is useful, but not necessary. At some point during our training, perhaps we should all be forced to do without the latest and greatest advances. If we do, we might even discover what they are good for.

—Andreas Mauer. "A Diet of Limitless Technology."
Costs of Care, 2014. (www.costsofcare.org)

VALUE-BASED CARE AND THE ROLE OF REGULATION

It has not traditionally been the role of individual clinicians to assess the value of new technologies at the point-of-care. In the past, this role has fallen to payers who can chose to either provide insurance coverage or withhold it. The biggest payer of all, of course, is the government. In the United States, the Centers for Medicare and Medicaid Services have rarely exercised the option of withholding coverage for low-value technologies. Particularly after the failure of the Clinton health reform plan, amidst widespread public concern about rationing, the government has even been wary to provide guidance on value of healthcare technologies.

This was not always the case. For 23 years, just prior to the defeat of the Clinton health plan, the Congressional Office of Technology Assessment (OTA) systematically studied and reported on the value of technologies to guide public decision making. Before being abolished in 1995 by the 104th US Congress over concerns about its necessity, the OTA published 750 scientific reports—at least 100 of which were devoted to cost-effectiveness of healthcare technologies—in order to guide public decision making (the archives of this office are maintained by the Federation of American Scientists).[38] Still, very few recommendations over the tenure of the OTA translated into payment decisions.

After a 15-year hiatus, in 2010 the Affordable Care Act somewhat renewed the role of government in appraising healthcare value by establishing two bodies—the Independent Payment Advisory Board (IPAB) and the Patient Centered Outcomes Research Institute (PCORI). IPAB is a 15-member body of experts who are given the specific charge of developing proposals that decrease growth in Medicare spending. Nonetheless, these proposals must fall within a highly restricted set of options. They are forbidden from making recommendations that raise revenues, increasing cost sharing for Medicare patients, restrict benefits, or restrict eligibility.[50] The only option left on the table appears to be reducing payments to providers—an indirect and politically unpopular way of limiting low-value technology. The reach of PCORI is also limited. PCORI provides funding to compare the clinical effectiveness of overlapping technologies, but it does not have regulatory authority or advise any one decision-making body.[51] Furthermore, the clunky name of PCORI is not a coincidence. PCORI does not have the words "value" or "cost" in the title because by law, they are explicitly forbidden from using CEA in their recommendations. Nonetheless, some have argued that PCORI is still able to demote some technologies with inferior value on the basis of comparative effectiveness alone.[52]

Unlike PCORI, the US Food and Drug Administration (FDA) does have regulatory authority, but only with regard to safety. The FDA must approve almost all forms of technological progress, including new drugs and devices as well as new applications of existing technology. Nonetheless, it is poorly positioned to influence the cost dimension of the value equation. In 2004, bevacizumab (trade name Avastin, Genentech USA Inc) was first approved by the FDA to treat certain types of metastatic cancer. A few years later the same class of medications were also found to be effective in treating an eye condition called macular degeneration. Rather than extending approval to use bevacizumab for macular generation, a new medication called ranibizumab (trade name Lucentis, Genentech USA Inc) was approved by the FDA for the new indication.

Both bevacizumab and ranibizumab are made by Genentech. Both were shown to be equally effective in treating macular degeneration. Both are even administered the same way. The only difference appeared to be that bevacizumab cost $50 per dose and ranibizumab cost $2000 per dose—a cumulative difference that sums to hundreds of millions of dollars of Medicare spending annually.[53] Similar examples of low-value technologies with unproven efficacy passing FDA approval abound. New devices may face even less scrutiny with regard to efficacy than drugs.[54]

By contrast, an equivalent agency in the United Kingdom does have regulatory purview over the value of new technologies. The National Institute for Health and Care Excellence (NICE) was established in 1999 to promote diffusion of high-value technology within the United Kingdom's National Health Service and to ensure taxpayer money was being invested for maximum health benefit.[55] A core activity of NICE is appraising the incremental cost-effectiveness ratios (ICERs) of new technologies with regard to societal willingness to pay thresholds. An ICER of less than £20,000 to 30,000 per QALY is considered worth paying for. Technologies exceeding this amount are sometimes considered but must be justified based on other strong considerations (exceptions have been made for certain end-of-life cancer drugs). Other technologies that exceed the willingness to pay are ultimately not covered by the National Health Service. Some of these decisions, such as restricting the use of bevacizumab in renal cell carcinoma, have been highly controversial.[56] Nonetheless, the United Kingdom has asserted a strong government role in limiting the influence of low-value technology on cost growth.

Controversy in regulating the cost of technology and a way forward

There are several legitimate reasons why regulating technology on the basis of cost is controversial. The first is that denying access to technology on the basis of cost is a way of rationing care. Even with a well-intended attempt to deploy resources equitably, it is possible that a regulator may inadvertently withhold high-value treatment from someone who needs it. In the United States the political intractability of this concern has prevented government from taking a more active role. Second, CEA is based on imperfect estimates that may be neither precise enough nor accurate enough in certain situations. Particularly for technologies that do not obviously extend life (like the DaVinci robot), the best effect measure is not obvious. Third, technology regulation may stifle innovation by making private investment into research and development less attractive. Many technology developers argue that the high prices of the drugs and devices they release are necessary to recoup their investment costs.

Despite these concerns, it is clear that technology is a major driver of cost growth and that many technologies that are low-value are major sources of waste. It is also clear that CEA is a powerful tool for discerning which technologies are likely to be valuable. In the absence of a stronger government role, several independent organizations have emerged to promote the use of CEA in guiding value-based care. The Institute for Clinical and Economic Review (conveniently abbreviated ICER) performs regular, rigorous, and publically available health-care technology appraisals.[57] Among other activities, ICER is currently leading a "Value Assessment Project" to develop a conceptual framework that payers can use to guide their assessment of the value of new technologies. A related effort is the Cost-Effectiveness Analysis Registry, part of the Center for Evaluation of

Value and Risk in Health (CEVR) at Tufts University. The registry includes over 3700 cost-utility analyses and allows both policymakers and researchers to easily search for utility weights (QALYs) and ICERs for CEA.[58]

Partly as a result of these independent efforts, the number of CEA publications has grown tremendously in recent years. A 20-year review of the Tufts CEVR registry found that the number of radiology-related CEAs that were published increased from an average of 1.6 per year between 1985 and 1995 to 9.4 per year between 1996 and 2005—56% of the articles were published between 2000 and 2005.[59] Clinical professional societies have begun promoting these studies among the evidence-based guidelines and practice bulletins they issue for their members (see also Chapter 14). Even in cases where CEA is not performed, the emerging focus on value is apparent. Since 2000, the American College of Radiology began publishing appropriateness criteria to guide use of imaging technologies. In 2014, both the American College of Cardiology and the American Society of Clinical Oncology announced that they planned to include value assessments in their practice guidelines.[60,61] As we mentioned in Chapter 5, dozens more professional societies have picked up the mantle by publishing lists of potentially low-value medical decisions as part of the Choosing Wisely campaign. More often than not, these lists describe applications of technologies that are low-value, even if the technologies themselves are worthwhile.

Therein lies the challenge for practicing clinicians. We must understand the contribution of technology to cost growth and be able to adopt recommendations that are guided by CEA. But at the end of the day it will be the marginal application of technology at the patient's bedside that will be truly valuable or wasteful. It is hard to issue a precise guideline on how many ultrasounds every pregnant woman needs. For some women, four ultrasounds will all be very valuable. For other women, the fourth ultrasound will be considerably less valuable than the third. The remaining chapters in this section of the book provide additional context for why the system in which clinicians practice makes it challenging to limit use of low-value technology. Part III will then detail several strategies to make care better.

KEY POINTS:

- The deployment of new technology is a driving force behind rising healthcare costs.
- While many new technologies are worth it on average, applications of these technologies may be wasteful at the margins.
- Cost-effectiveness analysis provides a means of measuring the value of new technology and considering value with respect to societal willingness to pay.
- In the absence of regulation of low-value technology, it will be increasingly important for clinicians to consider the use of new technologies carefully.

References:

1. Moore GE. Cramming more components onto integrated circuits. *Proc IEEE*. 1998;86(1):82-85.
2. Skinner JS. Health-care costs driven by expensive technology that doesn't work. *MIT Technol Rev*. 2013. http://www.technologyreview.com/news/518876/the-costly-paradox-of-health-care-technology/. Accessed August 28, 2014.
3. Proton Therapy Co-Operative Group: Facilities in Operation. http://www.ptcog.ch/index.php/facilities-in-operation. Accessed October 7, 2014.
4. Lawler E. Report on proton beam therapy from the Institute for Clinical and Economic Review (ICER) shows most uses not supported by evidence. http://www.icer-review.org/report-on-proton-beam-therapy-from-the-institute-for-clinical-and-economic-review-icer-shows-most-uses-not-supported-by-evidence-report-prepared-for-washington-state-health-care-authority/. Accessed September 13, 2014.
5. 100 Fastest-Growing Companies 2012: Intuitive Surgical - ISRG. Fortune. http://archive.money.com/magazines/fortune/fastest-growing/2012/snapshots/50.html. Accessed September 20, 2014.
6. Cortez MF, Adams S. Intuitive surgical declines on falling da Vinci sales. Bloomberg 2013. http://www.bloomberg.com/news/2013-07-09/intuitive-surgical-declines-on-falling-da-vinci-sales.html. Accessed September 20, 2014.
7. Gold J. Proton center closure doesn't slow new construction. *NPR.org*. http://www.npr.org/blogs/health/2014/10/01/352933758/proton-center-closure-doesn-t-slow-new-construction. Accessed October 4, 2014.
8. Rettig RA. Valuing lives. 1976. http://www.rand.org/pubs/papers/P5672.html. Accessed October 1, 2014.
9. National Kidney and Urologic Diseases Information Clearinghouse. Treatment methods for kidney failure: hemodialysis. http://kidney.niddk.nih.gov/Kudiseases/pubs/hemodialysis/. Accessed October 1, 2014.
10. Caplan A. Dialysis payment program is costly in too many ways. *MSNBC.com*. http://www.nbcnews.com/id/40842821/ns/health-health_care/t/dialysis-payment-program-costly-too-many-ways/. Accessed October 26, 2014.
11. Rettig RA. End-stage renal disease and the "cost" of medical technology. 1977. http://www.rand.org/pubs/papers/P6029.html. Accessed October 1, 2014.
12. Rettig RA. Medical innovation duels cost containment. *Health Aff*. 1994;13(3):7-27.
13. Blendon R, Altman SH. *Medical Technology: The Culprit behind Health Care Costs? Proceedings of the 1977 Sun Valley Forum on National Health*. Hyattsville, MD: Washington: U.S. Dept. of Health, Education, and Welfare, Public Health Service, Office of Health Research, Statistics, and Technology, National Center for Health Services Research, Health Resources Administration, Bureau of Health Planning; for sale by the Supt. of Docs., U.S. Govt. Print. Off.; 1979. http://catalog.hathitrust.org/Record/000736376. Accessed October 1, 2014.
14. Congressional Budget Office. Technological change and the growth of health care spending—CBO. 2008. http://www.cbo.gov/publication/41665. Accessed September 11, 2014.
15. Newhouse JP. Medical care costs: how much welfare loss? *J Econ Perspect*. 1992;6(3):3-21.
16. Peden EA, Freeland MS. Insurance effects on US medical spending (1960–1993). *Health Econ*. 1998;7(8):671-687.
17. Lowenstein R. The quality cure? *The New York Times*, March 13, 2005. http://www.nytimes.com/2005/03/13/magazine/13HEALTH.html. Accessed September 11, 2014.
18. Cheney RB, Reiner J. *Heart: An American Medical Odyssey*. New York, NY: Scribner; 2013.
19. Cutler DM. *Your Money Or Your Life: Strong Medicine for America's Health Care System*. Oxford: Oxford University Press; 2005.
20. Heidenreich PA, McClellan M. Trends in treatment and outcomes for acute myocardial infarction: 1975-1995. *Am J Med*. 2001;110(3):165-174.
21. Serruys PW, Kutryk MJB, Ong ATL. Coronary-artery stents. *N Engl J Med*. 2006;354(5):483-495.
22. Cutler DM, McClellan M. Is technological change in medicine worth it? *Health Aff*. 2001;20(5):11-29.

23. Cutler DM, McClellan M, Newhouse JP, Remler D. *Pricing Heart Attack Treatments*. Cambridge, MA. National Bureau of Economic Research; 1999. http://www.nber.org/papers/w7089. Accessed September 22, 2014.
24. Cutler DM, McClellan M. Is technological change in medicine worth it? *Health Aff*. 2001; 20(5):11-29.
25. Cutler DM, Meara E. *The Technology of Birth: Is It Worth It?*. Cambridge, MA. National Bureau of Economic Research; 1999. http://www.nber.org/papers/w7390. Accessed October 5, 2014.
26. Meltzer D. Accounting for future costs in medical cost-effectiveness analysis. *J Health Econ*. 1997;16(1):33-64.
27. Greene MF. Obstetricians still await a Deus ex Machina. *N Engl J Med*. 2006;355(21):2247-2248.
28. MacDorman MF, Menacker F, Declercq E. Cesarean birth in the United States: epidemiology, trends, and outcomes. *Clin Perinatol*. 2008;35(2):293-307.
29. Truven Health Analytics. *The Cost of Having a Baby in the United States*. 2013. http://transform. childbirthconnection.org/wp-content/uploads/2013/01/Cost-of-Having-a-Baby1.pdf.
30. Amin AP, Spertus JA, Cohen DJ, et al. Use of drug-eluting stents as a function of predicted benefit: clinical and economic implications of current practice. *Arch Intern Med*. 2012;172(15):1145-1152.
31. Millman J. The drug that's forcing America's most important—and uncomfortable—health-care debate. *The Washington Post*, July 24, 2014. http://www.washingtonpost.com/blogs/wonkblog/wp/2014/07/24/the-drug-thats-forcing-americas-most-important-and-uncomfortable-health-care-debate/. Accessed October 8, 2014.
32. Hershey J, Asch D, Jepson C, Baron J, Ubel P. Incremental and average cost-effectiveness ratios: will physicians make a distinction? *Risk Anal*. 2003;23(1):81-89.
33. Weinstein MC, Stason WB. Foundations of cost-effectiveness analysis for health and medical practices. *N Engl J Med*. 1977;296(13):716-721.
34. Kim JJ, Goldie SJ. Health and economic implications of HPV vaccination in the United States. *N Engl J Med*. 2008;359(8):821-832.
35. Consumer Price Index (CPI). http://www.bls.gov/cpi/. Accessed October 13, 2014.
36. Lipscomb J. Time preference for health in cost-effectiveness analysis. *Med Care*. 1989;27(suppl 3):S233-S253.
37. Zeckhauser R, Shepard D. *Where Now for Saving Lives?* Cambridge, MA: John Fitzgerald Kennedy School of Government, Harvard University; 1976.
38. Technology Assessment and Congress. OTA Arch. http://ota.fas.org/technology_assessment_and_congress/. Accessed October 13, 2014.
39. Pliskin JS, Shepard DS, Weinstein MC. Utility functions for life years and health status. *Oper Res*. 1980;28(1):206-224.
40. Weinstein MC, Torrance G, McGuire A. QALYs: the basics. *Value Health*. 2009;12(suppl 1):S5-S9.
41. EuroQol—About Us. http://www.euroqol.org/euroqol-group/about-us.html. Accessed October 13, 2014.
42. Burström K, Johannesson M, Diderichsen F. A comparison of individual and social time trade-off values for health states in the general population. *Health Policy*. 2006;76(3):359-370.
43. Gafni A. The standard gamble method: what is being measured and how it is interpreted. *Health Serv Res*. 1994;29(2):207-224.
44. Ubel PA, Loewenstein G, Scanlon D, Kamlet M. Value measurement in cost-utility analysis: explaining the discrepancy between rating scale and person trade-off elicitations. *Health Policy Amst Neth*. 1998;43(1):33-44.
45. Hirth RA, Chernew ME, Miller E, Fendrick AM, Weissert WG. Willingness to pay for a quality-adjusted life year: in search of a standard. *Med Decis Mak*. 2000;20(3):332-342.
46. Eichler H-G, Kong SX, Gerth WC, Mavros P, Jönsson B. Use of cost-effectiveness analysis in health-care resource allocation decision-making: how are cost-effectiveness thresholds expected to emerge? *Value Health*. 2004;7(5):518-528.
47. Newhouse JP. US and UK health economics: two disciplines separated by a common language? *Health Econ*. 1998;7(suppl 1):S79-S92.

48. Löthgren M, Zethraeus N. Definition, interpretation and calculation of cost-effectiveness acceptability curves. *Health Econ.* 2000;9(7):623-630.
49. Petrou S, Trinder J, Brocklehurst P, Smith L. Economic evaluation of alternative management methods of first-trimester miscarriage based on results from the MIST trial. *Int J Obstet Gynaecol.* 2006;113(8):879-889.
50. Oberlander J, Morrison M. Failure to launch? The Independent Payment Advisory Board's uncertain prospects. *N Engl J Med.* 2013;369(2):105-107.
51. Selby JV, Beal AC, Frank L. The Patient-Centered Outcomes Research Institute (PCORI) national priorities for research and initial research agenda. *JAMA.* 2012;307(15):1583-1584.
52. Bagley N. Who says PCORI can't do cost effectiveness? *The Incidental Economist.* Oct 14, 2013. http://theincidentaleconomist.com/wordpress/who-says-pcori-cant-do-cost-effectiveness/. Accessed October 14, 2014.
53. Pollack A. Clinical trial says avastin as effective as lucentis for macular degeneration. *The New York Times,* April 28, 2011. http://www.nytimes.com/2011/04/29/business/29eye.html. Accessed September 11, 2014.
54. Dhruva SS, Bero LA, Redberg RF. Strength of study evidence examined by the FDA in premarket approval of cardiovascular devices. *JAMA.* 2009;302(24):2679-2685.
55. NICE. Provider of national guidance and advice to improve health and social care. https://www.nice.org.uk/. Accessed September 13, 2014.
56. Malik NN. Controlling the cost of innovative cancer therapeutics. *Nat Rev Clin Oncol.* 2009; 6(9):550-552.
57. Institute for Clinical and Economic Review. http://www.icer-review.org/. Accessed October 14, 2014.
58. CEA Registry Website Blog. https://research.tufts-nemc.org/cear4/. Accessed October 14, 2014.
59. Otero HJ, Rybicki FJ, Greenberg D, Neumann PJ. Twenty years of cost-effectiveness analysis in medical imaging: are we improving? *Radiology.* 2008;249(3):917-925.
60. Anderson JL, Heidenreich PA, Barnett PG, et al. ACC/AHA statement on cost/value methodology in clinical practice guidelines and performance measures: a report of the American College of Cardiology/American Heart Association Task Force on Performance Measures and Task Force on Practice Guidelines. *Circulation.* 2014;CIR.0000000000000042.
61. ASCO in Action Brief: Value in Cancer Care. ASCO.org. http://www.asco.org/advocacy/asco-action-brief-value-cancer-care. Accessed October 15, 2014.

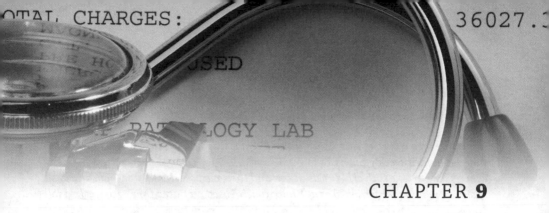

CHAPTER 9

Primary Care Shortage Crisis: Lost Opportunities to Deliver Value

David Margolius and Andrew F. Morris-Singer

*D*r Jones knocked on the exam room door, where her last patient of the day awaited her. "Enter," a voice said within. She did and found Mr White assembling his medication bottles on the desk to his right. Dr Jones met Mr White 7 years ago when she was an internal medicine resident rotating on the inpatient cardiology service. She became his primary care physician after that first hospitalization, but until recently, she rarely felt that she added any value to his well-being.

"How are you today, Mr White?" she asked, sitting next to him at the desk. "I am happy to report that I have just one concern!" he replied. He looked well. His bare ankles were slim, not swollen, and he spoke without needing to take a breath between every couple of words—a vast improvement from prior visits.

In the early days of their relationship, Mr White had spent nearly as much time in the hospital as he did at home. His heart failure and its episodic exacerbations were his identity: swollen legs and shortness of breath tethered him to a hospital bed when he missed a day's pills or ate too much salt. Dr Jones tried desperately to help him, but years of rushed visits and occasional phone calls did little to keep him out of the hospital. The helplessness she had felt frustrated her and her colleagues; most chose to become specialists rather than stay in primary care.

The frustrations ended when Dr Jones' clinic went through a transformation. Inspired by a new model of primary care—the "patient-centered medical home"—the clinic management reorganized the practice to facilitate team-based care, better access, and more contact with patients between visits. The days of delivering care through 15-minute appointments spaced out over months were over. Dr Jones and her team—a nurse, *medical assistant, and clerk—began meeting weekly to figure out the best way to improve the well-being of the entire group of patients assigned to her team.*

Mr White was a special case, given how often he was hospitalized. The team decided that he needed weekly phone calls from someone with time to ensure that he knew exactly how to take each of his medications and their purpose. Malik, the team's medical assistant who was also trained as a "health coach," used protected time each week to call Mr White. Each week, they would discuss Mr White's symptoms, medications, and anything else that came up. Within weeks, the intervention was successful: Mr White was able to adhere to his diet and medications and no longer required stints in the hospital. Malik calls Mr White weekly to this day.

"Well then," Dr Jones said, "Let's spend this visit discussing what matters to you."

Robust primary care is critical to any healthcare system delivering high-value care. In systems with greater numbers of primary care providers, the outcomes are better: lower rates of hospitalization, better patient experience, and lower overall costs.[1] Unfortunately, the predominant US payment structure does not reward some of the most important work done in primary care, including thoughtful diagnosis, listening, counseling, and coordination of care. Too often Dr Jones and her colleagues must fit more patients into their schedule each day—propagating the cycle of burnout and fewer trainees choosing primary care careers.

Fortunately, hope for the future of primary care exists. A handful of practices across the United States have transformed using team-based care, patient-centeredness, and local partnerships with payers to fund innovations and feedback population-level data.[2] Spreading these innovations to all components of the US healthcare system is the difficult task ahead—one that will require systemic changes (such as new reimbursement methods), as well as new models of clinical care. In order to staff these new innovative practices, new forms of training will be necessary. The primary care provider of the near future will be able to care for a population of patients, not only through face-to-face visits, but also via e-mail, phone calls, and participation on a team.

WHY IS PRIMARY CARE CRITICAL TO DELIVERING VALUE?

Primary care serves as the foundation of high-value healthcare systems in most wealthy nations of the world, as well as in specific communities within the United States. However, when it comes to the overall makeup of the US healthcare system, it seems that primary care stands as an afterthought despite its proven benefits.[1] According to the late health policy expert, Barbara Starfield, robust primary care must be composed of four pillars: first-contact care, continuity of care over time, comprehensiveness (addressing all aspects of patients' care needs rather than focusing only on a specific organ system), and coordination of care with other parts of the health system (Figure 9-1).[3] Each pillar not only defines primary care but also is critical for this domain of healthcare to deliver value.

First-contact care requires that primary care be ideally delivered where patients first access the healthcare system. Unfortunately, in the United States, a growing number of people are not able to obtain timely appointments to primary care and instead go to the emergency department (ED)—which is much more expensive. From 1997 to 2007 in the United States, the number of ED visits increased by 23%, and ED visits for Medicaid patients increased by 84%.[4] Dr Stephen Pitts and colleagues from Emory University found that two-thirds of ED visits were made after-hours or during the weekends.[5] This is unsurprising given that only 29% of primary care practices in the United States see patients after-hours, compared to 89% of practices in the United Kingdom, and 97% of practices in the Netherlands.[6] Not providing timely access to care counteracts much of the value that primary care offers: catching disease processes early and preventing costly ED visits and hospitalizations. One study estimates nearly half of ED visits could be prevented with timely access to primary care.[7]

Continuity of care refers to maintaining a relationship with the same provider or team over time. Most patients appreciate greater continuity of care: it is associated with higher patient satisfaction with their providers and outpatient visits, especially for the most vulnerable patients.[8] Providers also value continuity of care.[9] In addition to its effects on overall patient and provider satisfaction, continuity of care leads to better outcomes, including improved delivery of preventive care, fewer hospitalizations, reduced costs, and lower overall mortality.[10,11] However, continuity of care requires both an adequate supply of providers as well

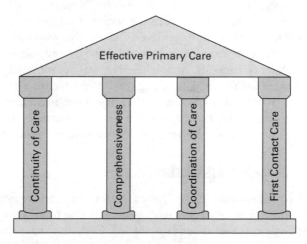

Figure 9-1. The four pillars of effective primary care.

as an organized system of care delivery, two attributes the US healthcare system currently lacks.

Comprehensiveness of care requires that primary care be capable of addressing the wide scope of issues that affect patients and families. Robust primary care should reduce the need for referral to specialists, but the reality is quite the opposite: providers in the United States are more likely to refer to specialists than other wealthy countries.[12] In turn, nearly half of visits to specialists in the United States are for routine follow-up and preventive care services that could have been performed by primary care providers.[13] This is problematic because of the higher cost of these visits and the greater tendency of specialists to order expensive tests, procedures, and medications. In one study, cardiologists were more likely than generalists to prescribe brand-name medications when generic formulations were available.[14]

Coordination of care means primary care takes responsibility for managing patients' health needs through the full spectrum of settings where care is delivered. For example, primary care coordinates transitions of care, such as when a patient moves from the hospital to their home or from their home to a long-term care facility, communicating with the variety of specialists and other personnel involved in the patient's care. In an international survey of patients with complex care needs, patients in the United States who had a primary care provider reported some of the best care coordination. Unfortunately, in the United States, those patients with complex care needs—who could most benefit from care coordination—were least likely to report having a regular primary care provider.[15]

Health systems built on a robust foundation of primary care that demonstrate the four pillars have been consistently shown to deliver higher value care overall. Medicare beneficiaries residing in areas with more full-time equivalent primary care physicians per capita had lower all-cause mortality, lower rates of preventable hospitalizations, and lower Medicare spending.[16] In a study of US metropolitan areas, regions with higher ratios of primary care physicians to specialists had lower total utilization of healthcare services.[17] Given this evidence, calls abound to increase the capacity of primary care systems in the United States to deliver the type of first-contact, continuous, comprehensive, and coordinated services that have been associated with such high-value care. However, efforts to revitalize US primary care face a number of challenges that have been mounting for decades: a growing demand for primary care services, a worsening primary care workforce shortage, and a reimbursement system that does not value primary care services.

THE SUPPLY/DEMAND MISMATCH

The demand for primary care in the United States has been steadily increasing over the years and is forecasted to accelerate largely due to an aging population with an increasingly complex set of care needs.[18] Even prior to insurance expansion brought on by the Affordable Care Act (ACA) (see Chapter 2), the demand for primary care was expected to surge, particularly in rural and underserved areas that already face considerable shortages in primary care capacity—work-load could increase by 29% between 2005 and 2025.[19] Demand for primary care will likely be further heightened as both public and private healthcare purchasers demand more proactive and preventive services for employees and beneficiaries to avoid utilization of more costly downstream health services.[20]

How many primary care providers will it take to serve these growing care needs? Estimates vary greatly but share two common features. First, the estimates focus on primary care physician services rather than nonphysician providers, given that physicians constitute over three-fourths of the primary care currently deliv-ered in the United States.[21] Second, the estimates warn that demand for primary care services will soon far outstrip supply, leaving the United States with signifi-cant shortages of primary care, especially given the health insurance expansion of the ACA. Recent estimates of this developing shortage range from a need for 20,000 to 50,000 primary care physicians over the next decade (Figure 9-2).[21-23] Despite increasing calls for policy solutions to account for the potential for nonphysician members of the primary care workforce to help fix the projected shortages, almost all policy proposals assume that physicians will continue to supply the vast majority of primary care services in the United States for the foreseeable future.

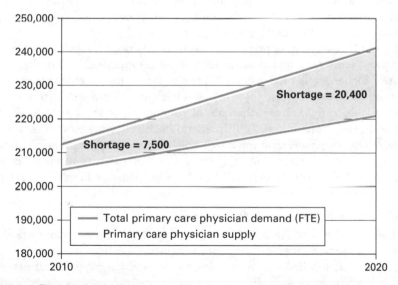

Figure 9-2. The primary care shortage.
Notes: Data are from Health Resources and Service Administration (HRSA) of the US Department of Health and Human Services. National demand projections assume that in 2010 the national supply of primary care physicians was adequate except for the approximately 7500 FTEs needed to de-designate the primary care HPSAs.

Too much outflow, insufficient inflow

In growing numbers, individual providers are retiring early or switching to part-time work. Reasons for this trend are greater care demands on providers' plates, enhanced time pressures, chaotic work environments, and increasing regulatory requirements.[24] Moreover, the workforce is aging. One-third of current primary care physicians will reach retirement age within the next decade.[25]

Burnout is experienced by up to half of primary care physicians, a disproportionately high rate compared to specialists.[26] By 2016, the number of adult primary care physicians leaving the workforce will exceed the number of physicians entering the workforce—making the burden on existing and incoming primary care providers even greater.[18]

Given the rate of departure from the profession, expanding the workforce will depend on more students choosing a primary care career. Unfortunately, graduates of US medical schools have been increasingly unlikely to do so, with less than 20% of them opting to choose primary care careers, nearly a 25% drop since the 1980s.[27] Reasons for the decline include a culture of primary care "bad-mouthing" at many medical schools, dissatisfaction with primary care clinical experiences where students regularly observe burnout among both attendings and residents, and the "hidden curriculum" that glorifies specialty careers and hospital-based health services.[28-30] An even greater influence may be the remarkably lower financial return on investment of choosing a primary care career—specialists' salaries are 267% that of primary care providers.[31] When coupled to the average educational debt of $160,000 to $200,000 among graduating medical students, physicians will usually opt for careers with higher salaries.[32]

The resulting shortage of primary care services is unequally distributed around the nation, with rural and urban underserved communities facing disproportionately higher levels of shortages.[33] Despite increasing investments in federally qualified health centers, physicians rarely choose to practice in this setting. Between 2006 and 2008, less than 5% of residency graduates went to practice in underserved communities.[34] With federal health insurance expansion under the ACA, the supply-demand mismatch will worsen—after state law expanded health insurance in Massachusetts, the number of patients receiving care at community health centers increased by 31% while the number of primary care clinicians remained steady.[35]

Reigniting the primary care workforce pipeline

What will it take to create an expanded reinvigorated primary care workforce? Given the aforementioned primary care provider-specialist income gap, efforts to revitalize the pipeline that do not involve substantial payment reform have little chance of success. According to the Council on Graduate Medical Education, an advisory group authorized by congress to make recommendations to the Department of Health and Human Services, primary care salaries will need to be at least 70% that of specialists in order to entice graduating medical students to pursue primary care careers.[27] In addition to increasing primary care salaries, efforts have been made to increase loan forgiveness for trainees choosing primary careers, specifically in underserved areas. The National Health Service Corps offers loan forgiveness and salary supplementation for primary care providers, and due to new investments from the ACA and the Recovery Act, the number of National Health Service Corps providers has tripled since 2008.[36]

Changes at the medical school level will also be needed, such as admissions policy changes that prioritize student characteristics associated with greater levels of eventual primary care practice and service in underserved communities.[31,37,38] Given publicly funded medical schools' greater tendency to graduate students into both primary care and service to underserved communities, efforts to expand US medical school capacity should prioritize funding to public programs.[37] The Title VII program of Section 747 legislation authorized Health Resources and Service Administration (HRSA) to award grants aimed at improving the quality of primary care training in medical schools and residency programs.[39] Even though the program has been successful in encouraging trainees to pursue generalist careers, legislators often threaten to decrease its funding.[39]

Additionally, it will be critical for this next generation of primary care physicians to have skills and competencies aligned with the components of transformed practice.[40] A number of residency programs are supplementing clinical competencies with communication, quality improvement, and practice-based learning skills integral to team-based care.[41] However, given that funding for residency programs flows through hospitals, outpatient training receives less emphasis than inpatient training, often resulting in graduates that are poorly trained for outpatient practice.[42] Additionally, the outpatient clinics in which residents practice primary care are usually subpar, specifically in the domain of continuity of care, compared to other clinic models, which further discourages graduates from choosing primary care careers.[43,44] The solution to the workforce problem, therefore, will involve reforming the way residency programs are funded to encourage more outpatient training and improving the actual care delivered by resident-based clinics to prepare trainees to work in transformed primary care practices.

An example of the latter is learning collaboratives.[45] Mirroring the efforts of quality improvement experts in nonacademic settings, the collaboratives are a space to accelerate transformation in care delivery and provider training among participating practices. One example is the "I3 collaborative," first launched in 2003 to improve chronic disease management among 10 academic primary care practices. Early on, the collaborative resulted in a nearly fourfold reduction in congestive heart failure ("CHF") hospitalizations through sharing best practices and optimizing the roles of nonprovider team members; since then, the collaborative doubled in size and has since taken on a variety of other quality improvement and cost control initiatives.[46,47] The model has spread to collaboratives in Colorado, Massachusetts, and Pennsylvania.[48-50]

Revitalizing primary care will require more than just addressing the shortage of physicians—these efforts must coexist with efforts to recruit nonphysician providers to primary care. Primary care delivered through teams, including nonphysician providers, nurses, pharmacists, social workers, and medical assistants, could alleviate the projected provider shortage, but would require liberalized scope-of-practice laws and payment reform to compensate nonphysician services.[51] If preventive and chronic care services are shared with nonprovider members of the primary care team, each practice could care for larger numbers of people, ensuring linkage to primary care for a greater percentage of the population.[52]

Ultimately, as much as the increasing engagement of a diverse set of health professionals on the primary care team represents glimmers of hope to the looming primary care service shortage in this nation, transforming the primary care team poses profound challenges. First, the traditional, siloed approach to health professions training—where different professions spend little time interacting during their training—does not support the new model. Second, new care teams will produce other unforeseen inefficiencies and costs associated with coordinating information and care between an increasingly large team. Third, the model causes concern that the physician will be increasingly relegated to a background role, separated from patients by a layer of other health professionals. We do not know what this will mean for patient satisfaction, the doctor-patient relationship, patient safety, and trainees' interest in primary care careers. What we do know is that the current model of primary care delivery is untenable.

Non-MDs to the rescue ... or maybe not

Nurse practitioners (NPs) and physician assistants (PAs) provide disproportionate degrees of primary care services to minority populations, particularly in underserved and rural populations.[53] Because of their lower average salaries, shorter length of training, and greater ability to shift specialties mid-career, NPs and PAs seem like one workforce solution to the primary care shortage.[54] Yet, just like the trend in graduating physicians, less and less of these professionals are entering primary care careers: one-half of NPs and one-third of PAs currently practice primary care.[21,54] Wide-ranging scope of practice laws and reimbursement policies also limit what nonphysician providers can do and get paid for doing.[55] For example, some states allow NPs to practice independently from physicians while other states require that physicians directly supervise NPs at least a portion of the time.[56] In Missouri, each time an NP sees a new patient, a physician must see the patient within 2 weeks of that first visit.[56] Onerous policies like these will need to be amended in order to enable NPs to make up some of the primary care shortfall. Yet even with these proposed changes to more fully include NPs and PAs in the primary care workforce, the ratio of primary care clinicians to population is still predicted to fall over time.[57]

Costs of the primary care shortage

The consequences of the worsening primary care shortage manifest in both direct and indirect ways. Directly, they present problems of access to services: difficulty establishing a new primary care provider, increased wait times to obtain an appointment and overall rushed visits. Three years after Massachusetts expanded insurance coverage, studies show about half of adult primary care physicians are not accepting new patients, wait times are lengthening, and a majority of practices face difficulty filling physician vacancies.[58] This trend is also playing out nationally, with 20% of Americans overall reporting difficulty accessing a regular source of primary care.[59] Indirectly, the shortage causes higher overall health costs, greater rates of preventable hospitalizations for conditions like heart failure, and a greater burden of care carried by the remaining pool of primary care providers.[24,60-62]

Story From the Frontlines—"The Hidden Cost of Lacking Primary Care"

When I first met Cassie, a cheerful 21-year-old, she was comfortably sprawled across her hospital bed in leopard-print pajamas. The TV was on, and she had a book in hand, though she was not paying much attention to either. She had recently moved to Boston from Florida, and she seemed happy to have company, even from a second-year medical student.

She had come into the ER for a sprained ankle. Her x-rays came back negative for a fracture, and she was given an ankle brace. But the routine check-up also revealed heart murmurs and low blood sugar. The doctor decided to keep her for more tests.

Cassie was, in fact, no stranger to hospitals. She was diagnosed with Type I diabetes when she was seven, and, ever since, she has struggled to keep her sugar levels steady. She had been admitted to the hospital a total of 17 times for severely dysregulated blood sugar levels. "I had real trouble doing the blood checks regularly," she told me. "The pump helped though. I was on the pump for 2 years during middle school, but my clothes wouldn't fit right, and people made fun of me." She paused and fidgeted with her book. "There was one time when the principal yanked out the pump because he thought it was a beeper. Yeah ... after that I took it out, and my sugar was never really under control ever since."

When asked whether her doctor in Florida had helped with the adherence issues, she laughed. "Oh no, I can't afford insurance. So I was under this plan they have for poor people. You wait 6 months for an appointment, and then wait 6 hours just to see a doctor for 10 minutes. Not worth it." In fact, she had moved to Boston primarily because Massachusetts offers more affordable healthcare than Florida. "I had to give up a lot," she explained. "I'm really close with my family. Now, my family and friends are far, but I need this."

As we talked, I realized how much a primary care provider (PCP) could have helped Cassie even beyond her diabetes. Her family has a history of mental illness—both her grandmother and her mother have bipolar disorder—and Cassie suffers from severe personality shifts, she says, when her blood sugar levels are low. Despite the blatant warning signs, she has never been recommended for a psychiatric evaluation. Until recently, she was also involved in an abusive relationship. She endured months of brutal beatings, until her mother noticed bruises and called the police.

In the media, we often hear heartbreaking stories about patients who die or become severely handicapped due to lack of access to healthcare. Cassie's case is different; she is relatively healthy despite her many hospitalizations and traumatic experiences. Yet her story speaks to the often overlooked, subtler consequences of inadequate coverage. A PCP could have coached Cassie by offering tips on adherence and checking-in on her regularly. Her doctor may have noticed the bruises, suspected domestic violence, and saved her from the brutal beatings sooner. A watchful PCP would recommend a psychiatric evaluation. An earlier investment in primary care could have significantly lessened Cassie's suffering.

Ironically, such an investment could actually have made Cassie's healthcare substantially cheaper. Virtually all of Cassie's care back home in Florida was provided through the ED, and only after the catastrophic sugar highs and lows had already dealt serious damage to her body. The cost of these 17 ambulance rides and hospitalizations easily exceeded the price of regular care through a dedicated PCP. Early investment in primary care may simultaneously reduce suffering, as well as costs.

Cassie remained apprehensive about the future. She told me, "The doctors here are nice. They seem like they care." In the meantime, she will be applying to colleges in the Boston area. With reliable healthcare under her belt and her blood sugar in control, Cassie hopes to pursue nursing school.

—David Mou. "The Hidden Cost of Lacking Primary Care."
Costs of Care, 2010. (www.costsofcare.org)

POOR INVESTMENT IN PRIMARY CARE AND THE NEED FOR REIMBURSEMENT REFORM

A key impediment to robust primary care in the United States is the fee-for-service reimbursement system, which rewards providers who perform procedures over providers who do not. The result is a primary care delivery model with short appointments, high burnout rates among providers, and relatively poor care outcomes.

In 1992, Medicare began reimbursing providers based on a fee schedule set by the resource-based relative-value scale. The Relative Value Unit Committee (RUC) compiles physician survey data to estimate time, mental effort and judgment, technical skill, physical effort, and stress for each physician service. The committee recommends a numerical value for each service (called a *relative value unit* [RVU]) to the Centers for Medicare and Medicaid Services (CMS). The RUC is a body appointed by the American Medical Association and is not a governmental body; however, CMS accepts nearly all of the committee's recommendations for RVUs. This value, along with a factor for geographical variation, determines Medicare payments for each service. The RUC is composed of 31 members, 21 of which are named by specialty societies. Although primary care is represented by three specialty societies, primary care providers make up a startling minority of voters.[63] Most private insurers base their payments to providers from current Medicare payments, thus the values chosen by this specialist-heavy committee are pervasive throughout the US healthcare system.[64]

As a result of this method for selecting reimbursements, from 1995 to 2005, the value placed on office visits did not increase, while many procedures received increased compensation. During this same period, the volume of procedures increased dramatically.[65]

In addition to the obvious drawbacks of a payment system that emphasizes quantity over quality and invasive procedures over "cognitive" services, this payment framework has uniquely disadvantaged primary care providers since a number of their services have not been reimbursed at all (see also Chapter 15). In a snapshot of his primary care practice, Dr Richard Baron, current President of the American Board of Internal Medicine, observed that physicians engaged in 23.7 telephone calls, 16.8 e-mails, and 12.1 prescription refills per day.[66] In addition, physicians reviewed 19.5 lab reports and 11.1 imaging reports per day. All of these recorded activities were separate from what went on during office visits and critical to both care coordination and comprehensiveness—yet, none of them were reimbursed.[66] Although Medicare has recently allowed for certain care coordination activities to be reimbursed starting in 2014, administrative and documentation requirements may be onerous and other integral services performed by primary care providers will continue to go unpaid.

A final hurdle is the lack of reimbursement for team-based care or care that occurs outside of traditional patient appointments. The RUC, in most cases, places value only on services delivered by physicians in face-to-face encounters. Therefore, innovative primary care services that devote time to caring for patients outside of the office setting (discussed in the next section) go unreimbursed, as do most visits with other members of the care team, such as social workers and pharmacists. To support such activities practices must obtain grants or cross-subsidize them through other practice services. However, it is unlikely that a large proportion of American primary care practices will be willing or able to find extra money for these services. For them, practice transformation will require sustained financial investment.[67]

Greasing the wheels of change

Efforts to bend the healthcare cost curve in the United States and improve overall quality have sought to replace volume-based payments with value-based payments (see Chapter 15). Accountable care organizations (ACOs) and patient-centered medical homes (PCMHs) now exist as entities to organize a new model of care delivery and support a reformed model of provider reimbursement.[68] Establishing a robust foundation of primary care to proactively manage patients' health and prevent unnecessary downstream costs is no longer just a moral imperative, it is a requirement for financial survival.[20]

A growing coalition of commercial payers, state-based health reform efforts, the Department of Defense, and Medicare and Medicaid innovation grants are putting more investment in primary care.[69] The PCMH has played a central role, allowing new enhanced payments for a more robust set of primary care services. New payments include higher encounter fees, care coordination fees, and quality improvement bonuses which can earn providers as much as $91,000 of additional revenue per year.[70] In addition to providing enhanced funding, some payers have increasingly provided performance data and decision support tools to participating practices to enable them to better identify and correct gaps in care.[68,71]

However, the investment may be insufficient considering that primary care physicians currently earn half of what specialists earn.[72-74] Also, by leaving the fee-for-service model of reimbursement in place, these payments may do little to change the chaotic, "hamster wheel" nature of clinic.[75] Hope for primary care payment reform means the United States must break from the volume-based model of payment and instead adopt risk-adjusted "comprehensive payment for comprehensive care."[76,77] In addition, practice transformation is a local process of change needing to cater to local factors and resources to be most successful—an enhanced payment structure must support local variation.[75] Allowing practices to choose their own areas of clinical quality improvement—as opposed to a federal agency choosing improved diabetes screening as a measure for all practices—is an example of such a policy that would support local transformation efforts.

Perhaps as a result of the slow speed at which larger payers have reformed primary care payment, significant numbers of primary care providers are opting out of traditional third-party payment models and establishing direct financial relationships with patients and employers. These arrangements include concierge practices and, more recently, a model called direct primary care. Concierge practices and direct primary care are similar in that they offer better access to appointments and the ability for patients to call and e-mail with their provider; these practices also serve only a fraction of patients that traditional practices serve.[78,79] In order for the model to be financially sustainable, these smaller practices charge a scheduled retainer fee to patients or employers, which is usually not covered by insurance. For those who can afford the fee, this type of primary care has the potential to be everything promised by Starfield's four pillars; however, the lower average panel size of each provider could spell an even worse primary care shortage were the model to spread significantly.

DELIVERY REFORM AND REDESIGNING PRACTICES

Despite the hurdles imposed by the reimbursement system, inspiring examples of transformed primary care exist throughout the country. Numerous healthcare systems have successfully redesigned their care delivery models to provide higher-value care (Table 9-1). Group Health, a healthcare system based in Washington State, piloted a transformed primary care practice and at 21 months observed a 29% reduction in unnecessary ED visits and 6% fewer hospitalizations compared to patients in usual care practices.[80] Southcentral Foundation, located in Alaska, similarly achieved a 50% reduction in ED visits and hospitalizations through its own decades-long journey of care delivery transformation that began in 1999.[81] The common features of these, and other, successful vanguards of primary care delivery transformation is that they have all sought to deliver better first-contact care, continuity, comprehensiveness, and care coordination—Starfield's four pillars of primary care.

A key aspect of the value of primary care is its accessibility—delays in access have been shown to lead to more emergency room visits, a worse patient experience, and higher mortality.[7,82,83] Systems that have successfully transformed their delivery models have all adopted some version of advanced access in order to meet the needs of their patients with same-day care.[84] They have accomplished this by matching supply to demand (of available appointments) to prevent developing the long waitlists that are common to most primary care practices. Realizing that this balancing act could be accomplished without merely adding more primary care appointments or decreasing patient panel sizes, these practices have been able to leverage the full capacity of the care team to deliver services outside of the traditional face-to-face appointments with providers.[67]

One area in which this has played a critical, enabling role has been in the management of patients' chronic diseases, such as diabetes and congestive heart failure. The chronic care model, developed by Dr Ed Wagner, Senior Investigator at the Group Health Research Institute, emphasizes the use of alternative "touches" to the typical office visit in order to enable a team to provide proactive chronic disease management to a panel of patients.[85] In addition to harnessing a team-based approach, the model combines a number of essential features to

Table 9-1 **Primary care problems and innovations**

Problem	Innovation
Unplanned visits with overfull agendas	Previsit planning Preappointment laboratory tests
Inadequate support to meet the patient demand for care	Sharing the care Expanded nurse or medical assistant rooming protocol Standing orders Extended responsibility for health coaching, care coordination, and integrated behavioral health to nonphysician members of the team Team responsibility for panel management
Great amounts of time spent documenting and complying with administrative and regulatory requirements	Scribing Assistant order entry Standardized prescription renewal
Computerized technology that pushes more work to the physician	In-box management Verbal messaging
Teams that function poorly and complicate rather than simplify the work	Improving team communication through: Co-location Huddles Regular team meetings Improving team functioning Systems planning Work flow mapping

Source: Reproduced, with permission, from Sinsky CA et al. In search of joy in practice: A report of 23 high-functioning primary care practices. *Ann Fam Med.* 2013;11(3):272-278.

help practices develop high-quality chronic illness management: commitment to patient self-management support, clinical information systems, provider decision support, healthcare organization, and engaging community resources.[85]

The commitment to provide proactive care to patients should also encompass preventive care. Pioneering practices use nonclinician members of the care team to play an important role in preventive care via *panel management*. This means constantly reviewing a registry to identify overdue preventive care opportunities, such as cancer screenings and vaccinations, and chronic disease management opportunities, like overdue lab tests and diabetic foot screenings, for a defined panel of patients.[86] Imagine the potential improvements in the influenza vaccination rate for adults over age 65, from the current 50%, if all primary care practices transformed to include panel management.[87]

In addition to advanced access, the chronic care model, and panel management, an element of successful primary care delivery systems is complex care management—delivering interdisciplinary care to the highest risk patients to prevent unnecessary visits to the ED or hospitalizations. Frequently involving

24/7 support from lower cost community health workers and other nonclinician members of the care team, this "high touch" care often focuses on some of the psychosocial issues facing patients, like housing, mental health and substance abuse that play a pivotal role in the large amount of care these "high utilizers" require.[88] Commonly referred to as the "hot spotters" model of care delivery, it has enabled many health systems that have adopted it to drastically reduce rates of hospitalization and ED use among the tiny fraction of patients that frequently account for a large portion of health spending in a particular community.[89]

Practices must possess accurate data about their patients and services in order to develop each of these elements of access, panel management, and complex care management. Not only does this require the practice to possess an electronic health record (EHR) with a registry function, but it must also be willing to use it to identify gaps in care and opportunities for improvement on either the individual patient or population level. Many successfully transformed practices are part of large organizations that purchase the EHR, since independent practices find that EHR software can be prohibitively expensive.[90]

Improving the specialist-primary care interface

An additional promising innovation in primary care delivery is platforms for greater collaboration between specialists and primary care providers. Project ECHO, a program in New Mexico, harnesses video-conferencing technology to connect specialists with frontline primary care providers, drastically enhancing underserved communities' access to a variety of complex specialty medications and interventions, reducing their need for costly long trips to see specialists in cities; the program delivers comparable rates of cure—for example, with hepatitis C—as those patients treated by specialist alone.[91] At San Francisco's county hospital, wait times for specialist appointments decreased by half with the implementation of a program called eReferral, which allows for Web-based dialogue between primary care providers and specialists, similarly reducing the demand for specialist appointments.[92]

The patient-centered medical home: hope for primary care?

In 2007, the primary care professional organizations crafted a joint model for primary care delivery called the *patient-centered medical home* (PCMH); prior to 2007, each organization had developed their own similar model for advanced primary care. The original description of the PCMH required the following characteristics: a personal physician for each patient, physician-directed medical practice, whole person orientation, care coordination, enhanced access, and payment reform (Figure 9-3)—many of the features we have described throughout this chapter. The medical home concept was not new. The American Academy of Pediatrics had first described medical homes in 1967. But, what was new was the momentum it created: the PCMH model received endorsements from large businesses, labor organizations, major national health plans, and the American

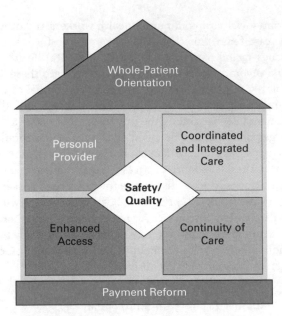

Figure 9-3. Components of the patient-centered medical home (PCMH).

Medical Association.[93] The announcement of the PCMH model created new hope for primary care. Major stakeholders now acknowledged that healthcare systems need robust primary care to provide value.

Apart from the momentum its introduction created, the PCMH serves two roles: a model for delivery reform and a mechanism for payment reform. As a model for delivery reform, the PCMH provides a clear goal for practices that are in the process of transforming the way they deliver primary care. The National Committee of Quality Assurance (NCQA) has created a certification process to label practices as level 1, level 2, or level 3 PCMHs. A number of consulting organizations, such as TransforMED, sprouted with the purpose of helping practices meet the must-pass elements to become an NCQA-certified PCMH.[94] As a mechanism for payment reform, some national and local health plans have agreed to pay primary care practices that are certified PCMHs a higher fee or capitated payment, with practices that achieve a higher level of PCMH receiving a proportionally higher payment. Therefore, at least in some parts of the country, the PCMH movement is creating primary care payment reform.

In the years since the PCMH movement launched, practices inspired by the model have had varying levels of success. A systematic review of PCMHs found that practice improvements lead to minimal increases in staff and patient satisfaction but no overall cost savings; however, the authors used a much broader definition of PCMH than the NCQA uses, so practices which made smaller scale change were included in the study.[95] On the other hand, practices that have fully embraced the PCMH model and even transformed beyond the required elements do achieve the triple aim: better patient experience, better population health, and lower overall costs.[81,96] Therefore, in order to mimic the successful primary care delivery reform of Group Health and Southcentral Foundation, practices will need to achieve at least the must-pass elements of the NCQA PCMH, and probably much more—a revolution that will require payment reform.

CONCLUSION

Although many barriers stand between the current state of primary care and a better, transformed primary care system, this journey is imperative so to capture the wide-reaching benefits provided by robust primary care. A healthcare system without a foundation in primary care is a system that is sinking, and without reform on local, state, and national levels, the US healthcare system will continue its trajectory toward the bottom. The good news is that pockets of innovation in primary care have sprouted all over the country, and their engagement of the full primary care team, novel uses of information technology and clear commitment to continuous improvement are giving hope and a sense of direction to all. Leaders in healthcare need only look at these examples to restore confidence that primary care can be rejuvenated and to learn how it can be done. For others working in healthcare, it is our job to understand the crucial role primary care plays in delivering value, and thus advocating for innovations that support it.

KEY POINTS:

- Healthcare systems with a foundation of robust primary care deliver more value than those without strong primary care.
- Effective primary care should be composed of four pillars: first-contact care, continuity of care over time, comprehensiveness (addressing all aspects of patients' care needs rather than focusing only on a specific organ system), and coordination of care with other parts of the health system.
- The shortage of primary care providers is expected to worsen as the population multiplies, ages, and gains health insurance. Team-based primary care can help address the shortage, as well as improve overall quality of care.
- Shining examples of innovative primary care prove that US healthcare can be redesigned.
- Health reform can only be fully realized with close linkage between education reform and care delivery transformation.

References:

1. Kringos DS, Boerma W, van der Zee J, Groenewegen P. Europe's strong primary care systems are linked to better population health but also to higher health spending. *Health Aff*. 2013;32(4):686-694.
2. Sinsky CA, Willard-Grace R, Schutzbank AM, Sinsky TA, Margolius D, Bodenheimer T. In search of joy in practice: a report of 23 high-functioning primary care practices. *Ann Fam Med*. 2013;11(3):272-278.
3. Starfield B. *Primary Care: Balancing Health Needs, Services, and Technology*. Oxford: Oxford University Press; 1998.
4. Tang N, Stein J, Hsia RY, Maselli JH, Gonzales R. Trends and characteristics of US emergency department visits, 1997-2007. *JAMA*. 2010;304(6):664-670.
5. Pitts SR, Carrier ER, Rich EC, Kellermann AL. Where Americans get acute care: increasingly, it's not at their doctor's office. *Health Aff*. 2010;29(9):1620-1629.
6. Schoen C, Osborn R, Doty MM, Squires D, Peugh J, Applebaum S. A survey of primary care physicians in eleven countries, 2009: perspectives on care, costs, and experiences. *Health Aff*. 2009;28(6):w1171-w1183.
7. California Health Care Foundation. Overuse of Emergency Departments Among Insured Californians. CHCF.org. 2014. http://www.chcf.org/publications/2006/10/overuse-of-emergency-departments-among-insuredcalifornians. Accessed January 3, 2014.
8. Nutting PA, Goodwin MA, Flocke SA, Zyzanski SJ, Stange KC. Continuity of primary care: to whom does it matter and when? *Ann Fam Med*. 2003;1(3):149-155.
9. Stokes T, Tarrant C, Mainous AG III, Schers H, Freeman G, Baker R. Continuity of care: is the personal doctor still important? A survey of general practitioners and family physicians in England and Wales, the United States, and The Netherlands. *Ann Fam Med*. 2005;3(4):353-359.
10. Saultz JW, Lochner J. Interpersonal continuity of care and care outcomes: a critical review. *Ann Fam Med*. 2005;3(2):159-166.
11. Wolinsky FD, Bentler SE, Liu L, et al. Continuity of care with a primary care physician and mortality in older adults. *J Gerontol*. 2010;65(4):421-428.
12. Starfield B, Chang H-Y, Lemke KW, Weiner JP. Ambulatory specialist use by nonhospitalized patients in us health plans: correlates and consequences. *J Ambulatory Care Manage*. 2009;32(3):216-225.
13. Valderas JM, Starfield B, Forrest CB, Sibbald B, Roland M. Ambulatory care provided by office-based specialists in the United States. *Ann Fam Med*. 2009;7(2):104-111.
14. Federman AD, Halm EA, Siu AL. Use of generic cardiovascular medications by elderly Medicare beneficiaries receiving generalist or cardiologist care. *Med Care*. 2007;45(2):109-115.
15. Schoen C, Osborn R, Squires D, Doty M, Pierson R, Applebaum S. New 2011 survey of patients with complex care needs in eleven countries finds that care is often poorly coordinated. *Health Aff*. 2011;30(12):2437-2448.
16. Chang C-H, Stukel TA, Flood AB, Goodman DC. Primary care physician workforce and Medicare beneficiaries' health outcomes. *JAMA*. 2011;305(20):2096-2104.
17. Kravet SJ, Shore AD, Miller R, Green GB, Kolodner K, Wright SM. Health care utilization and the proportion of primary care physicians. *Am J Med*. 2008;121(2):142-148.
18. Schwartz MD. Health care reform and the primary care workforce bottleneck. *J Gen Intern Med*. 2012;27(4):469-472.
19. Colwill JM, Cultice JM, Kruse RL. Will generalist physician supply meet demands of an increasing and aging population? *Health Aff*. 2008;27(3):w232-w241.
20. Grundy P, Hagan KR, Hansen JC, Grumbach K. The multi-stakeholder movement for primary care renewal and reform. *Health Aff*. 2010;29(5):791-798.
21. Health Resources and Services Administration (HRSA). Projecting the Supply and Demand for Primary Care Practitioners Through 2020; 2013. http://bhpr.hrsa.gov/healthworkforce/supply demand/usworkforce/primarycare. Accessed January 8, 2014.

22. Bodenheimer TS, Smith MD. Primary care: proposed solutions to the physician shortage without training more physicians. *Health Aff.* 2013;32(11):1881-1886.

23. Petterson SM, Liaw WR, Phillips RL Jr, Rabin DL, Meyers DS, Bazemore AW. Projecting US primary care physician workforce needs: 2010-2025. *Ann Fam Med.* 2012;10(6):503-509.

24. Grumbach K, Bodenheimer T. A primary care home for Americans: putting the house in order. *JAMA.* 2002;288(7):889-893.

25. Association of American Medical Colleges' Center for Workforce Studies. Physician specialty data; 2008. https://www.aamc.org/download/47352/data. Accessed January 8, 2014.

26. Shanafelt TD, Boone S, Tan L, et al. Burnout and satisfaction with work-life balance among US physicians relative to the general US population. *Arch Intern Med.* 2012;172(18):1377-1385.

27. Council on Graduate Medical Education Twentieth Report: Advancing Primary Care. 2010. http://ask.hrsa.gov/detail_materials.cfm?ProdID=4517. Accessed January 3, 2014.

28. Erikson CE, Danish S, Jones KC, Sandberg SF, Carle AC. The role of medical school culture in primary care career choice. *Acad Med.* 2013;88(12):1919-1926.

29. Peccoralo LA, Tackett S, Ward L, et al. Resident satisfaction with continuity clinic and career choice in general internal medicine. *J Gen Intern Med.* 2013;28(8):1020-1027.

30. Mahood SC. Medical education: beware the hidden curriculum. *Can Fam Physician Médecin Fam Can.* 2011;57(9):983-985.

31. The Robert Graham Center. Specialty and geographic distribution of the physician workforce: what influences medical student and resident choices? 2009. http://www.graham-center.org/online/graham/home/publications/monographs-books/2009/rgcmo-specialty-geographic.html. Accessed January 6, 2014.

32. Steinbrook R. Medical student debt—is there a limit? *N Engl J Med.* 2008;359(25):2629-2632.

33. Phillips RL Jr, Bazemore AM, Peterson LE. Effectiveness over efficiency: underestimating the primary care physician shortage. *Med Care.* 2014;52(2):97-98.

34. Chen C, Petterson S, Phillips RL, Mullan F, Bazemore A, O'Donnell SD. Toward graduate medical education (GME) accountability: measuring the outcomes of GME institutions. *Acad Med.* 2013;88(9):1267-1280.

35. Ku L, Jones E, Shin P, Byrne FR, Long SK. Safety-net providers after health care reform: lessons from Massachusetts. *Arch Intern Med.* 2011;171(15):1379-1384.

36. National Health Service Corps expands the primary care workforce. http://www.hhs.gov/news/press/2013pres/02/20130206a.html. Accessed January 7, 2014.

37. Mullan F, Chen C, Petterson S, Kolsky G, Spagnola M. The social mission of medical education: ranking the schools. *Ann Intern Med.* 2010;152(12):804-811.

38. Senf JH, Campos-Outcalt D, Kutob R. Factors related to the choice of family medicine: a reassessment and literature review. *J Am Board Fam Pract.* 2003;16(6):502-512.

39. Davis AK, Reynolds PP, Kahn NB Jr, et al. Title VII and the development and promotion of national initiatives in training primary care clinicians in the United States. *Acad Med.* 2008;83(11):1021-1029.

40. Thibault GE. Reforming health professions education will require culture change and closer ties between classroom and practice. *Health Aff.* 2013;32(11):1928-1932.

41. Batalden P, Leach D, Swing S, Dreyfus H, Dreyfus S. General competencies and accreditation in graduate medical education. *Health Aff.* 2002;21(5):103-111.

42. Warm EJ, Leasure E. Primary care and primary care training: mirror images. *J Gen Intern Med.* 2011;26(1):5-7.

43. Gupta R, Bodenheimer T. How primary care practices can improve continuity of care. *JAMA Intern Med.* 2013;173(20):1885-1886.

44. Keirns CC, Bosk CL. Perspective: the unintended consequences of training residents in dysfunctional outpatient settings. *Acad Med.* 2008;83(5):498-502.

45. Baxley EG, Stanek M, Association of Departments of Family Medicine. The AAMC Academic Chronic Care Collaborative: family medicine's participation and lessons learned. *Ann Fam Med*. 2007;5(2):183-184.
46. Reid A, Baxley E, Stanek M, Newton W. Practice transformation in teaching settings: lessons from the I3 PCMH collaborative. *Fam Med*. 2011;43(7):487-494.
47. Newton W, Baxley E, Reid A, Stanek M, Robinson M, Weir S. Improving chronic illness care in teaching practices: learnings from the I3 collaborative. *Fam Med*. 2011;43(7):495-502.
48. Colorado Family Medicine Residency PCMH Project. HealthTeamWorks. 2009. http://www.healthteamworks.org/medical-home/pcmh-residency.html. Accessed January 7, 2014.
49. Academic Innovations Collaborative—What We Do. Center for Primary Care, Harvard Medical School. https://primarycare.hms.harvard.edu/what-we-do/innovation/academic-innovations-collaborative. Accessed January 7, 2014.
50. Pennsylvania Academy of Family Physicians (PAFP): Residency Program & Community Health Center Collaboratives. http://www.pafp.com/pafpcom.aspx?id=347. Accessed January 7, 2014.
51. Auerbach DI, Chen PG, Friedberg MW, et al. Nurse-managed health centers and patient-centered medical homes could mitigate expected primary care physician shortage. *Health Aff*. 2013;32(11):1933-1941.
52. Altschuler J, Margolius D, Bodenheimer T, Grumbach K. Estimating a reasonable patient panel size for primary care physicians with team-based task delegation. *Ann Fam Med*. 2012;10(5):396-400.
53. Health Affairs Policy Brief. Nurse practitioners and primary care. 2013. https://www.healthaffairs.org/healthpolicybriefs/brief.php?brief_id=92. Accessed October 1, 2013.
54. Hooker RS, Cawley JF, Leinweber W. Career flexibility of physician assistants and the potential for more primary care. *Health Aff*. 2010;29(5):880-886.
55. Kaiser Commission on Medicaid and the Uninsured. Improving access to adult primary care in Medicaid: exploring the potential role of nurse practitioners and physician assistants. 2011. http://kaiserfamilyfoundation.files.wordpress.com/2013/01/8167.pdf. Accessed December 3, 2013.
56. Lugo NR, O'Grady ET, Hodnicki DR, Hanson CM. Ranking state NP regulation: practice environment and consumer healthcare choice. *Am J Nurse Pract*. 2007;11(4):8-24.
57. Grumbach K, Hart LG, Mertz E, Coffman J, Palazzo L. Who is caring for the underserved? A comparison of primary care physicians and nonphysician clinicians in California and Washington. *Ann Fam Med*. 2003;1(2):97-104.
58. Howell J, Sum A. Annual Physician Workforce Study: 2010. Massachusetts Medical Society; 2010. http://www.massmed.org/workforce. Accessed December 10, 2013.
59. Boukus ER, Cunningham PJ. Mixed signals: trends in Americans' access to medical care, 2007-2010. *Track Rep Cent Stud Health Syst Change*. 2011;(25):1-6.
60. Weiss LJ, Blustein J. Faithful patients: the effect of long-term physician-patient relationships on the costs and use of health care by older Americans. *Am J Public Health*. 1996;86(12):1742-1747.
61. Kronman AC, Ash AS, Freund KM, Hanchate A, Emanuel EJ. Can primary care visits reduce hospital utilization among Medicare beneficiaries at the end of life? *J Gen Intern Med*. 2008; 23(9):1330-1335.
62. United States Government Accountability Office. Primary care professionals—recent supply trends, projections, and valuation of services. US GAO, testimony before the US Senate; 2008.
63. American Medical Association. The RVS Update Committee. http://www.ama-assn.org/ama/pub/physician-resources/solutions-managing-your-practice/coding-billing-insurance/medicare/the-resource-based-relative-value-scale/the-rvs-update-committee.page.
64. Bodenheimer T, Grumbach K. *Understanding Health Policy*. 5th ed. New York, NY: McGraw Hill Professional; 2008.
65. Bodenheimer T, Berenson RA, Rudolf P. The primary care-specialty income gap: why it matters. *Ann Intern Med*. 2007;146(4):301-306.
66. Baron RJ. What's keeping us so busy in primary care? A snapshot from one practice. *N Engl J Med*. 2010;362(17):1632-1636.

67. Margolius D, Bodenheimer T. Transforming primary care: from past practice to the practice of the future. *Health Aff*. 2010;29(5):779-784.
68. Ignagni K. Health plan innovations in delivery system reforms. *Am J Manag Care*. 2013;19(4):260-262.
69. Patient-Centered Primary Care Collaborative. Benefits of implementing the primary care patient-centered medical home; 2012. https://www.pcpcc.org/sites/default/files/media/benefits_of_implementing_the_primary_care_pcmh.pdf. Accessed January 7, 2014.
70. Berenson RA, Devers K, Burton R. *Will the Patient-Centered Medical Home Transform the Delivery of Health Care?* Urban Institute; 2011. http://www.rwjf.org/en/research-publications/find-rwjf-research/2011/08/will-the-patient-centered-medical-home-transform-the-delivery-of.html. Accessed January 3, 2014.
71. Patel UB, Rathjen C, Rubin E. Horizon's patient-centered medical home program shows practices need much more than payment changes to transform. *Health Aff (Millwood)*. 2012;31(9):2018-2027.
72. Hoff T. The shaky foundation of the patient-centered medical home. *Am J Manag Care*. 2010;16(6):e134-e136.
73. Reform adds some financial assistance to increase physician, nurse workforce. Crains Detroit Bus. http://www.crainsdetroit.com/article/20100517/HEALTH/100519879/reform-adds-some-financial-assistance-to-increase-physician-nurse. Accessed January 7, 2014.
74. Medscape. Physician Compensation Report: 2012 Results. 2012. http://www.medscape.com/features/slideshow/compensation/2012/public. Accessed January 3, 2014.
75. Bitton A, Schwartz GR, Stewart EE, et al. Off the hamster wheel? Qualitative evaluation of a payment-linked patient-centered medical home (PCMH) pilot. *Milbank Q*. 2012;90(3):484-515.
76. Goroll AH, Berenson RA, Schoenbaum SC, Gardner LB. Fundamental reform of payment for adult primary care: comprehensive payment for comprehensive care. *J Gen Intern Med*. 2007;22(3):410-415.
77. Report of the National Commission on Physician Payment Reform. RWJF. 2013. http://www.rwjf.org/en/research-publications/find-rwjf-research/2013/03/report-of-the-national-commission-on-physician-payment-reform.html. Accessed January 7, 2014.
78. French MT, Homer JF, Klevay S, Goldman E, Ullmann SG, Kahn BE. Is the United States ready to embrace concierge medicine? *Popul Health Manag*. 2010;13(4):177-182.
79. Chase D. Health Plan Rorschach Test: Direct Primary Care. Forbes. 2014. http://www.forbes.com/sites/davechase/2013/07/06/health-plan-rorschach-test-direct-primary-care/. Accessed January 3, 2014.
80. Reid RJ, Coleman K, Johnson EA, et al. The Group Health medical home at year two: cost savings, higher patient satisfaction, and less burnout for providers. *Health Aff (Proj Hope)*. 2010;29(5):835-843.
81. Margolius D. Less tinkering, more transforming: how to build successful patient-centered medical homes. *JAMA Intern Med*. 2013;173(18):1702-1703.
82. Institute of Medicine. *Crossing the Quality Chasm a New Health System for the 21st Century*. Washington, DC: National Academy Press; 2001. http://search.ebscohost.com/login.aspx?direct=true&scope=site&db=nlebk&db=nlabk&AN=86916. Accessed January 3, 2013.
83. Prentice JC, Pizer SD. Delayed access to health care and mortality. *Health Serv Res*. 2007;42(2):644-662.
84. Murray M, Berwick DM. Advanced access: reducing waiting and delays in primary care. *JAMA*. 2003;289(8):1035-1040.
85. Bodenheimer T, Wagner EH, Grumbach K. Improving primary care for patients with chronic illness. *JAMA*. 2002;288(14):1775-1779.
86. Chen EH, Bodenheimer T. Improving population health through team-based panel management: comment on "electronic medical record reminders and panel management to improve primary care of elderly patients." *Arch Intern Med*. 2011;171(17):1558-1559.

87. McGlynn EA, Asch SM, Adams J, et al. The quality of health care delivered to adults in the United States. *N Engl J Med*. 2003;348(26):2635-2645.

88. Milstein A, Gilbertson E. American medical home runs. *Health Aff (Millwood)*. 2009; 28(5):1317-1326.

89. Gawande A. The hot spotters. *New Yorker*. January 24, 2011.

90. Baron RJ. Quality improvement with an electronic health record: achievable, but not automatic. *Ann Intern Med*. 2007;147(8):549-552.

91. Zigmond J. Project ECHO expands, spreads telehealth model. Mod Healthc. June 26, 2013. http://www.modernhealthcare.com/article/20130626/NEWS/306269952. Accessed January 3, 2014.

92. Chen AH, Murphy EJ, Yee HF Jr. eReferral—a new model for integrated care. *N Engl J Med*. 2013;368(26):2450-2453.

93. Rittenhouse DR, Shortell SM. The patient-centered medical home: will it stand the test of health reform? *JAMA*. 2009;301(19):2038-2040.

94. Robeznieks A. Blog: TransforMED pioneered medical home consulting. Mod Healthc. 2014. http://www.modernhealthcare.com/article/20130226/blogs03/302269997. Accessed January 3, 2014.

95. Jackson GL, Powers BJ, Chatterjee R, et al. The patient-centered medical home: a systematic review. *Ann Intern Med*. 2013;158(3):169-178.

96. Fernandopulle R. Learning to fly: building de novo medical home practices to improve experience, outcomes, and affordability. *J Ambulatory Care Manage*. 2013;36(2):121-125.

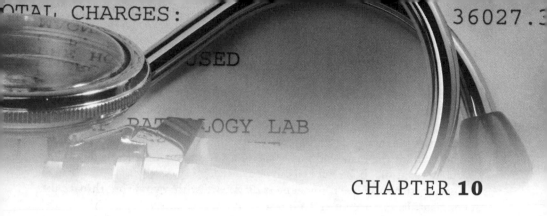

CHAPTER 10

Barriers to Providing High-Value Care

Cynthia D. Smith and Steven E. Weinberger

Jane, a 27-year-old woman, arrives to your busy clinic at the end of the day. She looks miserable and describes a lingering cold for the last few days, including sore throat, cough, congestion, and sneezing. Before you are even able to do an exam, she asks you for antibiotics. You examine her and decide she most likely has a virus, not a bacterial infection that would require antibiotics. In fact, you do not really think she will need any further diagnostic testing at all.

So you ask the patient why she wants antibiotics. She tells you that she is getting on an airplane the next day to go to a series of important meetings. She is worried about strep throat. "How will I get antibiotics if I get sicker?" she asks. You look at your watch and notice you are running 30 minutes behind schedule. You worry Jane will be upset if you do not give her what she wants. With a deep sigh, you quickly write her a prescription for azithromycin.

Antibiotics are among the most remarkable advances in modern medicine and have saved countless lives over the better part of the last century. However, when used incorrectly, antibiotics pose serious risks to both individual patients and the public health at large (we often wonder if the drug-resistant infections that catalyze the apocalypse in every modern Zombie movie are really that far off). Using antibiotics when they are not needed increases drug-resistance, leaving populations of patients vulnerable to resistant infections. Antibiotic overuse can also place individual patients at risk for allergic reactions, antibiotic-associated diarrhea, and other highly unpleasant and dangerous side effects.[1] These risks are well known to clinicians—as are the decades of clear evidence, guidelines, and quality measures that argue against prescribing antibiotics in certain conditions, such as routine sore throats and acute bronchitis.[2-4] Sir Alexander Fleming, the discoverer of penicillin, even warned in a 1945 *New York Times* article: "... the microbes are educated to resist penicillin and a host of penicillin-fast organisms is bred out.... In such cases the thoughtless person playing with penicillin is morally responsible for the death of the man who finally succumbs to infection with the penicillin-resistant organism. I hope this evil can be averted."[5,6]

And yet, currently when someone is diagnosed with a viral sore throat, like our patient Jane, antibiotics are prescribed approximately 60% of the time.[7] For acute bronchitis, patients are prescribed an antibiotic more than 70% of the time—a rate that has remarkably been increasing over time.[8] Why is this happening?

In many cases, clinicians overprescribe antibiotics knowingly and are "caving" to perceived patient demand. In a world that often forces clinicians to see more patients in less time (see Chapter 9), it may be easier to just write out a requested prescription rather than spend the time educating a patient about why she does not need the antibiotic that she specifically came to get. Now there is the added pressure that a patient may walk out of your office and immediately leave a negative review on one of the many public-facing doctor-rating websites (see Chapter 12). Nobody wants unsatisfied patients. However, as we discuss later in this chapter, perceived patient demand and actual patient demand do not always line up. It turns out that physician-patient communication—not antibiotic prescribing—is the most important factor related to patient satisfaction in acute bronchitis.[3]

Many different organizations have called for mandated "antimicrobial stewardship" programs across healthcare settings.[1,6] Antimicrobial steward-ship "refers to coordinated interventions designed to improve and measure the appropriate use of antimicrobial agents by promoting the selection of the optimal antimicrobial drug regimen including dosing, duration of therapy, and route of administration."[6] The major goals of these programs are to achieve the best clinical outcomes while minimizing toxicity and other adverse events, pro-tecting populations from emerging threats to public health, and reducing exces-sive costs.[1,6] In other words, improving healthcare value, as we have defined it throughout this book.

BARRIERS

Antibiotic stewardship is but one example that highlights both the many real cultural, operational, and financial barriers that currently hinder the deliv-ery of high-value care, as well as the extraordinary potential for improvements (Table 10-1). Addressing these barriers will require a combination of solutions, including delivery system reform as well as improved bedside communication, feedback, and clinical decision-support. We will introduce and examine the many barriers here and then will build upon proposed solutions throughout Part III.

Table 10-1 **Barriers to high-value care**

Barriers to High-Value Care	Examples
Misaligned financial incentives	A patient with viral pharyngitis is seen in the office because telephone care is not reimbursed.
Time pressure	A patient with a viral upper respiratory tract infection who asks for antibiotics is given a prescription because it takes less time than explaining why the patient does not need antibiotics.
Imprecise measurements	Insurance claims data do not account for clinical decision making based on individual patient characteristics, nor do they assess the quality of the patient experience.
Lack of education and training	Clinicians do not incorporate costs into decision making because they were not taught where to find costs of common tests and treatments.
Healthcare system fragmentation	A test done at another institution is repeated because the electronic medical records are not interoperable and the results are not available.
Local culture and hidden curriculum	The attending physician commends the medical student for working up a rare but unlikely diagnosis on his/her patient.
Discomfort with diagnostic uncertainty	Ordering the additional testing when the patient has a straightforward clinical diagnosis "just to be sure."
Fear of malpractice	Increased hospital admissions for atypical chest pain after a clinician was sued for a bad outcome when he/she sent a patient with chest pain home from the ED.
Patient expectations	A desire to please the patient by ordering advanced imaging for low back pain because the patient requests the study.

Misaligned financial incentives

Clinicians and policymakers do not always see eye to eye, but there is one thing that nearly everyone can agree on: a major barrier to improving value is a healthcare system that is replete with misaligned financial incentives. As we discussed in Chapter 3, the stakeholders (patients, providers, and payers) each consider the costs of care from their own perspective.

In most cases, US providers are paid more for doing more. Conversely, doing less can mean decreased revenue for a delivery system and lower salary for a clinician.[9] The fee-for-service payment model rewards clinicians for maximizing the number of patient encounters and procedures but often does not reimburse for important, value-added activities, like telephone follow-up and care coordination, that improve the quality of care.[10] As discussed in the last chapter (Chapter 9), compensation models for clinicians are typically based on relative value units (RVUs). Thus, even in delivery organizations that have risk-sharing contracts at the delivery system level (see Chapter 15), their clinicians are still strongly incentivized to provide as many services as possible.

If providers were reimbursed based on patient outcomes as opposed to the number of services they deliver, they would have stronger incentives to provide value-based care. But it is not only the clinicians - the vast majority of hospital executives, including those at nonprofit hospitals, are also compensated based on metrics related to productivity, rather than patient outcomes or community benefit.[11] There is substantial resistance to changing financial models at this point.

The cost structure of a typical healthcare setting is relatively rigid due to a high proportion of fixed costs (Chapter 4) that are minimally sensitive to small changes in patient volume, resource use, or the severity of patient illness.[12] At the same time, the operations of the hospital are designed to optimize revenue by delivering as many services as possible. In addition, more clinicians are employed by hospital systems than ever before and may be financially motivated to use their facilities and advanced technology.[9,13,14] Many health professionals are well-intentioned and trying to do all they can to take the best care possible for their patients, but it is hard to always do the right thing when placed in a system that floats on a river moving in the wrong direction.

As examined in Chapter 3, the situation becomes even more messy when considering the misaligned financial incentives of other stakeholders in the system, including payers, patients, pharmaceutical companies, and technology vendors. Each party is encouraged to charge different amounts to different customers, all creating "chaos behind a veil of secrecy."[15] Understanding the limitations of our current reimbursement models will help guide our work redesigning care delivery and realigning financial incentives with improved patient outcomes (see Chapter 15 on "Shifting Incentives").

Story From the Frontlines: "I'll Do It for $1100"

Where I am from, you can have someone killed for $5000. I will do it for $1100. I am a hand surgeon.

I practice (or practiced, by the time you read this) in an area that is what we often refer to as "underserved." Rather, the area isn't, but the people I treat are. I work in a large urban referral center that has a very high proportion of Medicaid, as well as unfunded patients. No one else in town will touch them. I am not blaming them—they are in private practice and they cannot cover their expenses if they are paid nothing or close to nothing for their time and supplies. While there may be an element of greed, it is not all greed. I know my colleagues in private practice and, almost without exception, I respect them all as physicians and people.

In my referral center, the hospital has favorable contracts with Medicaid that yield good revenue for the center from Medicaid patients. But, as a consequence, all of my procedures are "hospital-based" as opposed to "clinic-based." It is a semantic billing distinction that I do not completely understand myself (another part of the problem) and it allows the hospital to generate enough revenue to cover costs for an unquestionably needy population. For the patients with Medicaid, it allows us to care for them with little, if any out-of-pocket cost to them and keep the lights on. However, for patients with private insurance that is anything less than a top-of-the-line plan, procedures done in outpatient "hospital-based" clinics are not covered and are billed at very high rates that come out-of-pocket. A steroid injection for tendonitis can yield a bill in excess of $1000. Doing a simple wound "clean-up" or debridement can be north of $1100. I am on salary and do not make an extra nickel either way.

Which is why when Mr. Jones, an overweight diabetic with private insurance presented with a small local infection that I probably could have addressed in the office, I took him to the OR. His insurance company would only cover the costs if it were done upstairs, but would pay nothing if I did it in my clinic.

Once in the OR, the regional block he received did not work well (which happens) and his sedation was increased. The increased sedation made it difficult for him to breathe and he had to be ventilated emergently. He lost his airway. His oxygen saturation dipped below 60% of normal, briefly, and the anesthesiologists were able to right the ship and wake him up.

Ultimately, things went well. The patient's hand was healed and he didn't face a medical bill that would have decimated his financial health. However, I nearly killed him to save him $1110.

—Robert Gray. "I'll Do It for $1100."
Costs of Care, 2013. (www.costsofcare.org)

Time pressure

As the story that opens this chapter illustrates, time pressure is frequently identified by practicing clinicians as a significant barrier to delivering the best possible care. This is hardly surprising. Remember from Chapter 1 that it would take 21 hours a day for a primary care provider to provide all of the care recommended to meet his patients' acute, preventive, and chronic disease management needs.[16]

Often, the way clinicians deal with time pressure is by looking for ways to decrease their workload. For a busy emergency department (ED) physician with a packed waiting room, figuring out how to empty the stretcher in front of her may seem like the number one goal. Instead of ordering one test and then waiting for the result before ordering more, ordering several tests at once may be more expeditious. Pressure to reduce waiting times is one of the most significant sources of stress for ED staff.[17] Similarly, hospital physicians under pressure to decrease length of stay may order multiple tests and consultations simultaneously to expedite patient disposition. In a different era of practicing medicine, diagnoses were often clarified by just relying on a "tincture of time." In our hospitals and ambulatory offices, there is little patience for this approach despite the evidence that "watchful waiting" (sometimes referred to as "expectant management") is a feasible plan for patients with unexplained complaints and it does not result in delayed testing.[18] Indeed, as length of stay has decreased, there is some evidence that it does not actually result in overall cost savings, but instead merely shifts the increased costs to the ambulatory setting.[19]

In the ambulatory setting, time pressure also drives inappropriate use of tests and treatments. As our story illustrates, it can be quicker to write a prescription or order a test than it is to explain to a patient why these interventions may not be necessary. Shorter office visits, particularly those less than 15 minutes, are more likely to lead to inappropriate prescribing.[20] Recent studies exploring barriers to improved outcomes in hypertensive patients highlight the association of improved therapy adherence with strong patient-provider relationships.[21] Provider time might be better spent establishing and maintaining continuous healing relationships with patients than ordering tests and treatments that are unlikely to improve patient outcomes. In fact, this "time pressured" approach to care delivery may result in the creation of unnecessary additional workload from checking results, informing patients of results, and providing follow-up testing or treatment that occurs from the discovery of incidental findings. There are multiple components of care that are affected by time, including patient satisfaction, outcomes of chronic diseases, prescribing practices, physician satisfaction, and risk of malpractice claims.[22]

Throughout healthcare, poorly functioning work processes are created by unnecessary pauses and rework, delays, and established workarounds.[23] The inefficiency in hospital care delivery has created a system where nurses spend less than one-third of their working time performing direct patient care.[24] In turn, time pressure, burnout, and workload for nurses have been associated with patient safety risks.[25,26]

Healthcare system fragmentation

Clinicians may become accustomed to some of the pressures and flaws inherent in the current healthcare system, but the maddening fragmentation is starkly obvious to patients and their families. In healthcare provider offices, faxes—yes, faxes, in 2014—often provide vital documents such as discharge summaries or home care orders. These flimsy sheets of paper that often never make it to the provider or to the patient's chart, symbolize our antiquated and insufficient systems of communications in healthcare. Left with increasing provider specialization, poor continuity of care, and insufficient communication among providers, patients, and families, the modern-day US healthcare system is incredibly complex and fragmented—a single patient often receives care from multiple clinicians who work in different facilities.[19,27] This fragmentation may lead to duplication of tests and confusion about the care plan and often results in poor outcomes at a higher cost. In the United Kingdom, discontinuity of care was associated with decreased rates of cancer screening and prevention, and when these deficits were addressed in a national program, outcomes improved.[27]

Healthcare providers have been encouraged to transition to the use of electronic health records (EHR) through a Federal initiative called the "meaningful use" program in hopes that patient records could be more easily shared and communication among providers would be enhanced. However, the current EHR system has not lived up to this promise because electronic records at one health facility are rarely compatible with those at another facility.[28] Even within the same hospital system, it is not uncommon to find that the inpatient and outpatient electronic records are not connected. When information is not easily accessible, providers often opt to duplicate testing rather than spend the time trying to track down previous results.[29] Improving communication, continuity and access in such a way that incentivizes providers to have ongoing healing relationships with their patients would go a long way in combating the fragmented system, reducing waste and improving health outcomes.

Currently, considerable investments are made to improve healthcare by developing better drugs and devices. In many cases the gains of creating a more reliable system far outweigh any potential benefits of more effective therapeutics.[30] Let's consider a clinical example that has been highlighted by Dr Steven Woolf and colleagues from Virginia Commonwealth University in a 2005 "Annals of Family Medicine" article.[30] The use of aspirin by patients who have previously had a stroke or transient ischemic attack (TIA, sometimes referred to as a "mini-stroke") may reduce the incidence of a recurrent nonfatal stroke by 23%.[31] This is a remarkable benefit for a devastating disease. Yet, antiplatelet therapy is given to only 58% of eligible patients.[32] This means that for every 100,000 people that have suffered a prior

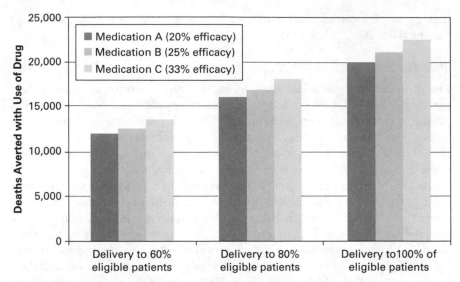

Figure 10-1. Care fragmentation leads to missed opportunities to save lives. (Original figure, based on data from Woolf SH, Johnson RE. The break-even point: when medical advances are less important than improving the fidelity with which they are delivered. *Ann Fam Med.* 2005;3(6):545–552.)

stroke or TIA, there will be 9660 additional strokes that could have been prevented if everyone was appropriately taking aspirin. The pharmaceutical industry invested heavily in creating antiplatelet drugs that are more effective than aspirin, developing clopidogrel and ticlopidine with extensive testing. These medications are about 10% to 12% more effective than aspirin at preventing stroke events. However, a proportional improvement of 74% in efficacy would be required to see benefits that would reach the same level as making sure that everyone that should get aspirin actually does (Figure 10-1).[30] As Dr Woolf and colleagues point out, "It is worth asking whether the resources expended for the antiplatelet trials might have prevented more vascular events if they were invested in better systems for the delivery of aspirin."[30]

As discussed in Chapter 16, efforts to improve healthcare delivery, consistency, and efficiency, such as the LEAN process improvement strategy, are increasingly taking hold across many healthcare settings. The promise to relieve patients and healthcare professionals of the broken processes of a healthcare system that handicaps the delivery of effective medical care is a welcome sign.

Imprecise measurement

Healthcare value is often defined differently in different contexts and is challenging to measure in a standard and precise way. As we discussed in Chapter 4, considering value as quality divided by cost may be oversimplified. In many situations we are missing good outcome measure definitions, as well as accurate patient-centered cost information. Even in conditions for which we have robust evidence about processes and measures that work, accurately showing improvement in outcomes can be fraught with challenges. There are serious technical issues involving the quality of available data (most of what we know about the health system comes from high-level insurance claims, not from detailed clinical records), as well as the methods involved in adjusting for appropriate differences between patients and considering the right time frame for tracking outcomes.[33] And that is only part of it. Outcomes are based on thousands of factors, only some of which we actually understand or are in our control. Decades of research have led to significantly improved outcomes in the treatment of acute myocardial infarction,[34] or a "heart attack," but even here where we reasonably know which processes lead to better outcomes— unlike nearly everything else we do in medicine—process improvements explained only 6% of the total outcome variance.[35] The other 94% remains a black box.

Often we think of "value-based care" as care that weighs the potential benefits of a given medical intervention against its costs and harms.[36,37] However, measuring cost in healthcare is incredibly complicated.[38-40] Furthermore, remember that value must also consider benefits and outcomes that are important to patients, which include patient satisfaction and care experiences.[41] Our ability to assess outcomes in a more comprehensive way that takes into account quality of life associated with particular conditions is woefully inadequate.[37] Thus, regardless of how high-value care is specifically defined, measuring each of its components can prove elusive.

This lack of measurement may actually be driving some areas of healthcare costs. In the rapidly progressing area of oncology, the absence of both suitable clinical research and integrated health economic studies has been cited as a major cost driver by an expert panel composed of healthcare professionals, cancer survivors and policy makers.[42] This deficiency has led to the alarming trend of declining access to evidence-based cancer care in developed countries.[42]

Even as the Affordable Care Act has attempted to help address these deficiencies with the creation of the Patient-Centered Outcomes Research Institute (PCORI), which aims to "help people make informed healthcare decisions, and improve healthcare delivery and outcomes, by producing and promoting high integrity, evidence-based information"[43] the law explicitly forbids PCORI from using "a dollars-per-quality adjusted life year (or similar measure that discounts the value of a life because of an individual's disability) as a threshold to establish what type of healthcare is cost effective or recommended"[44] (see Chapter 8).

Even in areas where high-quality data exist, providers may be uncomfortable interpreting results from comparative effectiveness and cost-effectiveness literature, as these types of analyses are relatively new and providers may have little training regarding how to interpret the results.[45] Even under the best conditions, the diffusion of high-quality evidence and guideline-recommended care into practices at the bedside is notoriously slow.[46-48]

Lack of knowledge and training

Further compounding the issue is that historically the medical education system has not placed sufficient emphasis on training physicians to practice in a cost-conscious fashion or to be good stewards of healthcare resources.[49,50] One study showed that less than a fourth of physicians tested came within 25% of the actual charge for 15 commonly ordered tests.[51] In addition, our current training model places a major emphasis in the inpatient setting, where medical interventions are readily available, easy to obtain and carry higher costs.[52] There is a general lack of reliable data in many delivery systems, creating a system where clinicians are constantly ordering off a menu with no prices, and then are shocked when they are shown the bill—if they are ever shown the bill.

The good news is that many providers are currently motivated to learn about healthcare value and have expressed a desire to be more cost-effective in their own practices.[51] Chapter 11 will explore the many arising strategies for educating clinicians in the delivery of high-value care. Beyond merely knowledge and training, what really may be needed is a more pervasive cultural change in our care delivery environments so that providing the appropriate amount of care is a team sport that is role-modeled, rewarded, and reinforced at the point-of-care.[52]

Local culture and the hidden curriculum

The knowledge and training gap in high-value care strengthens the effect of local culture and the hidden curriculum on clinical decision making.[53] The hidden curriculum is the informal mechanism by which trainees (and all healthcare providers) learn from their general clinical experience, peer interactions, and role models.[54] In this environment, traditional beliefs such as "more care is better care" and "the best doctors have the longest differential diagnosis" are allowed to flourish unchallenged.[52] In addition, cultural values affect the choice of teaching topics in our training programs, and discussing real world issues like cost has historically been considered less intellectual and academic.[49]

As Drs Lisa Rosenbaum and Daniela Lamas wrote in 2012 in *The New England Journal of Medicine*[55]:

Imagine your first medicine rotation. You present a patient admitted overnight with cough, fever, and an infiltrate on chest x-ray. After detailing a history and physical, you conclude, "This is a 70-year-old man with community-acquired pneumonia."
Dead silence.
"Perhaps," the attending finally says. "But what else could this be?"
Your face reddens. "Pulmonary embolism," you say. The resident nods. "Heart failure." Now you're talking. "Churg-Strauss," you add. "The patient does have a history of asthma."
The attending smiles. "How might you investigate these other possibilities?" he asks.
Next thing you know, the patient's lined up for a chest CT, lower extremity Dopplers, echo, and a rheum panel. You get honors. And so it begins.

This culture is pervasive and powerful. Much like the way that a poorly perceived patient safety culture has been linked to increased error rates,[56] it may not be possible to incorporate high-value care principles into practice unless this culture is acknowledged and addressed.[57] Every member of the healthcare team needs to be educated, empowered and rewarded for speaking up and identifying ways to make care safer and more cost-effective.

Discomfort with risk and diagnostic uncertainty

Providers and patients have expressed clear aversion to diagnostic uncertainty and often order additional confirmatory tests "just to be sure."[58] Both clinicians and patients often overvalue being certain and overestimate the ability of diagnostic tests to give us the answers we so desperately seek. In fact, clinicians may avoid considering options where information is missing or where the probability is unknown.[59] This tendency is sometimes called "ambiguity bias."

"Personal risk aversion" (as opposed to consideration of malpractice risk) has also been associated with an increased intensity of care for certain conditions including the decisions of emergency physicians to admit patients to the hospital with acute chest pain.[60] Those physicians who were personally less risk averse were more likely to discharge patients with acute chest pain from the ED than were physicians who were more risk averse. Self-reported physician risk-taking behaviors also predicted whether or not imaging was ordered for patients with abdominal pain, whereas malpractice fear did not.[61] Furthermore, clinicians who are less confident in their diagnostic accuracy have been shown to be more likely to request more resources.[62] In their quest for certainty, providers and patients tend to underestimate the downstream costs associated with confirmatory testing, including financial and opportunity costs, anxiety, false positive rates, incidental findings, overdiagnosis, and radiation exposure.[36,63] Commonly, reassurance is given as justification for further testing. A meta-analysis of trials in which patients with a low probability of disease were randomized to receive initial diagnostic testing versus a nontesting approach found no benefits of diagnostic testing on reducing illness worry or anxiety.[64] In fact, more testing frequently uncovers further unclear findings that send clinicians and their patients down a rabbit hole of more "recommended follow-up" tests, and ultimately may create increased undue worry and harms.[65]

Fear of malpractice liability

The effect of defensive medicine on overall healthcare costs has been estimated at $55.6 billion annually, or 2.4% of total healthcare spending in 2008.[66] Despite this relatively low estimate, defensive medicine is highly prevalent, particularly in areas of the country with high malpractice premiums, and may be a driver of variability in practice patterns throughout the nation. Fifty-two percent of practicing physicians participating in a national survey identified fear of malpractice as a major reason for ordering unnecessary tests on patients.[67] In Pennsylvania 93% of physicians reported practicing defensive medicine, which resulted in the combination of overuse of unnecessary services like imaging and consultation, and underuse of high-risk invasive procedures.[68] This study highlighted how pervasive the problem is in areas with high malpractice rates and the resultant twin problems of overuse and underuse of services.

Although both clinicians and patients perceive that fear of malpractice is a key driver of low-value care in this country and needs to be addressed, the effect of tort reform efforts on clinical decision-making has not been clearly demonstrated. Clinicians' concerns about malpractice risk may be much more significant than their actual risk. State tort reform laws that directly limit malpractice damage payments have had little impact on state healthcare expenditures.[69] Physicians who report a high level of malpractice concern are more likely to engage in defensive practices, but there is no correlation with their actual state-level indicators of malpractice risk.[70] Furthermore, physicians' fears of malpractice lawsuits are not eased by tort reforms.[71] In general, clinicians fear being sued, period. The amount of the payout is generally not the motivator for defensive medicine. It seems that "reducing defensive medicine may require approaches focused on physicians' perceptions of legal risk and the underlying factors driving those perceptions"[70] rather than truly on specific tort reforms.

The fact of the matter is that unfortunately, malpractice claims can be arbitrary and hard to prevent; 40% of malpractice claims do not involve any medical error at all.[72] Furthermore, more care is not better care, as tests and treatments have harms associated with them that may lead to malpractice. Also, lack of follow-up of abnormal test results can lead to malpractice litigation. Once again, there is a good reason to not order a test if you do not plan on appropriately following it up and acting on the results. The only effective ways to try to ward off malpractice claims may be to listen to your patients and carefully document decision making, including discussion of side effects and risks of all tests and treatments, and to have clear and open communication with patients and families following medical errors.[73]

Patient expectations

Both actual patient expectations and perceived patient expectations are drivers of unnecessary care. For instance, physicians often choose to give antibiotics even when they are not indicated, because they perceive the patient wants them. But this perception may be incorrect. In a study done in 10 academic EDs, physicians were five times more likely to prescribe antibiotics unnecessarily if they perceived that patients wanted them.[74] Interestingly, these physicians were correct about their patients' desires only a quarter of the time. Furthermore, patient satisfaction has not actually been linked to whether or not the patient receives an antibiotic prescription at all, but rather is tied to improved communication.[3,74] Nonetheless, much like with malpractice fears, perceived barriers may be just as powerful determinants of clinician behavior as real barriers.

A systematic review of patients with back pain showed that patients had explicit expectations of their providers. The most important of which were acknowledging their pain, performing a physical examination, providing a clear explanation of what was causing the pain, and defining a clear plan for treatment and follow-up. Some patients did indeed expect imaging and specialist referral, but these hopes had a lower effect on overall satisfaction.[75] In addition, a broad-based patient survey identified communication and follow-up as key influencers of patient satisfaction.[76] What patients really want is a clear diagnosis, shared decision making, and acknowledgment that their symptoms are real. Asking patients up front about their expectations and creating a clear follow up plan may constitute a practical approach to simultaneously avoiding unnecessary care and improving patient satisfaction (see also Chapter 12).

As we engage in our work to improve patient outcomes, we must be aware of the many barriers to high-value care and make a conscious effort to simultaneously address both individual and system-based obstacles.

KEY POINTS:

- Both systemic and bedside clinical barriers contribute to the difficulty clinicians experience in practicing high-value care. These barriers include misaligned financial incentives, time pressures, lack of knowledge, culture, malpractice litigation fears, and patient expectations.
- Clinicians may have more control over bedside barriers to high-value care than they do over systemic ones, though these different types of barriers are often interrelated and are more likely to be overcome if systemic and bedside barriers are addressed together.
- The improvement of healthcare value is complicated by difficulties with accurately defining and measuring the components of value, which include benefits, harms, and cost, as well as downstream effects and patient perspectives.
- Many clinical barriers can be overcome by engaging all members of the healthcare team, including patients and families, in discussions about high-value care principles and practice.

References:

1. Fridkin S, Baggs J, Fagan R, et al. Vital signs: improving antibiotic use among hospitalized patients. *MMWR Morb Mortal Wkly Rep*. 2014;63(9):194-200.
2. Smith SM, Fahey T, Smucny J, Becker LA. Antibiotics for acute bronchitis. *Cochrane Database Syst Rev*. 2014;3:CD000245.
3. Gonzales R, Bartlett JG, Besser RE, et al. Principles of appropriate antibiotic use for treatment of uncomplicated acute bronchitis: background. *Ann Intern Med*. 2001;134(6):521-529.
4. Cooper RJ, Hoffman JR, Bartlett JG, et al. Principles of appropriate antibiotic use for acute pharyngitis in adults: background. *Ann Intern Med*. 2001;134(6):509-517.
5. Penicillin finder assays its future. *New York Times*. June 26, 1945:21.
6. Policy Statement on Antimicrobial Stewardship by the Society for Healthcare Epidemiology of America (SHEA), the Infectious Diseases Society of America (IDSA), and the Pediatric Infectious Diseases Society (PIDS). *Infect Control Hosp Epidemiol*. 2012;33(4):322-327.
7. Barnett ML, Linder JA. Antibiotic prescribing to adults with sore throat in the United States, 1997-2010. *JAMA Intern Med*. 2013.
8. Barnett ML, Linder JA. Antibiotic prescribing for adults with acute bronchitis in the united states, 1996-2010. *JAMA*. 2014;311(19):2020-2022.
9. Poulsen G. The third path. Systemic change will focus on returning value. *Mod Healthc*. 2008;38(16):26-27.
10. Eisenberg JM, Williams SV. Cost containment and changing physicians' practice behavior. Can the fox learn to guard the chicken coop? *JAMA*. 1981;246(19):2195-2201.
11. Joynt KE, Le ST, Orav EJ, Jha AK. Compensation of chief executive officers at nonprofit US hospitals. *JAMA Intern Med*. 2014;174(1):61-67.
12. Rauh SS, Wadsworth EB, Weeks WB, Weinstein JN. The savings illusion—why clinical quality improvement fails to deliver bottom-line results. *N Engl J Med*. 2011;365(26):e48.
13. Eappen S, Lane BH, Rosenberg B, et al. Relationship between occurrence of surgical complications and hospital finances. *JAMA*. 2013;309(15):1599-1606.
14. Eneli I, Norwood V, Hampl S, et al. Perspectives on obesity programs at children's hospitals: insights from senior program administrators. *Pediatrics*. 2011;128(suppl 2):S86-S90.
15. Reinhardt UE. The pricing of U.S. hospital services: chaos behind a veil of secrecy. *Health Aff*. 2006;25(1):57-69.
16. Yarnall KSH, Østbye T, Krause KM, Pollak KI, Gradison M, Michener JL. Family physicians as team leaders: "time" to share the care. *Prev Chronic Dis*. 2009;6(2):A59.
17. Flowerdew L, Brown R, Russ S, Vincent C, Woloshynowych M. Teams under pressure in the emergency department: an interview study. *Emerg Med J*. 2012;29(12):e2.
18. Van Bokhoven MA, Koch H, van der Weijden T, et al. The effect of watchful waiting compared to immediate test ordering instructions on general practitioners' blood test ordering behaviour for patients with unexplained complaints: a randomized clinical trial (ISRCTN55755886). *Implement Sci*. 2012;7:29.
19. Kuo Y-F, Goodwin JS. Association of hospitalist care with medical utilization after discharge: evidence of cost shift from a cohort study. *Ann Intern Med*. 2011;155(3):152-159.
20. Tamblyn R, Berkson L, Dauphinee WD, et al. Unnecessary prescribing of NSAIDs and the management of NSAID-related gastropathy in medical practice. *Ann Intern Med*. 1997;127(6):429-438.
21. Zyczynski TM, Coyne KS. Hypertension and current issues in compliance and patient outcomes. *Curr Hypertens Rep*. 2000;2(6):510-514.
22. Dugdale DC, Epstein R, Pantilat SZ. Time and the Patient-Physician Relationship. *J Gen Intern Med*. 1999;14(Suppl 1):S34-S40.
23. Cain C, Haque S. Organizational workflow and its impact on work quality. In: Hughes RG, ed. *Patient Safety and Quality: An Evidence-Based Handbook for Nurses*. Advances in Patient Safety. Rockville, MD: Agency for Healthcare Research and Quality (US); 2008. http://www.ncbi.nlm.nih.gov/books/NBK2638/. Accessed July 13, 2013.

24. Hendrich A, Chow MP, Skierczynski BA, Lu Z. A 36-Hospital Time and Motion Study: how do medical-surgical nurses spend their time? *Perm J*. 2008;12(3):25-34.

25. Teng C-I, Shyu Y-IL, Chiou W-K, Fan H-C, Lam SM. Interactive effects of nurse-experienced time pressure and burnout on patient safety: a cross-sectional survey. *Int J Nurs Stud*. 2010; 47(11):1442-1450.

26. Holden RJ, Scanlon MC, Patel NR, et al. A human factors framework and study of the effect of nursing workload on patient safety and employee quality of working life. *BMJ Qual Saf*. 2011;20(1):15-24.

27. Griffith RS, Williams PA. Barriers and incentives of physicians and patients to cancer screening. *Prim Care*. 1992;19(3):535-556.

28. Abernethy NF, DeRimer K, Small PM. Methods to identify standard data elements in clinical and public health forms. *AMIA Annu Symp Proc*. 2011;2011:19-27.

29. Abbo ED, Volandes AE. Teaching residents to consider costs in medical decision making. *Am J Bioeth*. 2006;6(4):33-34.

30. Woolf SH, Johnson RE. The break-even point: when medical advances are less important than improving the fidelity with which they are delivered. *Ann Fam Med*. 2005;3(6):545-552.

31. Antithombotic Trialists' Collaboration. Collaborative meta-analysis of randomised trials of anti-platelet therapy for prevention of death, myocardial infarction, and stroke in high risk patients. *BMJ*. 2002;324(7329):71-86.

32. McGlynn EA, Asch SM, Adams J, et al. The quality of health care delivered to adults in the United States. *N Engl J Med*. 2003;348(26):2635-2645.

33. Quality of Care and Outcomes Research in CVD and Stroke Working Groups. Measuring and Improving Quality of Care A Report From the American Heart Association/American College of Cardiology First Scientific Forum on Assessment of Healthcare Quality in Cardiovascular Disease and Stroke. *Circulation*. 2000;101(12):1483-1493.

34. Krumholz HM, Wang Y, Chen J, et al. Reduction in acute myocardial infarction mortality in the united states: risk-standardized mortality rates from 1995-2006. *JAMA*. 2009;302(7): 767-773.

35. Bradley EH, Herrin J, Elbel B, et al. Hospital quality for acute myocardial infarction: correlation among process measures and relationship with short-term mortality. *JAMA*. 2006;296(1): 72-78.

36. Owens DK, Qaseem A, Chou R, Shekelle P, Clinical Guidelines Committee of the American College of Physicians. High-value, cost-conscious health care: concepts for clinicians to evaluate the benefits, harms, and costs of medical interventions. *Ann Intern Med*. 2011;154(3):174-180.

37. Gusmano MK, Callahan D. "Value for money": use with care. *Ann Intern Med*. 2011;154(3):207-208.

38. Sprague L. Seeking value in Medicare: performance measurement for clinical professionals. *Issue Brief George Wash Univ Natl Health Policy Forum*. 2013;(852):1-11.

39. Grove A. Peeling away health care's sticker shock. *Wired*. 2012. http://www.wired.com/business/2012/10/mf-health-care-transparency/. Accessed November 15, 2012.

40. Kaplan RS, Anderson SR. Time-driven activity-based costing. *Harv Bus Rev*. 2004. http://hbr.org/2004/11/time-driven-activity-based-costing/ar/1. Accessed September 4, 2013.

41. Rosenbaum L. The whole ball game—overcoming the blind spots in health care reform. *N Engl J Med*. 2013;368(10):959-962.

42. Sullivan R, Peppercorn J, Sikora K, et al. Delivering affordable cancer care in high-income countries. *Lancet Oncol*. 2011;12(10):933-980.

43. Patient-Centered Outcomes Research Institute. http://www.pcori.org/. Accessed May 22, 2014.

44. Neumann PJ, Weinstein MC. Legislating against use of cost-effectiveness information. *N Engl J Med*. 2010;363(16):1495-1497.

45. Galani C, Rutten FF. Self-reported healthcare decision-makers' attitudes towards economic evaluations of medical technologies. *Curr Med Res Opin*. 2008;24(11):3049-3058.

46. Goldberger JJ, Buxton AE. Personalized medicine vs guideline-based medicine. *JAMA*. 2013;309(24):2559-2560.

47. Hoffmann C, Graf von der Schulenburg JM. The influence of economic evaluation studies on decision making: a European survey. The EUROMET group. *Health Policy Amst Neth*. 2000; 52(3):179-192.

48. Evans BA, Snooks H, Howson H, Davies M. How hard can it be to include research evidence and evaluation in local health policy implementation? Results from a mixed methods study. *Implement Sci*. 2013;8:17.

49. Cooke M. Cost consciousness in patient care—what is medical education's responsibility? *N Engl J Med*. 2010;362(14):1253-1255.

50. Weinberger SE. Providing high-value, cost-conscious care: a critical seventh general competency for physicians. *Ann Intern Med*. 2011;155(6):386-388.

51. Tek Sehgal R, Gorman P. Internal medicine physicians' knowledge of health care charges. *J Grad Med Educ*. 2011;3(2):182-187.

52. Detsky AS, Verma AA. A new model for medical education: celebrating restraint. *JAMA*. 2012;308(13):1329-1330.

53. Moriates C, Shah N, Arora VM. Medical training and expensive care. *Health Aff*. 2013;32(1):196-196.

54. Hafferty FW, Franks R. The hidden curriculum, ethics teaching, and the structure of medical education. *Acad Med*. 1994;69(11):861-871.

55. Rosenbaum L, Lamas D. Cents and sensitivity—teaching physicians to think about costs. *N Engl J Med*. 2012;367(2):99-101.

56. Sexton JB, Helmreich RL, Neilands TB, et al. The safety attitudes questionnaire: psychometric properties, benchmarking data, and emerging research. *BMC Health Serv Res*. 2006;6:44.

57. Chassin MR. Improving the quality of health care: what's taking so long? *Health Aff*. 2013;32(10):1761-1765.

58. Jarvik JG, Hollingworth W, Martin B, et al. Rapid magnetic resonance imaging vs radiographs for patients with low back pain: a randomized controlled trial. *JAMA*. 2003;289(21):2810-2818.

59. Davis P, Gribben B, Scott A, Lay-Yee R. The "supply hypothesis" and medical practice variation in primary care: testing economic and clinical models of inter-practitioner variation. *Soc Sci Med*. 2000;50(3):407-418.

60. Pearson SD, Goldman L, Orav EJ, et al. Triage decisions for emergency department patients with chest pain: do physicians' risk attitudes make the difference? *J Gen Intern Med*. 1995;10(10):557-564.

61. Pines JM, Hollander JE, Isserman JA, et al. The association between physician risk tolerance and imaging use in abdominal pain. *Am J Emerg Med*. 2009;27(5):552-557.

62. Meyer AD, Payne VL, Meeks DW, Rao R, Singh H. Physicians' diagnostic accuracy, confidence, and resource requests: a vignette study. *JAMA Intern Med*. 2013;173(21):1952-1958.

63. Kendrick D, Fielding K, Bentley E, Kerslake R, Miller P, Pringle M. Radiography of the lumbar spine in primary care patients with low back pain: randomised controlled trial. *BMJ*. 2001;322(7283):400-405.

64. Rolfe A, Burton C. Reassurance after diagnostic testing with a low pretest probability of serious disease: systematic review and meta-analysis. *JAMA Intern Med*. 2013;173(6):407-416.

65. Barry MJ. Incidentaloma fatigue. *JAMA Intern Med*. 2014;174(6):851-852.

66. Mello MM, Chandra A, Gawande AA, Studdert DM. National costs of the medical liability system. *Health Aff (Proj Hope)*. 2010;29(9):1569-1577.

67. The ABIM Foundation, PerryUndem Research. Unnecessary tests and procedures in the health care system: what physicians say about the problem, the causes, and the solutions. Results from a National Survey of Physicians. 2014. http://www.choosingwisely.org/wp-content/uploads/2014/04/042814_Final-Choosing-Wisely-Survey-Report.pdf. Accessed May 2, 2014.

68. Studdert DM, Mello MM, Sage WM, et al. Defensive medicine among high-risk specialist physicians in a volatile malpractice environment. *JAMA*. 2005;293(21):2609-2617.

69. Hellinger FJ, Encinosa WE. The impact of state laws limiting malpractice damage awards on health care expenditures. *Am J Public Health*. 2006;96(8):1375-1381.

70. Carrier ER, Reschovsky JD, Katz DA, Mello MM. High physician concern about malpractice risk predicts more aggressive diagnostic testing in office-based practice. *Health Aff.* 2013;32(8):1383-1391.
71. Carrier ER, Reschovsky JD, Mello MM, Mayrell RC, Katz D. Physicians' fears of malpractice lawsuits are not assuaged by tort reforms. *Health Aff.* 2010;29(9):1585-1592.
72. Studdert DM, Mello MM, Gawande AA, et al. Claims, errors, and compensation payments in medical malpractice litigation. *N Engl J Med.* 2006;354(19):2024-2033.
73. Langel S. Averting medical malpractice lawsuits: effective medicine—or inadequate cure? *Health Aff.* 2010;29(9):1565-1568.
74. Ong S, Nakase J, Moran GJ, et al. Antibiotic use for emergency department patients with upper respiratory infections: prescribing practices, patient expectations, and patient satisfaction. *Ann Emerg Med.* 2007;50(3):213-220.
75. Verbeek J, Sengers M-J, Riemens L, Haafkens J. Patient expectations of treatment for back pain: a systematic review of qualitative and quantitative studies. *Spine.* 2004;29(20):2309-2318.
76. Anderson R, Barbara A, Feldman S. What patients want: a content analysis of key qualities that influence patient satisfaction. *J Med Pract Manag.* 2007;22(5):255-261.

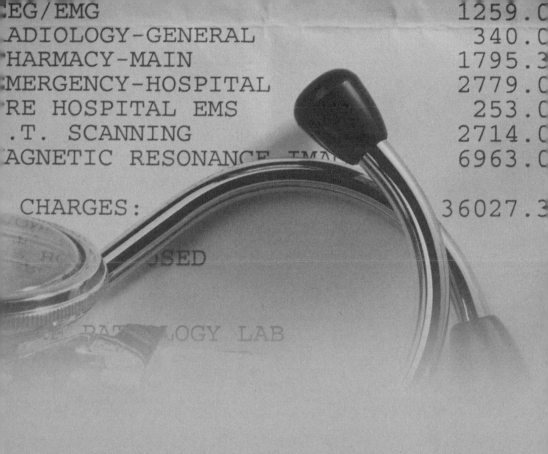

```
EG/EMG                              1259.C
ADIOLOGY-GENERAL                     340.C
HARMACY-MAIN                        1795.3
MERGENCY-HOSPITAL                   2779.C
RE HOSPITAL EMS                      253.C
.T. SCANNING                        2714.C
AGNETIC RESONANCE IMA               6963.C

CHARGES:                           36027.3

            SED

      PAT   LOGY LAB
```

PART III

Solutions and Tools

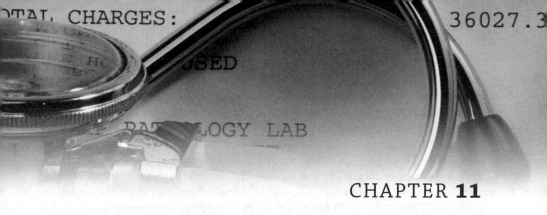

Building A Pipeline of Change: Teaching About Cost Awareness and Evidence-Based Medicine

In a large lecture hall of fellow clinicians-to-be, I was told that my job as a physician is not to be concerned with costs but rather to treat patients. My wrist, moving frantically left to right on my page taking notes, stopped. I looked up and my mind wandered: What an odd message to tell those who will be listening to ill people's symptoms, prescribing medicine, ordering tests, and orchestrating people's care to not worry about costs.

We have set up this dichotomy of treating the patient or being concerned with costs. We have soaked medicine with the belief that cost-conscious care is rationing at the bedside and the public is fed fear messages that clinicians who care about costs are limiting their care. How can we teach future clinicians to be so out-of-touch with one of the greatest concerns that many patients have when seeing a clinician? We know that people forgo medications because of high prices, medical bankruptcy plagues many, and that some cannot seek care due to cost. What other industries allow someone so crucially involved in controlling costs immunity from worrying about them? Does medicine's unique role of saving lives exempt it from keeping an eye on the register? Is good care not cost-conscious care?

Clinicians do not have the luxury to not care about costs.

—adapted from Sarah Jorgenson, Costs of Care, 2013

As Sarah Jorgenson eloquently highlights, teaching medical students how to consider costs while caring for patients is uncommon—in fact, clinicians are often taught to specifically ignore costs. But times are changing, and recently, there have been increasing calls for medical education to train cost-conscious physicians.[1] Educating physicians to be "cost aware" is now becoming a critical responsibility of medical schools and residency programs. The Accreditation Council of Graduate Medical Education (ACGME) has included cost awareness and stewardship into its systems-based practice competency; residents are asked "to incorporate considerations of cost awareness and risk-benefit analysis in patient and/or population-based care as appropriate."[2] To raise the visibility of this need, the American College of Physicians (ACP) has proposed that high-value, cost-conscious care be added as a standalone "7th core competency" of residency education.[3]

MEDICAL EDUCATION AND VALUE-BASED CARE

Although current efforts to integrate value-based care into medical training may appear new, it may be surprising to learn that such efforts actually date back to as early as 1975! In that year, Harvard Professor of Medicine Dr Howard Hiatt famously encouraged physicians collaborate with other experts and the public to protect the medical commons (see Chapter 5).[4] In 1984, UCSF Professor of Medicine Dr Stephen Schroeder and colleagues rigorously evaluated an educational intervention, which included a weekly lecture as well as audit and feedback, designed to reduce lab and radiology use at the University of California at San Francisco (UCSF). Unfortunately, there was no significant effect on total hospital charges.[5] One reason such prior efforts have not resulted in widespread change could be in part due to the local nature of the efforts, in addition to the myriad of cultural, operational, and systemic challenges such innovations have faced, including the need to align stakeholder interests and integrate novel material into already crowded curricula.

But now, cost-containment has become an urgent national priority that is increasingly spilling over into clinical education. For example, policymakers and accrediting organizations have all expressed concern that residency training does not produce cost-effective physicians. The Medicare Payment Advisory Commission (MedPAC), which advises Medicare on payment issues, has identified cost-consciousness as a critical deficiency in current residency training.[6] In fact, a MedPAC RAND Study in 2009 demonstrated that only 23% of 26 internal medicine residency programs reported their residents get training in cost-effectiveness.[7] A 2012 survey from the Association of Program Directors of Internal Medicine (APDIM) continues to highlight the lack of formal curricula in this area, finding that only 15% of programs had curricula related to cost, although an additional 50% of programs were thinking about starting one.[8] Furthermore, while the majority (85%) of program directors thought that graduate medical education has the responsibility to curtail the rising costs of care, just under half (47%) felt that their faculty working with residents model cost-conscious patient care.

The situation is no better in our nation's medical schools. Data from the 2013 Association of American Medical Colleges (AAMC) Graduation Medical Student

Questionnaire demonstrate that 63% of graduating students feel the training they received on healthcare economics was "inadequate."[9] Of all the topical areas assessed, training in healthcare economics was judged to be the worst. Given the lack of curricula at both the undergraduate and graduate level, it is worth considering what obstacles exist. In both the RAND and APDIM studies, a lack of qualified faculty to teach and role model cost-conscious care was cited as a major barrier. Furthermore, the culture of medical training environments creates what educators often refer to as the "hidden curriculum" (as discussed below). It is not just that we are not taught much about healthcare costs, but *the way that we're taught* may be actively training us to be bad stewards of healthcare resources.

Value-based care in the formal and hidden curricula

To address value-based education, it is important that we first understand how medical education is actually delivered in teaching hospitals. As Mayo Clinic Professor Fred Hafferty has recognized, there are several types of "curricula" that pass down knowledge and attitudes to medical trainees (Figure 11-1).[10] The most obvious and familiar to the casual observer is the "formal curriculum," which refers to the actual planned lessons or written curricular objectives and content that are delivered to medical trainees. When asked about curricula, this is often the component that is discussed. But, a powerful and surreptitious undercurrent is also at

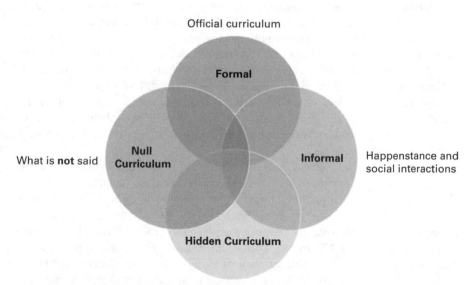

Figure 11-1. The formal, hidden, and null curriculum. (Adapted, with permission, from Dr. Shalini Reddy, University of Chicago. Data from Hafferty F. Measuring medical professionalism: A commentary. In: Stern DT, ed. *Measuring Medical Professionalism.* New York, NY: Oxford University Press; 2005.)

work in medical education, aptly named the "hidden curriculum." The hidden curriculum describes lessons that are not taught formally, but are learned through the transmission of norms, values, and beliefs conveyed in the classroom and the social environment. Medical education experts believe the hidden curriculum to be more powerful than the formal curriculum for instilling values, beliefs, and behaviors. Lastly, the "null curriculum" emphasizes that topics or issues that are *not* taught are deemed to not be important, thus often sending an unintended message to trainees.

To see how the hidden curriculum plays a major role in promoting a culture of overuse and waste, consider how medical trainees are often rewarded for suggesting rare diagnoses in the differential diagnoses for patients, and that many resident conferences, such as traditional morning reports, emphasize bizarre and very rare cases that require more intensive workups rather than focusing on the most likely diagnosis for the patient's chief complaint.[11] Residents are also more often criticized for sins of omission than for commission. For example, a resident is more likely to be asked why he or she did not order a certain test than to be questioned about why he or she *did* order a test. Moreover, questioning whether a test is needed, opens up a trainee to possible criticism for "not being thorough."[12]

In fact, there are many reasons that trainees may overorder tests and it is easy to see how these relate to the hidden and null curricula (Table 11-1).[13] Actively tackling these reasons for overuse in the training environment clearly map to several of the ACGME core competencies, most notably, systems-based practice, practice-based learning and improvement, interpersonal communication, and professionalism (see Table 11-1). Let us think about preemptive ordering. Systems inefficiencies in hospitals lead to an often-used workaround: to jump the gun and "preemptively" order a test just in case you might need it later, realizing that a delay in ordering could ultimately result in a postponed discharge.[14] As a result, many patients receive tests they do not necessarily need, which lead to both direct and indirect effects on patient safety. Unnecessary testing can lead to patient harm, as discussed throughout this book. In addition, if, say, an MRI was labeled as "urgent" when it is in fact not, a less sick patient may take priority in getting a scan over a patient who truly needed it.

Another reason physicians may overorder a test is that patients directly request the test (see Chapter 10).[15] While clinicians are often taught to be patient-centered and serve their patients, information asymmetry leads patients to make medical decisions that may not always be the most rational, or in their actual best interest. This is why the competency of interpersonal communication is so important (see also Chapter 12). In fact, studies have shown that through better communication, physicians are able to counsel patients to avoid unnecessary tests. In one study published in 1987, patients were randomized to receive immediate x-rays or a brief educational intervention for back pain.[16] After 3 weeks, fewer patients in the education group believed "everyone with back pain should have an x-ray" (44% education vs 73% x-ray). Patient outcomes were no different in both groups, and no serious diagnoses were missed.

Table 11-1 Top 10 reasons doctors overorder tests

Top 10	Problem	Solution	ACGME Competency	ABIM Charter Commitment
How we are taught	It's taboo for doctors to consider cost	Change culture	Systems-based practice	Improving access to care
		Create framework for considering costs as part of patient care paradigm		Just distribution of resources
Trying our best	We're worried ... and risk averse	Teach diagnostic strategies	Professionalism	Improving quality of care
			Practice-based learning and improvement	Improving access to care
Preemptive ordering	Ordering every-thing now is easier and saves time	Semiannual review of order-entry by workflow task force, composed of all members of care team	Systems-based practice	Just distribution of resources
Covering all bases	Doing more is equated with being thorough	Build cost-effectiveness data into workflow	Practice-based learning and improvement	Improving quality of care
General unawareness	We do not know how much things cost	Monthly "Costs of Care" morning report	Systems-based practice	Improving access to care
				Just distribution of resources
Broader ignorance	Costs are opaque	Build price-point examples into workflow	Systems-based practice	Improving access to care
				Just distribution of resources
Unaware of setting's effect on cost	Pricing is not intuitive	Institution-specific cheat sheets for commonly ordered tests	Systems-based practice	Improving access to care
				Just distribution of resources
Defensive medicine	Malpractice claims are real ... and exaggerated	Teaching module designed to differ-entiate standards of care versus evidence-based medicine	Systems-based practice	Patient welfare
			Practice-based learning and improvement	Improving access to care

(Continued)

Table 11-1 Top 10 reasons doctors overorder tests *(Continued)*

Top 10	Problem	Solution	ACGME Competency	ABIM Charter Commitment
Patient requests	The customer is always right	Communication module aimed at understanding and addressing requests	Professionalism Patient care Interpersonal and communication skills	Honesty with patients Maintaining appropriate relations with patients
Lack of oversight	Discomfort with third party oversight, among doctors and patients	Evidence-based demonstrations of better outcomes and lower costs through oversight	Systems-based practice	Professional responsibilities

Story From the Frontlines: On Being 100% Sure

As busy practitioners, we may forget that our trainees do not always have the skills to make cost judgments prior to ordering tests, especially when a test is just a computer-click away. As teachers, though, it is imperative we reinforce the fact that tests have costs and should only be used as adjuncts to our clinical assessments. The toughest thing to teach is what not to order.

Unfortunately, medical economics is not routinely taught in medical school and we either never learn it at all or we learn it informally from our mentors, if we are lucky. The emergency room is an area where we always seem to struggle with trying not to "miss a disaster." A chief resident came to me to discuss a woman who presented with left lower quadrant pain that was suspicious for ovarian torsion, a surgical emergency. If you suspect it, you operate. She underwent a pelvic ultrasound that was completely normal, and by the time the evaluation was completed, her pain had resolved. Discharge; end of story, right? No. The resident, still concerned, wanted to observe her in the Emergency Room for four more hours and repeat the ultrasound to "double-check."

"Why would you do that? What risk factors does she have for torsion?" I asked.

The resident responded, "None, but I want to be sure."

"If you're that worried, then we should go to the OR, not wait for another ultrasound," I advised.

"I'm not concerned enough for the OR, but don't we need to be 100% sure?" she asked.

"We can never be 100% sure 100% of the time, but if we use good judgment, we can be pretty darn close. The remaining uncertainty, you have to learn to deal with. She'll call again if the pain returns," I said.

It didn't.

In a time when there's constant worry about potential lawsuits, it's very difficult to embrace the concept of tolerating uncertainty. We are so used to being explorers trying to find the proverbial zebra, that it becomes harder to see the horse when it's staring us in the face. That's how these million-dollar workups occur when sometimes a tincture of time is the best treatment. I was fortunate to have teachers who helped instill the importance of clinical examination, who engaged me in understanding medical costs, but I am not perfect by any means. It is a continual learning process, which should be a formal part of medical training. Until then, all I can do is take baby steps, starting with myself and those I educate. Hopefully, many people taking many baby steps can work to reduce costs and provide better care, which, in the end, is our ultimate goal.

—Padma Kandadai. "On Being 100% Sure." Costs of Care, 2010. (www.costsofcare.org)

MOVING TOWARD COMPETENCIES FOR TEACHING VALUE-BASED CARE

Recently, the ACGME has launched a new institutional approach to accreditation based on the Clinical Learning Environment Review, or "CLER," with a focus on integrating residents into the hospital quality and safety mission, including value. For example, under the pathway of education on quality improvement, the ACGME states "the focus will be on the extent to which residents/fellows receive experiential learning in quality improvement that includes consideration of underuse, overuse, and misuses in the diagnosis or treatment of patients."[17] Early experiences with CLER site visits demonstrate that residents are seldom engaged in systems-based practice and even when they are, their efforts to improve quality and safety may not be well-integrated with the approach of their institution.[18]

In the summer of 2014, these gaps in physician skills for delivering high-value care prompted the Institute of Medicine (IOM) to issue a report that proposes radical changes in the structure and financing of graduate medical education.[19] In particular, the IOM committee recommended creating a new "GME Transformation Fund" to support efforts that help close the value-based care training gap. Based on lessons from the Transformation Fund pilot projects, they proposed tying how much an academic medical center gets paid to performance. In a *New England Journal of Medicine* article that summarizes their recommendations, committee chairs Gail Wilensky and Donald Berwick point out, "GME can and should be better leveraged than it has been to date for ... meeting the needs of the American people."[20]

In 2013, The ABIM Foundation convened a meeting of stakeholders around promoting high-value care education for trainees. At that meeting, the following competencies, designed to be interdisciplinary, were proposed for trainees (Table 11-2).

Table 11-2 Competencies proposed for Choosing Wisely

Competency	Skills
Know *why* to Choose Wisely	• Understand the potential clinical harms from low-value tests and procedures • Understand the ethical case for stewarding resources, including the potential impact of clinical decisions on patient affordability and system sustainability • Understand the professional obligation to communicate with peers and team members about the value of tests and procedures
Know *when* to Choose Wisely	• Understand the influence of culture on norms related to resource use • Understand the incentives for overuse in training and practice environments. • Understand metrics for systems accountability in delivering value and how these metrics may be used for practice-based improvement
Know *How* to Choose Wisely	• Demonstrate appropriate diagnostic reasoning and management of uncertainty • Use evidence to compare the risks and benefits (ie, value) of tests and treatments • Use information technologies and decision-support tools to choose high value tests and treatments • Communicate with patients about the affordability and value of care they are receiving

The need for interprofessional training

In addition to training physicians, there is a recognized need to train all health professionals in high-value care, particularly with a renewed focus on teamwork and interprofessional learning.

The Macy Foundation has been a leader in advocating for interprofessional education and collaborative practice as a way of achieving the elusive "triple aim": improving the patient experience of care, health of populations, and reducing the costs of healthcare.[21] While the concept of interprofessional education is not new and has been advocated for since the 1970s, a renewed interest in team-based care has emerged as a result of the Affordable Care Act and other drivers. To meet this need, the Inter-Professional Education Collaborative (IPEC) was formed through a joint effort of the Association of American Medical Colleges, American Association of Colleges of Nursing, American Association of Colleges of Osteopathic Medicine, American Association of Colleges of Pharmacy, American Dental Education Association, and the Association of Schools of Public Health. When the IPEC released its interprofessional core competencies, a key rationale was that team-based care represented a cost-effective way to meet patient, family, and community healthcare needs.[22] While initiatives to promote interprofessional learning are growing, high-value care educational initiatives have largely targeted physicians-in-training. This unfortunate oversight could actually undo some of the progress made by high-value care educational initiatives.

> Just as a single individual who fails to hand-wash may infect a patient and undo the diligent compliance of everyone else on the team, the efforts of some clinicians to cut wasteful practices may be quickly undone by a lack of understanding or skills from others in the healthcare system. The successful delivery of high-value care depends on major cultural shifts throughout the clinical environment, and [as Dr Ezekiel Emanuel has stated] the current healthcare cost situation calls for an "all-hands-on-deck" mentality.
>
> (From Moriates, Dohan, Spetz, Sawaya. Defining Competencies in Education in Healthcare Value: Recommendations from the University of California, San Francisco Center for Healthcare Value Training Initiative. Academic Medicine. 2014)

STRATEGIES FOR MEDICAL EDUCATION TO INTRODUCE VALUE-BASED CARE

As we consider how to incorporate value-based care into medical training, it is worth noting there is a wide range of strategies that could be employed, some of which are more feasible and impactful than others. In reality, to truly make lasting change in medical education, there is no easy solution. Medical educators will have to simultaneously employ multiple strategies to create true change.

Incorporation into high-stakes exams

Perhaps the most tried-and-true method of achieving widespread curricular change is to modify the high-stakes exams trainees are required to take to progress during medical training. At the medical school level, this includes the United States Medical Licensing Exam Step 1 and 2, as well as the associated Step 2 Clinical Skills examination. Following residency, physicians obtain specialty-specific certification through secure exams administered by the respective specialty board, such as the American Board of Internal Medicine or the American Board of Pediatrics. In recent years, this method has been proposed as a way of introducing new and emerging competencies, such as patient safety.[23] Similarly, this may be an important lever for generating importance of value-based decision-making.[24] Current high-stakes exams for medical students focus on basic or clinical science and do not include an emphasis on value-based care. Moreover, by design, sins of omission are more serious than sins of commission on the current USMLE Step 2 Clinical Skills examination, which promotes a practice of increasing diagnostic testing and working-up every symptom that a standardized patient reports.[25] In graduate medical education, in-training exams administered to internal medicine residents by the ACP have started to make inroads by including a high-value care sub-score to highlight if the examinee's choices on the test were the most appropriate and cost-effective.

Other allied health professions could also incorporate principles of healthcare economics and high-value care into their high-stakes exams. Many pharmacy students are currently exposed to basic economic principles in their pharmacy curriculums, but may have difficulty applying those theoretical concepts to actual patient care.[26] Nurses represent the largest labor force at the sharp end of patient care, and as such are well positioned to advocate for healthcare value. Unfortunately, nursing education, like medical education, has not yet formally integrated value-based care into their curricula or their high-stakes examinations.[27]

Embedding into clinical teaching and residency evaluation

In addition to high-stakes exams, residency programs have numerous other opportunities to integrate value into teaching. Dr Mitesh Patel (University of Pennsylvania) and colleagues at the University of Michigan highlight over 40 ways that value-based teaching could be integrated into residency programs (Table 11-3).[28] Apart from using structured formal teaching opportunities, Patel and colleagues also advocate for incorporating value-based instruction into clinical teaching, measurement and evaluation, and feedback. Natural "teachable moments" for high-value care on the wards could include attending rounds, discussions with social workers, and discharge planning for a patient. Using end-of-rotation evaluations, attending physicians could offer their assessment of trainee knowledge and integration of high-value care practices into their care plans. Lastly, feedback could come in the form of data-driven reports that target resource utilization.[29]

Table 11-3 Opportunities for residency programs to incorporate training in value-based care

Stage	Component	Incorporating Concepts of Value-Based Care
Structured teaching	Orientation and basic systems training	Inform residents of opportunities to help guide their assessment of value-based care when orienting them to the health system, providing basic computer training, and discussing available electronic and library resources
	Inpatient reports/conferences	Discussion of recent clinical cases should include prompts for residents to evaluate whether or not interventions provided value for the patient
	Outpatient reports/conferences	Compare the potential value of preventive care (eg, cancer screening) versus costly interventions when reviewing clinical guidelines and best practices
	Journal Club	Review of published studies should focus on how validation for an intervention was determined and an assessment of whether variation exists among various patient populations. Residents should discuss how these concepts are important for creating value for the patient and how study design might limit the translations from statistical significance to clinical significance
	Quality improvement curriculum	An ACGME requirement for residency programs that could be leveraged to provide structured teaching in core concepts of value-based care and their overlap with improving healthcare quality
	Online training modules	Advances in computer simulation and mobile technology provide platforms for creating online modules that provide an interactive method of demonstrating how concepts of value affect patient care
	Grand rounds (eg, Morbidity and mortality)	These patient cases are often presented to the entire department and help set the path toward changes in health system practices. Incorporating a review of when value was added or opportunities were missed might help to integrate these concepts into system redesign

(Continued)

Table 11-3 Opportunities for residency programs to incorporate training in value-based care *(Continued)*

Stage	Component	Incorporating Concepts of Value-Based Care
Clinical teaching	Attending teaching rounds	As one of the cornerstones of clinical teaching during residency training, this provides an opportunity for the attending to demonstrate the importance of considering value when making management decisions. Attending physicians should be trained to teach and discuss these concepts for every patient
	Bedside interactions with patients	Residents learn much of their lifelong practice habits during clinical interactions with patients in residency. They should be required to consider and discuss concepts of value with the patient. For example, when obtaining patient consent for a procedure, residents should incorporate concepts of value into the discussion of risks and benefits of the procedure
	Staffing a patient	Whether in the inpatient or outpatient setting, residents often see the patient first and then present or "staff" a patient with an attending. Their assessment and plan should highlight how their recommendations for care provide or do not provide value to the patient.
	Social work issues	Often barriers to care that involve affordability or access are passed on to social workers. Integrating residents into this process, such as mandating daily attendance at social work rounds, helps them to understand the importance of evaluating and addressing these issues
	Discharge planning	Transitions in care provide opportunities for residents to review medical management thus far and to determine prioritization of future patient care. Residents should be required to utilize concepts of value to help identify which interventions provide the most value to the patient and how to best reduce the chances of medical error or long-term side effects.
Measurement/ evaluation	Attending evaluations	Evaluations of resident performance should include a section on whether the resident demonstrated integration of concepts from value-based care. Attendings might offer the best perspective on evaluating the resident's high-level management of patient care
	Senior resident evaluations	Senior residents are most involved with more junior residents' decisions regarding medical interventions. They offer the best perspective on evaluating the junior resident's day-to-day management of patient care.

	Trainee evaluations	Residents are expected not only to learn about concepts of patient care, but also to teach these concepts to more junior residents and medical students. Trainees sometimes provide the only evaluations of resident performance in teaching. Therefore, trainees, both junior residents and medical students, should evaluate their resident's performance in teaching concepts of value in patient care
	Online evaluation modules	As mentioned above, computer simulation and mobile technology have created a platform for use of online modules to teaching concepts of patient care. A powerful component of these modules is the ability to evaluate residents while using the modules. These performance scores can be reviewed immediately after the module by residents and can be used by the resident program to evaluate whether changes in residency training are impacting training in these topics
	In-training examinations	Many residency programs use these exams to help residents gauge their knowledge and preparation for board examinations. While the actual test is often from a centralized organization, this timepoint provides an opportunity for the resident program to administer a supplemental questionnaire or evaluation focused on topics that reflect changes in the program's training
	Board examinations	There are certification exams that residents take after completion of residency. While the residency program does not have control over these, they do often offer board preparation sessions. As board certification exams change to reflect concepts in value, residency programs can integrate teaching on these concepts during preparation sessions
Feedback	Program director	A discussion regarding a resident's overall performance during residency is often only conducted during the meeting with the residency program director. Based on the evaluation and measurement methods above, the program director can provide feedback on a resident's ability to incorporate concepts of value into patient care
	Attending/senior resident	At the end of a rotation, the attending and senior resident provides feedback on the resident's clinical performance as well as their performance in other areas such as communication, professionalism, and time management. There should be a requirement for feedback on the resident's ability to assess and provide value-based care
	Data-driven report cards	Price transparency and resource utilization are two areas that have received attention as opportunities to help improve healthcare value. While the application of each of these needs further study within the clinical realm, they offer a powerful objective indicator of how the resident is providing value-based care

Reproduced from Patel MS, Davis MM, Lypson ML. The VALUE framework: training residents to provide value-based care for their patients. *J Gen Intern Med.* 2012;27(9):1210-1214. Table 2. With kind permission from Springer Science and Business Media.

E-learning and social media

The explosion of e-learning and social media provides new exciting opportunities to further facilitate value-based care learning. Disruptive innovators in the educational space include Sal Khan, whose Khan Academy video-based tutorials have now infiltrated medical education through a partnership with the AAMC.[30] The Institute for Healthcare Improvement's Open School has directly marketed their electronic modules to learners, spreading concepts of quality and patient safety to more than 200,000 learners in at least 65 countries worldwide.[31] Likewise, the success of "MOOCs," or Massive Online Open Courses, through sites such as Coursera have fueled some to suggest the future of medical education lies in this mechanism.[32] Recently, the Brookings Institution has launched a collaboration between the Khan Academy and the Richard Merkin Initiative at the Engelberg Center for Health Care Reform to develop a MOOC aimed at improving clinician education about healthcare payment and delivery.[33] While it is unproven whether these methods will actually be successful in truly changing practices, the increasing spread of social media and MOOCs into mainstream medical education highlights such innovations in value-based education will continue to spread. It is noteworthy that the first known dedicated "tweet chat" on value-based care education on the popular micro-blog service Twitter attracted 68 participants who generated 489 tweets in 1 hour, resulting in a reach of over 1 million impressions.[34]

The *"COST" framework* for value-based care interventions in medical education

Since the principles related to the delivery of value-based care (or the lack thereof) are so widely prevalent in every aspect of medical practice, strategies to compel real behavior change should simultaneously target multiple different areas throughout medical education. One way to categorize these targets is the *"COST"* framework (developed by our Costs of Care organization), comprised of culture, oversight, systems change, and training (see Table 11-4).[35] While many educational interventions target training alone, successful programmatic interventions can have a more impactful and sustained change on practice patterns if they are coupled with objectives in other areas, such as changing the overuse culture, adding attending oversight, and/or embedding a long-term systems change to promote value-based care. In other words, value-based care training must be baked in throughout the training environment, rather than merely added as a layer of icing on top.

- *Culture:* Perhaps the most critical element for true practice change, a cost-conscious culture refers to the institutional and organizational values that are consistent with value-based care. Changing the culture is not easy. Early value-based care interventions that have tackled culture were often multifactorial, addressing many targets all at once and involving the support of senior leadership. At Banner Health Good Samaritan Hospital a local competition was created to solicit trainee suggestions for the best

Table 11-4 COST framework for educational interventions for high-value care

	Interventions	Description	Example
C	*Culture*	Valuing cost-consciousness and resource stewardship at the individual and team level	Hospital-wide campaign led by peer-champions to reduce lab tests overuse
O	*Oversight*	Requiring accountability for cost-conscious decision-making at both a peer and organizational level	Requiring attending to review labs residents order to reduce overuse
S	*Systems Change*	Creating systems to make cost-conscious decisions using institutional policy, decision-support tools, and clinical guidelines	Electronic health record displays cost of lab tests next to order for specific test or prioritizes display so high-value option is displayed first
T	*Training*	Providing knowledge and skills clinicians need to make cost-conscious decisions	Lecture or workshop on ordering of lab tests

ways to promote high-value care, with the winners being given resources from the institution to turn their suggestions into reality.[35] Another similar example is the "Caring Wisely" program at UCSF, as described in Chapter 16. Celebrating efforts to improve value can be a powerful way to create cultural change. As Dr George Halvorson, prior chief executive officer for Kaiser Permanente, has highlighted, something that is openly celebrated will naturally become a key component of that group's culture.[36]

- *Oversight:* Oversight refers to the use of attending physicians or other "overseers" to ensure effective stewardship of resources. Examples of such oversight are abundant in the medical workplace. Antibiotic stewardship programs—which usually require pre-approval by an infectious disease service prior to use of an antibiotic that is associated with drug resistance—have become commonplace in hospitals, and the Centers for Disease Control and Prevention has called for mandated antimicrobial stewardship programs across healthcare settings.[37,38] In contrast to the proliferation of antibiotic stewardship programs, oversight is underutilized in other areas for preventing overuse and promoting value-based care. In teaching hospitals, lab utilization patterns are largely driven by interns, but attending oversight is frequently lacking, representing "a missed opportunity to reduce practice variation and improve patient care."[39]

- *Systems change:* Reengineering the process of care so that value-based care decisions are embedded into the workflow is perhaps one of the most powerful ways to promote value-based care and educate trainees in the process. Typically, this has been accomplished through the use of electronic health records and decision support, although less technological options are also possible. This could include making the prices of various tests available at the point-of-care, or enabling the prioritization of default options that are the highest value for a specific set of care options. For example, in a study aptly named "surgical vampires," the very low tech option of a weekly announcement to surgical residents and attending physicians on the charges of the prior week's laboratory services led to a reduction of over $50,000 costs in 11 weeks![40]

• *Training:* Beneath all of the efforts discussed above, a firm foundation of teaching and training to ensure mastery of principles and practices associated with value-based care must be in place. Education is likely necessary but insufficient to create lasting change. A recent systematic review of interventions to educate residents on cost-effectiveness demonstrated that most educational methods were didactic, and evaluation was limited.[41] Novel educational methods should also be employed that appeal to adult learners.

The "COST" framework is useful for educational as well as operational interventions, and will be revisited again in Chapter 16.

RESOURCES FOR MEDICAL EDUCATORS TO TEACH VALUE-BASED CARE

There are an increasing number of resources that can be used by medical educators to teach value-based care. For example, the Choosing Wisely Campaign, led by the ABIM Foundation, brought together an unprecedented number of medical specialty societies to issue their "top five" things "that physicians and patients should question" (available at www.choosingwisely.org; see also Chapter 5).[42] Many faculty report frequently downloading the lists to share with their trainees.[43] Likewise, the American College of Radiology has issued a set of Appropriateness Criteria that are designed to help clinicians decide on the most appropriate radiological tests for a certain condition (see also Chapter 14).[44]

Didactic education is also now available to educators free-of-charge. One notable curriculum is the ACP High-Value Care Curriculum.[45] The ACP and the Alliance for Academic Internal Medicine partnered together to produce a high-value care curriculum for internal medicine trainees, which has received over 17,000 downloads within the first 18 months of its release. The curriculum is case-based, available for free online (www.highvaluecarecurriculum.org), and designed to be used by a faculty champion to train their learners. In addition, an independent quality improvement project on high-value care led by the learners is encouraged and tools are provided.

The Teaching Value Project, which was funded by the ABIM Foundation and led by our Costs of Care team, is an online resource of video vignettes followed by interactive web-based modules that are designed to share fundamental principles of value-based care (www.teachingvalue.org).[46]

Drexel University College of Medicine, with funding from the ABIM Foundation, has created a series of interactive communication modules focusing on how to communicate Choosing Wisely recommendations from nine medical specialty societies to patients. The modules are available free-of-charge on the Choosing

Wisely website (www.choosingwisely.org) and include short video examples demonstrating effective physician-patient communication related to Choosing Wisely topics, in addition to pre- and post-tests to assess knowledge acquistion.[47] Another resource that medical educators may find helpful is actually designed primarily for patients: *Consumer Reports* houses a wealth of information on the "best buy" for certain drugs for various medical conditions (http://www.consumerreports.org/health/best-buy-drugs/index.htm) (see also Chapter 13).[48]

A groundswell of enthusiasm and efforts related to integrating high-value care into medical education has emerged across the country. To try to capture these local innovations and bright ideas, the Teaching Value and Choosing Wisely Challenge was launched by Costs of Care and sponsored by the ABIM Foundation.[35] From April 2013 to June 2013, bright ideas and innovations from medical educators were solicited to show how to best promote principles of stewardship among medical trainees. The results of the first annual challenge were quite robust and included 74 submissions from 14 specialties. Themes of the submissions reflected promising strategies to integrate and sustain high-value care teaching and practice into training programs. Several of the major themes are discussed in greater detail here.

Competition and gamification

Dr Robert Fogerty at Yale University used a friendly competition, the "Interactive Cost Awareness Exercise (I-CARE)," to inspire attendings, residents, interns, and students to incorporate cost-conscious thinking into solving a traditional morning report case. Evaluation of I-CARE has shown higher ratings than the traditional morning report and overall favorable reviews by both attendings and residents. Attending physicians had significantly lower costs ($1027.45 vs $4264.00, $p = .02$) and higher diagnostic accuracy than trainees.[49]

High-yield case vignettes

Through the "Do No Harm Project," developed at the University of Colorado, faculty work closely with trainees to identify and develop cases, protect a full day for writing time for trainees, and ultimately publish examples on the Web.[50] According to their website, the use of a traditional tool—clinical vignettes—provides a "potent way to humanize the harms of medical overuse and provide a persuasive counterbalance to the 'more is better' culture." This effort has been so successful that it was recently translated into a formal journal series called "Teachable Moments" in *JAMA Internal Medicine*.[51]

Linking didactic and experiential learning

Other submissions highlighted the importance of providing experiential learning that drives home the lessons of didactic teaching. A medical student at Tufts

School of Medicine extolled the benefits of spending a full day with the billing department in order to understand how the care she provides gets interpreted by medical coders.[35] Another medical student from University of Pennsylvania highlighted a new elective for medical students in which they are asked to compare a real patient's true cost of care to the ideal cost of care.[52]

Process improvement efforts

Several programs used quality improvement tools to drive change in this area, specifically by tackling areas of overuse. For example, Dr Valerie Ng, a lab medicine physician at Alameda County, California, has worked on "right sizing" medical tests through advocacy and working with clinicians to identify tests of low-value that should not be ordered.[53] Similarly, several trainees tackled specific projects that eschewed overuse of medical interventions. A resident at UCSF used quality improvement techniques to reduce the ordering of unnecessary liver ultrasounds for hepatitis C patients at San Francisco General Hospital.[35]

Coaching and role modeling

Just as the hidden curriculum highlights the power of observing role models' behavior, explicit role modeling can be used to infuse value-based care among trainees. One specific example is University of Toronto professor Dr Allan Detsky's "Celebrating Restraint" model in which he highlights that if we were to train faculty to specifically reward restraint, our trainees would get a very different message than the current implicit standards.[54] A unique University of Colorado program goes so far as to use one-on-one coaching to promote efficiency during a month-long elective hospital medicine rotation.[35]

Dr Gurpreet Dhaliwal, an influential clinician from the San Francisco Veterans Affairs Medical Center, notes that, "Attending physicians have a responsibility not only to talk the talk but also to walk the walk if we hope to help create a generation of physicians who come to understand that the best doctors are often defined by restraint rather than action."[55] He acknowledges that there are many remaining challenges and discomforts with this approach, particularly in the high-stakes atmosphere of teaching hospitals, but he also advises that he has "discarded one of the stock phrases for excessive testing: 'this is a teaching hospital.' I now think 'this is a teaching hospital—so we are *not* doing an unindicated test or treatment.'"[55]

Price transparency, feedback, and dashboards

Price transparency through electronic health records was a common theme of several submissions, potentially resulting in fewer ordering of low-value tests.[56] In addition, many submissions also tackled the idea of using specific feedback at the point-of-care, either through decision support or through apps that would let you know how much money has been spent in the workup during the first

48 hours of admission. A faculty member at Johns Hopkins University proposed providing trainees with dashboards that include utilization practices so to benchmark their practices against the institution and other trainees.

CONCLUSION

Although medical education on value-based care has traditionally been lacking and prior efforts have often failed to yield palpable results, current forces at play have made training in value-based care an imperative for tomorrow's health professions workforce. While trainees are faced with numerous barriers to implementing value-based care in their current practice, a myriad of educational strategies and methods can assist in embedding this new competency in the current education of health professionals. New educational frameworks and ideas from innovators can assist in rapid adoption of the most successful initiatives.

KEY POINTS:

- Medical educators have traditionally been relatively silent on issues related to healthcare costs and value, but more recently, multiple forces—from healthcare leaders to policies and regulations to professional groups—have called on educators to address this deficiency.
- The hidden curriculum in medical training, taught implicitly through the transmission of norms, values, and beliefs, plays a major role in ingraining medical practices, and must be adequately addressed to achieve high-value care.
- Successful education programs in clinical training environments should address multiple targets including culture, oversight, systems, and training ("COST").
- Many resources and inspirational examples are emerging for medical educators to teach high-value care in diverse settings and across the spectrum of health professional learners.

References:

1. Cooke M. Cost consciousness in patient care—what is medical education's responsibility? *N Engl J Med*. 2010;362(14):1253-1255.
2. ACGME Common Program Requirements. https://www.acgme.org/acgmeweb/Portals/0/PF Assets/ProgramRequirements/CPRs2013.pdf. Accessed March 29, 2014.
3. Weinberger SE. Providing high-value, cost-conscious care: a critical seventh general competency for physicians. *Ann Intern Med*. 2011;155(6):386-388.
4. Hiatt HH. Protecting the medical commons: who is responsible? *N Engl J Med*. 1975;293(5):235-241.
5. Schroeder SA, Myers LP, McPhee SJ, et al. The failure of physician education as a cost containment strategy. Report of a prospective controlled trial at a university hospital. *JAMA*. 1984;252(2):225-230.

6. Hackbarth G, Boccuti C. Transforming graduate medical education to improve health care value. *N Engl J Med*. 2011;364(8):693-695.

7. How are we preparing residents for the 21st century. http://www.medpac.gov/documents/Jul09_ResidencyPrograms_CONTRACTOR_CB.pdf.

8. Patel MS, Reed DA, Loertscher L, McDonald FS, Arora VM. Teaching residents to provide cost-conscious care: a national survey of residency program directors. *JAMA Intern Med*. 2014;174(3):470-472.

9. AAMC Graduation Questionnaire 2013. https://www.aamc.org/download/350998/data/2013gqallschoolssummaryreport.pdf. Accessed March 3, 2014.

10. Stern DT. *Measuring Medical Professionalism*. New York, NY: Oxford University Press; 2006.

11. Moriates C, Shah N, Arora VM. Medical training and expensive care. *Health Aff*. 2013;32(1):196-196.

12. Rosenbaum L, Lamas D. Cents and sensitivity—teaching physicians to think about costs. *N Engl J Med*. 2012;367(2):99-101.

13. Shah N. Top 10 Reasons Doctors Over-Order. CommonHealth. 2010. http://commonhealth.wbur.org/2010/09/top-ten-doctor-overorder. Accessed November 15, 2012.

14. Abbo ED, Volandes AE. Teaching residents to consider costs in medical decision making. *Am J Bioeth*. 2006;6(4):33-34.

15. Wilson IB, Dukes K, Greenfield S, Kaplan S, Hillman B. Patients' role in the use of radiology testing for common office practice complaints. *Arch Intern Med*. 2001;161(2):256-263.

16. Deyo RA, Diehl AK, Rosenthal M. Reducing roentgenography use. Can patient expectations be altered? *Arch Intern Med*. 1987;147(1):141-145.

17. CLER Pathways to Excellence. http://www.acgme.org/acgmeweb/Portals/0/PDFs/CLER/CLER_Brochure.pdf. Accessed on March 6, 2014.

18. Nasca TJ, Weiss KB, Bagian JP. Improving clinical learning environments for tomorrow's physicians. *N Engl J Med*. 2014;370(11):991-993.

19. Institute of Medicine. *Graduate Medical Education That Meets the Nation's Health Needs*. Washington, DC: National Academies Press; 2014.

20. Wilensky GR, Berwick DM. Reforming the financing and governance of GME. *N Engl J Med*. 2014;371(9):792-793.

21. Macy Foundation. Transforming Patient Care: Aligning Interprofessional Education with Clinical Practice Redesign. http://macyfoundation.org/docs/macy_pubs/TransformingPatientCare_ConferenceRec.pdf. Accessed on March 6, 2014.

22. Association of American Medical Colleges. Core Competencies for Interprofessional Collaborative Practice. 2011. https://www.aamc.org/download/186750/data/core_competencies.pdf. Accessed on March 6, 2014.

23. Kachalia A, Johnson JK, Miller S, Brennan T. The incorporation of patient safety into board certification examinations. *Acad Med*. 2006;81(4):317-325.

24. Marcotte L, Moriates C, Milstein A. Professional organizations' role in supporting physicians to improve value in health care. *JAMA*. 2014;312(3):231-232.

25. Zuger A. The real world is not an exam. *Well Blog, The New York Times*. Feb 10. 2014. http://well.blogs.nytimes.com/2014/02/10/the-real-worldis-not-an-exam/. Accessed February 16, 2014.

26. Rattinger GB, Jain R, Ju J, Mullins CD. Principles of economics crucial to pharmacy students' understanding of the prescription drug market. *Am J Pharm Educ*. 2008;72(3). http://www.ncbi.nlm.nih.gov/pmc/articles/PMC2508734/. Accessed April 5, 2014.

27. Kurtzman ET. A transparency and accountability framework for high-value inpatient nursing care. *Nurs Econ*. 2010;28(5):295-306.

28. Patel MS, Davis MM, Lypson ML. The VALUE Framework: training residents to provide value-based care for their patients. *J Gen Intern Med*. 2012;27(9):1210-1214.

29. Dine CJ, Miller J, Fuld A, Bellini LM, Iwashyna TJ. Educating physicians-in-training about resource utilization and their own outcomes of care in the inpatient setting. *J Grad Med Educ*. 2010;2(2):175-180.

30. Medical Education Community Collaborates with Khan Academy to Help Prepare Students for New MCAT® Exam. https://www.aamc.org/newsroom/newsreleases/332152/040213.html. Accessed on March 6, 2014.

31. IHI Open School. http://www.ihi.org/education/IHIOpenSchool/Courses/Pages/OSInTheCurriculum.aspx. Accessed on March 6, 2014.

32. Harder B. Are MOOCs the future of medical education? *BMJ*. 2013;346(2):f2666-f2666.

33. Involving Clinicians in Payment and Delivery Reform: The Role of Social Media and MOOCs. Brookings Institute. http://www.brookings.edu/events/2014/02/19-involving-clinicians-payment-delivery-reform. Accessed April 5, 2014.

34. #MedEd Healthcare Social Media Analytics. Symplur. http://www.symplur.com/healthcare-hashtags/MedEd/analytics/?hashtag=MedEd&fdate=10%2F17%2F2013&shour=18&smin=0&tdate=10%2F17%2F2013&thour=19&tmin=0&ssec=00&tsec=00&img=1. Accessed April 5, 2014.

35. Shah NT, Levy A, Moriates C, Arora VM. Wisdom of the crowd: bright ideas and innovations from the teaching value and Choosing Wisely competition. *Acad Med*. 2015 [in press].

36. Halvorson GC. KP inside: 101 Letters to the People of Kaiser Permanente. CreateSpace Independent Publishing Platform; 2012.

37. Boyles TH, Whitelaw A, Bamford C, et al. Antibiotic stewardship ward rounds and a dedicated prescription chart reduce antibiotic consumption and pharmacy costs without affecting inpatient mortality or re-admission rates. *PloS One*. 2013;8(12):e79747.

38. Fridkin S, Baggs J, Fagan R, et al. Vital signs: improving antibiotic use among hospitalized patients. *MMWR*. 2014;63(9):194-200.

39. Iwashyna TJ, Fuld A, Asch DA, Bellini LM. The impact of residents, interns, and attendings on inpatient laboratory ordering patterns: a report from one university's hospitalist service. *Acad Med*. 2011;86(1):139-145.

40. Stuebing EA, Miner TJ. Surgical vampires and rising health care expenditure: reducing the cost of daily phlebotomy. *Arch Surg*. 2011;146(5):524-527.

41. Varkey P, Murad MH, Braun C, Grall KJH, Saoji V. A review of cost-effectiveness, cost-containment and economics curricula in graduate medical education. *J Eval Clin Pract*. 2010;16(6):1055-1062.

42. Choosing Wisely. An Initiative of the ABIM Foundation. http://www.choosingwisely.org/. Accessed October 7, 2013.

43. Wolfson D. Teaching Choosing Wisely® in Medical Education and Training: The Story of a Pioneer. *The Medical Professionalism Blog*. http://blog.abimfoundation.org/teaching-choosing-wisely-in-meded/. Accessed March 29, 2014.

44. American College of Radiology. ACR Appropriateness Criteria Overview. 2013. http://www.acr.org/~/media/ACR/Documents/AppCriteria/Overview.pdf. Accessed March 4, 2014.

45. American College of Physicians. ACP High-Value Care Curriculum. 2013. http://hvc.acponline.org/curriculum_list.html. Accessed January 4, 2014.

46. Costs of Care, ABIM Foundation. Teaching Value Project. http://www.teachingvalue.org/. Accessed August 4, 2013.

47. Communication Modules. Choosing Wisely. http://www.choosingwisely.org/resources/modules/. Accessed March 29, 2014.

48. Consumer Health Choices. Consumer Reports Health. http://consumerhealthchoices.org/. Accessed July 7, 2013.

49. Fogerty RL, Heavner JJ, Moriarty JP, Sofair AN, Jenq G. Novel integration of systems-based practice into internal medicine residency programs: the Interactive Cost-Awareness Resident Exercise (I-CARE). *Teach Learn Med*. 2014;26(1):90-94.

50. The Do No Harm Project. Division of General Internal Medicine. University of Colorado Denver. http://www.ucdenver.edu/academics/colleges/medicalschool/departments/medicine/GIM/education/DoNoHarmProject/Pages/Welcome.aspx. Accessed February 5, 2013.

51. Caverly TJ, Combs BP, Moriates C, Shah N, Grady D. Too much medicine happens too often: the teachable moment and a call for manuscripts from clinical trainees. *JAMA Intern Med.* 2014;174(1):8-9.

52. Penn Med Student Recognized for "Bright Idea" in Education. http://www.uphs.upenn.edu/news/News_Releases/2013/10/daughtridge/. Accessed March 6, 2014.

53. May TA, Clancy M, Critchfield J, et al. Reducing unnecessary inpatient laboratory testing in a teaching hospital. *Am J Clin Pathol.* 2006;126(2):200-206.

54. Detsky AS, Verma AA. A new model for medical education: celebrating restraint. *JAMA.* 2012;308(13):1329-1330.

55. Dhaliwal G. Bringing high-value care to the inpatient teaching service. *JAMA Intern Med.* 2014;174(7):1021-1022.

56. Feldman LS, Shihab HM, Thiemann D, et al. Impact of providing fee data on laboratory test ordering: a controlled clinical trial. *JAMA Intern Med.* 2013;173(10):903-908.

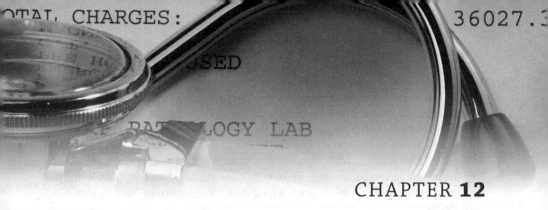

CHAPTER **12**

The Role of Patients: Shared Decision Making, e-Patients, and Consumer-Directed Healthcare

The [first doctor] never asked me what I wanted. He did not mention my needs or treatment goals. He did not know—or seem to care—that my hope was to extend my quality time on this planet rather than merely linger. He did not care about the toll of the treatments on my body and my remaining days …

Thank goodness my [second doctor] was not like that specialist. Instead of ignoring my wishes and goals, my doctor was embracing them and keeping me as informed as possible. She'd discussed the diagnosis, prognosis, and possible treatments, and she'd asked me about how I wanted to proceed. Together, the two of us chose a treatment regimen that would slow tumor growth, while protecting what was precious to me: my quality of life. Too many other patients have doctors like that [first] specialist. A cancer-survivor friend told me that her oncologist once said, "I wish I could just treat the cancer; patients get in the way." Another friend, with stage IV cancer, was advised by her oncologist to skip a three-hour car ride to visit her new granddaughter because she'd miss a chemo appointment— one that would do nothing to change the fatal nature of her advanced disease.

—*Amy Berman, RN*[1]

The gap between the way many patients wish healthcare decisions could be made and the way these decisions are actually made is tremendous. According to a 2014 survey conducted by the Altarum Institute, nearly all patients expect to be in control of medical decisions. Only 7% of adult, nonelderly patients wanted their physicians to be in the lead role.[2] Despite this clear preference, the same survey found that the vast majority of patients let the doctor take charge of care decisions nonetheless.

Among the many complex factors that go into medical decision making, there is a widespread perception that the values of patients often get pushed to the bottom. *Patient experience* (a term that is increasingly replacing the more narrow term *patient satisfaction*) is a core component of delivering value-based care. As we have mentioned many times in this book, defining value as a ratio of physical outcomes to costs is too simplistic. At the end of the day, care that improves some health outcomes while ignoring a patient's treatment goals or putting her through a miserable experience may not be worth it. And yet, meaningfully involving patients in our decisions is a goal that continues to frequently evade our profession.

There are surely many reasons for this, but Dr Alvan Feinstein, a Yale physician credited with helping to start the field of clinical epidemiology, hit the nail on the head when he pointed out the great irony of what clinicians often consider "hard" vs "soft" data: "A doctor's observation of whether the patient has tenderness in a knee is regarded as objective and is therefore 'harder' than the patient's report of the pain experienced when he walks."[3] These words may ring as true in 2014 as they did in the early 1960s when they were first articulated. In the clinical world, directly observed data continues to take precedence over more subjective, but equally important reports of patient experience.

As online health information empowers patients to make informed choices, the paternalistic clinician-patient relationship that was once widely accepted is being increasingly called into question, and in many cases is falling away entirely toward a more collaborative relationship (Table 12-1). Clearly, the best care

Table 12-1 Patient-physician interactions

Model for Patient-Physician Interaction	Physicians' Role	Patients' Role	Knowledge "Flow"	Objective
Paternalistic	Directive	Passive	One-way knowledge transfer (physician to patient)	Compliance of patient to physicians' directive
Autonomous	Receptive	Directive	One-way knowledge transfer (patient to physician)	Compliance of physician to patients' directive
Shared decision making	Informative	Informative	Two-way knowledge exchange	Equity in the decision making process
Collaborative decision making	Supportive	Proactive	Knowledge building that goes beyond clinical issues (Shared learning by exchanging information)	Optimal action plan to improve health

Source: Reproduced, with permission, from O'Grady L, Jadad A. Shifting from shared to collaborative decision making: a change in thinking and doing. *J Participat Med.* 2010 Nov 8;2:e13.

results when informed patients and knowledgeable clinicians work together and are on the same page. A recent study demonstrated that there is a significant difference between merely telling patients information explicitly, and actually explaining clinical reasoning. Many patients mistakenly believe that a procedure called percutaneous coronary intervention (PCI) will prevent a myocardial infarction (MI or "heart attack"). Researchers at the Cleveland Clinic and the University of Michigan tested patients beliefs after they received "no information," "explicit information" (simply told that PCI does not prevent MI), and "explanatory information" (detailed explanation of why PCI does not prevent MI).[4] Perhaps, not surprisingly, patients who received explanatory information were significantly less likely to choose PCI and significantly more likely to instead choose a more optimal medical therapy for their care (Figure 12-1).

In this chapter, we describe efforts to enable better *"shared decision making"* and discuss what the rise of the empowered *"e-patient"* may mean for modern healthcare delivery. We briefly review the promise and pitfalls of consumer-directed health plans. Lastly, we examine emerging efforts to better measure and report patient experiences, both to inform value-based care and to create necessary accountability.

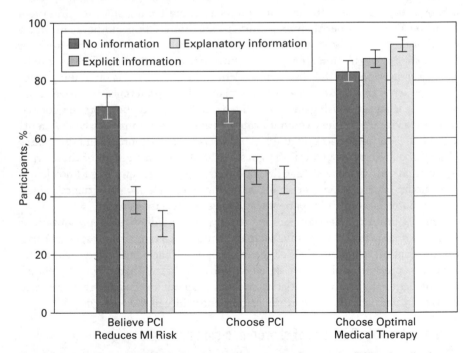

Figure 12-1. Patient beliefs concerning percutaneous coronary intervention (PCI) and medication. (Reproduced, with permission, from Rothberg MB, Scherer L, Kashef MA, et al. The effect of information presentation on beliefs about the benefits of elective percutaneous coronary intervention. *JAMA Intern Med.* 2014;174(10):1623-1629. Copyright © 2014 American Medical Association. All rights reserved.)

SHARED DECISION MAKING

The term "shared decision making" (SDM) has been used for decades, though not everyone who invokes this term is talking about the same thing. SDM was first introduced into the clinical lexicon by the 1982 President's Commission for the Study of Ethical Problems in Medicine and Biomedical and Behavioral Research.[5] As it turns out, since that time there have been at least 342 articles published on SDM, many of them using different definitions. Most notably, the concepts of patient values and options appeared in only half of the definitions. Dartmouth Professor Glyn Elwyn and his colleagues nicely sum up the modern intention of SDM thusly: "an approach where clinicians and patients share the best available evidence when faced with the task of making decisions, and where patients are supported to consider options, to achieve informed preferences."[6]

One way to promote SDM is through the use of tools called "decision aids," which can be used by patients to communicate to clinicians about their preferences for treatment options. Decision aids come in many complementary formats, including by paper, web, or video.[7] Some clinicians utilize multiple formats at once. A routine use of SDM is to guide expectant mothers on the use of prenatal screening tests that can uncover genetic problems such as Down syndrome before a baby is born. Some mothers would prefer to avoid testing since few interventions are available other than pregnancy termination. Other mothers absolutely feel that they need to know. And some are unsure whether they want to know or not. Complicating matters, the information from these tests (like all tests) can be equivocal or imprecise. The Dartmouth Center for Shared Decision Making helps guide patients through these and other challenging, "preference-sensitive" decisions (see Chapter 7) using an online video and companion booklet. The booklet contains a visual aid to help communicate risk and a questionnaire to help patients articulate their preferences (Figure 12-2). The Dartmouth Center maintains a large library of decision aids on over 30 topics.[8] A 2009 Cochrane review of these types of decision aids concluded that decision aids can lead to improved knowledge, more accurate perceptions of risk, decisions more consistent with patients' values, reduced internal conflict for patients, and fewer undecided patients.[9]

The design of the decision aid is critically important. Visual representations such as icon arrays and bar graphs seem to be most effective for conveying statistical information to patients.[10] The type of statistics to include also requires careful thought—presenting absolute risk reductions is far better than reporting relative risk reductions, and some statistics such as "number needed to treat" seem to overly confuse patients and may undermine the utility of the decision aid.[10]

Evidence and applications of shared decision making

Studies of SDM interventions have demonstrated improved care, including greater patient satisfaction.[11] A randomized controlled trial recently published in *Health Affairs* compared patients who received enhanced support (phone coaching

Most testing labs will report a specific risk for each condition. For example, a 1 in 10 risk means that for every 10 women who have this result, one will have a child with the condition, while the other nine will not.

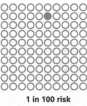

1 in 10 risk

Similarly, a 1 in 100 risk means that for every 100 women who have this result, one will have a child with the condition, while the other 99 will not.

1 in 100 risk

1. Am I prepared to deal with the worry that I may feel if I have a positive screening result?

   ☐ Yes   ☐ No   ☐ I'm not sure

2. If I have a positive screening result, would I consider having a CVS or amniocentesis to get a definite answer? (Remember: CVS and amniocentesis both have a risk of miscarriage)

   ☐ Yes   ☐ No   ☐ I'm not sure

3. Would I consider terminating my pregnancy if I find out that my baby definitely has Down syndrome, trisomy 18, or a neural tube defect?

   ☐ Yes   ☐ No   ☐ I'm not sure

4. If I decide to continue my pregnancy, would knowing that my baby has one of these conditions help me to prepare for his or her birth?

   ☐ Yes   ☐ No   ☐ I'm not sure

5. If I decide to continue my pregnancy, would I want to have time during my pregnancy to consider an adoption plan?

   ☐ Yes   ☐ No   ☐ I'm not sure

6. Would I rather find out after my baby's birth if he or she has one of these conditions?

   ☐ Yes   ☐ No   ☐ I'm not sure

Figure 12-2. A sample decision aid. (Adapted, with permission, from *Prenatal Screening: Is It Right For You?* Copyright © 2013 Dartmouth-Hitchcock, Lebanon, NH.)

with decision aids) during decision making for preference-sensitive decisions to those who did not. SDM resulted in lower overall medical costs, lower hospital admissions, and fewer preference-sensitive surgeries than patients who received usual care.[12] The introduction of a decision aid for hip and knee osteoarthritis at Group Health Cooperative (a nonprofit health system in Seattle, Washington) was associated with lower costs (12%-21%), largely due to fewer patients opting to undergo surgery once they were fully informed about the trade-offs.[13] Based on these and other emerging studies, it has been estimated that use of SDM for just 11 procedures nationwide could save $9 billion in 10 years.[14]

Given the promise of SDM to improve value, the Maine Health Management Coalition (a multi-stakeholder collaborative led by big employers and other large healthcare "purchasers") has proposed placing healthcare services into three tiers according to a traffic stoplight scheme: "green" services are evidence-based with a high healthcare return on investment, "yellow" services are preference-sensitive and require decision support (perhaps in the form of an SDM tool), and "red" services are supply-sensitive with little or no evidence to support their use (Figure 12-3). Yellow services are actively paired with decision aids, often embedded directly into the electronic medical record or the clinician's order-entry system, and integrated into value-based health insurance benefit designs. As a

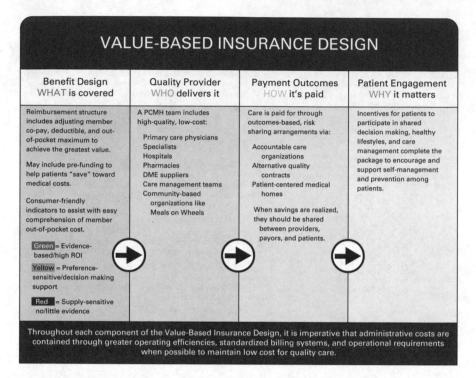

Figure 12-3. Value-based insurance design and patient engagement. (Reproduced, with permission, from Maine Health Management Coalition.)

result, SDM is now a major component of an ambitious plan to reduce healthcare costs while improving value in the state of Maine.

Although purchasers and other stakeholders have great interest in SDM, clinicians are often concerned about the extra work it can involve. Few of us are clamoring for more to do. In fact, a systematic review demonstrated that the most common barrier to adoption of SDM was time constraints.[15] Some decision aids are also obviously better than others—in the same study clinicians cited a lack of applicability due to characteristics of either the patient or the clinical situation. Despite the benefits to patients, these barriers are considerable and not easy to surmount. A 2010 Cochrane review found little evidence of effective ways to engage clinicians to adopt SDM and noted that further study of SDM is warranted.[16]

The Affordable Care Act (ACA) encourages greater use of SDM in healthcare. According to Section 3506 of the ACA, an independent entity to develop standards and certify patient decision aids will be funded. In addition, the Center for Medicare and Medicaid Innovation has been authorized to evaluate models of SDM on relevant outcomes.[14] Furthermore, the ACA authorized the creation of the Patient Centered Outcomes Research Institute (PCORI), which enables funding of research related to SDM involving patient stakeholders as part of its patient-centered research priorities.[17]

HISTORY OF THE E-PATIENT MOVEMENT

While SDM represents one way to bridge the gap between patient preferences and clinical decisions, the rise of the e-patient movement represents a parallel trend toward greater patient involvement in decisions regarding care. Although it is often assumed that "e-patients" refer to patients who access healthcare information electronically, the term was originally coined by physician author Tom Ferguson in reference to patients who are "equipped, enabled, empowered and engaged in their health and health care decisions."[18] His initial efforts led to the formation of the Society of Participatory Medicine, which is a professional organization that many e-patients are affiliated with. In addition to the characteristics outlined by Ferguson, a recent study of e-patients identified two more qualities[19]:

- *Evaluating:* Evaluating encompasses how e-patients find information, and critically assess the source of that information (ie, Web page vs healthcare professional), determining which sources are most trustworthy based on their assessment.
- *Equal:* E-patients expect to be equal members of the healthcare team. If clinicians or the healthcare system does not support this premise, e-patients will make an effort to position themselves to assert equal power, but without the open and honest relationship that is also valued.

Difference between empowered patients and e-patients

"Patient empowerment" refers to patients who are able to "take charge of their health and their interactions with health care professionals."[20] Patients can be empowered in a context-specific way. For example, during the doctor visit, empowered patients may ask questions such as "Why?" to engage in a constructive dialogue and express their opinions. In contrast, e-patients will likely look up their condition to ask informed questions and could even propose their own treatment plans based on what they have read. Given the increasing ubiquity of credible health information online, the term "e-patient" is often colloquially used to refer to those who are most technology savvy and engaged in digital health (also referred to as an "internet patient").[21]

Profiles of well-known e-patients

- E-PATIENT DAVE deBronkart was diagnosed with advanced kidney cancer in 2007. As a result of his illness, he started on his journey toward empowerment, often employing technology, and "participatory medicine" to beat the odds.[22] Because of his background in marketing and data analysis, upon receiving his diagnosis, he began doing his own research and connecting with other patient communities online. These online discussions informed his decision to work with his physician to try laparoscopic removal of his cancer followed by participation in a clinical trial using immunotherapy, which eventually resulted in complete cure. He kept an active blog chronicling his treatments and recovery.[23] After learning about Tom Ferguson's definition of e-patients using technology to advance their care, he joined the e-patient movement as "e-Patient Dave" and became a founding cochair of the Society for Participatory Medicine. He is now an international spokesman for the e-patient movement and author of *Let Patients Help: A Patient Engagement Handbook*.[24] He has had a major impact on discussions on how to improve data transparency for patients, particularly highlighting the inaccuracies of billing data, and has also helped define meaningful use standards to include patient access to records.[25]

- JESSIE GRUMAN was a three-time cancer patient who drew upon her own experience battling Hodgkin disease, cervical cancer, and colorectal cancer to lead the Center for Advancing Health, a Washington-based policy nonprofit that focuses on patient engagement.[26] As a PhD in social psychology, she built on her experience, as well as conducted structured interviews with over 200 others who have received devastating diagnoses, to author *AfterShock: What To Do When the Doctor Gives You—Or Someone You Love—A Devastating Diagnosis*, which offers patients a 10-step approach to make informed decisions.[27] Gruman served on numerous boards and advisory panels, including as an Advisory Panel member on Medicare Education for the Centers for Medicare and Medicaid Services of the US Department of Health and Human Services.

- REGINA HOLLIDAY became a patient advocate through caring for her husband who was suffering from metastatic kidney cancer. Regina's husband ultimately died at age 39 as a result of his cancer in June 2009. She had requested to see his medical records upon transferring him from one hospital to another, but was told that she would have to pay 73 cents a page and wait 21 days, which her husband did not have at that time.[28] Inspired by her husband's challenge to "Go after them," Regina used her talent as an artist to paint a mural telling the story of her husband's ordeal upon his passing. Her artwork shows intricate details such as the patient unable to see his record, a clock with no hands representing no sense of urgency in healthcare, and a doctor with his hands tied because he was unable to take action. She also subsequently conceived and created the "The Walking Gallery," a collection of murals and painted jackets that people wear in which the painting highlights a specific issue or story related to healthcare. As a result of her artwork, she is now recognized as a voice for patients in making health records transparent and immediately available.[29] In addition, her advocacy efforts have attracted national media attention, which has also led to her being likened to the "Rosa Parks of Healthcare."[30]

Reactions to e-patients

While the e-patient movement has given patients a voice in healthcare discussions that they were previously absent from, reactions to e-patients from clinicians have not been universally welcoming. Ultimately, for e-patients to successfully advocate for their preferences, clinicians have to be willing to listen and respond. In some cases, resistance to e-patients is buoyed by an archetypal patient who may not have reasonable or well-informed demands.

Many physicians are not excited when patients present them with information they found on the Internet. In one study, physicians felt unprepared to respond to questions regarding Internet information, and often felt this placed

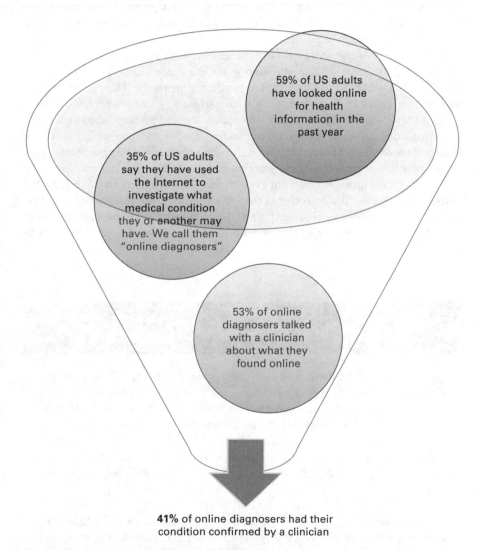

Figure 12-4. Internet as a diagnostic tool. (Original figure, using data from Pew Research, data obtained from http://www.pewinternet.org/2013/10/10/e-patients-and-their-hunt-for-health-information/.)

additional responsibility on them to clarify the information.[31] Physicians perceived Internet information led to confusion, distress, and could result in potential harms through self-diagnosis or self-treatment. It has even been suggested that clinicians "employ disciplinary strategies" to enforce traditional patient roles and further alienate patients who use the Internet.[32] This bias is readily apparent to patients as well. Although the majority of patients now use the Internet as a primary source of health information (Figure 12-4), one study found that patients are reluctant to bring up the information that they have found on the Internet with their physicians for fear of being perceived as "problem patients" or overstepping bounds.[32]

In addition to resistant clinicians, others in healthcare are quick to point out the "digital divide" that exists among patients. For example, e-patients by definition are technology savvy, which limits the generalizability of their perceptions for those that are not facile with technology or face certain barriers such as literacy and reading. A second concern related to some e-patients and patient advocacy groups arises from growing corporate sponsorship and the potential for conflicts of interest. Often, funding sources are not made transparent on websites of patient advocacy organizations—those directly sponsored by pharmaceutical companies may not even include the company name or logo.[33,34] Lastly, even e-patients acknowledge that like their health professional counterparts, they are unable to represent all patients through a single voice and it is important to consider an e-patient's voice more like an "n of 1" trial, on a case-by-case basis.[35]

Story From the Frontlines: Is That Really Necessary?

A close encounter with a jungle rock while mountain biking sent my husband back to our cruise ship with a deep gash on his shin. Our ship's doctor cleaned it, stitched it and sent him to our room with antibiotic cream. Two days later, with red streaks around the wound and swelling puffing up around his stitches, his foot and ankle looked like a balloon with toes. A day of oral antibiotics followed by a few rounds of IV antibiotics on the ship got us to the end of the cruise and back to the states, but things still looked bad.

Landing near midnight, we headed straight for the ER for a dose of American medicine. Efficient service quickly led to a very pleasant doctor assessing the situation.

"Yes" she said, "That's definitely infected. Let's start by getting an ultrasound."

"Why," we asked, "would we get an ultrasound?"

She replied that we had just taken a long plane ride and it could be a blood clot.

We said, "It looked exactly like this before we got on the plane. We have a $5000 deductible and really would prefer not to spend $300-400 for an ultrasound if it can be avoided." She said, "I'm sure it would cost a lot more than that!" and agreed that we could proceed without it.

Then she said, "Well, let's get him admitted." We asked why he needed to be admitted since they could clean up the wound and get him an IV antibiotic right there in the ER. She said they would watch him overnight to make sure he was doing all right. Having some idea of exactly how much he would be watched after midnight on a weekend, we suggested that since we lived 10 minutes away I would watch him and rush him back if things went south. She agreed that we seemed like responsible people who could be trusted to come back if necessary. The next step was to remove the stitches and clean the wound. This was going to be quite painful and the doctor said they had a new pain med that works really well. Then, finally catching on, she looked back and said, "On second thought, we can just add some morphine to his IV. That will work and it's a lot less expensive."

An hour later, armed with four prescriptions we headed home. We filled the oral antibiotic ($16 at a local pharmacy) but skipped the antibiotic ointment (we already had this from the boat) and the Vicodin and Naproxyn since over-the-counter ibuprofen was managing the pain just fine. The wound slowly healed and all is well with the injury, but certainly not with our healthcare system. We got great customer service, but how many thousands of dollars would have been spent on this one event absent a few probing questions? Yet how many patients have the background and temperament to ask challenging questions, especially in the midst of a health crisis? Certainly, for the doctor all the incentives point in the direction of more care. A well-intentioned desire to be thorough combines with fear of malpractice and the fee for service system where erring on the side of doing more results in greater revenues for the care providers.

Patients can't solve this, even if they are armed with "skin in the game" and a handful of quality and cost measures. It has to be treating physicians and their teams who consider and discuss with patients the cost/value tradeoffs of their care recommendations. I believe most doctors would be sincerely concerned about the implications their recommendations have on their patients' financial health if they really understood what these expenditures meant to them. Hopefully, this particular ER doc now has an altered perspective.

—Ann Rabinow. "Is That Really Necessary."
Costs of Care, 2014. (www.costsofcare.org)

CONSUMER-DIRECTED HEALTHCARE

Consumer-directed healthcare plans "refer to insurance that provides financial incentives for consumers to become involved in purchasing decisions regarding their health care."[36] They have been proposed as a way to control health spending by having patients assume greater control and risk over how they choose to spend their funds on healthcare.[37] Proponents of consumer-directed healthcare argue that healthcare spending has not been curbed because normal market forces that control costs and improve quality do not exist since patients do not have enough "skin in the game." Therefore, by giving patients more responsibility and control over choosing healthcare, patients will be in the best position to choose healthcare services that maximize quality and minimize cost.

A major component of consumer-directed healthcare is healthcare savings accounts (see Chapter 2), which provide patients with the option of paying directly for healthcare services from pretax income. The Medicare Prescription Drug, Improvement, and Modernization Act in 2003 facilitated creation of Health Savings Accounts through tax incentives for those who had high-deductible health plans. With the passage of the ACA, the increasing focus on high-deductible plans made consumer-directed healthcare more popular as a way to expand insurance while also controlling costs. Indeed, compared to patients in traditional healthcare plans, patients in a consumer-directed healthcare plan do seem more likely to ask about cost and choose a less expensive treatment option.[37]

However, this impulse can go too far. One critique of consumer-driven health plans is that they incentivize patients to forgo valuable care, particularly for those with low income or low health literacy.[38] For example, because of out-of-pocket costs, these vulnerable patients sometimes delay seeking care to the point of harm. Jonathan Oberlander, a political scientist at the University of North Carolina, Chapel Hill, has stated "Consumer-driven health care is badly named, because it's certainly not driven by consumers."[39] Another critique concerns the availability of accurate and actionable information to help guide patients in making value-based decisions. As we discussed in Chapter 3, patients are rarely able to access transparent quality and price information, though a variety of public and private solutions to this problem are emerging.

HealthcareBlueBook.com provides searchable, "fair market" cash prices for tests, procedures, visits, and a variety of other healthcare services. The website also enables patients to look at data by zip code to get the nearest "best buy."[40] Fairhealth.org was originally funded by insurance companies as a result of a New York State legal investigation into how healthcare insurance determined out-of-network reimbursement.[41,42] It is now a third party independent database of doctors' fees that aims to increase price transparency for the public. Castlighthealth.com contracts with employers to give their employees access to prices of healthcare services. It quickly made waves as its initial public offering resulted in a rush of investors and a valuation of more than $3 billion, highlighting the interest in healthcare price transparency for large businesses who insure employees and other major healthcare purchasers.[43]

Of course, price is only one component of the big picture. Many websites also aim to provide patients with information on healthcare quality as well as patient experiences. In fact, today when you search for a physician by name on Google, Bing, or other search engines, their professional Web page is typically buried underneath a slew of physician-rating sites. In addition, several organizations rate quality of care at the hospital or delivery system level, including the Leapfrog Group and the Consumer Union (publisher of *Consumer Reports*).

MEASURING AND REPORTING PATIENT EXPERIENCE

Increasingly, patient experience is being viewed as a critical component of measuring and reporting quality of care. While some believe this may be a passing fad, Harvard Medical School Professor Dr Thomas Lee has argued, "measurement of what matters to patients is here to stay" (Dr Lee also currently serves as Chief Medical Officer of a private company called Press Ganey that profits from developing instruments that measure patient experience).[44] He goes on to explain how "patient experience" is different from the "patient satisfaction" surveys that have been used by health systems for decades. The idea is not to measure amenities, like food and parking. Instead the intention is to track data such as patients' confidence in their clinicians (as measured by their likelihood of recommending hospitals or doctors to family/friends), perceptions of care coordination, and whether they feel their clinicians are listening to their concerns.

Until recently, hospitals collected patient information individually but there was no national standard that allowed valid comparisons to be made between clinicians and provider organizations. In 2002, two federal agencies (the Center for Medicare and Medicaid Services and the Agency for Healthcare Research and Quality) partnered to develop and test the Hospital Consumer Assessment of Healthcare Providers and Systems or HCAHPS.[45] The result was a 32-item survey and data collection methodology that is now widely used to allow meaningful comparisons of hospitals, create incentives for hospitals to improve quality of care, and enhance public accountability of hospitals for delivering quality. The survey is typically administered to a random sample of patients who were recently discharged from the hospital and asks questions similar to those highlighted by Dr Lee: how well doctors and nurses communicate with patients, how well hospital staff help patients manage pain, and whether key information is provided at discharge. Since 2008, results from the survey have been publically reported—10 of the HCAHPS measures are formatted on the Medicare *Hospital Compare* website (www.medicare.gov/hospitalcompare), allowing consumers or other interested parties to quickly review patient experience data (Figure 12-5).

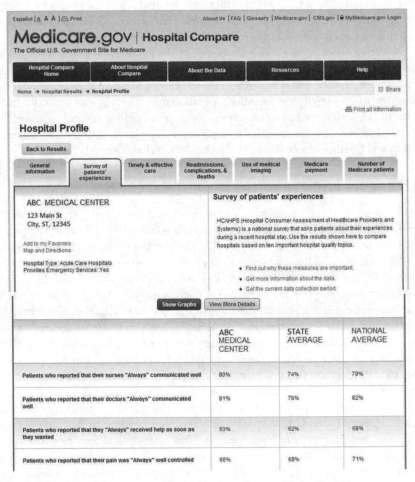

Figure 12-5. Medicare's hospital compare website and patient experience. (Screenshot from Medicare.gov.)

Patient-reported measures: linking patient experience and value

Recently, the link between HCAHPS measures and value was made explicit. The Medicare Hospital Value-Based Purchasing program links hospital payments to performance on a set of quality measures (see also Chapter 15). In 2014, patient experience of care (derived from HCAHPS) now comprises 30% of the total score determining these payments.[45] While this represents a bold step, it may just be the beginning. The growing use of *patient-reported measures* (PRMs, or sometimes patient-reported outcome measures) enhances the possibilities for both driving accountability and delivering value.

While surveys like HCAHPS ask general questions after care has been received ("Did you understand how to take your medications?"), PRMs ask very specific questions about a patient's condition at multiple intervals over the course of treatment. For a patient in need of a hip replacement, relevant questions might include, "How much pain do you have?" or "Are you able to climb stairs?" The same questions are ideally asked both before and after surgery. Patients considering surgery can then compare their own responses to others in order to decide if the surgery is right for them. The same questions would also ideally be asked at several intervals postoperatively (3 months, 6 months, 9 months, etc) to make sure the healthcare system is truly delivering the functional improvements that the patient originally sought out.

Of course PRMs and other types of patient experience data are not easy to collect. With PRMs in particular, the need to collect and track individual patient data can be burdensome and time consuming. It also means that healthcare organizations need to stay in touch with patients longer than they usually do currently (though the general drive toward population health management, as we have discussed in Chapters 4 and 9, may change this). According to Institute for Healthcare Improvement Vice President Kathy Luther, some groups like single orthopedic practices are testing PRMs using pencil and paper while others have more sophisticated "patient portals."[46] Including PRMs in clinical workflow, perhaps through integration into electronic health record (EHR) systems will be key to making them pragmatic. The US Department of Health and Human Services has already taken steps to ensure this by including PRMs as part of a program called "Meaningful Use" that provides healthcare delivery organizations with incentive payments for complying with best practices for EHRs.[47]

An additional challenge will be creating PRMs that are meaningful for all of the conditions that we care for as clinicians and interpreting PRMs in the context of the multiple simultaneous conditions that so many of our patients have. To date, some of the best-developed and studied PRMs relate to joint replacements. The federally funded FORCE-TJR Project, led by Dr David Ayers from the University of Massachusetts, is prospectively tracking PRMs for 30,000 patients who have undergone joint replacement surgery over the course of several years.[48] Early data from this effort has already brought valuable insight into the optimal timing to undergo surgery—interestingly, while most patients benefit from surgery significantly, those who wait the longest and are most disabled prior to surgery do not seem to benefit at all.[49]

In the years to come, more and more research dollars will be directed toward developing PRMs. We have already mentioned PCORI, a new federal funding agency created by the ACA. Another large organization, the International Consortium for Health Outcomes Measurement (ICHOM), founded by Harvard Business School, the Boston Consulting Group, and the Karolinska Institute, is developing standard patient outcome measure sets for conditions ranging from coronary artery disease to prostate cancer.[50] Ultimately, we agree with Dr Lee. Measurement of patient experience is critical to delivering value-based care and it is clearly here to stay.

CONCLUSION

As patients become more involved in healthcare, movements that empower and enable patients to participate in healthcare decision making and costs of care are emerging. Through increased emphasis on SDM, the rise of the "e-patient," and the emergence of consumer-driven healthcare, patients are being asked to take a greater responsibility for interfacing with the healthcare system to ensure high-quality and high-value care. At the same time, delivery organizations are being asked to take greater responsibility for measuring and reporting patient experience.

KEY POINTS:

- Shared decision making (SDM) is a potential tool to empower patients to take a more active role in their care by articulating their preferences of care, which can be one way to improve value of care.
- e-Patients represent activated, engaged patients who are savvy with technology and able to advocate effectively for care. The emergence of e-patients highlights the need for clinicians to effectively partner with patients.
- Efforts to provide patients with greater responsibility of their healthcare spending, through consumer-directed health plans, have become progressively popular as a potential way to promote costs savings.
- Measuring patient experience is an increasingly recognized component of delivering value-based care.

References:

1. Berman A. Living life in my own way—and dying that way as well. *Health Aff.* 2012;31(4):871-874.
2. Lynch W, Perosino K, Stover M. Altarum Institute Survey of Consumer Health Care Opinions. Accessed June 7, 2014. http://altarum.org/sites/default/files/uploaded-related-files/Spring_2014_Survey_of_Consumer_Health_Care_Opinions.pdf.
3. Katz J. Professor, Harvard School of Public Health and former mentee of Dr. Alvan Feinstein. 2014.
4. Rothberg MB, Scherer L, Kashef M, et al. The effect of information presentation on beliefs about the benefits of elective percutaneous coronary intervention. *JAMA Intern Med.* 2014;174(10): 1623-1629.
5. Institute of Medicine. Making health care decisions. https://repository.library.georgetown.edu/bitstream/handle/10822/559354/making_health_care_decisions.pdf?sequence=1. Accessed June 7, 2014.
6. Elwyn G, Laitner S, Coulter A, Walker E, Watson P, Thomson R. Implementing shared decision making in the NHS. *BMJ.* 2010;341:c5146.
7. Barry MJ, Edgman-Levitan S. Shared decision making—pinnacle of patient-centered care. *N Engl J Med.* 2012;366(9):780-781.
8. Decision Aid Library. Center for Shared Decision Making. Dartmouth-Hitchcock. http://patients.dartmouth-hitchcock.org/shared_decision_making/decision_aid_library.html. Accessed June 19, 2014.
9. Stacey D, Bennett CL, Barry MJ, et al. Decision aids for people facing health treatment or screening decisions. *Cochrane Database Syst Rev.* 2011;(10):CD001431.
10. Zipkin DA, Umscheid CA, Keating NL, et al. Evidence-based risk communication: a systematic review. *Ann Intern Med.* 2014;161(4):270-280.
11. Walsh T, Barr PJ, Thompson R, Ozanne E, O'Neill C, Elwyn G. Undetermined impact of patient decision support interventions on healthcare costs and savings: systematic review. *BMJ.* 2014;348:g188.
12. Veroff D, Marr A, Wennberg DE. Enhanced support for shared decision making reduced costs of care for patients with preference-sensitive conditions. *Health Aff.* 2013;32(2):285-293.
13. Arterburn D, Wellman R, Westbrook E, et al. Introducing decision aids at Group Health was linked to sharply lower hip and knee surgery rates and costs. *Health Aff.* 2012;31(9):2094-2104.
14. Oshima Lee E, Emanuel EJ. Shared decision making to improve care and reduce costs. *N Engl J Med.* 2013;368(1):6-8.
15. Gravel K, Légaré F, Graham ID. Barriers and facilitators to implementing shared decision-making in clinical practice: a systematic review of health professionals' perceptions. *Implement Sci.* 2006;1:16.
16. Légaré F, Ratté S, Stacey D, et al. Interventions for improving the adoption of shared decision making by healthcare professionals. *Cochrane Database Syst Rev.* 2010;(5):CD006732.
17. Caramenico A. Patient-centered care, shared decision-making gets $30M in funding. *FierceHealthcare.* http://www.fiercehealthcare.com/story/patient-centered-care-shared-decision-making-gets-30m-funding/2012-06-19. Accessed May 19, 2014.
18. About E-Patients. http://e-patients.net/about-e-patientsnet. Accessed June 1,2014.
19. Hewitt-Taylor J, Bond CS. What e-patients want from the doctor-patient relationship: content analysis of posts on discussion boards. *J Med Internet Res.* 2012;14(6):e155.
20. Roberts KJ. Patient empowerment in the United States: a critical commentary. Health Expect. *Int J Public Particip. Health Care Health Policy.* 1999;2(2):82-92.
21. E-patient. Wikipedia Free Encycl. 2014. http://en.wikipedia.org/w/index.php?title=E-patient&oldid=607524527. Accessed May 14, 2014.
22. Cooney E. The excellent patient. *Boston Globe,* May 18, 2009. *Boston.com.* http://www.boston.com/news/health/articles/2009/05/18/the_excellent_patient/. Accessed June 7, 2014.
23. deBronkart D. My cancer story—short version. New life e-patient Dave 2008. http://patientdave.blogspot.com/2008/06/my-cancer-story-short-version.html. Accessed June 7, 2014.

24. deBronkart D, Sands DD. *Let Patients Help!* Lexington: CreateSpace Independent Publishing Platform; 2013.

25. Versel N. Ease of patient access, privacy called central to "user-friendly" EMRs. *FierceEMR.* http://www.fierceemr.com/story/ease-patient-access-privacy-called-central-user-friendly-emrs/2009-06-18. Accessed June 7, 2014.

26. Jessie Gruman. Wikipedia Free Encycl. 2014. http://en.wikipedia.org/w/index.php?title=Jessie_Gruman&oldid=572643729. Accessed June 7, 2014.

27. Gruman J. *AfterShock: What to Do When the Doctor Gives You—Or Someone You Love—A Devastating Diagnosis.* New York, NY: Walker & Company; 2007.

28. Shapiro J. A widow paints a health care protest. *NPR.org.* http://www.npr.org/2009/11/09/120028213/a-widow-paints-a-health-care-protest. Accessed June 7, 2014.

29. A wife's vow: access to your record can save your life. http://www.healthit.gov/profiles/access-to-medical-records. Accessed June 7, 2014.

30. Millenson ML. Will Regina Holliday become health care's Rosa Parks? *The Health Care Blog.* http://thehealthcareblog.com/blog/2012/05/05/will-regina-holliday-become-health-care%E2%80%99s-rosa-park/. Accessed June 7, 2014.

31. Ahmad F, Hudak PL, Bercovitz K, Hollenberg E, Levinson W. Are physicians ready for patients with Internet-based health information? *J Med Internet Res.* 2006;8(3):e22.

32. Broom A. Virtually he@lthy: the impact of internet use on disease experience and the doctor-patient relationship. *Qual. Health Res.* 2005;15(3):325-345.

33. Colombo C, Mosconi P, Villani W, Garattini S. Patient organizations' funding from pharmaceutical companies: is disclosure clear, complete and accessible to the public? An Italian survey. *PloS One.* 2012;7(5):e34974.

34. Ball DE, Tisocki K, Herxheimer A. Advertising and disclosure of funding on patient organisation websites: a cross-sectional survey. *BMC Public Health.* 2006;6:201.

35. Gruman J. Is a single patient representative in a group sufficient? *KevinMD.com.* 2014. http://www.kevinmd.com/blog/2014/01/single-patient-representative-group-sufficient.html. Accessed June 7, 2014.

36. Buntin MB, Damberg C, Haviland A, et al. Consumer-directed health care: early evidence about effects on cost and quality. *Health Aff.* 2006;25(6):w516-530.

37. Goodman JC. *Consumer Directed Health Care.* Rochester, NY: Social Science Research Network; 2006. http://papers.ssrn.com/abstract=985572. Accessed May 11, 2014.

38. Woolhandler S, Himmelstein DU. Consumer directed healthcare: except for the healthy and wealthy it's unwise. *J Gen Intern Med.* 2007;22(6):879-881.

39. Gross T. Terry Gross interviewing Jonathan Oberlander, associate professor, University of North Carolina, Chapel Hill. Fresh Air, NPR. 2007.

40. Mathews AW. Lifting the veil on pricing for health care. *Wall Street Journal*, October 28, 2012. http://online.wsj.com/news/articles/SB10001424052748704222704574499623333862720. Accessed May 12, 2014.

41. Bernstein N. Health insurers switch baseline for out-of-network charges. *The New York Times*, April 23, 2012. http://www.nytimes.com/2012/04/24/nyregion/health-insurers-switch-baseline-for-out-of-network-charges.html. Accessed May 12, 2014.

42. Kates W. "FAIR Health" database will allow people to compare health care costs. *Huffington Post.* http://www.huffingtonpost.com/2009/10/27/fair-health-database-will_n_335773.html. Accessed May 12, 2014.

43. de Brantes F. Castlight is model of price transparency for health plans. *Modern Healthcare.* http://www.modernhealthcare.com/article/20140329/MAGAZINE/303299942. Accessed June 8, 2014.

44. Lee T. Patient experience will drive a renewal of professionalism. *Health Aff.* Blog. http://healthaffairs.org/blog/2013/09/18/patient-experience-will-drive-a-renewal-of-professionalism/. Accessed August 25, 2014.

45. HCAHPS—Hospital Survey. http://www.hcahpsonline.org/home.aspx. Accessed August 25, 2014.

46. Institute for Healthcare Improvement. How do patient-reported measures contribute to value in health care? http://www.ihi.org/communities/blogs/_layouts/ihi/community/blog/itemview. aspx?List=7d1126ec-8f63-4a3b-9926-c44ea3036813&ID=92. Accessed August 25, 2014.

47. How to attain meaningful use. http://www.healthit.gov/providers-professionals/how-attain-meaningful-use. Accessed August 25, 2014.

48. FORCE TJR. http://www.force-tjr.org/. Accessed August 25, 2014.

49. Lazar K. Knee and hip surgery registries yield clues for more successful treatments. *The Boston Globe. BostonGlobe.com.* 2014. https://www.bostonglobe.com/lifestyle/health-wellness/2014/06/29/knee-and-hip-surgery-registries-yield-clues-for-more-successful-treatments/Fd48ealbP1QZHckhLMhY9L/story.html. Accessed August 25, 2014.

50. International Consortium for Health Outcomes Measurement. Who we are. http://www.ichom.org/who-we-are/. Accessed August 25, 2014.

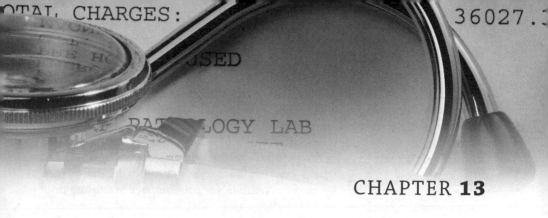

CHAPTER 13

High-Value Medication Prescribing

*T*he rush-hour traffic on the 405 freeway in Los Angeles seemed even worse than usual and Andrew Martin's thoughts began to drift back to his workday and the big construction deal that he had been working on for a month but was now falling through. Suddenly he began to feel a dull, constant pressure in his chest that travelled down his left arm. He took a few deep breaths, but the pressure seemed to get worse and began to feel like it was suffocating him. He pulled off the freeway and drove to the closest emergency room. As a previously healthy 55-year-old man he infrequently saw a primary care provider and did not take any medications. The emergency department (ED) physician said that it seemed like a panic attack, but that he should be admitted overnight to get some tests in order to "just make sure that this isn't your heart." Although that statement made him even more nervous, Mr Martin's chest pain resolved shortly after arriving at the hospital.

He spent the night under telemetry monitoring in an observation unit located next door to the ED. The next morning a cardiologist stopped by his bed and told him that based on his blood work (two negative troponin tests obtained 8 hours apart) and his normal ECGs, he was not having a heart attack, but that his cholesterol drawn this morning was found to be high. His 10-year risk of cardiovascular disease (derived from the Framingham risk calculator)[1] was approximately 15%, so the cardiologist recommended that he start on a statin. Mr Martin agreed to take this medication and the cardiologist wrote him a prescription for Lipitor (atorvastatin calcium; Pfizer Inc) 40 mg by mouth, once daily. Mr Martin left the hospital and went straight to his closest pharmacy to fill the prescription. When the pharmacist entered the prescription she told him that this medication will cost him $191 each month. Mr Martin is worried about his cholesterol and the fact that the cardiologist told him that he is at risk of having a real heart attack one day, but he thinks back to his failed construction deal and his tight financial situation. "Never mind for now, I will have to come back another time," Mr Martin tells the pharmacist, leaving the drug store without his prescription.

Unfortunately, the out-of-pocket costs of medications have led many patients to forgo recommended treatments. Patients like Mr Martin are often not aware that less costly statins exist and they may feel embarrassed about bringing up an inability to pay for this medication with a healthcare provider. Although the majority of patients report a desire to talk to their doctors about out-of-pocket drug costs, only 15% of patients say they have ever done so.[2] The discomfort caused by discussing costs is not only common for patients, but healthcare providers as well. In one study, 79% of physicians wished that they could discuss costs with patients but reported unease with the topic, insufficient time, and doubts about viable solutions.[3] These discussions are vital, however, since cost-related medication underuse is prevalent in the United States, particularly among the uninsured (Figure 13-1).[4] This chapter will review a number of potential mediators at both the clinician and health system level that can help patients navigate this concerning problem. We should note upfront that evidence suggests the most effective and consistent way to reduce the risk of cost-related nonadherence is to provide patients with any form of prescription drug coverage.[5]

On the quality side of the value equation, many patients are not benefiting from their prescription plans due to complicated regimens. More than half of all patients above 65 years old take three or more prescription medications.[4] While most of these patients likely have appropriate indications for a number of their medications, patients with the same chronic illnesses have highly variable levels

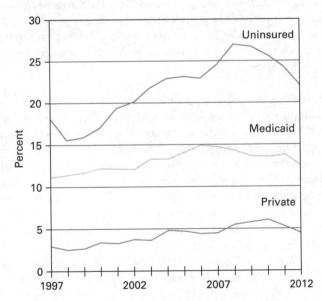

Figure 13-1. Delay or nonreceipt of prescription drugs. (Reproduced from National Center for Health Statistics. *Health, United States, 2012.* Hyattsville, MD; 2013. Available at /nchs/hus/htm. Accessed May 31, 2013.)

of medication complexity.[6] The problem is that complex prescription regimens are clearly associated with reduced compliance compared to simple regimens.[7]

High-value prescribing entails providing the simplest medication regimen that minimizes physical and financial risk to the patient while achieving the best outcome. In other words, decreasing either cost, complexity, or risk of medications can improve value. Ideally, providers should aim to decrease all three simultaneously.

UNDERUSE OF MEDICATIONS DUE TO COST AND COMPLEXITY

Medication nonadherence results in poor disease management and costly complications,[8] including increased ED visits, psychiatric admissions, nursing home placements, and decreased overall health status.[9-11] Patients are not just failing to fill that prescription for loratadine for their season allergies, but also essential medications such as hypoglycemics, diuretics, bronchodilators, and antipsychotics.[3] The data suggest that more than one million adults diagnosed with diabetes may be taking less hypoglycemic medications than prescribed because of cost, and an additional 750,000 people with diabetes may be cutting back on their medications at least once per month.[3] Incredibly, these numbers do not even include the patients that are noncompliant for a myriad of other reasons, including medication regimen complexity and other psychosocial factors.

If you see patients in a clinical setting, then you undoubtedly see patients who are not taking their medications as prescribed due to costs. Bearing in mind this overwhelming prevalence of cost-related medication nonadherence, clinicians should consider this as a possible cause whenever a patient "fails" to respond to pharmacotherapy. Instead, clinicians often reply to these "medication failures" by prescribing more medications, ultimately exacerbating the underlying problem of unaffordability. Relying on patients to mention their nonadherence or their financial difficulties will not suffice. About one-third of chronically ill adults who underuse prescription medications due to medication costs never talk with clinicians about this issue.[3]

Contributing to the problem of medication underuse is the increasing complexity of medication regimens. The medical management for congestive heart failure now includes a cocktail of different drugs consisting of aspirin, angiotensin converting enzyme inhibitors (ACE inhibitors), β-blockers, statins, and diuretics. A review of the studies on barriers to medication adherence in the elderly[12] found that four studies showed taking more drugs led to worse overall adherence,[13-16] and a single study reported the opposite.[17] It is not simply about the total pill count: medication regimens can also vary significantly in complexity due to multiple dosage forms, frequency of dosing, and additional usage directions.[6] In patients with poorly controlled diabetes, taking diabetic medications more than twice daily led to decreased adherence and worsened blood sugar control (as measured by hemoglobin A1c).[18] In another study compliance improved from 59% on a three-time daily regimen to 84% on a once-daily regimen, leading the authors to declare, "Probably the single most important action that healthcare providers can take to improve compliance is to select medications that permit the lowest daily prescribed dose frequency."[7]

Medication complexity is a *modifiable risk factor* to adherence; therefore, efforts should be made to provide patients with the simplest appropriate regimen. Clinicians could consider combination pills that include two or more common medications and doses, which decreases pill burden and may provide better compliance for patients with chronic conditions, such as hypertension.[19] Combination pills may be cheaper than the component medication separately. However, this strategy requires caution since some combination pills can be inappropriately expensive. In these instances the trade-off between medication complexity and cost burden will need to be carefully weighed lest you replace one medication adherence problem with another.

Of course, clinicians must also consider whether or not their patient can appropriately understand the medication regimen in the first place. Health literacy is low in many US populations and a lot of patients have limited English proficiency. Dr David Margolius shared a parable about misinterpreted medication instructions in a *Los Angeles Times* Op-Ed: "The story of 'once' is a cautionary tale that—best as I am able to tell from Google—was adapted from a Spanish soap opera. In one version, a doctor prescribes a patient a 30-day supply of a medication. Three days later, the patient returns for a refill. 'How can this be?' the doctor wonders. The Spanish-speaking patient responds, 'I took the pills exactly as the bottle said to: '11 daily.' The doctor scrutinized the pill bottle: 'Take once daily.' But 'once' read and pronounced 'ohn-say' means 11 in Spanish. The patient had taken 11 pills daily, just as the bottle label said—in Spanish. The patient lives in that story, but in other versions he is hospitalized or even dies."[20]

It is imperative that providers take into account their patients' ability to pay for, understand, and comply with their medication regimen, otherwise their efforts to provide thoughtful and effective medical care may be easily undermined.

WHY DO WE SEE LOW-VALUE PRESCRIBING?

The tools and strategies we highlight in this chapter are designed to help clinicians and their patients address the challenges presented by the costs and complexity of therapeutic options. However, there are several barriers to high-value prescribing that will require systems-level solutions, beyond the individual patient-clinician encounter. Chapter 3 reviewed the challenge of price transparency and Chapter 12 discussed some of the emerging tools to help patients better understand the cost and quality of care they are receiving. Although medication costs are often easier to discern prior to purchase than diagnostic tests and other health services, prices may vary in equally frustrating and arbitrary ways. For example, oral contraceptive pills, one of the most frequently prescribed medications for women of reproductive age, can vary by an order of magnitude in monthly cost to the patient, depending on the coverage plan, formulation, and pharmacy that is selected.[21] This variation in pricing makes it challenging for both patients and care providers to track lower cost options and has left a gap in medical education, with many clinicians feeling unprepared to deal with medication costs.[3]

Our fee-for-service reimbursement system also presents a notable challenge to high-value prescribing (see Chapter 15). This is particularly evident in cases where both medical and surgical management may be appropriate. Because performing procedures generates more reimbursement than prescribing medications, opportunities to use a high-value medication may be overlooked or dismissed. The evidence for this exists at the systems level—as we point out in Chapter 7, many procedures in the United States are performed at variable rates in different regions, sometimes varying more than 20-fold, without an apparent medical explanation or benefit.[22] An all too common example is joint arthritis, which depending on the patient's individual case and goals of care might be managed conservatively with medication and physical therapy or surgically with an elective knee, shoulder, or hip replacement. Recent data suggest that the skewed incentives to operate may be leading to unnecessary surgery in many parts of the country, where medical therapy may have been more appropriate.[23]

Sometimes an expensive medication can be worth it if it helps avoid an even more expensive, risky, or otherwise undesirable surgery. As an extreme example, medical hormonal therapy costs significantly more than bilateral orchiectomy (removal of testes) for men with prostate cancer. Although both hormonal therapy and castration are reasonable approaches, the very expensive hormonal therapy appears worth it and creates positive value for men with prostate cancer by enabling them to avoid a highly undesirable surgery.[24]

The influence of the pharmaceutical industry on prescribing practices has recently drawn increased scrutiny within academic medicine. Through a combination of lobbying efforts and targeted marketing, the industry as a whole spends more than one-third of all sales revenue (approximately $100 billion) on promoting the use of their products.[25] While advertising in itself may not be necessarily problematic, tensions arise when industry incentives to maximize shareholder profits are misaligned with the patient and caregiver incentives to deliver high-value care.

A 2003 survey of third-year medical students revealed that over 93% of them reported accepting food from a pharmaceutical company. At that time, resident physicians also commonly interacted with pharmaceutical companies, which altered their prescribing behaviors.[26] Even exposure to small pharmaceutical promotional items subtly influences medical students' attitudes toward the advertised product.[27] The Institute of Medicine (IOM) and the Association of American Medical Colleges (AAMC) both recommended drastically curtailing commercial involvement in medical education.[28-30] In response, numerous medical schools, residency programs, and academic medical centers have limited industry access to medical training, although this ban is far from complete.[31,32] The American Medical Student Association (AMSA) has created a "PharmFree" scorecard that publically compares conflict of interest policies across academic medical centers (available at http://www.amsascorecard.org), which has also helped catalyze these policies. Recent studies provide encouraging evidence that these medical school policies are associated with changing student attitudes toward marketing,[27] and lead to more conservative future prescribing practices.[33] Despite these inroads in the undergraduate and postgraduate educational arenas, the world of continuing medical education (CME) remains substantially sponsored by the pharmaceutical industry. This seems less likely to change significantly anytime soon because the Accreditation Council for Continuing Medical Education (ACCME) has considered but rejected ending commercial support,[34] which in 2011 equaled approximately $736 million.[35] Of note, this does represent a dramatic decrease from the peak of $1.2 billion in CME commercial support, back in 2006.[34,35]

Outside of education, in the "real world" of private practice physician offices and community hospitals, the lunchtime visits from pharmaceutical representatives and the invited dinner lectures are often a daily occurrence. Payers have a unique ability to drastically influence this situation by creating a policy that would ban their providers from these relationships. One move in that direction is the new "Physician Payments Sunshine Act," which requires public reporting of payments to physicians and teaching hospitals from pharmaceutical and medical device companies. This law includes meals, honoraria, travel expenses, and grants. The data started being published on a public website in 2014.[36] Perhaps this will help prove the adage, "sunshine is the best disinfectant."

SCREENING PATIENTS FOR FINANCIAL BURDEN OF MEDICATIONS

As already discussed, patients are usually uncomfortable initiating conversations about medication costs with their physicians. There are a number of reasons for this discomfort, but patients say that an important contributor is the perception that their clinicians are unwilling or unable to help them with this problem.[3] Perhaps this is because providers have never asked them about their medication adherence or their financial situations. Eighty-five percent of patients reported they have never discussed out-of-pocket costs with their physicians, and only 16% of patients believe that their physician was aware of the magnitude of their out-of-pocket costs.[2] There is little wonder as to why patients think that this is not a priority to their providers. Maybe the reality is that with the many challenges and competing urgencies that clinicians face, it frankly is not. But it absolutely should be. It is central to the care for many patients. And patients who are not asked by their providers about the problem of medication costs have a more global, negative perception regarding their clinicians' overall interest and potential ability to assist them.[3]

At least equally concerning, patients adopt other strategies—in addition to underuse of medications—to cope with the burden of high medication costs (Figure 13-2). These include cutting back on necessities such as food or heat to

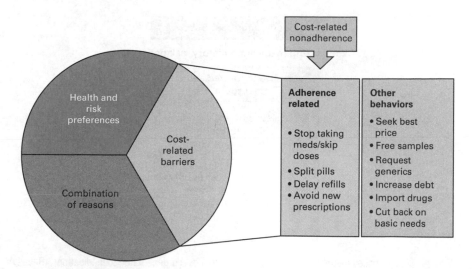

Figure 13-2. Relationship between medication nonadherence and cost-related behaviors. (Reproduced from Briesacher BA, Gurwitz JH, Soumerai SB. Patients at-risk for cost-related medication nonadherence: review of the literature. *J Gen Intern Med.* 2007;22(6):864-871. With kind permission from Springer Science and Business Media.)

pay for medications. Many take on increased debt.[37] This strain on household budgets can cause further erosion of personal health. According to one study, almost a quarter of Medicare patients without prescription drug coverage had cut back on food or clothing because of medication costs.[38] As the Haitian proverb goes, we may be "washing our hands and then drying them in the dirt" by prescribing medications that aim to help with medical conditions but that are actually compelling older patients with chronic conditions to forgo necessities, eat less healthily, and increase their debt burden.

The first step for clinicians to address this common problem is to ask simple questions to screen patients for financial burdens associated with their medications. We propose three specific questions to ask patients while taking a medical history (Figure 13-3)[39]:

1. Do your medications cost too much?
2. Have you ever cut back on medications because of cost?
3. Have you ever cut back on other things (eg, food, leisure) due to high drug costs?

Making such screening routine, much like is done with advanced directives, could help alleviate the patient or physician discomfort with this topic.[40]

This paradigm of screening patients for medication-related financial harm applies to hospitalized patients as well. In one survey of hospitalized adults, 23% reported cost-related underuse in the year prior to admission.[41] Yet, few patients (16%) who were prescribed medications at discharge knew how much

Screening for Cost Burden

When taking medication history, ask patients:

1	"Do your medications **cost too much?**"
2	"Have you ever **cut back** on medications because of cost?"
3	"Have you ever cut back on **other things (eg, food, leisure)** due to high drug costs?"

Figure 13-3. Proposed method for screening patients for cost burden related to medications. (Rupali Kumar, Neel Shah, Andy Levy, Mark Saathoff, Jeanne Farnan, Vineet Arora. GOT MeDS: designing and piloting an interactive module for trainees on reducing drug costs. Society of General Internal Medicine Presentation, April 2013.)

they would pay at the pharmacy, and almost none of them had spoken to their inpatient (4%) or outpatient (2%) providers about the cost of newly prescribed drugs.[41] Any benefit from a hospitalization could be too easily unraveled by careless discharge prescriptions that a patient cannot appropriately fill. Not taking medication costs into account can easily lead to preventable and unnecessarily costly readmissions. In one case recently presented at an M&M (Mortality and Morbidity) conference, a patient was readmitted to the hospital for anticoagulation treatment of his cancer-related deep vein thrombosis after he was unable to afford the out-of-pocket costs of Enoxaparin injections. His previous inpatient medical team had neither taken this possibility into consideration nor tried to obtain a prior authorization.

TOOLS FOR DETERMINING MEDICATION COSTS

Healthcare providers require clear information regarding the relative efficacy and price of medications. Fortunately, there are many tools and resources available for both physicians and patients. These include websites such as www.consumer reports.org, mobile applications like Epocrates and Lowestmed.com, and drug store discount generic drug lists (as discussed below).

Consumer Reports has created a number of "Best Buy Drug Reports" listed by condition and by specific drug name (Figure 13-4).[42] Their statin list points out that, "Statins can vary widely in cost—from as little as $12 per month (and even less if your drug is available on a drug store's discount generic list) to more than

The Best Statin at the Best Price

Consumer Reports Best Buy Drugs are in blue and **bold black**. We recommend these drugs because they are effective, generally safe, and cost less. Work with your doctor to choose the best statin and dose for you.

- If you need to lower your LDL cholesterol less than 30%, look at the drugs listed in blue.
- If you need to lower your LDL cholesterol more than 30%, look at the drugs listed in bold black.

Generic Name and Dose	Brand Name[1]	Average Cost Per Month[2]	% of LDL Cholesterol Lowered	Reduces Heart Attack Risk[3]
Atorvastatin 10 mg	Generic	$114	34–38%	Yes
Atorvastatin 20 mg	Generic	$155	42–46%	Yes
Atorvastatin 40 mg	**Generic**	**$160**	**47–51%**	**Yes**
Atorvastatin 80 mg	**Generic**	**$164**	**46–54%**	**Yes**
Atorvastatin 10 mg	Lipitor	$130	34–38%	Yes
Atorvastatin 20 mg	Lipitor	$178	42–46%	Yes
Atorvastatin 40 mg	Lipitor	$191	47–51%	Yes
Atorvastatin 80 mg	Lipitor	$199	46–54%	Yes
Fluvastatin 20 mg	Lescol	$135	22%	Likely
Fluvastatin 40 mg	Lescol	$132	25%	Likely
Fluvastatin sustained release 80 mg	Lescol XL	$172	35%	Likely
Lovastatin 10 mg	**Generic**	**$12**	**21%**	**Yes**
Lovastatin 20 mg	**Generic**	**$16**	**24–27%**	**Yes**
Lovastatin 40 mg	**Generic**	**$51**	**31%**	**Yes**
Lovastatin 80 mg	Generic	$103	39–48%	Yes
Lovastatin sustained release 20 mg	Altoprev	$409	30%	Unknown
Lovastatin sustained release 40 mg	Altoprev	$515	36%	Yes
Lovastatin sustained release 60 mg	Altoprev	$490	40%	Yes

Generic Name and Dose	Brand Name[1]	Average Cost Per Month[2]	% of LDL Cholesterol Lowered	Reduces Heart Attack Risk[3]
Pravastatin 10 mg	Generic	$35	18–25%	Yes
Pravastatin 20 mg	Generic	$32	23–29%	Yes
Pravastatin 40 mg	Generic	$46	26–34%	Yes
Pravastatin 80 mg	Generic	$71	30–37%	Yes
Pravastatin 20 mg	Pravacol	$142	23–29%	Yes
Pravastatin 40 mg	Pravacol	$208	26–34%	Yes
Pravastatin 80 mg	Pravacol	$199	30–37%	Yes
Rosuvastatin 5 mg	Crestor	$163	39–46%	Yes
Rosuvastatin 10 mg	Crestor	$161	43–50%	Yes
Rosuvastatin 20 mg	Crestor	$163	52–55%	Yes
Rosuvastatin 40 mg	Crestor	$161	55–60%	Yes
Simvastatin 10 mg	Generic	$38	26–33%	Yes
Simvastatin 20 mg	**Generic**	**$68**	**30–40%**	**Yes**
Simvastatin 40 mg	**Generic**	**$68**	**35–45%**	**Yes**
Simvastatin 80 mg	Generic	$59	40–50%	Yes
Simvastatin 10 mg	Zocor	$120	26–33%	Yes
Simvastatin 20 mg	Zocor	$191	30–40%	Yes
Simvastatin 40 mg	Zocor	$198	35–45%	Yes
Simvastatin 80 mg	Zocor	$207	40–50%	Yes

This series is produced by Consumer Reports and *Consumer Reports Besy Buy Drugs*, a public information project supported by grants from the Engelberg Foundation and the National Library of Medicine of the National Institutes of Health. These materials were also made possible by a grant from the State Attorney General Consumer and Prescribe Education Grant Program which is funded by the muti-state settlement of consumer fraud claims regardng the marketing of the prescription drug Neurontin. This brief should not be viewed as a substitute for a consultation with a medical or health professional. It is provided to enhance communication with your doctor, not replace it. Neither the National Library of Medicine nor the National Institutes of Health are responsible for the content or advice herein.

Figure 13-4. Consumer Reports' Statin list comparing efficacy and costs. (Copyright 2007 Consumers Union of U.S., Inc. Yonkers, NY 10703-1057, a nonprofit organization. Reprinted with permission from *Consumer Reports® Best Buy Drugs* for educational purposes only. www.ConsumerReports.org.)

[1] "Generic" indicates a drug sold by generic name.
[2] Prices reflect nationwide retail average for December 2011, rounded to the nearest dollar. Information derived by Consumer Reports Best Buy Drugs from data provided by Wolters Kluwer Pharma Solutions. Wolters Kluwer is not involved in our analysis or recommendations.
[3] Nonfatal and fatal heart attack plus deaths attributed to heart disease.

$500. Most people who take them must continue to do so for years—perhaps for the rest of their life—so the cost can be an important factor to consider."[43]

The AARP (formerly the American Association of Retired Persons) has released their own user-friendly "Drug Savings Tool" that helps patients determine if there is a "less expensive, but equally effective medication you can use instead," as well as whether there is "a comparable drug with fewer side effects."[44,45] For example, the tool shows that the "heartburn" medication Prilosec 20 mg costs an average of $220 per month, and suggests that "you and your doctor consider" alternatives such as the generic equivalent omeprazole 20 mg, which only costs $24 per month. It also provides basic information and recommendations about heartburn drugs in general and advises, "Not everyone needs to take a proton pump inhibitor (PPI) drug." Here are some of the clear instructions and information the website gives patients: "So before you turn to a PPI, make sure you really need it. If you have occasional, mild heartburn and have not been diagnosed with GERD, you should first try lifestyle changes, like reducing how much alcohol and caffeine you drink, quitting smoking, eating smaller meals and losing weight if you need to. If those do not work, try an inexpensive over-the-counter antacid..."[44]

Many health insurers now also offer tools that tell members how much a drug is likely to cost them under their specific plan. Examples include myCigna.com[46] and Humana-medicare.com.[47] These tools let patients search drugs by either name or health condition and provide advice. This is important because different insurance plans have diverse formularies and preferred medications. It would not be fair to expect clinicians to know the ins-and-outs of the many insurance plans and their idiosyncratic formularies, but clinicians, as well as office and hospital staff, can and should take responsibility for simply pointing their patients toward these appropriate, readily available, high-quality resources.

COST-SAVING MEDICATION STRATEGIES USED BY PAYERS

Payers have an invested interest in controlling medication expenditures. Spending in the United States for prescription drugs was a remarkable $234.1 billion in 2008,[48] and medication costs compose a significant component of rising outpatient expenditures for both Medicare and privately insured patients.[48,49] For brand-name drugs, the recent growth in spending is primarily due to increased charged prices, whereas for generic drugs it is due to the rising number of filled prescriptions.[49]

One of the most widely implemented strategies by payers to control medication expenditures is to create several medication tiers with differing amounts of cost sharing for patients. The majority of beneficiaries are now covered by plans that employ incentive-based formulas designed to encourage use of lower cost medications (a *formulary* is the full list of medications that the health plan will pay for). In 2009, over three-quarters (78%) of workers with employer-sponsored coverage were in plans with three or more tiers of cost sharing for prescription drugs, which is almost three times the proportion that were in 2000.[48] These tiers

Table 13-1 **Payer prescription cost-saving strategies**

Strategy	Definition
Tiered formularies	• Grouping the required copayments by (usually three or more) increasing "tiered" amounts, based on the cost of the medication to the payer. Generic medications are typically in the lowest tier.
Coinsurance	• Requiring patients to pay a fixed percentage of the total cost of the medication.
Prior authorization	• Requiring formal permission from the payer before certain drugs can be dispensed.
Step therapy	• Requiring use of lower-cost medications prior to providing coverage for more expensive alternatives.
Closed formularies	• Covering a restricted, specific set of medications within each therapeutic class (while not covering others).
Mandatory generic substitution	• Requiring substitution of generic medications when possible.
Reference pricing	• A cap on the amount a plan will pay for prescriptions within a specific therapeutic class.

resulted in average copayments (in 2009) of $10 for generics, $27 for preferred drugs (typically negotiated by the payer at lower cost), $46 for nonpreferred drugs, and $85 for fourth-tier drugs.[48]

Less commonly, plans may require beneficiaries to pay coinsurance—a percentage of the total cost of the prescription. This more direct "skin in the game" approach can be controversial since patients seldom have the knowledge to determine when a medication is truly necessary and worth the increased price. Payers utilize a number of other cost-saving measures (Table 13-1), including prior authorization (requiring permission before certain drugs can be dispensed), step therapy (requiring use of lower-cost medications prior to providing coverage for more expensive alternatives), closed formularies, mandatory generic substitution, and reference pricing (a cap on the amount a plan will pay for a prescription with a specific therapeutic class).[50]

Medicare Part D

Medicare is the largest public payer of prescription drugs and was responsible for 22% of total US prescription spending in 2008.[48] The Medicare Part D drug coverage plan uses a number of approaches for cost containment. These include cost sharing, formulary coverage that varies considerably across plans, and utilization management restrictions such as prior authorization, step therapy, or quantity limits.[51] Since Medicare is the largest purchaser in the United States, one may assume that they have significant purchasing power and could therefore effectively negotiate medication prices. In truth, Medicare is actually prohibited by law from directly negotiating drug prices or rebates with manufacturers to control costs. On the campaign trail prior to the 2008 election, presidential candidate Barack Obama had denounced this restraint as a costly result of pharmaceutical industry lobbying. However, in 2009, his administration struck a deal that delivered pharmaceutical support for the Accountable Care Act in exchange for a promise that federal law would continue to prohibit Medicare from negotiating drug prices.[52,53] By one estimate, this policy may result in hundreds of billions of dollars in excess costs for Medicare and US tax payers over the next 10 years.[52] The pharmaceutical industry contends that higher prices are necessary for new medication research and development, which often require high long-run investments.[54]

As mentioned previously, many of the strategies used by payers involve some level of prescription drug cost sharing. A summary of the evidence of drug cost sharing concluded that for every 10% increase in cost sharing, overall prescription drug spending decreases by 2% to 6%, depending on the class of drugs and patient condition.[55] This is a good time for a reminder that these strategies—although variably effective at decreasing healthcare expenditures—are not without consequences. For some chronic conditions, higher cost sharing for prescription drugs is associated with greater use of even more expensive medical services such as ED visits and hospitalizations.[50] Greater cost sharing for asthma medications has been associated with a reduction in medication use among children, leading to higher rates of asthma hospitalizations.[56] As discussed in Chapter 2, cost sharing results in potentially both positive and negative effects and needs to be carefully balanced.

COST-SAVING MEDICATION STRATEGIES FOR PROVIDERS AND PATIENTS

Choosing generic medications

There are many approaches for both providers and patients to achieve lower drug costs. One of the most obvious, but unfortunately underused, strategies is to choose generic drugs when they are available. Generic medications have been proven to be effective. Systematic reviews and meta-analyses have not shown any convincing differences in efficacy compared to brand-name medications.[57] Not only are generics as efficacious as branded medications, but in practice they may actually be better; some studies have shown improved medication compliance when using generic medications.[58]

Generic medications are significantly cheaper than brand-name medications, oftentimes by more than a factor. Many large chain stores (eg, Costco, Target, WalMart, Kmart, BJ's, Sam's Club) have a number of generic medications for $4 per month or $10 per three-months. Even if the patient has private insurance, it may be even less expensive for him or her to use a $4 plan rather than paying a co-pay at a different pharmacy. Providers can help their patients find available "$4 drugs" by referring to lists online, such as www.target.com/pharmacy/generics.

Although prescribing generic medications is a win-win proposition for patients and payers, healthcare providers have famously failed to deliver. In 2011, more prescriptions for Lipitor (atorvastatin calcium; Pfizer Inc) were written than for generic simvastatin.[59] Remember our patient, Mr Martin from the beginning of our chapter? US primary care physicians' use of branded statins results in $5.8 billion excess spending each year.[59] In one study, about 4 out of 10 physicians admitted to sometimes or often prescribing brand-name medications to a patient when a generic is available "because the patient wanted it."[60] As anybody that has watched primetime television knows, patients (just like clinicians) are flooded with direct-to-consumer advertising for brand-only products. Pharmaceutical spending on direct advertising was $10.9 billion in 2009, which has increased astronomically over the last few years.[48] But that isn't the only way that the pharmaceutical companies influence the use of brand-name drugs. The physicians that were more likely to "acquiesce to patient demands" for brand-name medications were also more likely to have received food and beverages in the workplace from pharmaceutical companies, and they sometimes or often met with industry representatives to "stay up to date."[60] It also was notable that older physicians (those in practice more than 30 years) were significantly more likely than younger physicians (those in practice less than 10 years) to prescribe brand-name medications for patients that asked.[60]

Clinicians should take personal responsibility for prioritizing generic medications for their patients, but based on the barriers and prior failures of clinicians to deliver on this proposition, systems-level interventions such as those mentioned earlier may be necessary to augment these efforts. Due to the convincing association between industry relationships and brand-name medication prescribing, insurers (both private and public) could consider banning healthcare providers from accepting food and beverages in the workplace.[60]

There are other systems-level or institutional changes that can be effective in promoting generic drug ordering. The pharmacy at the Veterans Affairs (VA) medical center has a closed formulary and wields primary control over medication decisions. There are specific algorithms in place governing the use of certain medications. For instance, a patient may need to fail the maximum dose of simvastatin prior to providers being allowed to prescribe the more powerful, but more expensive, rosuvastatin. Importantly, providers do retain the ability to override these rules in rare situations, such as patient-specific idiosyncratic responses, although it usually involves having to convince the pharmacist to approve the request. If we look at diabetic patients covered by Medicare or the VA—both are governmental payers—whose medications do you think cost more? Despite performing similarly on diabetic quality metrics, brand-name drug use for Medicare patients with diabetes was two to three times that of VA patients, resulting in an excess of more than $1 billion for Medicare in 2008.[61] The VA is able to do this for the same reason that Britain can: it is a closed health system involving a single payer and thus can easily institute a formulary. In California, Kaiser Permanente has a similar system and has been able to achieve generic prescribing rates as high as 98% when a generic is available and appropriate.[62]

For inpatient care, hospitals can create similar situations of mini-closed healthcare systems and pharmacy-controlled formularies. Formularies are meant to represent a listing of the drugs of choice, as determined by their clinical efficacy, their relative safety—including adverse drug reactions, side effects, interactions, the potential for errors, and the risk of patient harm—and their cost.[63] An increasingly utilized strategy by hospitals is therapeutic interchanges. An interchange is automatically switching one drug for another within the same therapeutic class (eg, ranitidine for famotidine), or from different classes but with similar pharmacological effect and potency. One specific type of therapeutic interchange is generic substitution, which refers to switching automatically between a branded drug and an equivalent generic version. These standardized approaches can make considerable impact on medication ordering within hospitals.

Outside of closed healthcare systems, payers such as Medicare or commercial insurers can implement varying cost sharing mechanisms (as described earlier) meant to encourage patients to use generics or lower cost medications. The problem here is that many patients lack the knowledge of when cheaper alternatives exist. Consider my sister who was recently given a prescription for ciprofloxacin eardrops from an urgent care clinic. She happened to casually mention to me over the phone that the pharmacy told her it was "not covered" by her private insurance and would cost her approximately $120 out-of-pocket. This seemed outrageous for a common medication, so I told her to call the pharmacy and ask some questions about why this may be. An hour later she was given a prescription for a different (but effective) formulation of the ciprofloxacin eardrop, costing her just $15. She says that she had no idea that this was possible and that if she hadn't spoken to me that day she would have just grumbled and paid the $120. Patients should not need a brother that is a physician—and happens to be writing a chapter about "High-Value Medication Prescribing"—just to avoid unnecessarily paying an extra $100 for a medication.

Other cost-saving tactics

Generic medications are not always available for the condition or indication needed, but there are a number of other cost-saving tactics patients and providers can try. We have used the mnemonic "GOT MeDS" to describe these different strategies (Figure 13-5).[39] These cost-saving strategies include ordering three-month supplies of medications in bulk from pharmacies or by e-mail, and considering cheaper available medications in the same class. Regularly reviewing patients' medication lists and removing any unnecessary medications or those that have not been effective is another important strategy to minimize unnecessary costs and harms for patients.

Cost-Saving Strategies: GOT MeDS?	
G	**G**enerics: prescribe when possible; educate patients on safety/efficacy
O	**O**rdering in bulk: 3-month supplies of drugs from pharmacy or by mail
T	**T**herapeutic alternatives: over-the-counter meds; cheaper meds in same class
Me	**Me**dication review: regularly review med list; remove unnecessary meds
D	**D**iscount drugs: $4 drugs (Walmart, Target, etc.); discount cards
S	**S**plitting pills: prescribe higher dose and advise patients to split pills

Figure 13-5. Cost-saving strategies: "GOT MeDS." (Rupali Kumar, Neel Shah, Andy Levy, Mark Saathoff, Jeanne Farnan, Vineet Arora. GOT MeDS: designing and piloting an interactive module for trainees on reducing drug costs. Society of General Internal Medicine Presentation, April 2013.)

Story From the Frontlines: "The Right Medication at the Right Price"

I arrived in the office one morning to find the following message on my desk: "Mrs Smith called, wants you to know that the once-a-month pill you ordered for her costs $15, cannot afford this every month, order something else. She says she's already paying too much for the other pill you ordered."

What had I ordered? Vitamin D 50,000 units once a month and Alendronate 70 mg once a week. She was retired and had good insurance. Her insurance had paid for the bone density test that had found the severe osteopenia, and the blood test that had identified the severe Vitamin D deficiency. It had paid for the routine, yearly well-woman exam. So what was the problem?

It turns out that she had a three-tier pharmacy co-pay plan. The generic level was $15 for a 30-day supply. So, she was paying $30 per month for four pills of Alendronate and one pill of Vitamin D. Total yearly cost was $360.

A mail-away pharmacy service could provide a 90-day supply of both medications for $60. Total yearly cost = $240.

But, it still seemed obscene to me that 12 pills of Vitamin D would cost her $120 per year.

As I investigated further, I called her pharmacist at the local drug store to learn about out-of-pocket costs for these medications. The Alendronate would cost more, but 12 pills of Vitamin D (a whole year's supply) would cost only $20 if she just paid for it herself and didn't use her insurance!! Total yearly cost = $140.

Just a few more phone calls and I found out which pharmacies in my area had the cheapest prices (Target, Wal-Mart, Costco, BJ's). I found out that they offered $4 generics for a 30-day supply, or $10 for a 90-day supply. If she paid out-of-pocket, she could get both of her medications there. Total yearly cost = $60. Bingo!!!

The following week, she brought me a bunch of gorgeous, sweet-smelling peonies from her garden and a box of homemade brownies (the thick, moist, melt in your mouth kind).

She gave me a hug and thanked me. She told all of her friends. I now actively direct my patients to use these pharmacies. I advise them to look for the $10 gift card coupons that some pharmacies offer in the newspapers for buying a new prescription there. I tell them that loyalty to any particular pharmacy should only go so far. I encourage my patients to ask their pharmacists every time they get a prescription filled what their medications would cost if they paid for it themselves, and then to do so if it's in their favor.

Most patients tell me they did not know they could get such information, or that their pharmacist is required to tell them if they ask, or that they can pay for medications without using their insurance.

It takes time and effort on our part to collect the necessary information to inform our patients about their drug costs. But there are also definite rewards—like that box of brownies—and the unending gratitude and trust that our patients show us when they know that we really are on their side.

—Luisa Kontoules. "The Right Medication at the Right Price."
Costs of Care, 2010. (www.costsofcare.org)

One area that is tricky to parse is that of pharmaceutical drug samples. Pharmaceutical samples are widely used for promotion and marketing, and some argue that they are an important resource for defraying the costs to some patients.[64] However, research has shown that these free drug samples are actually much more likely to go to wealthy, insured Americans rather than those in need.[65] This supports the view that these drug samples truly serve as a marketing tool, and not as a safety net. In addition, it turns out that individuals that receive samples have higher prescription expenditures than those that do not use samples.[66] An explanation for this may be that samples ultimately drive up prescription costs since many of the patients end up on name-brand medications. Therefore, short-term economic relief may actually lead to a larger long-term financial burden. Furthermore, samples usually comprise the newest agents on the market and may expose patients to risks that have not yet been identified in clinical trials. As Drs Susan Chimonas (researcher at Columbia University) and Jerome Kassirer (former editor of the *New England Journal of Medicine*, and Professor at Tufts University) point out, "The experience with Vioxx is a case in point. By 2002, only three years after Vioxx was introduced, it became the most widely distributed sample, and two years later the drug was withdrawn from the market because of an excess risk of myocardial infarctions and strokes. Needless to say, Vioxx was not the only drug given extensively as samples and later found to enhance risk."[67]

Another cost-saving strategy may be splitting pills in half by prescribing a higher dose. For instance if a patient has an indication to take simvastatin 40 mg daily, it is possible to write a prescription for "Simvastatin 80mg tabs, take ½ tab by mouth daily." This would likely save overall money for the patient. However, if employing this strategy it is imperative that the instructions are made completely clear to the patient and that the patient will be able to appropriately understand and comply with these special instructions.

CONSERVATIVE PRESCRIBING

Of course the best way to prevent costs and complications from medications is to avoid prescribing them when they are unnecessary. This approach has been called "conservative prescribing." Harvard researcher Dr Gordon D. Schiff and colleagues have described a number of principles of conservative prescribing (Table 13-2), which broadly include: thinking beyond drugs, practicing more strategic prescribing, maintaining heightened vigilance regarding adverse effects, approaching new drugs and new indications cautiously and skeptically, working with patients for a more deliberative shared agenda, and considering longer-term, broader effects.[68]

In many ways our medical system is biased toward the initiation of medications for the treatment of all diseases even when nondrug alternatives, such as exercise, physical therapy, diet changes, or smoking cessation, can be beneficial. Even a "tincture of time" can be an effective management strategy for a number of common complaints, including back pain, sinusitis, and otitis media. As we previously discussed, patients may come to healthcare providers already

Table 13-2 Principles of conservative prescribing

Principle	Strategy	Example/Notes
Think beyond drugs	Seek nondrug alternatives first	• Prescribe exercise, physical therapy, diet changes, smoking cessation, orthotics, or surgery when appropriate.
	Consider potentially treatable underlying causes of problems rather than just treating the symptoms with a drug	• Consider if impotence could be a sign of marital discord, a pituitary problem, diabetes, or drug effect.
	Look for opportunities for prevention rather than focusing on treating symptoms or advanced disease	• Tobacco control and smoking cessation efforts (with or without medications) save many more lives than costly chemotherapies for smoking-related cancers.
	Use the test of time as a diagnostic and therapeutic trial whenever possible	• Evidence supports delayed strategy of diagnosis for rhinosinusitis, otitis media, back pain, and many other conditions.
Practice more strategic prescribing	Use only a few drugs and learn to use them well	• Studies have shown that having a more limited personal formulary is associated with higher-quality prescribing, and less risk for errors.
	Avoid frequent switching to new drugs without clear compelling evidence-based reasons	• Avoid the frequent but often irrational practice of switching inpatient antibiotics frequently without clear indications.
	Whenever possible, start treatment with only one drug at a time	• Temper the urge to start treatment with medications for a new patient's hypertension, urinary tract infection, dyspepsia, headaches, and toenail infection—all on one visit.
Maintain heightened vigilance regarding adverse effects	Have a high index of suspicion for adverse drug effects	• Consider whether "fibromyalgia" pain could actually be statin-induced myopathy, or whether worsening heart failure could be due to an NSAID or rosiglitazone.
	Educate patient about possible adverse effects to ensure that they are recognized as early as possible	• Better-informed patients are more likely to recognize adverse effects early.
	Be alert to clues that you may be treating or risking withdrawal symptoms	• Caffeine or other analgesics are used to treat headaches but ultimately can cause daily headaches.

Table 13-2 **Principles of conservative prescribing** *(Continued)*

Principle	Strategy	Example/Notes
Approach new drugs and new indications cautiously and skeptically	Learn about new drugs and new indications from trustworthy unbiased sources	• Avoid education from pharmaceutical representatives or "experts" with conflicts of interest. Instead turn to independent drug bulletins (eg, Medical Letter) or specialists with reputations for integrity and conservative approaches.
	Do not rush to use newly marketed drugs	• In pre-marketing trials, only carefully selected patients are exposed, who are often younger and not already taking multiple medications. There are many examples of medications that were found to have serious side effects following their widespread release, such as COX2 inhibitors and thiazolidinediones.
	Be certain that the drugs improve actual patient-centered clinical outcomes rather than just treating or masking a surrogate marker	• Many randomized trials show statistically significant improvements in surrogate markers such as laboratory or radiologic findings, but may lack proof of meaningful clinical benefit.
	Be vigilant about indications creep	• Avoid prescribing medications for extrapolated indications, such as assuming that because gabapentin may work for postherpetic neuralgia, it is worth trying for headaches.
	Do not be seduced by elegant molecular pharmacology or drug physiology	• Sophisticated molecular structure designs do not always reliably predict how it will behave in humans. For instance, Torcetrapib was designed to block cholesteryl ester transfer protein and thereby increase HDL levels; however, in large trials it failed to slow atherosclerosis and actually increased mortality.
	Beware of selective reporting of studies	• Trials with positive results are much more likely to be published than trials with negative results. Positive selectivity is even truer for the literature supplied by pharmaceutical representatives, which should be assumed to highlight benefits and downplay risks.

(Continued)

Table 13-2: **Principles of conservative prescribing** *(Continued)*

Principle	Strategy	Example/Notes
Work with patients for a more deliberative shared agenda	Do not hastily or uncritically succumb to patient requests for drugs, especially drugs that they have heard advertised	• With the growth of direct-to-consumer advertising, clinicians are under greater pressure from their patients to prescribe advertised drugs, but taking the path of least resistance and prescribing without an appropriate discussion and indication is dangerous.
	Avoid mistakenly prescribing additional drugs for refractory problems, failing to appreciate the potential for patient nonadherence	• Studies have shown that in most instances of poorly controlled hypertension, patients are not taking their prescribed medications.
	Avoid repeating prescriptions for drugs that a patient has previously tried unsuccessfully or that caused an adverse reaction	• Providers frequently unknowingly prescribe a drug that has previously failed to benefit the patient or that has caused an adverse reaction due to a lack of an accurate longitudinal medication history.
	Discontinue treatment with drugs that are not working or are no longer needed	• Many conditions or patients are unresponsive to particular drugs, and providers need to look for such response failures and discontinue treatments as soon as they are recognized.
	Work with patients' desires to be conservative with medications	• Some patients actually prefer to avoid medications. Leading meaningful discussions with these patients and providing honest education can earn the patients' trust in your judicious approach to limiting drug therapy and may convince them to more readily accept treatment recommendations when medications are truly essential.
Consider longer-term, broader effects	Think beyond short-term beneficial drug effects to consider longer-term benefits and risks	• Dopamine antagonists such as chlorpromazine and haloperidol, which caused tardive dyskinesia, continue to haunt us as examples of drugs that were dramatically effective but were later found to cause irreversible structural brain damage.
	Look for opportunities to improve prescribing systems, changes that can make prescribing and medication use safer	• Implementing well-designed computerized provider order entry or improved patient or laboratory monitoring systems has been shown to improve drug treatment, often more than the marginal impact of many new "breakthrough" drugs.

Source: Adapted, with permission, from Schiff GD, Galanter WL, Duhig J, et al. Principles of conservative prescribing. *Arch Intern Med.* 2011;171(16):1433-1440. Copyright © 2011 American Medical Association. All rights reserved.

requesting a specific medication based on a direct-to-consumer television or magazine advertisement. Although it may be easier to just jot out the requested prescription, the costs—both financially and physically—of this practice make it dangerous. It is much better to have an informed discussion with the patient about the appropriate indications, alternatives, and possible side effects.

Conservative prescribing is particularly important for elderly patients where the tendency to prescribe medications as a first response has led to the common problem of polypharmacy.[69-71] Patients at nursing homes, oftentimes with life-limiting diseases and poor prognoses, may take a list of medications for primary or secondary prevention without consideration about whether or not they will ever live long enough to see any benefits. A framework for considering medication appropriateness for patients late in life advocates for including patients' remaining life expectancy and goals of care, along with an estimated time until benefit of the medication, as major components to consider when contemplating starting or stopping medications in the elderly.[71] For instance, while some medications for symptom relief, such as pain medications, have a very short time-to-benefit and can be very beneficial for patients at the end of their lives, other medications, such as statins, have a time-to-benefit of many years and therefore are unlikely to add any value for patients late in life.[71] Without benefits, all that is left are costs and burdens. These include financial costs, adverse effects (indeed, elderly patients are more sensitive to medications and are at higher risks for adverse effects), and excessive pill burdens. Members of the healthcare team, including clinicians and pharmacists, can each play an important role in reducing polypharmacy for the elderly.[70]

There are countless opportunities for clinicians to provide high-value medication prescribing for patients, ensuring that patients can afford, understand, and comply with their regimens. All healthcare professionals can take responsibility for familiarizing themselves with the available tools and tactics for determining medication costs, appropriate alternatives, and specific cost-saving strategies.

KEY POINTS:

- Out-of-pocket medication costs place a substantial financial burden on many patients and lead some to pursue measures for cost savings, including nonadherence to recommended medications.
- Clinicians can ask simple questions in order to screen patients for financial burdens associated with their medications (see Figure 13-3).
- A number of tools and resources exist to help patients and providers determine drug costs and possible cheaper, effective alternatives.
- Strategies, such as using equivalent generic medications, can yield significant cost savings for patients. Also clinicians can follow conservative prescribing practices that help minimize unnecessary costs and harms from medications.

References:

1. 10-year CVD Risk Calculator (Risk Assessment Tool for Estimating Your 10-year Risk of Having a Heart Attack Version). http://hp2010.nhlbihin.net/atpiii/calculator.asp. Accessed June 8, 2013.

2. Alexander GC, Casalino LP, Meltzer DO. Patient-physician communication about out-of-pocket costs. *JAMA.* 2003;290(7):953-958.

3. Piette JD, Heisler M, Wagner TH. Cost-related medication underuse: do patients with chronic illnesses tell their doctors? *Arch Intern Med.* 2004;164(16):1749-1755.

4. National Center for Health Statistics. *Health, United States, 2012.* Hyattsville, MD: 2013. /nchs/hus.htm. Accessed May 31, 2013.

5. Briesacher BA, Gurwitz JH, Soumerai SB. Patients at-risk for cost-related medication nonadherence: a review of the literature. *J Gen Intern Med.* 2007;22(6):864-871.

6. Libby AM, Fish DN, Hosokawa PW, et al. Patient-level medication regimen complexity across populations with chronic disease. *Clin Ther.* 2013;35(4):385-398.e1.

7. Eisen SA, Miller DK, Woodward RS, Spitznagel E, Przybeck TR. The effect of prescribed daily dose frequency on patient medication compliance. *Arch Intern Med.* 1990;150(9):1881-1884.

8. Chan M. Reducing cost-related medication nonadherence in patients with diabetes. *Drug Benefit Trends.* 2010;22(3):67-71.

9. Tamblyn R, Laprise R, Hanley JA, et al. Adverse events associated with prescription drug cost-sharing among poor and elderly persons. *JAMA.* 2001;285(4):421-429.

10. Soumerai SB, Ross-Degnan D, Avorn J, McLaughlin TJ, Choodnovskiy I. Effects of Medicaid drug-payment limits on admission to hospitals and nursing homes. *N Engl J Med.* 1991;325(15):1072-1077.

11. Soumerai SB, McLaughlin TJ, Ross-Degnan D, Casteris CS, Bollini P. Effects of limiting Medicaid drug-reimbursement benefits on the use of psychotropic agents and acute mental health services by patients with schizophrenia. *N Engl J Med.* 1994;331(10):650-655.

12. Gellad WF, Grenard JL, Marcum ZA. A systematic review of barriers to medication adherence in the elderly: looking beyond cost and regimen complexity. *Am J Geriatr Pharmacother.* 2011;9(1):11-23.

13. Chapman DRH, Petrilla AA, Benner JS, Schwartz JS, Tang SSK. Predictors of adherence to concomitant antihypertensive and lipid-lowering medications in older adults. *Drugs Aging.* 2008;25(10):885-892.

14. Gray SL, Mahoney JE, Blough DK. Medication adherence in elderly patients receiving home health services following hospital discharge. *Ann Pharmacother.* 2001;35(5):539-545.

15. Turner BJ, Hollenbeak C, Weiner MG, Ten Have T, Roberts C. Barriers to adherence and hypertension control in a racially diverse representative sample of elderly primary care patients. *Pharmacoepidemiol Drug Saf.* 2009;18(8):672-681.

16. Stoehr GP, Lu S-Y, Lavery L, et al. Factors associated with adherence to medication regimens in older primary care patients: the steel valley seniors survey. *Am J Geriatr Pharmacother.* 2008;6(5):255-263.

17. Gazmararian JA, Kripalani S, Miller MJ, Echt KV, Ren J, Rask K. Factors associated with medication refill adherence in cardiovascular-related diseases. *J Gen Intern Med.* 2006;21(12):1215-1221.

18. Odegard PS, Gray SL. Barriers to medication adherence in poorly controlled diabetes mellitus. *Diabetes Educ.* 2008;34(4):692-697.

19. Bangalore S, Kamalakkannan G, Parkar S, Messerli FH. Fixed-dose combinations improve medication compliance: a meta-analysis. *Am J Med.* 2007;120(8):713-719.

20. Margolius D. Rx for a medical near-miss. *Los Angeles Times*, June 3, 2013. http://www.latimes.com/news/opinion/commentary/la-oe-margolius-prescription-drugs-20130603,0,4406907.story. Accessed June 10, 2013.

21. Clear Health Costs. The price of birth control. http://clearhealthcosts.com/widget-blog/. Accessed July 11, 2013.
22. Weinstein JN, Lurie JD, Olson P, Bronner KK, Fisher ES, Morgan TS. United States trends and regional variations in lumbar spine surgery: 1992-2003. *Spine*. 2006;31(23):2707-2714.
23. Fisher ES, Bell J-E, Tomek IM, Esty AR, Goodman DC. Trends and regional variation in hip, knee, and shoulder replacement. The Dartmouth Institute for Health Policy and Clinical Practice; 2010. http://www.dartmouthatlas.org/downloads/reports/Joint_Replacement_0410.pdf. Accessed July 10, 2013.
24. Chon JK, Jacobs SC, Naslund MJ. The cost value of medical versus surgical hormonal therapy for metastatic prostate cancer. *J Urol*. 2000;164(3 Pt 1):735-737.
25. World Health Organization. Pharmaceutical industry. *WHO*. http://www.who.int/trade/glossary/story073/en/. Accessed July 11, 2013.
26. Zipkin DA, Steinman MA. Interactions between pharmaceutical representatives and doctors in training: a thematic review. *J Gen Intern Med*. 2005;20(8):777-786.
27. Grande D, Frosch D, Perkins A, et al. Effect of exposure to small pharmaceutical promotional items on treatment preferences. *Arch Intern Med*. 2009;169(9):887-893.
28. Austad KE, Avorn J, Franklin JM, Kowal MK, Campbell EG, Kesselheim AS. Changing interactions between physician trainees and the pharmaceutical industry: a national survey. *J Gen Intern Med*. 2013;28(8):1064-1071.
29. Association of American Medical Colleges. Industry funding of medical education: report of an AAMC Task Force; 2008. https://members.aamc.org/eweb/upload/Industry%20Funding%20of%20Medical%20Education.pdf. Accessed June 9, 2013.
30. Institute of Medicine (U.S.). *Conflict of Interest in Medical Research, Education, and Practice*. Washington, DC: National Academies Press; 2009.
31. Fugh-Berman A, Brown SR, Trippett R, et al. Closing the door on pharma? A national survey of family medicine residencies regarding industry interactions. *Acad Med*. 2011;86(5):649-654.
32. Kao AC, Braddock C 3rd, Clay M, et al. Effect of educational interventions and medical school policies on medical students' attitudes toward pharmaceutical marketing practices: a multi-institutional study. *Acad Med*. 2011;86(11):1454-1462.
33. King M, Essick C, Bearman P, Ross JS. Medical school gift restriction policies and physician prescribing of newly marketed psychotropic medications: difference-in-differences analysis. *BMJ*. 2013;346(5):f264-f264.
34. Steinbrook R. Future directions in industry funding of continuing medical education. *Arch Intern Med*. 2011;171(3):257-258.
35. ACCME Annual Report Data—2011. http://www.accme.org/news-publications/publications/annual-report-data/accme-annual-report-data-2011. Accessed June 10, 2013.
36. Agrawal S, Brennan N, Budetti P. The sunshine act—effects on physicians. *N Engl J Med*. 2013;368(22):2054-2057.
37. Heisler M, Wagner TH, Piette JD. Patient strategies to cope with high prescription medication costs: who is cutting back on necessities, increasing debt, or underusing medications? *J Behav Med*. 2005;28(1):43-51.
38. Safran DG, Neuman P, Schoen C, et al. Prescription drug coverage and seniors: how well are states closing the gap? *Health Aff*. 2002; Suppl Web Exclusives:W253-W268
39. Kumar R, Shah N, Levy A, Saathoff M, Farnan J, Arora V. GOT MeDS: designing and piloting an interactive module for trainees on reducing drug costs. *Poster Present Soc Gen Intern Med*. April 2013.
40. Moriates C, Shah NT, Arora VM. First, do no (financial) harm. *JAMA*. 2013;310(6):577-578.
41. Choudhry NK, Saya UY, Shrank WH, et al. Cost-related medication underuse: prevalence among hospitalized managed care patients. *J Hosp Med*. 2012;7(2):104-109.
42. Safe and effective drug recommendations from Best Buy Drugs. http://www.consumerreports.org/health/best-buy-drugs/index.htm. Accessed June 9, 2013.

43. Consumer Reports Health—Statins. http://www.consumerreports.org/health/best-buy-drugs/statins.htm. Accessed June 9, 2013.
44. AARP Drug Savings Tool. AARP. http://drugsavings.aarp.org/. Accessed May 14, 2013.
45. AARP launches drug-pricing tool. Mod Healthc. http://www.modernhealthcare.com/20101110/NEWS/311109992/. Accessed May 14, 2013.
46. myCigna. https://my.cigna.com/web/public/guest?#mycigna-benefits. Accessed June 9, 2013.
47. Medicare Plans & Benefits: Affordable Medicare Coverage at Humana. http://www.humana-medicare.com/. Accessed June 9, 2013.
48. Prescription Drug Trends Fact Sheet. May 2010 Update. http://kff.org/health-costs/fact-sheet/prescription-drug-trends-fact-sheet-may-2010/. Accessed May 15, 2013.
49. Bundorf MK, Royalty A, Baker LC. Health care cost growth among the privately insured. *Health Aff*. 2009;28(5):1294-1304.
50. Goldman DP, Joyce GF, Zheng Y. Prescription drug cost sharing: associations with medication and medical utilization and spending and health. *JAMA*. 2007;298(1):61-69.
51. Centers for Medicare & Medicaid Services. Your guide to Medicare prescription drug coverage. http://www.medicare.gov/Pubs/pdf/11109.pdf. Accessed June 6, 2013.
52. Strengthen Medicare: end drug company price setting. *Health Aff* Blog. http://healthaffairs.org/blog/2013/05/28/strengthen-medicare-end-drug-company-price-setting/. Accessed June 9, 2013.
53. Hamburger T. Obama gives powerful drug lobby a seat at healthcare table. *Los Angeles Times*. http://www.latimes.com/features/health/la-na-healthcare-pharma4-2009aug04,0,4078424,full.story. Published August 4, 2009. Accessed June 10, 2013.
54. Congressional Budget Office. Research and development in the pharmaceutical industry; 2006. http://www.cbo.gov/sites/default/files/cbofiles/ftpdocs/76xx/doc7615/10-02-drugr-d.pdf. Accessed July 10, 2013.
55. Eibner C, Goldman DP, Sullivan J, Garber AM. Three large-scale changes to the Medicare program could curb its costs but also reduce enrollment. *Health Aff*. 2013;32(5):891-899.
56. Karaca-Mandic P, Jena AB, Joyce GF, Goldman DP. Out-of-pocket medication costs and use of medications and health care services among children with asthma. *JAMA*. 2012;307(12):1284-1291.
57. Kesselheim AS, Brookhart MA, Lee JL, et al. Clinical equivalence of generic and brand-name drugs used in cardiovascular disease: a systematic review and meta-analysis. *JAMA*. 2008;300(21):2514-2526.
58. Shrank WH, Hoang T, Ettner SL, et al. The implications of choice: prescribing generic or preferred pharmaceuticals improves medication adherence for chronic conditions. *Arch Intern Med*. 2006;166(3):332-337.
59. Green JB, Ross JS, Jackevicius CA, Shah ND, Krumholz HM. When choosing statin therapy: the case for generics. *JAMA Intern Med*. 2013:1-4.
60. Campbell EG, Pham-Kanter G, Vogeli C, Iezzoni LI. Physician acquiescence to patient demands for brand-name drugs: results of a national survey of physicians. *JAMA Intern Med*. 2013:1-3.
61. Gellad WF, Donohue JM, Zhao X, et al. Brand-name prescription drug use among veterans affairs and Medicare Part D patients with diabetes. A national cohort comparison. *Ann Intern Med*. 2013;159(2):105-114.
62. Pharmacy. Kaiser Permanente®. http://businesshealth.kaiserpermanente.org/manage-costs/pharmacy/. Accessed June 9, 2013.
63. Grissinger M. The truth about hospital formularies, Part 1. *Pharm Ther*. 2008;33(8):441.
64. Wolf BL. Drug samples: benefit or bait? *JAMA*. 1998;279(21):1698-1699.
65. Cutrona SL, Woolhandler S, Lasser KE, Bor DH, McCormick D, Himmelstein DU. Characteristics of recipients of free prescription drug samples: a nationally representative analysis. *Am J Public Health*. 2008;98(2):284-289.
66. Alexander GC, Zhang J, Basu A. Characteristics of patients receiving pharmaceutical samples and association between sample receipt and out-of-pocket prescription costs. *Med Care*. 2008;46(4):394-402.

67. Chimonas S, Kassirer JP. No more free drug samples? *PLoS Med.* 2009;6(5):865.
68. Schiff GD, Galanter WL, Duhig J, et al. Principles of conservative prescribing. *Arch Intern Med.* 2011;171(16):1433.
69. Fulton MM, Riley Allen E. Polypharmacy in the elderly: a literature review. *J Am Acad Nurse Pract.* 2005;17(4):123-132.
70. Rollason V, Vogt N. Reduction of polypharmacy in the elderly: a systematic review of the role of the pharmacist. *Drugs Aging.* 2003;20(11):817-832.
71. Holmes HM, Hayley DC, Alexander GC, Sachs GA. Reconsidering medication appropriateness for patients late in life. *Arch Intern Med.* 2006;166(6):605-609.

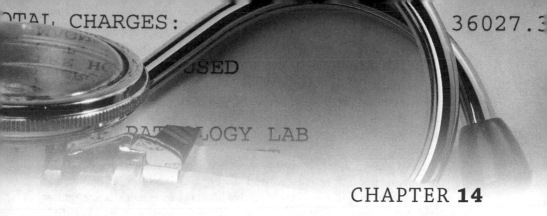

CHAPTER 14

Screening and Prevention: Balancing Benefits with Harms and Costs

"Oh, and one more thing: it is now time for you to get another colonoscopy," Dr Brown said to his patient Mrs Mary Moore, as she was packing up her purse and getting ready to leave the exam room. "We recommend that everyone gets a colonoscopy every 5 to 10 years, so I will have my nurse call you to set-up an appointment for you with the gastroenterologist here in town. Okay?"

"Umm, okay, sure," Mrs Moore, an 86-year-old widowed woman with severe congestive heart failure, hesitantly answered.

"Great! It is always a pleasure seeing you Mrs Moore, thanks for coming today. See you at your next appointment," Dr Brown smiled as he left.

Dr Brown has known Mrs Moore for more than 30 years. He has helped her through difficult times over the years such as the death of her spouse, and has taken care of her chronic hypothyroidism and more recently her worsening congestive heart failure. Mrs Moore truly respects Dr Brown and is thankful for their therapeutic relationship.

A colonoscopy involves inserting a small camera on a telescope-like instrument through the rectum in order to examine the interior of a person's large bowels. In general, the goal of a screening colonoscopy is to discover and remove polyps that can be precursors to cancer. But since progression from a polyp in the colon to a cancer is a slow process, it takes many years for patients to realize benefits from a colonoscopy procedure.[1] Also the procedure is expensive, preparation can be uncomfortable because of the need to take powerful laxatives in order to remove the fecal matter from the bowel, and there are risks of damaging the intestines during the procedure. Therefore, the US Preventive Services Task Force (USPSTF) advises against routine colon cancer screening in patients over 75 years and any screening in patients over 85.[2] Nevertheless, Medicare pays for routine screening colonoscopies regardless of age, paying doctors more than $100 million for nearly 550,000 screening colonoscopies in 2009, with around 40% of those for patients over 75.[3] But the cost is not only monetary: life-threatening complications such as perforating the bowel significantly increase with advancing age.[4] Therefore, an 86-year-old patient with a life-limiting disease like congestive heart failure is more likely to suffer from the risks of a colonoscopy than to ever see the potential downstream benefits.

Overscreening patients for disease is a massive and growing problem in the United States. Elderly patients, often with multiple life-limiting diseases and/ or advanced dementia, frequently undergo screening testing that will never benefit them.[5] Approximately 50% of woman older than 80 years continue to receive breast cancer screening, and more than half of patients older than 75 years report that their physicians continue to recommend routine screening.[6]

For younger patients, colonoscopies may also present a personal monetary hurdle. Although insurance plans cover the costs of colonoscopy as a preventive test, if an abnormality is found (such as a polyp or growth) then some no longer consider it a "screening test," and patients may be responsible for paying their entire deductible or copay.[7] For patients on a high-deductible health plan (see Chapter 2), this could mean that the patient is responsible for the entire cost of the procedure, which may be up to thousands of dollars. The American Cancer Society (ACS) recommends: "If you are getting a screening colonoscopy, be sure to find out how much you will have to pay if something is found (and biopsied or removed) during the exam. This can help you avoid any surprise costs."[7] This clearly illustrates the tension between patient affordability and societal stewardship; screening is cost-effective at the societal level and improves population health, but has the potential to be expensive for the individual patient and very rarely improves individual health.

Many colonoscopies are performed unnecessarily, and not only in elderly patients. Following a negative screening colonoscopy, the recommendation is to not repeat the test within 7 to 10 years. However, in a large study, nearly half of patients underwent a repeated examination in fewer than 7 years, suggesting an epidemic of unhelpful colonoscopies.[8] In the right setting—a patient in the appropriate target group and obtained at recommended intervals—colonoscopies can be incredibly valuable, life-saving procedures, but too often these procedures are performed in situations without likely benefit. With no realized benefit, the only things left are unpleasant bowel preps, discomfort, risks, and costs.

DEFINING AN EFFECTIVE SCREENING TOOL

Effective screening tests should meet a number of conditions[9]:

- Designed to detect asymptomatic and early stage disease
- Highly *sensitive* and highly *specific* (see below) to pick up most cases of true disease and avoid *false-positives*

- Targeted toward populations with a higher disease prevalence (high *positive predictive value*)
- Relatively safe and cost-effective to society (as defined by "willingness to pay" thresholds that vary by country or health system)
- Screen for diseases in which early identification and treatment have been demonstrated to improve clinical outcomes

In 1968, the World Health Organization published formal guidelines for the principles of screening, often referred to as "Wilson's Criteria" after the lead author, Dr James M.G. Wilson (Table 14-1).[10] These tenets form the foundation for screening tests.

There are different types of screening strategies that are commonly used in society, including:

- *Mass screening*: the screening of an entire population or a subgroup, offered to all, irrespective of the risk status of the individual.

  Examples include pap screening at age 21 regardless of sexual history; or HIV screening for all adolescents and adults aged 15 to 65 years (as recommended by the USPSTF).
- *High-risk or selective screening*: screening conducted only among populations at a particular risk for the disease.

  For instance, many genetically linked disorders are part of prenatal testing for specific patient groups (eg, cystic fibrosis in Northern European patients; Tay Sachs in Ashkenazi Jewish patients). Another example is early breast and ovarian cancer screening in women with a genetic disorder that puts them at high risk for these diseases (BRCA+ mutation).

Table 14-1 World Health Organization (WHO) principles of screening guidelines

• The condition should be an important health problem.
• There should be a treatment for the condition.
• Facilities for diagnosis and treatment should be available.
• There should be a latent stage of the disease.
• There should be a test or examination for the condition.
• The test should be acceptable to the population.
• The natural history of the disease should be adequately understood.
• There should be an agreed policy on whom to treat.
• The total cost of finding a case should be economically balanced in relation to medical expenditure as a whole.
• Case-finding should be a continuous process, not just a "once and for all" project.

Source: Reproduced, with permission, from Wilson JMG, Jungner G. *Principles and Practice of Screening for Disease.* Geneva: World Health Organization, 1968.

- *Multiphasic screening*: a technique of screening populations that combines the application of two or more screening tests (a "battery of screening tests") to a large population at one time instead of carrying out separate screening tests for single diseases.

    This strategy is often employed by Health Maintenance Organizations (HMOs) and corporate wellness programs to screen for "metabolic syndrome" disorders, and are also used frequently for prenatal immunity screening (single blood collection in first trimester to test rubella, hepatitis B, HIV, and other diseases).

Brief biostatistics review

It is vital that clinicians have a firm grasp on interpreting the basic test characteristics of all diagnostic tests. Sensitivity and specificity both measure a test's validity. They describe the test's ability to correctly detect people with or without the disease in question.[11] Therefore, they are critical to the evaluation of screening tests and thresholds. Let us briefly visit these concepts now. The equations for each of these biostatistical terms are presented in Table 14-2.

The *sensitivity* of a test is its ability to detect people who actually have the disease. A test that is 100% sensitive would always identify every person with that disease. Very sensitive tests are required in situations where the consequences of a *false-negative* result (a negative test result obtained in a case where the person does

Table 14-2 **Biostatistical terms and equations**

Term	Definition	Equation
Sensitivity	The ability to detect people who *do* have the disease.	$\dfrac{\text{Number testing positive who have the disease (TP)}}{\text{Total number tested who have the disease (TP+FN)}} \times 100$
Specificity	The ability to detect people who *do not* have the disease.	$\dfrac{\text{Number testing negative who do not have the disease (TN)}}{\text{Total number tested who do not have the disease (TN+FP)}} \times 100$
Positive Predictive Value (PPV)	The likelihood that a person with a positive test result actually has the disease.	$\dfrac{\text{Number who test positive and have the disease (TP)}}{\text{Total number who test positive (TP+FP)}} \times 100$
Negative Predictive Value (NPV)	The likelihood that a person with a negative test result truly does not have the disease.	$\dfrac{\text{Number who test negative and do not have the disease (TN)}}{\text{Total number who test negative (TN+FN)}} \times 100$

Source: Data from Glaser AN. *High-Yield Biostatistics*, 3rd ed. Philadelphia: Lippincott Williams & Wilkins; 2005.

actually have the disease) would be extremely serious.[11] For instance, screening donated blood for HIV, in which a highly sensitive test is required to ensure that there are not any false-negative cases leading to accidental transmission of HIV.

Highly sensitive tests are good for ruling out disease. In other words, if a highly sensitive test is negative, one can rest assured that it is exceedingly unlikely that they have the disease in question.

Of course, finding everyone who have the disease is only half of the issue. A test that *always* returned positive may indeed be a true-positive for every person with the disease (therefore, "highly sensitive"), but it would also be positive for every-one without the disease (false-positive); thus, it would remain a worthless test.

The *specificity* of a test is its ability to detect people who *do not* have the disease. Tests that are highly specific are needed particularly in situations where a false-positive test would cause significant harm. For instance, prior to starting a toxic chemotherapy regimen for cancer, the patient and physician need to be quite certain that the test result is true and the patient does indeed have cancer.

Highly specific tests help rule in disease. That is, that if a highly specific test is positive for a certain disease then there is substantial confidence that the patient does in fact have that disease.

Ideally, screening tests will maximize both sensitivity and specificity, but in practice there is almost always a trade-off between the two; sensitivity is increased at the cost of specificity, and vice versa. This is usually because patients with a disease and without a disease are on a continuum and the two groups often overlap each other.[11] The test must have a "cut-off" point that is chosen based on the specific test characteristics. Where that cut-off point is chosen may lead to either more missed cases (false-negatives) or more incorrect diagnoses (false-positives). A commonly used strategy is to perform a highly sensitive and rather cheap test first to identify all patients that may have a disease, and then follow up with a more specific (and usually more expensive) test to eliminate false-positive results. This approach is used for HIV testing.

Sensitivity and specificity are very important concepts when designing or evaluating diagnostic tests, and when determining whether a test should be ordered in the first place. But once a test is performed, the individual patient and clinician want to answer a different question altogether. The patient wants to know, based on this test result, how likely is it that I do or do not have the disease. The answer of this question requires knowing the *predictive values* of the test.

The *Positive Predictive Value (PPV)* is the proportion of positive results that are true-positives. If a patient tests positive for HIV, the question is: "Given the posi-tive test, how likely is it that I actually have HIV?" The PPV answers this question.

The *Negative Predictive Value (NPV)* is the proportion of negative results that are true-negatives. If the HIV test returns negative, the question is: "Given the negative test, how likely is it that I really do not have HIV?" The NPV answers this question.

The predictive values vary according to the prevalence of the disease in a specific population group. Using the blood test CA-125 to screen for ovarian

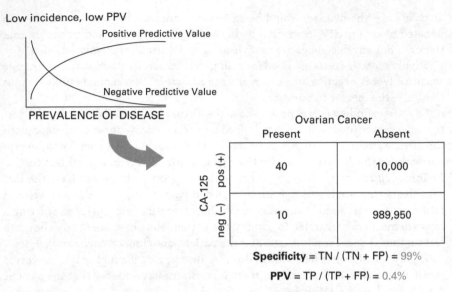

Specificity = TN / (TN + FP) = 99%

PPV = TP / (TP + FP) = 0.4%

Figure 14-1. An example of a highly specific test but with a low positive predictive value due to low disease prevalence in a population.

cancer may be an excellent example of predictive values and the concept of the trade-offs between sensitivity and specificity. CA-125 may be up to 99% specific, but it is less than 80% sensitive. Since the population prevalence is so low, this results in an abysmal 0.4% PPV, thus rendering it unhelpful as a mass screening tool.[12] As Figure 14-1 shows, with these test characteristics if 100,000 women were screened, there would be approximately 10,040 positive results. The problem is that this would be a false-positive for 10,000 of these women, potentially subjecting them to further testing, undue worry, and invasive procedures.

LIMITATIONS AND BIASES IN SCREENING

There are various limitations that are inherent to screening tests and are important for clinicians to consider when interpreting these studies. The apparent effects from screening will always be more favorable than real effects seen in a population.[13] This is because screening-detected cases include cases that were diagnosed earlier, progress more slowly, and may never actually cause a clinical problem. There are a number of biases that we review below that inflate the survival of screen-detected cases. The key is to understand the important difference between survival rates and mortality. Whereas mortality rates define the number of people that die of a certain cause in a given year, survival rates calculate the percentage of people with a disease who are still alive a set amount of time after diagnosis. Preventing death, curing the disease, or *making the diagnosis earlier* can all increase survival rates.[14]

Consider this illustrative story by Indiana University School of Medicine professor Dr Aaron Carroll from the *Incidental Economist* blog[14]:

Let's say there's a new cancer of the thumb killing people. From the time the first cancer cell appears, you have 9 years to live, with chemo. From the time you can feel a lump, you have 4 years to live, with chemo. Let's say we have no way to detect the disease until you feel a lump. The 5-year survival rate for this cancer is about 0, because within 5 years of detection, everyone dies, even on therapy.

Now I invent a new scanner that can detect thumb cancer when only one cell is there. Because it's the United States, we invest heavily in those scanners. Early detection is everything, right? We have protests and lawsuits and now everyone is getting scanned like crazy. Not only that, but people are getting chemo earlier and earlier for the cancer. Sure, the side effects are terrible, but we want to live.

We made no improvements to the treatment. Everyone is still dying 4 years after they feel the lump. But since we are making the diagnosis 5 years earlier, our 5-year survival rate is now approaching 100%! Everyone is living 9 years with the disease. Meanwhile, in England, they say that the scanner doesn't extend life and won't pay for it. Rationing! That's why their 5-year survival rate is still 0%.

The mortality rate is unchanged. The same number of people are dying every year. We have just moved the time of diagnosis up and subjected people to 5 more years of side-effects and reduced quality of life. We haven't done any good at all. We haven't extended life, we've just lengthened the time you have a diagnosis.

Lead-time bias

Dr Carroll's "thumb cancer" example highlights the problem of *lead-time bias* from screening tests. Since we determine the length of survival from the time of diagnosis, and screen-detected cases are diagnosed earlier than those detected by signs and symptoms, the measured survival length often increases with screening, even if that patient ends up dying at the same exact time they would have died without the screening test. The patient seems to have lived longer with cancer, but in reality they simply knew about the cancer longer. In Figure 14-2, the patient develops cancer in March 2013 and dies in January 2016. The only difference is that with a screening test, the diagnosis was made in January 2014; without the test, the diagnosis was made based on symptoms in July 2015. With the screening test, the patient is said to have survived for 2 years with cancer. Without the screening test, the patient is considered to have survived for only 6 months with cancer. But the reality is that she died the same date regardless. She simply was aware of the existence of her disease longer.

Lead-time bias helps explain why the commonly used metric of 5-year survival rates to judge the value of cancer screening can potentially be misleading.[15]

Length-time bias

Another issue is that screening overestimates survival duration due to the relative excess identification of slowly progressing disease, a phenomenon known as *length-time bias*. Screening tests disproportionately find slow-growing cancers compared to rapidly advancing cancers due to a much larger window of

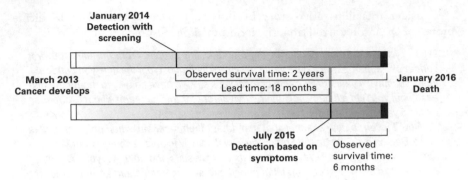

Figure 14-2. Lead-time bias example.

opportunity to identify these diseases in an asymptomatic state.[13,15] In other words, "the probability of detection is directly proportional to the length of time during which they are detectable (and thereby inversely proportional to the rate of progression)."[13] The most important consequence is that the very nature of screening tests selects for cancers that inherently have a better prognosis.[15]

Figure 14-3 demonstrates this concept, showing how slower growing tumors that are much less likely to kill someone within the given time-span are much

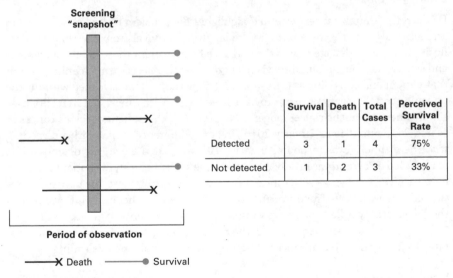

Figure 14-3. Length-time bias.

Notes: A total of seven patients (lines) are depicted. The length of the line represents the length of the clinical course. Even though the prevalence of disease is nearly the same in this hypothetical cohort, patients that survive during the period of observation (blue lines) are more likely to be detected during a "screening snapshot" than patients that die during the period of observation (black lines). This can skew perceived survival rates.

more likely to be picked up by screening tests, compared to rapidly progressive disease that both develops and causes death within the screening interval.

The extreme of this is "overdiagnosis," which is discussed in detail further below. Overdiagnosis refers to finding a lesion that is so indolent that if it were untreated it would never go on to cause problems for the individual. In 2012, the USPSTF recommended against routine prostate cancer screening using the prostate-specific antigen (PSA) test for exactly this reason. Before this guideline, PSA testing was widespread. In an effort to curb overuse of PSA, the USPSTF pointed out the multiple harms of overdiagnosis in their recommendations, including the small risk of death from unnecessary surgery.[16]

Healthy volunteer bias

There is often something fundamentally different about people who agree to participate in prevention and early detection programs from those who do not. In general, folks that opt to participate in screening or prevention programs tend to be more health-conscious. On average, they are more likely to exercise, they smoke and drink less, and they come from higher socioeconomic classes compared to those that do not participate in these programs.[15] Therefore, at baseline this self-selected group of people seem to live longer in general than those that do not participate in these types of programs. In fact, this is such a common finding that epidemiologists have labeled it the *"healthy volunteer effect."*[15]

In the Prostate, Lung, Colorectal, and Ovarian (PLCO) cancer screening trial—a large, multicenter program that randomized more than 150,000 men and women between 55 and 74 years to a screening or a control arm over many years—the standardized all-cause mortality rate was 43 in participants, whereas the expected standard would be 100.[17] Why did the men and women who chose to enroll in this study die so much less frequently (regardless of randomization to the screening arm) than would be expected in the general population? Well, it turns out that these subjects were better educated, more physically active, more likely to be married, and less likely to be current smokers than the average public.[17]

ENTHUSIASM FOR CANCER SCREENING IN THE UNITED STATES

Americans are generally "enthusiastic" about cancer screening.[18] This is true for people in other countries as well. In the United Kingdom, people expressed a clear preference to undergo diagnostic testing for cancer at all risk levels—88% of people surveyed said that they would want to undergo diagnostic testing for cancer even if the risk that their symptom actually represented cancer was only 1%.[19] When it comes to cancer, often emotion prevails over cold hard science.[20,21] However, interestingly, this fervor for cancer screening does not extend to other healthcare issues, such as heart disease, which actually kills many more women than breast cancer.[20]

This is not necessarily surprising. There exist many persuasive stories and messages of people touting that a screening test "saved my life." There is no doubt that this is sometimes true and that certain screening tests have made a substantial contribution to lives being saved. But, over the course of 30 years, screening mammography has had a limited effect on breast cancer mortality in the United States.[22] Although the introduction of mammography has been associated with a doubling of early-stage breast cancer cases detected each year (from 112 to 234 cases per 100,000 women), the rate at which women present with late-stage cancer has only decreased by 8% (from 102 to 94 cases per 100,000 women). Therefore, it seems that only 8 of the additional 122 early-stage cancers diagnosed by screening mammography would have been expected to progress to advanced disease.[22] In an impressively large, comprehensive trial performed in Canada, nearly 90,000 women between the ages of 40 to 59 were randomized in the 1980s to either get annual screening mammography for 5 years or no mammography at all. The results were released in 2014 and, perhaps shockingly, revealed that there was no significant difference in death from breast cancer in both groups (500/44,925 women died in the mammogram group; 505/44,910 women died in the no mammogram group).[23] How can this happen? Well, remember the limitations of screening testing including lead-time and length-time biases. It has been suggested that as many as one-in-three women with breast cancer detected by screening are "overdiagnosed"—they had tumors detected on screening that would never have led to meaningful clinical symptoms—translating to 1.3 million women in the United States over the past 30 years.[22,24] This means the reality is that most women with screen-detected breast cancer that claim to have had their "life saved" have *not* likely had their life saved by screening.[25] Instead, it is much more likely that these women were diagnosed early with no effect on their mortality, or they were overdiagnosed, such that their cancer would not have ever resulted in clinically meaningful disease.[25]

The issue becomes even clearer as we look at screening in the elderly—the group that may be least likely to see long-term benefits from screening and most likely to experience harms. Many older adults think that "it would be strange" to stop cancer screening at any point during their lifetime.[26] Stopping screening feels like a major decision, whereas just continuing to go along with screening may not. Due to these deeply ingrained ideals, some have worried that "a physician's recommendation to stop [screening] may threaten patient trust."[26] As a result, as many as half of women over 80 years old continue to undergo breast cancer screening.[6] Not surprisingly, the largest predictor about whether or not a patient undergoes a screening test is whether their physician recommended the test to them.[6] More than 50% of men and women over the age of 75 report that their physicians continue to regularly recommend screening.[6]

It is clear that clinicians are not immune to the phenomenon of "misfearing," the term used to describe the human tendency to fear instinctively rather than factually.[20] Healthcare professionals demonstrate an inordinate fear of missing cancer, which undoubtedly shapes some of their overzealous screening practices.

In the United States, more screening is happening more frequently... even when the screening test is considered inappropriate. A large cross-sectional national study comparing outpatient visits in 1999 to visits in 2009 found that while 6 of 9 underuse indicators improved, only 2 of the 11 overuse indicators got better, and in fact one of the metrics—prostate cancer screening among men older than 74 years old—got significantly worse.[27]

Even patients with advanced cancer and limited life expectancies undergo screening.[28] Almost 10% of women with advanced non-breast cancer underwent a subsequent mammogram, and 15% of men with advanced non-prostate cancer underwent prostate cancer screening with a blood test (PSA).[28] This is crazy!

One driver may be that many clinicians are drilled with quality indicators that indiscriminately focus on screening rates. In the Veteran Affairs healthcare system, an age-based measure for colorectal cancer encourages testing in patients aged 50 to 75. With this program, an unhealthy 75-year-old man was more likely to get a colonoscopy than a healthy 76-year-old man.[29] This highlights the need for future quality measures to focus on clinical benefit rather than simply age, and also to balance measures of underuse with those that gauge overuse.

Clinicians may be able to reduce non-beneficial screening by including frank and informed discussions of risks and benefits, including complications and potential burdens, in their patient counseling.[26] In reality, clinicians rarely discuss the possibility of overdiagnosis and overtreatment when recommending cancer screening.[30] In contrast to much of the data highlighting emotions driving screening overuse, in a survey of Americans aged 50 to 69 years old, most of whom had undergone screening, over half of patients said they would not agree to screening if it resulted in more than one overtreated person per one cancer death averted, and almost all of them (87%) would not agree if more than 20 received overtreatment per one death averted.[30]

"Wow," wrote Dartmouth Institute researcher Dr H. Gilbert Welch in an accompanying editorial.[31] "That implies that millions of Americans might not choose to be screened if they knew the whole story; however, most do not."

THE HARMS OF SCREENING AND OVERTESTING

Although some fear that recommendations to avoid certain screening tests are driven by concerns over costs—that, bluntly, lives are being lost to save money—costs are very rarely the reason that guidelines set limits on screening.[32] Many of the boundaries placed on screening guidelines are driven by the patient harms that result from screening. "Harms from screening programs are real; the burden of these harms can be disputed, but their existence cannot."[32]

Screening can lead to physical complications caused by the test (for instance, colon perforation from colonoscopy, as mentioned in the introduction), anxiety over abnormal results, overdiagnosis, and a snowballing effect of further testing, workups, and treatments.

One particularly dramatic example comes from a patient I admitted to the hospital. A healthy 84-year-old woman underwent a routine colonoscopy and then immediately developed severe abdominal pain and hypotension (low blood pressure). She was transferred to our emergency department and underwent two CT scans and an ultrasound to determine that she had a splenic hematoma (bleeding resulting in a collection of blood in her spleen). This required an overnight hospital stay for monitoring and resulted in significant pain for the patient. In fact, over a month following discharge, she continued to experience pain from this complication.

Splenic hematoma is a rare complication of colonoscopy, but occurs more frequently in females and the elderly. Most concerning about this case was that when asked, our patient stated that she was not aware that if cancer were found from this test that she would possibly have required colorectal surgery and chemotherapy, which she thought she probably would not have wanted to pursue anyways. Just like Ms Moore in the beginning of this chapter, she had never discussed the possible downsides of this screening procedure, nor the fact that colonoscopy is generally not recommended for routine screening at her age.[2]

Another serious complication from screening tests is the risk of false-positive results. Being told that you have cancer or HIV can cause profound psychological distress that can actually persist for years.[33,34] And these situations are unfortunately all too common. Over the course of 10 years, one out of every three women screened for breast cancer, who do not actually have breast cancer, will have an abnormal test result that requires additional evaluation.[35]

Screening tests can also lead to incorrect labeling, inconvenience, expense, and physical harm due to follow-up tests. Although there are screening tests for many different diseases and conditions, let us once again consider the case of cancer. The word "cancer" is an extremely loaded term, fraught with automatic connotations and emotional responses. Many patients have described situations where immediately following a clinician uttering the word "cancer," they felt that they were briskly overwhelmed and not able to pay attention to or hear anything else that was said. But many conditions that currently include the word "cancer" do not truly represent life-threatening diseases. Leaders from the National Cancer Institute have called for removing the term "cancer" (or "carcinoma") for any lesions that do not present a reasonable likelihood of lethal progression if left untreated, such as many premalignant conditions including ductal carcinoma in situ (DCIS).[36] The idea is that patients are likely to behave differently if their disease is appropriately framed with the correct implied degree of seriousness. For example, many forms of thyroid nodules and thyroid "cancer" are not truly dangerous. Since 1975, the incidence of thyroid cancer has nearly tripled, but the mortality rate has not changed.[37] These patients often undergo frequent follow-up ultrasound tests to monitor this abnormality, which is a huge source of radiology revenue, but has no demonstrated impact at all on mortality.[38,39] "The epidemiology of the increased incidence ... suggests that it is not an epidemic of disease but rather an epidemic of diagnosis."[37] Sound familiar?

SCREENING RECOMMENDATIONS AND DISCREPANCIES IN GUIDELINES

Over the past few decades, guidelines have taken hold and proliferated at an astounding pace. The Agency for Healthcare Research and Quality (AHRQ) sponsors the National Guideline Clearinghouse (www.guideline.gov). As of January 2014, there were 2498 individual guideline summaries included in this index.[40] Guidelines are important tools to help inform clinicians and provide advice, but it would serve us well to remember that guidelines are written by groups with different stakeholders and viewpoints. This results in biases that sometimes shape recommendations. Commonly, different groups come up with directly opposing recommendations. As a general rule, the USPSTF tends to be more conservative compared to many advocacy groups. For example, in 2008 the USPSTF found that two colorectal screening tests—fecal DNA testing and CT colonography—were lacking in evidence, while the ACS endorsed these tests.[32]

In 2009, the USPSTF recommended against "routine" mammography for women aged 40 to 49 years, suggesting instead that physicians first address women in this age group's "values regarding specific benefits and harms." This recommendation led to vocal and sharply polarized opinions in the medical literature and public press. Both sides flung allegations of harming women.[41] No doubt, the stakes are high.

As each guideline organization evaluated the same evidence through their own lenses, different recommendations emerged. Currently, "guidelines issued by four highly respected organizations provide conflicting recommendations about the appropriate interval for screening mammography of women aged 40 to 74 years at average risk of breast cancer."[42] USPSTF recommends mammography every 2 years for women at average risk aged 50 to 74 years. The ACS and American College of Radiology (ACR) guidelines call for annual screening mammography in average risk women aged 40 years and older—without a stop date. The American College of Obstetricians and Gynecology (ACOG) recommends annual mammography, but hedge by stating that biennial mammography may be "more appropriate or acceptable" for some women.

The costs associated with these discrepant screening strategies is enormous; the United States could likely save more than $6 billion annually on breast cancer screening if practices followed the USPSTF guidelines rather than actual practices (Figure 14-4).[43]

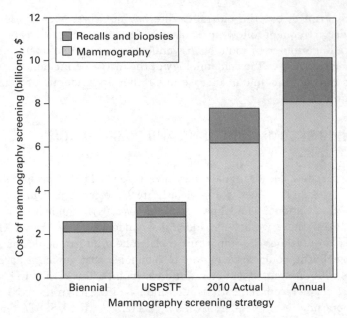

Figure 14-4. The costs of guideline-discordant mammography practices. (Reproduced, with permission, from O'Donoghue C, Eklund M, Ozanne EM, Esserman LJ. Aggregate cost of mammography screening in the United States; comparison of current practice and advocated guidelines. *Ann Intern Med.* 2014;160(3):145-153. Copyright © 2014, The American College of Physicians.)

Moreover, conflicting guidelines can lead clinicians to feel vulnerable to malpractice. What happens if they follow the USPSTF guidelines and then a patient claims to have a delayed diagnosis of breast cancer that may have been seen a year earlier if her physician had used the ACS recommendations? This has led some to propose "safe harbor" legislation that would provide liability protection to physicians that comply with approved guidelines or protocols.[42,44] Although this may make clinicians more comfortable—and possibly more likely to adhere to guidelines in general—one study found that applying proposed "safe harbor" legislation to closed malpractice claims would have reversed the findings in the physician's favor less than 1% of the time.[45] Despite fear and the perception of malpractice liability, clinicians are frankly extremely unlikely to be sued for following a specific guideline.

By the way, for comparison sake, we will note that the United Kingdom's breast cancer screening program recommends mammography every 3 years for women aged 50 through 70 years.[46]

Political contexts

The US Congress created the Agency for Healthcare Policy and Research (AHCPR, which later became AHRQ) in 1989 and charged it with creating a public-private partnership to develop, disseminate, and evaluate clinical practice guidelines. But in 1995, Congress very nearly defunded the agency in response to lobbying by back surgeons who disagreed with the guidelines the group had created for the treatment of low back pain.[47] The threat to defund the program was likely not an empty one. Other governmental bodies, such as the National Center for Health Care Technology and the congressional Office of Technology Assessment, have been defunded due to political sensitivities surrounding this type of activity.[47]

In the court of public opinion, the harms of overscreening are very rarely considered.[48] The framing of these harms is controversial even among scientists, as thresholds to quantify harm from overscreening are imprecise.[49] Despite the 2009 mammography guideline update, it does not appear there was any subsequent decrease in utilization, suggesting a lack of public acceptance.[50] Many have noted that when considering cancer screening programs, "politics trounces science."[51]

As the issues surrounding the production of guidelines in the United States become increasingly contentious, political fights can even lead to judicial disputes. One dramatic example has been labeled "The Lyme Wars," pitting most of American medicine and the Infectious Disease Society of America (IDSA) against a faction consisting of self-proclaimed "Lyme-literate" patients, advocates, politicians, and physicians, led by the International Lyme and Associated Diseases Society,[52] who promote the idea of "chronic Lyme disease." A number of political groups have sprouted up to purportedly increase awareness and raise funds for "chronic Lyme disease." The Lyme Action Network widely released a patient-facing pamphlet called "It Might Be Lyme" that listed various nonspecific symptoms that may be harbingers for this disputed entity.[52] The battle became so heated that in May 2008, the attorney general of Connecticut performed an antitrust investigation into the development of Lyme disease treatment guidelines released by the IDSA, one of the largest medical societies in the United States.[53]

Likely prompted by the increased scrutiny, political contexts, and high-wired reactions enveloping guidelines these days, in June 2013, the National Heart, Lung, and Blood Institute announced that it would discontinue its nearly 4-decade participation in the development of clinical guidelines.[54]

Shifting guidelines to improve value and decrease harms of overtesting

A number of suggestions have been made over the last few years to reform guidelines in order to improve value and decrease harms of overtesting. One that has seemed to take hold is for recommendations to routinely be graded by a standardized rubric. The Grading of Recommendations Assessment, Development, and Evaluation (GRADE) system (www.gradeworkinggroup.org) classifies recommendations as strong or weak based on the strength of the evidence and patient outcomes.[55] GRADE does not allow for "expert opinion." In the absence of evidence, or if there is clearly conflicting evidence, no recommendation is made. This is actually a paradigm shift, considering that more than half of guideline recommendations currently by IDSA and those issued by the American Heart Association/American College of Cardiology are based solely on expert opinion and do not have evidence to back them up.[56-58]

Other systems for grading evidence have been developed by the USPSTF (Table 14-3) and AHRQ.[59]

One of the problems with guidelines based on "expert opinion" is that many have expressed concerns about conflicts of interest among members of guideline groups.[47,60] According to a 2002 survey, 87% of clinical guideline authors had some form of interaction with the pharmaceutical industry—more than half had received financial support.[61] Interestingly, only 7% of participants believed that their own relationship with industry influenced their recommendations, 19% felt that their coauthors' recommendations were influenced by such relationships.[61] The Institute of Medicine has recommended that "groups that develop clinical practice guidelines should generally exclude as panel members individuals with conflicts of interest and should not accept direct funding for clinical practice guideline development from medical product companies or company foundations."[47]

Despite the sharpening focus on healthcare value, guidelines notably often do not explicitly consider the cost denominator of the value equation at all in their analyses or recommendations.[62] This has prompted some leaders to call for more widespread inclusion of cost considerations and information in guidelines, which could help inform clinicians, the public, and policymakers regarding interventions that are most likely to provide high-value care for patients.[63]

Table 14-3 United States Preventive Services Task Force (USPSTF) recommendation grades

Grade	Definition
A	The USPSTF recommends the service. There is high certainty that the net benefit is substantial.
B	The USPSTF recommends the service. There is high certainty that the net benefit is moderate, or there is moderate certainty that the net benefit is moderate to substantial.
C	Clinicians may provide this service to selected patients depending on individual circumstances. However, for most individuals without signs of symptoms there is likely to be only a small benefit from this service.
D	The USPSTF recommends against the service. There is moderate or high certainty that the service has no net benefit or that the harms outweigh the benefits.
I Statement	The USPSTF concludes that current evidence is insufficient to assess the balance of benefits and harms of the service.

Since guidelines are complicated documents that require careful analyses and considerations that rely on a breadth of skill and knowledge, a multidisciplinary team that include expertise in epidemiology, statistics, economics, and health-care policy should be included in effective guideline groups.[60,64] Some have also advocated for including patients and explicitly addressing patient preferences in guideline considerations.[65]

Of course, creating the guidelines is only part of the issue. For guidelines to be effective, they must convince clinicians to adhere to their recommendations in the correct situations. There are various barriers to guideline adherence, including lack of awareness, familiarity, or agreement.[66] Guideline groups and healthcare systems should concentrate on efforts to improve observance of appropriate guidelines. Some suggested strategies involve including prioritized checklists of recommendations and clear implementation strategies that rely on systems rather than individual clinicians.[64] Part of the challenge with guideline implementation is that guidelines are typically optimized for the average patient and it is widely accepted that there will always be exceptional patients that do not fit the criteria of the recommendations. The problem is that *most* patients view themselves as exceptional. As Yale cardiologist and health researcher Dr Harlan Krumholz eloquently puts it, "guidelines should inform but not dictate, guide but not enforce, and support but not restrict."[67]

Appropriateness criteria

A new breed of guidelines is now emerging: Appropriateness Criteria. The ACR launched their ACR Appropriateness Criteria during the 1990s in an immense effort to define national guidelines for proper imaging usage. In 2013, the ACR Appropriateness Criteria addressed over 197 clinical conditions with more than 900 variants, providing expert guidance for clinicians to weigh potential benefits and risks—including radiation and costs—when choosing imaging modalities for a given clinical scenario.[68] The ACR Appropriateness Criteria are reviewed and updated at least biennially. More recently, a similar effort has emerged by the American College of Cardiology (ACC). The ACC Appropriate Use Criteria are "intended to define 'when to do' and 'how often to do' a given procedure in the context of scientific evidence, the healthcare environment, the patient's profile and a physician's judgement."[69] Appropriateness Criteria often address more detailed scenarios than practice guidelines, thus are able to differentiate between subtle differences.[69] They also generally consider a much broader context that may more accurately capture possible harms of testing. Appropriateness Criteria have the potential to emerge as instrumental tools in clinicians' efforts to deliver high-value care. Similarly, the ABIM Foundation's Choosing Wisely campaign (www.ChoosingWisely.org) reframes the most common way guidelines are used; instead of listing guidelines for what to do, the campaign lists guidelines for what not to do.

Story From the Frontlines: "Failing Grades for Doing the Right Thing"

Mrs Smith is a 40-year-old woman who has always had her annual pap smears. With the change in pap smear guidelines, she does not need a pap smear this year. Mrs Smith comes in for her annual well-woman visit and she expects a pap smear—she has always thought that screening for cervical cancer was very important and she is a little worried over this new recommendation and expresses this concern to her physician.

So a pap smear is performed. This takes less time than counseling her about why the pap smear guidelines have changed. And it makes the patient happy because it makes her feel safe.

The test shows mild dysplasia, so she returns to the office for another appointment including a colposcopy and biopsy. Mild dysplasia is confirmed on the biopsy and the patient is told that this does not need treatment, but that she should have another pap smear in six months. She is a little anxious, but relieved that this abnormality was "caught in time."

So the patient had anxiety, expense, discomfort, and a couple of extra procedures over this. It turns out that she is happy that her doctor did not follow the guidelines—after all, in her view, he found something and now he will follow it closely. But ... the pap smear did not need to be done in the first place, and the results of mild dysplasia are very unlikely to be significant in this case. (Most mild dysplasias resolve spontaneously without any needed treatment. Furthermore, progression from mild to cancer is very slow so progression would be discovered within the recommended interval.)

As a physician, what do we have to believe in? This is just my opinion, but I think that physicians have to believe in educating their patients about why certain tests do not need to be done—I also think we have an obligation to the society as a whole to be good stewards of healthcare dollars. It does take more work to teach patients about why a test may not need to be performed—in fact it takes longer to explain this than to just do the test.

In my current system, the grade on my "report card"—which I receive every month and shows each physician listed with the number of patients seen and amount of charges generated—is lower for doing the right thing rather than the more expensive thing. There is no column for following guidelines or saving patients money by choosing a more conservative and less costly treatment. But I choose to try and do the right thing, and to follow appropriate guidelines when I can.

—Lauren Demosthenes. "Failing Grades For Doing The Right Thing." Costs of Care, 2013. (www.costsofcare.org)

PREVENTIVE SERVICES

Preventive care refers to measures taken to prevent diseases from occurring. Simple examples include hand washing, smoking cessation and obesity counseling, immunizations, and exercise. As discussed in Chapter 1, Americans commonly lack adequate preventive care.[70] Remember that one of the reasons is that it is estimated it would take a primary care provider 21 hours per day just to provide all of the care recommended to meet their patients' acute, preventive, and chronic disease management needs.[71]

Missed prevention opportunities result in many downstream diseases that are costly both in physical and fiscal terms. Thirty-eight percent of all deaths in the United States are attributable to four behaviors—smoking, unhealthy diet, lack of physical activity, and problem drinking.[72,73]

There are many preventive measures and treatments that have been proven to be cost-effective, and many that have not (Table 14-4). Some measures such as childhood immunizations and smoking cessation have convincingly been shown to not only be "cost-effective" but cost-saving.[73,74] It is estimated that up

Table 14-4 Cost-effectiveness of selected clinical preventative measures and treatments

Cost-Effectiveness Ratio	Preventative Intervention
<0 (cost-saving)	Haemophilus influenzae type b vaccination of toddlers and other childhood vaccinations
	One-time colonoscopy screening for colorectal cancer in men 60 to 64 years old
	Advising at-risk adults to take aspirin
	Smoking cessation advice and help to quit
	Screening adults for alcohol misuse and brief counseling

(Continued)

Table 14-4 **Cost-effectiveness of selected clinical preventative measures and treatments (*Continued*)**

Cost-Effectiveness Ratio	Preventative Intervention
$0 to $13,999/QALY*	Newborn screening for medium-chain acyl-coenzyme A dehydrogenase deficiency
	High-intensity smoking-replase prevention program, as compared with a low-intensity program
	Chlamydia screening (sexually active adolescents and young women)
	Colorectal cancer screening (adults age 50 and older)
	Influenza immunization (adults age 50 and older)
	Pneumococcal immunization (adults age 65 and older)
	Vision screening in preschool age children
$14,000 to $34,999/QALY	Intensive tobacco-use prevention program for seventh and eighth graders
	Cervical cancer screening (all women)
	Counseling women of childbearing age to take folic acid supplements
	Counseling women to use calcium supplements
	Injury prevention counseling for parents of young children
	Hypertension screening (all adults)
> $40,000/QALY	Screening all 65-year-olds for diabetes as compared with screening 65-year-olds with hypertension for diabetes ($590,000/QALY)
	Antibiotic prophylaxsis (amoxicillin) for children with moderate cardiac lesions who are undergoing urinary catheterization (increases cost and worsens health)

*QALY = Quality-Adjusted Life Year.
Source: Adapted from Cohen J, Neumann P, Weinstein M. Does preventative care save money? Health economics and the presidential candidates. *N Engl J Med.* 2008;358:7 and Table 6-2 of Institute of Medicine (US) Roundtable on Evidence Based Medicine, Yong PL, Saunders RS, Olsen LA, et al. *The Healthcare Imperative: Lowering Costs and Improving Outcomes: Workshop Series Summary.* Washington DC: National Academies Press (US); 2010.

to $55 billion of annual wasted healthcare spending is due to missed prevention opportunities.[73,75]

Many tools exist to help clinicians determine appropriate preventive services for their patients:

- AHRQ provides a tool for clinicians (the Electronic Preventive Services Selector [ePSS]) to search for USPSTF graded recommendations: www.epss.ahrq.gov/PDA
- Vaccine recommendations are available via the CDC: www.cdc.gov/vaccines/schedules/Schedulers/adult-scheduler.html

TOWARD HIGH-VALUE SCREENING, DIAGNOSTIC TESTING, AND PREVENTIVE CARE

Screening and diagnostic tests are important in the provision of high-value care because these tests result in many physical and financial costs for patients. The ACP has identified a number of clinical situations in which a test does not reflect high-value care, and have suggested principles for the "appropriate use of screening and diagnostic tests to foster high-value, cost-conscious care."[76]

Diagnostic tests should not be performed if the results will not change management.[76] Sounds simple enough, but this guiding principle seems to often be ignored in clinical practice. Healthcare professionals should also recognize that when the pretest probability of disease is low, the likelihood of a false-positive test result is higher than the likelihood of a true-positive result. Remember the example of CA-125 screening for ovarian cancer (Figure 14-1), where despite the test having very high sensitivity, in patients with a low pretest probability it is nearly certain that a positive result will represent a false-positive—one that can cause incredible amounts of worry and distress—rather than true disease.

As emphasized throughout this chapter, clinicians and patients should always consider the potential downstream costs that may be incurred if a test is performed. These costs can include profound monetary, physical, emotional, and psychosocial effects.

Geriatricians have recommended incorporating *lag time to benefit* into prevention decisions for older adults.[77] Lag time to benefit is the length of time between a preventive intervention and the time when improved health outcomes are seen. As opposed to only asking, "how much will this test or treatment likely help?" lag time to benefit also addresses "when will it help?" This second question is at least as important as the first for older adults. If an older adult is expected to likely die before the time that any benefit from the intervention will be realized, then administering that intervention exposes them to the immediate risks without providing any upside.[77] A general approach suggested by UCSF geriatrician Dr Sei J. Lee and colleagues involves estimating the patient's life expectancy (online calculators can be used, such as www.eprognosis.ucsf.edu), and then estimating the preventive intervention's lag time to benefit to determine the most appropriate strategy (Figure 14-5).[77] The lag time to benefit is available for some widely used screening procedures or primary prevention treatments. If unavailable, the lag time to benefit can be estimated by reviewing Kaplan-Meier survival curves for the intervention and control groups; the point at which the curves last separate provides a qualitative estimate of the lag time to benefit.

"Incorporating time lag estimates into screening guidelines would encourage a more explicit consideration of the risks and benefits of screening for breast and colorectal cancer."[1] This time lag concept can also be important in reviewing medication lists in the elderly and minimizing unnecessary pills that are unlikely to significantly help during their lifetime, but could contribute to adverse side effects or medication interactions (see Chapter 13).

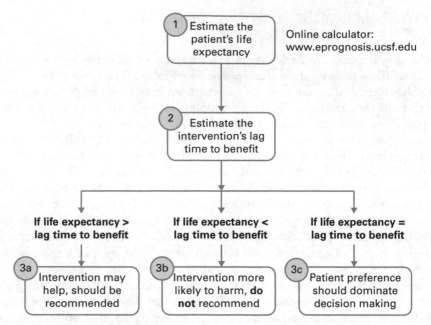

Figure 14-5. Incorporating lag time to benefit in preventive measures for older adults. (Figure created based on framework from Lee SJ, Leipzig RM, Walter LC. *JAMA* 2013;310(24):2609-2610.)

In addition, UCSF geriatricians Drs Louise Walters and Kenneth Covinsky have proposed a framework for incorporating individualized decision making into cancer screening recommendations in the elderly.[78] They advocate for more informed cancer screening decisions by "detailing the benefits and harms that need to be weighed when making screening decisions. Patient preferences then act like a moveable fulcrum of a scale to shift the magnitude of the harms or benefits that are needed to tip the decision toward a screening option."[78]

In fact, clear communication between medical staff and patients improves appropriate screening by reducing underuse, overuse, and misuse.[79] For instance, a simple decision aid for mammography screening of women 75 years and older improved women's decision making about this study.[80] However, there are many important barriers to this strategy, including a reimbursement system that makes it easier to just order a test than to have a detailed conversation with patients (see Chapters 10, 12, and 15), and quality metric programs that only focus on screening rates rather than "appropriateness." Despite these obstacles, it is incredibly important to consider the potential risks and benefits, as well as the patient's overall goals of care, to avoid a patient preference misdiagnosis.[81] Currently, the USPSTF (http://www.uspreventiveservicestaskforce.org) offers several "how to talk to patients" guides, ranging from recommendations on how to stop cancer screening in an elderly population to how to tailor screening to individuals when evidence is insufficient.

Bottom line: Clinicians should carefully weigh all potential benefits, risks, and costs of interventions and discuss these openly and honestly with patients, creating an alliance that allows for real shared decision making (see also Chapter 12). To achieve this, clinicians need to have a firm grasp of how to evaluate and interpret test characteristics, and should have a clear understanding of their individual patients' values and interests.

KEY POINTS:

- Screening tests aim to detect asymptomatic and early stage disease in an accurate and cost-effective manner. This goal must be balanced with the known harms associated with screening, including false-positives, overdiagnosis, and accruing downstream costs (both physical and fiscal) for patients.
- Clinicians should understand basic test characteristics and limitations, as well as their individual patient's goals and values, prior to recommending a screening test.
- Clinical guidelines are important resources for clinicians, but must be critically interpreted based on the level of evidence and consideration of possible limitations. Many new Appropriateness Criteria guidelines are emerging to help clinicians address both overuse and underuse of specific tools.
- It is important to consider lag time to benefit and overall prognosis of elderly patients when deciding on potential screening, diagnostic, or treatment recommendations.

References:

1. Lee SJ, Boscardin WJ, Stijacic-Cenzer I, Conell-Price J, O'Brien S, Walter LC. Time lag to benefit after screening for breast and colorectal cancer: meta-analysis of survival data from the United States, Sweden, United Kingdom, and Denmark. *BMJ*. 2013;346(12):e8441-e8441.
2. US Preventive Services Task Force. Screening for colorectal cancer: U.S. Preventive Services Task Force recommendation statement. *Ann Intern Med*. 2008;149(9):627-637.
3. Redberg RF. Squandering medicare's money. *The New York Times*, May 25, 2011. http://www.nytimes.com/2011/05/26/opinion/26redberg.html. Accessed November 15, 2012.
4. Gatto NM, Frucht H, Sundararajan V, Jacobson JS, Grann VR, Neugut AI. Risk of perforation after colonoscopy and sigmoidoscopy: a population-based study. *J Natl Cancer Inst*. 2003;95(3):230-236.
5. Walter LC, Lindquist K, Nugent S, et al. Impact of age and comorbidity on colorectal cancer screening among older veterans. *Ann Intern Med*. 2009;150(7):465-473.
6. Bellizzi KM, Breslau ES, Burness A, Waldron W. Prevalence of cancer screening in older, racially diverse adults: still screening after all these years. *Arch Intern Med*. 2011;171(22):2031-2037.
7. American Cancer Society. Colorectal cancer screening—state and federal coverage laws. http://www.cancer.org/cancer/colonandrectumcancer/moreinformation/colonandrectumcancer

earlydetection/colorectal-cancer-early-detection-screening-coverage-laws. Accessed September 14, 2013.

8. Goodwin JS, Singh A, Reddy N, Riall TS, Kuo Y. Overuse of screening colonoscopy in the medicare population. *Arch Intern Med*. 2011;171(15):1335-1343.

9. American College of Physicians. ACP high-value care curriculum. 2013. http://hvc.acponline.org/curriculum_list.html. Accessed January 4, 2014.

10. Wilson JMG, Jungner G, World Health Organization. Principles and practice of screening for disease. 1968. http://apps.who.int/iris/handle/10665/37650?mode=full&submit_simple=Show+full+item+record. Accessed January 15, 2014.

11. Glaser AN. *High-Yield Biostatistics*. Philadelphia, PA: Lippincott Williams & Wilkins; 2005.

12. Buys SS, Partridge E, Black A, et al. Effect of screening on ovarian cancer mortality: the Prostate, Lung, Colorectal and Ovarian (PLCO) cancer screening randomized controlled trial. *JAMA*. 2011;305(22):2295-2303.

13. American College of Physicians. ACP: effective clinical practice—primer on lead-time, length, and overdiagnosis biases. http://www.acponline.org/clinical_information/journals_publications/ecp/marapr99/primer.htm. Accessed January 23, 2014.

14. The Incidental Economist. http://theincidentaleconomist.com/wordpress/survival-rates-are-not-the-same-as-mortality-rates/. Accessed March 6, 2014.

15. Croswell JM, Ransohoff DF, Kramer BS. Principles of Cancer Screening: Lessons from History and Study Design Issues. *Semin Oncol*. 2010;37(3):202-215.

16. United States Preventive Services Task Force. Talking with your patients about screening for prostate cancer. 2012. http://www.uspreventiveservicestaskforce.org/prostatecancerscreening/prostatecancerscript.pdf. Accessed March 15, 2014.

17. Pinsky PF, Miller A, Kramer BS, et al. Evidence of a healthy volunteer effect in the prostate, lung, colorectal, and ovarian cancer screening trial. *Am J Epidemiol*. 2007;165(8):874-881.

18. Schwartz LM, Woloshin S, Fowler FJ Jr, Welch HG. Enthusiasm for cancer screening in the United States. *JAMA*. 2004;291(1):71-78.

19. Banks J, Hollinghurst S, Bigwood L, Peters TJ, Walter FM, Hamilton W. Preferences for cancer investigation: a vignette-based study of primary-care attendees. *Lancet Oncol*. 2014;15(2):232-240.

20. Rosenbaum L. "Misfearing"—culture, identity, and our perceptions of health risks. *N Engl J Med*. 2014;370(7):595-597.

21. Allemang J.When emotion prevails over cold, hard science in public policy. *The Globe and Mail*. December 2, 2011. http://www.theglobeandmail.com/life/health-and-fitness/when-emotion-prevails-over-cold-hard-science-in-public-policy/article4243441/. Accessed February 3, 2014.

22. Bleyer A, Welch HG. Effect of three decades of screening mammography on breast-cancer incidence. *N Engl J Med*. 2012;367(21):1998-2005.

23. Miller AB, Wall C, Baines CJ, Sun P, To T, Narod SA. Twenty five year follow-up for breast cancer incidence and mortality of the Canadian National Breast Screening Study: randomised screening trial. *BMJ*. 2014;348(9):g366-g366.

24. Jorgensen KJ, Gotzsche PC. Overdiagnosis in publicly organised mammography screening programmes: systematic review of incidence trends. *BMJ*. 2009;339(1):b2587-b2587.

25. Welch HG, Frankel BA. Likelihood that a woman with screen-detected breast cancer has had her "life saved" by that screening. *Arch Intern Med*. 2011;171(22):2043-2046.

26. Torke AM, Schwartz PH, Holtz LR, Montz K, Sachs GA. Older adults and forgoing cancer screening: "I think it would be strange". *JAMA Intern Med*. 2013;173(7):526-531.

27. Kale MS, Bishop TF, Federman AD, Keyhani S. Trends in the overuse of ambulatory health care services in the united states. *Arch Intern Med*. 2013;173(2):142-148.

28. Sima CS, Panageas KS, Schrag D. Cancer screening among patients with advanced cancer. *JAMA*. 2010;304(14):1584-1591.

29. Saini SD, Vijan S, Schoenfeld P, Powell AA, Moser S, Kerr EA. Role of quality measurement in inappropriate use of screening for colorectal cancer: retrospective cohort study. *BMJ*. 2014; 348(2):g1247-g1247.

30. Wegwarth O, Gigerenzer G. Overdiagnosis and overtreatment: Evaluation of what physicians tell their patients about screening harms. *JAMA Intern Med*. 2013;173(22):2086-2087.

31. Welch H. Informed choice in cancer screening. *JAMA Intern Med*. 2013;173(22):2088-2088.

32. Woolf SH, Harris R. The harms of screening: new attention to an old concern. *JAMA*. 2012;307(6):565-566.

33. Bond M, Pavey T, Welch K, et al. Psychological consequences of false-positive screening mammograms in the UK. *Evid Based Med*. 2013;18(2):54-61.

34. Bhattacharya R, Barton S, Catalan J. When good news is bad news: psychological impact of false positive diagnosis of HIV. *AIDS Care*. 2008;20(5):560-564.

35. Elmore JG, Barton MB, Moceri VM, Polk S, Arena PJ, Fletcher SW. Ten-year risk of false positive screening mammograms and clinical breast examinations. *N Engl J Med*. 1998;338(16):1089-1096.

36. Esserman LJ, Thompson IM, Reid B. Overdiagnosis and overtreatment in cancer: an opportunity for improvement. *JAMA*. 2013;310(8):797-798.

37. Davies L, Welch H. Current thyroid cancer trends in the united states. *JAMA Otolaryngol Neck Surg*. 2014;140(4):317-322.

38. Davies L, Welch HG. Increasing incidence of thyroid cancer in the United States, 1973-2002. *JAMA*. 2006;295(18):2164-2167.

39. Welch HG, Black WC. Overdiagnosis in Cancer. *J Natl Cancer Inst*. 2010;102(9):605-613.

40. National Guideline Clearinghouse. Guideline Index. http://www.guideline.gov/browse/index. aspx?alpha=A. Accessed January 17, 2014.

41. Marmot MG. Sorting through the arguments on breast screening. *JAMA*. 2013;309(24):2553-2554.

42. Kachalia A, Mello MM. Breast cancer screening: conflicting guidelines and medicolegal risk. *JAMA*. 2013;309(24):2555-2556.

43. O'Donoghue C, Eklund M, Ozanne EM, Esserman LJ. Aggregate cost of mammography screening in the United States: comparison of current practice and advocated guidelines. *Ann Intern Med*. 2014;160(3):145-153.

44. The Value of Clinical Practice Guidelines as Malpractice "Safe Harbors." RWJF. http://www. rwjf.org/en/research-publications/find-rwjf-research/2012/04/the-value-of-clinical-practice-guidelines-as-malpractice--safe-h.html. Accessed January 24, 2014.

45. Kachalia A, Little A, Isavoran M, Crider L-M, Smith J. Greatest impact of safe harbor rule may be to improve patient safety, not reduce liability claims paid by physicians. *Health Aff*. 2014;33(1):59-66.

46. What does the NHS Breast Screening Programme do? http://www.cancerscreening.nhs.uk/ breastscreen/screening-programme.html. Accessed January 24, 2014.

47. Institute of Medicine (US). *Conflict of Interest in Medical Research, Education, and Practice*. Washington, DC: National Academies Press; 2009.

48. Gøtzsche PC. *Mammography Screening: Truth, Lies and Controversy*. London: Radcliffe Pub; 2012.

49. Cuzick J. Breast cancer screening—time to move forward. *The Lancet*. 2012;379(9823):1289-1290.

50. Pace LE, He Y, Keating NL. Trends in mammography screening rates after publication of the 2009 US Preventive Services Task Force recommendations. *Cancer*. 2013;119(14):2518-2523.

51. Reynolds H. In mammogram debate, politics trounces science. *Bloomberg*. 2012. http://www. bloomberg.com/news/2012-07-31/in-mammogram-debate-politics-trounces-science.html. Accessed January 25, 2014.

52. Specter M. The Lyme wars. *New Yorker*. 2013. http://www.newyorker.com/reporting/ 2013/07/01/130701fa_fact_specter. Accessed March 5, 2014.

53. Johnson L, Stricker RB. The Infectious Diseases Society of America Lyme guidelines: a cautionary tale about the development of clinical practice guidelines. *Philos Ethics Humanit Med*. 2010;5:9.

54. Gibbons GH, Shurin SB, Mensah GA, Lauer MS. Refocusing the agenda on cardiovascular guidelines: an announcement from the National Heart, Lung, and Blood Institute. *Circulation*. 2013;128(15):1713-1715.

55. Brozek JL, Akl EA, Alonso-Coello P, et al. Grading quality of evidence and strength of recommendations in clinical practice guidelines. Part 1 of 3. An overview of the GRADE approach and grading quality of evidence about interventions. *Allergy*. 2009;64(5):669-677.

56. Khan AR, Khan S, Zimmerman V, Baddour LM, Tleyjeh IM. Quality and strength of evidence of the Infectious Diseases Society of America clinical practice guidelines. *Clin Infect Dis*. 2010;51(10):1147-56.

57. Lee DH, Vielemeyer O. Analysis of overall level of evidence behind Infectious Diseases Society of America practice guidelines. *Arch Intern Med*. 2011;171(1):18-22.

58. Tricoci P, Allen JM, Kramer JM, Califf RM, Smith SC. Scientific evidence underlying the ACC/AHA clinical practice guidelines. *JAMA*. 2009;301(8):831-841.

59. Owens DK, Lohr KN, Atkins D, et al. AHRQ series paper 5: grading the strength of a body of evidence when comparing medical interventions—Agency for Healthcare Research and Quality and the effective health-care program. *J Clin Epidemiol*. 2010;63(5):513-523.

60. Sniderman AD, Furberg CD. Why guideline-making requires reform. *JAMA*. 2009;301(4):429-431.

61. Choudhry NK, Stelfox HT, Detsky AS. Relationships between authors of clinical practice guidelines and the pharmaceutical industry. *JAMA*. 2002;287(5):612-617.

62. Schwartz JT, Pearson SD. Cost consideration in the clinical guidance documents of physician specialty societies in the united states. *JAMA Intern Med*. 2013;173(12):1091-1097.

63. Drozda JP. Physician specialty society clinical guidelines and bending the cost curve: comment on "cost consideration in the clinical guidance documents of physician specialty societies in the united states". *JAMA Intern Med*. 2013;173(12):1097-1098.

64. Pronovost PJ. Enhancing physicians' use of clinical guidelines. *JAMA*. 2013;310(23):2501-2502.

65. Montori VM, Brito J, Murad M. The optimal practice of evidence-based medicine: incorporating patient preferences in practice guidelines. *JAMA*. 2013;310(23):2503-2504.

66. Cabana MD, Rand CS, Powe NR, et al. Why don't physicians follow clinical practice guidelines? A framework for improvement. *JAMA*. 1999;282(15):1458-1465.

67. Krumholz HM. The new cholesterol and blood pressure guidelines: perspective on the path forward. *JAMA*. 2014;311(14):1403-1405.

68. American College of Radiology. ACR Appropriateness Criteria overview. 2013. http://www.acr.org/~/media/ACR/Documents/AppCriteria/Overview.pdf. Accessed March 4, 2014.

69. American College of Cardiology Foundation. Appropriate Use Criteria: what you need to know. http://www.cardiosource.org/~/media/Files/Science%20and%20Quality/Quality%20Programs/FOCUS/E1302_AUC_Primer_Update.ashx. Accessed March 4, 2014.

70. McGlynn EA, Asch SM, Adams J, et al. The quality of health care delivered to adults in the United States. *N Engl J Med*. 2003;348(26):2635-2645.

71. Yarnall KSH, Østbye T, Krause KM, Pollak KI, Gradison M, Michener JL. Family physicians as team leaders: "time" to share the care. *Prev Chronic Dis*. 2009;6(2):A59.

72. Mokdad AH, Marks JS, Stroup DF, Gerberding JL. Actual causes of death in the United States, 2000. *JAMA*. 2004;291(10):1238-1245.

73. Institute of Medicine (US). *The Healthcare Imperative: Lowering Costs and Improving Outcomes: Workshop Series Summary*. Washington, DC: National Academies Press; 2010.

74. National Commission on Prevention Priorities. *Preventive care: a national profile on use, disparities, and health benefits. Partnership for Prevention*; 2007.

75. Institute of Medicine. *Best Care at Lower Cost : The Path to Continuously Learning Health Care in America*. Washington, DC: National Academies Press; 2012.

76. Qaseem A, Alguire P, Dallas P, et al. Appropriate use of screening and diagnostic tests to foster high-value, cost-conscious care. *Ann Intern Med*. 2012;156(2):147-149.

77. Lee SJ, Leipzig RM, Walter LC. Incorporating lag time to benefit into prevention decisions for older adults. *JAMA*. 2013;310(24):2609-2610.

78. Walter LC, Covinsky KE. Cancer screening in elderly patients: a framework for individualized decision making. *JAMA*. 2001;285(21):2750-2756.
79. Holden DJ, Harris R, Porterfield DS, et al. *Enhancing the Use and Quality of Colorectal Cancer Screening*. Rockville, MD: Agency for Healthcare Research and Quality; 2010. http://www.ncbi.nlm.nih.gov/books/NBK44526. Accessed September 30, 2013.
80. Schonberg MA, Hamel M, Davis RB, et al. Development and evaluation of a decision aid on mammography screening for women 75 years and older. *JAMA Intern Med*. 2014;174(3):417-424.
81. Mulley AG, Trimble C, Elwyn G. Stop the silent misdiagnosis: patients' preferences matter. *BMJ*. 2012;345(6):e6572-e6572.

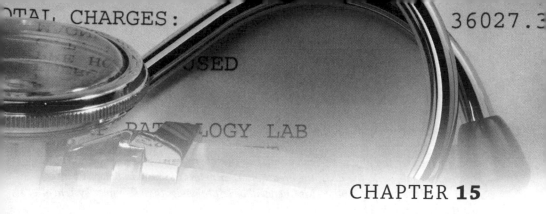

CHAPTER 15

Shifting Incentives: Moving Reimbursement from Volume to Value

*M*s Grace Chen knows to avoid the perfume section in the department store. At 53-years-old, she has lived with asthma her entire life. Scented perfumes and other "triggers" can suddenly cause her airways to spasm, sending her into a fit of wheezing. Today, she is not entirely sure what set off her symptoms, but she could feel her chest tightening up as it became more and more difficult to catch her breath, a sensation that she has experienced many times before. She reached into her purse to take out her inhaler and took a few puffs. She still felt like she was trying to breathe through a snorkel to get the air down to her lungs. Realizing that she may need help, she asked her son to drive her to a nearby urgent care clinic.

At the urgent care clinic, Ms Chen is evaluated by a physician, given a breathing treatment, and undergoes an electrocardiogram (EKG). Following the breathing treatment, she continues to have significant wheezing and shortness of breath, so the urgent care clinic physician coordinates for an ambulance to take her to an emergency room across town. Ms Chen has had to visit the ER for her asthma before, but it has been a number of years since the last episode that was this bad.

In the ER, she is promptly placed in a room and evaluated by an emergency medicine physician. Ms Chen undergoes further breathing treatments. A chest x-ray is taken, blood is drawn for labs, and another EKG done. Her labs are ok, her chest x-ray is clear, and her EKG remains normal. The physician then decides to obtain a chest CT (computed tomography) scan "just to be sure nothing was missed." The CT scan does not reveal any significant abnormalities. Following more breathing treatments and an intravenous administration of solumedrol (a steroid), she improves. She ultimately is discharged home with self-care instructions, including directions for using her home inhalers and a prescription for oral steroids.

In Ms Chen's mind, this entire shortness-of-breath experience was a single event, caused by a single disease—an asthma exacerbation likely triggered by an environmental allergen. However, the urgent clinic will bill separate fees for the physician evaluation, the breathing treatment, and the EKG. The hospital will send another bill that charges separate fees for the physician evaluation, the chest x-ray, chest CT, the intravenous steroids, the lab work, the EKG, the breathing treatments, and the radiologist's interpretation of the imaging studies. Ms Chen will be left to navigate the complex system of healthcare costs herself.

Medicine is a noble profession, built on the altruistic motivations of caretakers. But, it is hard to ignore the fact that perverse incentives that require clinicians to "do more" to get paid will predictably result in more medical care. As in Ms Chen's case, treatments and procedures are paid for a la carte, whether or not they are actually necessary or help the patient. Ms Chen very likely did not warrant a chest CT scan for her asthma exacerbation, but the hospital will be paid for it anyway. Even if the physicians' motivation to order the study had absolutely nothing to do with making more money for himself or his medical center, there sure were no incentives for him *not* to order that test, or more broadly, to consider the value of the care he was delivering. The Institute of Medicine (IOM) recognized this problem in their seminal "Crossing the Quality Chasm" report: "Even among health professionals motivated to provide the best care possible, the structure of the payment incentives may not facilitate the actions needed to systemically improve the quality of care, and may even prevent such actions."[1]

"We already have pay for performance," UCSF healthcare leader Dr Robert M. Wachter has quipped. "We pay more for the performance of procedures, hospitalizations, and office visits, and so that's precisely what medicine produces."[2] In this chapter we discuss how different payment systems can help incentivize a necessary shift from a healthcare system that is reimbursed for volume (seeing more patients and doing more tests) to a system that is reimbursed for value (making patients better off) (Table 15-1).

FEE-FOR-SERVICE: PAYING FOR WHAT YOU GET, OR GETTING WHAT YOU PAY FOR

Fee-for-service (FFS) describes a payment structure in which each healthcare service is billed and paid for separately. The physician or hospital is paid for each office visit, hospitalization, intravenous medication, x-ray, EKG, or other services delivered. Under traditional FFS, individual physicians and healthcare systems are financially rewarded for providing more care, even when this care does not demonstrate actual benefit. This "you eat what you treat" system may create a perverse incentive to provide patients with unnecessary care.

Table 15-1 Payment models for primary care services

Payment Model	Key Attribute	Key Advantages	Key Disadvantages
Fee-for-service	Payment for each patient encounter (typically an office visit)	• Predominant payment method, familiar to physicians and patients • Has served many medical specialties well • Incentivizes performance of specific, targeted activities • Rewards physician industriousness	• Does not directly reward key primary care functions, especially coordination or comprehensive care of patients with multiple chronic conditions • Inadequate or infeasible for rewarding enhanced access (eg, after hours, telephone or e-mail communication) • Does not facilitate practice redesign to better serve patient needs
Capitation	Periodic (eg, monthly) payment per patient	• Creates clear accountability between primary care clinician and patient • Provides the financial flexibility for clinician to redesign and invest in personnel and technology needed to provide other primary care functions (eg, enhanced access, care coordination)	• Case mix payment adjustment and capitation rate-setting challenges • Incentives potentially to withhold services • Unpopularity of capitation with some patients (and many physicians)
Salary	A fixed amount paid regularly for personally provided professional services	• Theoretically physician can act in patient's best interests without concerns about financial self-interest • Within a group, administratively straightforward and a base for additional performance incentives	• "Time is money"—physician still needs to allocate time among competing patients' needs • Generosity of salary depends on financial well-being of the group—so physician not really indifferent to payers' incentives • Does not explicitly reward industriousness • Administratively not feasible for most third party payers

Source: Reproduced from Berenson RA, Rich EC. US approach to physician payment: the deconstruction of primary care. *J Gen Intern Med*. 2010;25(6):613-618. With kind permission from Springer Science and Business Media.

The FFS system may have some virtues: As Harvard Medical School economist Michael Chernew put it, "[FFS] rewards hard work and productivity and incentivizes physicians not to stint on care. It avoids placing physicians at financial risk if they care for sick patients and facilitates financing systems that allow patients unconstrained choice of provider (eg, physicians, allied health professionals, and hospitals)."[3] Of course, the flipside of incentivizing physicians "not to stint on care" is that it can encourage the overuse of care, particularly without checks-and-balances to counteract this impulse. Erring on the side of overdoing it has become so ingrained in clinical practice that judiciously ordering tests and referrals is often seen as more cognitively taxing for clinicians. Moreover, there is a common perception that doing so may increase the risk of malpractice repercussions (see Chapter 10). Since FFS pays each clinician and/or health system separately, it also indirectly enables the type of fragmented and duplicative care that Ms Chen experiences. FFS alone provides no financial motivation to coordinate care, or to avoid unnecessary referrals.

In addition to potentially incentivizing too much care, the actual amounts that are paid out under most American FFS systems can be highly arbitrary. Prior to 1989, reimbursements paid to clinicians for the same service varied tremendously by specialty and geographic region based on what was considered "usual, customary, and reasonable" for the local market.[4] A first step toward more value-based payments was standardizing the process for determining these amounts. The relative value unit (RVU) has now become the standard of FFS productivity and is used by many health systems to determine physician compensation.[5] As we discussed in Chapter 9, FFS payments and the RVU weighting system disadvantages more cerebral parts of care delivery such as prevention and diagnosis compared to more procedure-based practices. As a result, FFS payment systems are often blamed as the engine driving the "hamster on a treadmill" phenomenon (running faster just to stand still) that is lamented by many primary care providers.[6]

PAY FOR PERFORMANCE: A CARROT USED AS A STICK?

In a classic psychology experiment in the 1970s, researchers recruited a group of preschoolers that liked to draw.[7] Some of the children were told that if they drew pictures for the study, they would be given a certificate with a gold seal and ribbon. The other children were not given any such expectation. Each child was invited to a separate room to draw for 6 minutes. Afterwards, the children that were told they would be given a reward were presented their certificate as promised. Over the next few days, the preschoolers were surreptitiously watched from behind one-way mirrors to see how much they would continue drawing on their own accord. The group of children that had expected and received a reward spent about half as much time spontaneously drawing as the other kids. Perhaps even more surprising, judges that did not know who drew which pictures independently rated the art drawn by children expecting a reward as less aesthetically pleasing. Once children expected a reward for drawing, it seems that they felt less interested in doing it "for free" and they put less effort into it.

As demonstrated by this example, the interplay of *intrinsic motivation* (motivation that arises inside the individual) and *extrinsic motivation* (motivation that arises from outside of the individual) is complicated. If a student is driven to get good grades because he feels fulfilled when he turns in good work, then he seems to be responding to intrinsic motivation, even if the grades themselves represent a reinforcing extrinsic motivator. On the other hand, if he achieves good grades primarily because his parents demand that he does well and that he is accepted to a particular university, then this would be in response to extrinsic motivation.

Promising premise and early results

The idea that health services should no longer be simply paid based on quantity, but rather should focus on quality, is logical and attractive. Taken on the surface level, "pay for performance" (P4P) is a no-brainer. P4P is built on the simple concept of providing clinicians or health systems more money for hitting specified targets, such as achieving a certain percentage of diabetic patients in a practice that have good blood sugar control. Sounds good, right? Well, as with most things, the closer one looks, the more complicated P4P actually becomes. In other words, the devil may be in the details.[8]

Studies on P4P thus far have shown inconsistent results.[9] In one notably positive study, P4P hospitals in Medicare's Premier Hospital Quality Incentive Demonstration (HQID) had greater improvement over the first 2 years in multiple metrics of quality, including measures for heart failure, acute myocardial infarction, and pneumonia, compared to their colleagues.[10] But, over time these gains diminished and may have completely disappeared.[9,11] And, frustratingly, risk-adjusted mortality (an important bottom-line measure of performance) between hospitals participating in the program and those that did not remained similar over the course of the first 6 years.[12] In 2011, the Cochrane group published two systematic reviews that failed to show convincing evidence that financial incentives can improve patient outcomes.[13,14] A separate systematic review published in *Annals of Internal Medicine* around the same time concluded, "the effect of P4P targeting individual practitioners on quality of care and outcomes remains largely uncertain."[15] Even if it is possible that P4P may have the power to change healthcare professional behaviors,[13] many of the most visible programs implemented thus far have not translated into what we really care about: better health outcomes for our patients.

Perhaps if we look across the pond we will find more encouraging results. After all, the United Kingdom introduced the Quality and Outcomes Framework—a P4P program on a grand scale—more than a decade ago, back in 2004. This program tied about a quarter of family practitioners' income to measures of their performance.[16] With incentives that large, as you may imagine, "much changed overnight" in medical clinics in the United Kingdom.[16] Family practitioners increased nursing staffing, creating programs for chronic disease that were much more proactive, such as nurse-run, protocol-driven clinics for some diseases like diabetes. Many hired more administrative staff to provide rapid access to performance data. They also started using full electronic medical records, since these were required for payments to be made. The pace of improvement in the quality of care for asthma and diabetes picked up considerably.[17] It seemed that the program had kick-started the engine of improvement and may have created an inflection point in the quality of care. Then by 2007, the rate of improvement had slowed and started to level off. Even more concerning, aspects of care that were not associated with an incentive actually declined in quality for patients.[17]

In one of the most encouraging study results for proponents of P4P, the introduction of a P4P program in 24 English hospitals seemed to result in improvements in risk-adjusted 30-day mortality for pneumonia, heart attacks, and heart failure over the first 18 months.[18] This was the ultimate feather in the cap of P4P, as it seemed that if implemented correctly incentives might just actually save lives after all. However, yet again, these benefits evaporated over time. During the following 2 years, the hospitals not participating in the program caught up to P4P hospitals, resulting in no measurable mortality difference any more between these groups.[19]

Well, if incentives or "bonuses" may not reliably work, how about invoking penalties for poor outcomes? Would the natural instinct of loss aversion be more motivating to clinicians or health systems? Maybe ... maybe not.

Back in 2008, Medicare introduced a policy that reduced payments for hospital-acquired infections.[20] Some states responded to this no-pay-for-poor-performance measure aggressively and slashed hospital-acquired infection rates.[21] But a 2012 study published in the *New England Journal of Medicine* found that overall the policy had no measurable effect on the rates of central catheter-associated bloodstream infections and catheter-associated urinary tract infections across US hospitals.[22]

Taken together, it appears that P4P programs are helpful in catalyzing, but not sustaining, meaningful change. It is clear that at the very least P4P is not a "magic bullet" and if it is to improve care, payment reforms must be paired with sustainable reforms in care delivery.[16] Moreover, even if we believe there should be some incentives for quality, determining appropriate metrics and fair schema is not straightforward.

Concerns and challenges

Is it a motivation problem, in the first place?

"The quality improvement literature has pinpointed many causes of quality breeches in medical care: fatigue; poorly designed workflow and care systems; undue commercial influence; knowledge gaps; memory lapses; reliance on inappropriate heuristics; poor interpersonal skills and insufficient teamwork, to name just a few," wrote health policy expert, Dr Steffie Woolhandler, and behavioral economist, Dan Ariely.[23] "But 'not trying' is rarely cited. Yet P4P implicitly blames lack of motivation for poor quality care."

The current healthcare system is built on the backs of hardworking, well-intentioned health professionals. It does seem hard to argue that dangling some more dollars on a string would somehow get them to try even harder. But much as was seen following the introduction of the UK program, it is possible that the potential power of P4P is not in trying to drive personal motivation, but rather in fomenting delivery system changes and innovations (such as the implementation of electronic health records and the creation of nurse-led chronic disease clinics). This may be even truer at the hospital or health system level.

Could P4P undermine intrinsic motivation and result in negative effects?

Tangible rewards, particularly monetary ones, seem to weaken, or "crowd-out," intrinsic motivation.[24] There are many examples from the emerging behavioral economics literature. Remember how a shiny certificate had the power to possibly squash preschoolers' inherent joy of drawing? Another frequently cited example of motivational crowd-out evaluated monetary payments for blood donors. When money was offered, blood donations actually decreased, leading many to argue that by introducing financial rewards, the stronger altruistic motivations of the donors were being replaced by the weaker monetary one.[24,25] The intuition here is that many people donate blood because it is socially recognized as "the right thing to do." Fewer people decide to donate blood because it is a desirable way to make money.

Some physicians fear that measuring and rewarding physicians may similarly sap motivation.[26,27] Still, not all rewards are bad all the time, particularly when there are multiple competing motivations. "For instance, when the Italian government gave blood donors paid time off work, donations increased. The law removed an obstacle to altruism."[24]

So, it seems the salient question then is whether or not the volume-based payment system is currently "an obstacle to altruism," and does P4P help remove this barrier?

What is the correct amount of money in P4P bonuses and penalties?

The United Kingdom has provided up to a quarter of potential income in their initial schema, but most P4P programs in the United States have used much smaller incentives. One of the leading concerns has been that large financial incentives would induce efforts to "game the system." Even without overt misplay, substantial incentives could cause harm by creating undue focus on the limited areas of clinical practice that are being measured and incentivized. Due to these concerns, a change in the income structure that would reduce the percentage tied to P4P in the United Kingdom "has been widely welcomed."[16] On the other side of the spectrum, incentives that are too small may not even garner physicians' attention.

In a national survey performed in 2008, one-in-six physicians did not even know whether P4P was incorporated in their compensation or not.[28] Of course, it is hard for financial incentives to promote change if physicians are not even aware of their existence nor how it is that they get paid. The challenge is finding the amount of incentive that is large enough to invoke change, but not so lucrative as to create a singular focus.

The other issue is whether to pay for meeting a set standard goal or for relative improvement. In one early natural experiment, physician groups whose performance was initially lowest improved the most following the introduction of P4P, whereas physician groups that were already performing above the bonus threshold at baseline improved the least—yet, those that were above the bonus threshold at baseline captured three-quarters of the bonus payments.[29] Therefore, the way the incentive is structured is important since it could potentially lead to the greatest improvers not being rewarded, while also possibly allowing good performers to rest on their laurels rather than create further improvements. Moreover, if the lowest performers who have the greatest potential for clinical benefits from improvements are penalized for not hitting a specific target despite making incremental changes, then it could further denigrate their ability to improve.

Do we even know how to accurately measure quality or value?

Not everything important can be measured and not everything measured is important. Large parts of clinical practice just cannot be accurately computed or benchmarked, leaving quality metrics to be made up of only those things that can be rather easily quantified. Even more concerning, there is some evidence that quality may deteriorate for non-incentivized measures like continuity of care.[30] Thus, rewarding a narrow set of indicators could in fact decrease overall global quality. This may be "the medical equivalent of teaching to the test."[31] As we begin to focus on value, the problem becomes even more acute. Remember from Chapters 4 and 10 that there are numerous complications with defining and measuring value.

In addition, there are also serious concerns about the validity of the current data and the problem of accurate attribution to specific practices. Based on a study analyzing nearly 1.8 million Medicare claims in 2000 through 2002, patients saw a median of two primary care physicians and five specialists working in four different practices.[32] Only about a third of the visits each year were with a patient's assigned physician, and a third of patients changed their assigned physician from one year to another. The unfortunate reality is "the Centers for Medicare and Medicaid Services (CMS), despite heroic efforts, cannot accurately measure any physician's overall value, now or in the foreseeable future."[33]

What are the potential "side effects" of P4P?

Even if P4P is relatively new in the world of medicine, it is not a new concept. Perhaps the first real experiment of P4P was in the mid-1800s in England. British schools and teachers were paid on the basis of the results of student examinations, with the goal of improving educational outcomes. What happened, though, is curricula narrowed to only focus on the tests, and teachers quickly figured out that the way to get students to perform well was via rote memorization of test specifics. Soon enough, "testing bureaucracy had burgeoned, cheating and cramming flourished, and public opposition had grown dramatically."[34] In the United States, attempts at performance-based pay for schools in the 1960s similarly resulted in cheating scandals and failures.[34] These days, merit pay remains a very controversial topic in education.

As we can see, there are many possible "side effects" of P4P that need to be considered. For example, clinicians motivated to meet specific goals may practice "cherry picking" by attempting to preferentially see and treat patients that are already the healthiest. In the 1980s, pediatric residents that were paid for each clinic visit saw more patients, and their patients had fewer visits to the emergency department, compared to their colleagues that were "salaried."[35] But as it turned out, almost all of the differences were because the residents that were paid for each clinic visit enrolled more healthy patients and performed many more well child visits, thus had "stacked the deck" in their favor.

P4P programs can also create a tunnel vision focus on only things that are measured. For instance, an emergency department may concentrate on processes related to pneumonia care since these will be measured and reported, while not necessarily pay attention to the quality of care for patients with other critical ailments, such as gastrointestinal bleeds.

Another possible unintended effect is the creation of a "check-the-box" mentality that meets measures but does not actually improve care. With the introduction of quality measures, standard forms that include checkboxes are naturally created to "capture" these processes, but this can encourage people to "just check the box" and say that they did something like smoking cessation if they met some minimum requirement, even if they did not really provide substantive counseling.

Creating financial incentives: general recommendations

Financial incentives, when designed and used properly, can be a motivational tool to help drive behavior. It is important that the incentives align well with the shared purpose of the organization and clinician, and thereby avoid the problem of motivational crowd-out.

In the Geisinger Health System in Pennyslvania, physician incentives are designed to reward teamwork and collaboration. For example, endocrinologists' goals are based on good control of glucose levels for all diabetic patients in the system, not just those they see.[36] Moreover, a collaborative approach is encouraged by bringing clinicians together across disciplinary service lines to plan, budget, and evaluate one another's performance. These efforts are partly credited with a 43% reduction in hospitalized days and $100 per member per month in savings among diabetic patients.[37] At UCSF, even a modest financial incentive (of up to

$1200 per year) offered to residents and fellows has proven effective. Specific quality improvement project goals are determined collaboratively between the trainees and medical center leadership.[38] The engagement of UCSF frontline physicians in defining their own annual goals and in leading the intervention programs helps ensure dedicated buy-in and loyalty to the program (see also Chapter 16).

Healthcare leaders, Drs Thomas Lee (Harvard and now also Chief Medical Officer at Press Ganey) and Delos "Toby" Cosgrove (Chief Executive Officer and President at Cleveland Clinic), have made a number of recommendations for creating incentives that lead to sustainable changes in care delivery[36]:

- Avoid attaching large sums to any single target.

    Much like with the local UCSF program, small incentives that are well applied tend to catch clinicians' attention and drive change. Theoretically, intrinsic motivation is engaged whenever one "measures" quality and reports it, thus even without paying, no one wants to be at the bottom. Even on the health system level, incentives that target only 1% of Medicare payments, which itself is only a fraction of overall reimbursement, have driven national efforts to reduce readmissions.[39]

- Watch for conflicts of interest.

    Financial incentives that are focused solely on reducing costs, rather than improving quality or patient safety, can create real or perceived conflicts of interest. Doctors should not stand to gain by shortchanging patients. In addition, "'Gain sharing' programs, in which the organization shares with physicians the savings from improved performance, have not been successful at most hospitals, in part because of their complexity."[36]

    This does not mean that aligning incentives to support the reduction of unnecessary care will necessarily cause harm to patients by promoting doctors to withhold care. Dr Lee noted in a separate article that "…my years of experience as a physician leader of a large health care system with many large capitated contracts suggests that physicians simply will not withhold care that they believe patients need, even if the costs of that care hurt them financially. They will be upset as they contemplate the fiscal impact of needed care, but they will not withhold it."[40]

    Regardless, it appears unwise to create incentives that may create apparent conflicts of interest or could reasonably lead to clinician resentment.

- Reward collaboration.

    Good healthcare requires the dedicated effort of many different individuals working together. "Physicians (like most people) naturally prefer that their compensation be based on behaviors that they alone control, such as whether they order tests in specific circumstances—but that approach does not encourage teamwork."[36] It seems more effective to create goals that depend on collaboration across individuals and departments. It is likely that the endocrinologists at Geisinger may have opted for the metric to be based solely on diabetic patients that they see themselves, but by making them responsible for glucose control across the organization they now are encouraged to think about larger system changes and to work with other departments and clinicians.

Let us not forget that the overall goal of these incentives is better care for as many patients as possible.

• Communicate.

Financial incentive programs should be continually appraised and modified. It is vital clinicians participate in this process and that the goals and shared purpose of the program are clearly communicated.

When appropriate extrinsic motivators align or interact synergistically with intrinsic motivation, it can promote high levels of performance and satisfaction.[41] We believe that it is important to engage frontline clinicians in the creation and design of financial incentives that will affect them. To best appeal to clinicians' intrinsic motivation, it seems that P4P measures should be developed in consultation with clinicians and based on meaningful, clearly communicated goals for improving patient care.[26]

MOVING FROM VOLUME TO VALUE

"Perhaps the only health policy issue on which Republicans and Democrats agree is the need to move from volume-based to value-based payment for healthcare providers," wrote health policy experts Drs Robert Berenson (the Urban Institute) and Deborah Kaye (Johns Hopkins) in 2013.[33]

The Affordable Care Act (ACA) strives to encourage healthcare value by simultaneously improving quality of care and driving down unsustainable healthcare costs. These goals are enacted through a variety of Medicare "purchasing" strategies that include global, population-based payments to accountable care organizations (ACOs); bundled payments for high cost, high variation services and procedures like hip-replacement; a value-based purchasing (VBP) program for all hospitals paid by Medicare; and a physician value-based payment modifier (PVBPM) for individual physician services. These programs are intended to encourage physicians to work with their peers, systems, hospitals, other professionals, and their patients to hit quality targets while optimizing resource use.[42] Clearly there is an expectation that clinicians shoulder responsibility to develop and support strategies for mitigating inappropriate resource use.

Public reporting of quality and cost

Starting in 1991, the New York State Department of Health began publicly reporting risk-adjusted mortality rates for patients that underwent heart bypass surgery. This initially led to intense media attention and scrutiny for the lowest performers. Many hospitals were prompted to improve their cardiac surgery programs, and statewide mortality fell substantially as a result.[43] In addition, surgeons with the highest mortality rates were much more likely to retire or leave their practices.[43,44] Differences between hospitals still remained though. In fact, patients that picked a top-performing hospital or surgeon had approximately half the chance of dying as did those who picked a hospital or surgeon from the bottom part of the list.[44] Nevertheless, market share did not seem to change based on performance.[44] The other critical issue was that as surgeons became increasingly concerned about their performance scores, they began turning away the sickest patients, thus exacerbating racial and ethnic disparities.[45]

As this example highlights, public performance reporting seems to generate behavioral changes in both individual clinicians and health organizations, generally improving quality of care, albeit not without some unintended consequences.[45,46] This is despite the fact that patients and families do not seem to be paying much attention to public reporting and there is little actual impact by these programs on the selection of healthcare providers.[46]

In an effort to empower the public with information on quality and costs,[47] CMS has freely released a treasure trove of accessible data at www.data.medicare. gov. This website includes the public-facing resource "Hospital Compare" (www. hospitalcompare.hhs.gov), which features easily searchable results comparing hospitals across a variety of metrics, including patient experience; readmissions, complications, and deaths; use of medical imaging; and Medicare payments. Now within minutes, the public can find out how a specific hospital, by name, compares to state and national averages across an array of domains. Notably for the discussion of value, this includes markers of overuse, such as the percentage of "outpatients with low back pain who had an MRI without trying recommended treatments first, such as physical therapy," along with the explanation, "if a number is high, it may mean the facility is doing too many unnecessary MRIs for low back pain."[48]

CMS will soon provide individual and group physician-level performance scores through their Physician Compare program (www.medicare.gov/physician compare).[49,50] Indeed, the "wall obscuring physician performance difference" is finally starting to crumble.[50] The effect of this more extensive and transparent public reporting program is yet to be seen.

Medicare's value-based purchasing program

Despite some of the criticisms and concerns regarding P4P, in 2012 the federal government introduced their VBP program, which is basically a P4P system for all hospitals paid by Medicare. In effect, the ACA required that 1% of Medicare hospital payments be dispersed based on "value," under the Medicare VBP Program. This incentive amount will gradually rise to 2% in 2017. Once again, this is likely an important shift in the right direction of paying for good healthcare rather than just more healthcare, although it does come with all of the baggage of the disappointing previous results of P4P.

The seemingly marginal amount of reimbursement currently linked to value (1%-2%) has been sufficient in getting the attention of most medical centers, given the substantial proportion of revenue that comes from Medicare payments.

The initial quality indicators included clinical process measures for pneumonia, acute myocardial infarction, congestive heart failure, healthcare-associated infections, and patient experience measures. In 2014, risk-adjusted mortality, hospital-acquired conditions, patient safety, and satisfaction measures (largely based on patient survey responses to programs like Hospital Consumer Assessment of Healthcare Providers and Systems survey [HCAHPS]) were added.

Opponents are concerned that unintended consequences may include practitioners or health systems avoiding sicker and/or poorer and/or minority patients. These concerns have largely failed to be substantiated, and in fact there is suggestion that P4P may work particularly well for hospitals that serve poor patients.[51] There remains, however, concerns about not rewarding relative improvement, which, as discussed above, could result in the lowest performing hospitals having further resources taken away and possibly creating a vicious cycle that impedes development.

The physician value-based payment modifier

Medicare's PVBPM applies to individual physicians and physician groups still in traditional FFS Medicare—the lion's share of physicians. For groups as small as 10, it ties payment updates to performance on composite measures of quality and resource use. The reward formula is simple. Performance is assessed in two dimensions (quality and cost), with physicians that perform above average in both dimensions receiving payments, those that are worse than average or choose not to participate will be paid less, and physicians with average performance will see no change.[42]

In 2014, CMS sent Quality and Resource Use reports to show physicians how their performance on the measures to be used in the PVBPM compares to peers. Eligible physicians will now receive an annual report of their performance on cost and quality measures.[52]

Beginning in 2015, quality reporting will transition from a voluntary program to a mandatory one—the Medicare Physician Quality Reporting Initiative ("PQRI")—which will require that by 2017 all physicians report on quality measures applicable to their practice.[53] To facilitate reporting, CMS aims to consolidate efforts for a number of programs so that physicians can report once and qualify for the physician quality and reporting system incentive program, the meaningful use requirements, and the value modifier.[52] If physicians elect to not participate, their Medicare payments will be reduced by 1.5% beginning in 2015 and the reductions will continue to increase thereafter.[53]

Bundled and global payments

A way to potentially drive more thoughtful resource utilization that does not reward unnecessary care or complications is through *prospective or bundled payment systems*. Among the calls for payment reform to hospitals and physicians, most suggest some form of bundled payments to physicians, with specific approaches ranging in scope. If we consider reimbursements to a hospital, rather than paying a discrete fee for each service rendered (FFS), the payer may instead pay a specific amount for each day in the hospital (*per diem*), for each episode of hospitalization (eg, *diagnosis related groups* [DRGs]), for each patient in their community considered to be under their care (*capitation*), or the hospital could be given a fixed fee for all services performed on every patient during a full year (*global budget*) (Table 15-2).

For example, a hospital could be paid one fee for childbirth, regardless of how the baby is delivered and the number and type of interventions or resources used. Bundled payments could theoretically encourage reductions in hospital-acquired complications as these would lead to increased costs, length of stay, and spent resources.

Global or bundle payments could also potentially combine payments across different providers and settings (Figure 15-1). In our opening vignette, Ms Chen's insurance was billed separately from the urgent care clinic and the emergency department, with itemized charges for each service rendered. However, under a bundled payment structure, this single episode of asthma exacerbation would

Table 15-2 Common payment methods

Payment Terms	Definition
Capitation	The payment of a fee to a healthcare provider providing services to a number of people, such that the amount paid is determined by the number of total patients. A specific fee is paid "per head" for the provision of a defined package of service for a specified time period.
Fee-for-service	A payment system where healthcare services are unbundled and paid for separately. A specific price is set for each service.
Global payment	A fixed payment is made for all services for a specified period of time (usually 1 year). The Veterans Health Administration, Department of Defense, and Kaiser Permanente hospitals are paid via global budgets, where every service performed on every patient during a year is aggregated into a single payment.
Payment by episode of illness	The physician or hospital is paid one sum for all service delivered during one illness. Medicare's diagnosis related group (DRG) system for hospital reimbursement is an example of payment by episode of illness, with the amount of reimbursement based on the patient's diagnosis.
Per diem payment	A hospital is paid a bundled fee for all services delivered to a patient during a single day.
Salary	Clinicians or other health personnel are paid a fixed amount for predetermined hours of work or responsibilities.

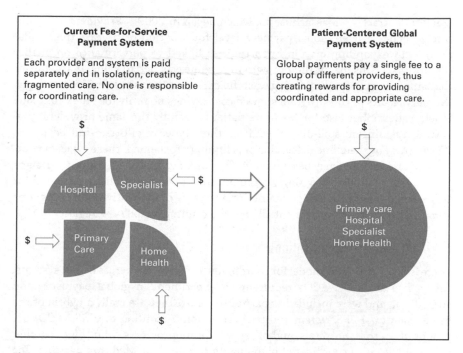

Figure 15-1. Fee-for-service versus global payments.

result in a single payment that would be shared across the two settings and providers. This is meant to incentivize the creation of coordinated care systems that work together and share information.

Let us consider a second example. If Mr Adams, a 65-year-old man, suffers a heart attack, his care associated with this medical event may span multiple different healthcare settings and providers. He could be seen in an emergency department, be hospitalized under the care of a hospitalist physician, undergo a procedure by a cardiologist, work with physical therapy, be discharged to a skilled nursing or rehabilitation facility, and see his primary care physician for a post-discharge follow-up appointment. If all of these entities are paid a single fee for the treatment of Mr Adams' heart attack, it will benefit these providers and systems if they all work together to take care of Mr Adams. Also, any unnecessary testing or procedures will come out of the group's bottom line. Evidence is accruing to support what seems like an obvious conclusion: delivery system integration can improve care and decrease spending for patients, particularly when there is a strong emphasis on primary care and when healthcare providers accept greater financial risks for the outcomes of their care.[54]

Risk sharing and shared savings force health systems to have "skin in the game." One early and successful example is the Blue Cross Blue Shield "Alternative

Quality Contract" in Massachusetts, which began in 2009.[55] Providers were contracted under a fixed global payment level for a period of 5 years (plus inflation), with expanding margin opportunities linked to performance on quality (Figure 15-2). This meant their growth in revenue was tied to value. It also meant that any savings from eliminating wasteful care were theirs to keep. Interestingly, the early results of this program showed cost savings not only for Blue Cross Blue Shield patients but also for Medicare patients seen by the same providers, suggesting a significant spill-over effect from these types of efforts.[56] Indeed, as the *Washington Post* headline discussing this finding proclaimed, these types of coordinated care savings "may be contagious."[57] Similar value-based insurance designs (VBID) are becoming increasingly common. The University of Michigan Center for Value-Based Insurance Design maintains a registry of innovative VBID programs at various stages of development all over the country (http://vbidregistry.org/).

Accountable care organizations

There is a new emerging model for coordinated care delivery across health systems, referred to as ACOs. ACOs represent an experiment in global payments and shared risk, and were included as part of the ACA. They are really a hybrid of the more traditional FFS system and true capitation. According to CMS: "ACOs are groups of doctors, hospitals, and other healthcare providers, who come together voluntarily to give coordinated high quality care to their Medicare patients. The goal of coordinated care is to ensure that patients, especially the chronically ill, get the right care at the right time, while avoiding unnecessary duplication of services and preventing medical errors."[58] When an ACO delivers high-value care

Unique contract model:
• Accountability for quality and resource use across full care continuum
• Long-term (5 years)

Controls cost growth:
• Global population-based budget
• Shared risk: 2-sided symmetrical
• Health status adjusted
• Annual inflation targets designed to achieve total medical expense growth at or below general economic growth

Improved quality, safety & outcomes:
• Robust performance measure set creates accountability for quality, safety & outcomes across continuum
• Substantial financial incentives for high performance and for improvement

Performance on quality
Inflation (cumulative)
Identify savings within budget

PERFORMANCE-BASED PAYMENT OPPORTUNITIES

INITIAL GLOBAL PAYMENT LEVEL

Year 1   Year 2   Year 3   Year 4   Year 5

Figure 15-2. Key components of the Alternative Quality Contract model. (Reproduced, with permission, from Dana Gelb-Safran, ScD.)

by accomplishing both high quality and low costs, then it shares in the savings that it achieves.

Two initial Medicare models of shared savings were designed. In one model, healthcare systems are eligible to share in savings but do not bear any risk for losses during the first 2 years. These ACOs are eligible for approximately 50% of savings accrued by the Medicare program after they surpass a fixed savings threshold. The second model involves healthcare organizations taking both upside and downside risk sharing from the start. These organizations are eligible for a larger percentage of shared savings. This model more closely approximates capitation. Similar private insurance ACO models have also emerged, with multiple insurance plans entering into contracts with providers using a shared risk payment model, making providers eligible for both bonuses and financial penalties.[59]

Some of the early results of the ACOs have been optimistic, showing gains in healthcare quality[60] and possible slowing of associated healthcare cost growth,[61] but it is important to keep in mind the sober words of former CMS administrator Dr Don Berwick that ACOs are a "promise, not a panacea."[62]

"[ACO's] logic is strong: offer primary care physicians and group practices shared savings and risk in an environment that also gives them the flexibility to place resources where patients need them, rather than dancing to the fee-for-service tune," wrote Dr Berwick in 2012.[62] "As they learn how to coordinate care and anticipate needs, costs should decline further for the right reason, because patients get better care."

Still, not everyone holds such a rosy view of ACOs. Voicing concerns about "echoing" the HMO "managed care fiasco," some warn that perhaps what is even worse than FFS is "fee-for-*non*-service."[31]

The Center for Medicare and Medicaid Innovation (CMMI)

The CMS Innovation Center was created by the ACA in 2010, and tasked with testing payment and delivery system models that could improve the quality of care and simultaneously slow the rate of cost growth for Medicare, Medicaid, and the Children's Health Insurance Program.[63] Promising models can be expanded nationwide by the authority of the Secretary of Health and Human Services, as long as the model either reduces spending without reducing the quality of care, or improves the quality of care without increasing spending—in other words, improving "value."[64] This program is meant to "overcome antireform inertia" by allowing the diffusion of successful programs without requiring congressional approval.[65]

The Innovation Center is currently focused on the following priorities[64]:

- Testing new payment and service delivery models
- Evaluating results and advancing best practices
- Engaging a broad range of stakeholders to develop additional models for testing

The innovation models include ACOs, bundled payments for care improvement, primary care transformation (particularly patient-centered medical homes—see Chapter 9), and initiatives to speed the adoption of best practices. CMS has also contracted with expert groups to develop and test different payment model strategies, utilizing simulations of the impact of these models.[66] The aim of the Innovation Center is to catalyze swift evolution of programs by performing rapid-cycle iterative evaluations that help strengthen implementation.[67]

TRANSITIONING FROM FEE-FOR-SERVICE TO VALUE-BASED PAYMENTS

In 2013, a group known as Catalyst for Payment Reform created a national scorecard on payment reform.[68] Their initial survey showed that only about 11% of healthcare dollars paid to doctors and hospitals were tied to "value-oriented" measures, with the other 89% represented by traditional FFS payments.[68] The evolution may have begun, but there is a long way to go before medical payments in the United States are truly based on value rather than volume.

In March 2012, the Society of General Internal Medicine convened a National Commission on Physician Payment reform, chaired by Dr Steven Schroeder and honorary chair, former senator Dr William H. Frist. The group included physicians from various specialties, along with experts in health policy and delivery. The 2014 report called for a 5-year transition from the current FFS reimbursement model to a blended payment system.[69] The Commission endorsed the principles of bundling and full capitation, "which transfers much of the insurance function, including financial risk and gain, to care providers."[70] Interestingly, the pragmatically minded Commission also advocated for some preservation of FFS. For clinicians to take on these risks, it will be essential that change is incremental. Moreover, clinicians will need to be supported in the transition to models that focus more on longitudinal care, coordination across domains, and responsibility for population health. If the payment system is to meaningfully shift, then the delivery system will need to adapt simultaneously.

It is important to understand that payment reform is not an either/or proposition but instead a continuum of financial risk. There are a spectrum of options between volume and value (Figure 15-3). As clinicians assume increasing levels of risk for a larger portion of total care, the incentives are greater not only for efficiency and coordination, but also for "stinting on care."[70] Some hope that safeguards can be put in place, such as publicly reported quality metrics that include measures of underuse, which will allow for more ambitious forms of capitation to be successful without the threat of encouraging the withholding of necessary care.[70]

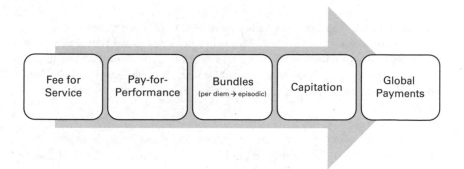

Figure 15-3. Moving from fee-for-service to global payments.

Story From the Frontlines: "The High Price of Kidney Stones These Days"

I wish I could share the photo of my 4mm boomerang shaped kidney stone. I labored for 2 months, back in early 2009, to pass it, the second stone in 5 years.

During my ordeal with these stones, I had the following healthcare encounters, tests, medicines, lab and imaging tests:

- At least five sets of blood work, with CBC and chemistry profiles, and parathyroid studies
- Several urine tests, including urinalysis and urine culture, and two 24-hour urine studies (a third 24-hour urine test was recommended, but I declined)
- Two CT scans
- One MRI
- Four specialist visits, two primary care visits, two ER visits (involving IVs, pain meds, lab studies)
- Prescriptions for antibiotics (despite no evidence of an infection) and Flomax
- Lab analysis of my kidney stone

The actual cost generated by these things evades me, because until recently I have been a passive, insured healthcare consumer. Now that I work on healthcare issues as a patient safety advocate, I am more aware of overuse and the costs associated with it. More care does not mean better care and it is depleting our healthcare resources. My estimate for all of the items listed is at least $15,000—and it actually was probably more. Luckily, my out-of-pocket costs were insignificant since my copays have always been very small.

The point of my story is that the outcome, my passed tiny kidney stone, would have been the same if I had paid $0, instead of generating all of these costs. At the time I thought I was doing the right thing, but by the time I visited an endocrinologist, and he ordered the exact same tests that my urologist had done within a few months before that visit, I knew it was time to say "whoa."

—Kathy Day. "The High Price of Kidney Stones These Days." Costs of Care, 2014. (www.costsofcare.org)

CONCLUSION

Healthcare is financed in the United States through a complicated, byzantine system that has slowly developed and evolved over the course of decades to center primarily around employment-based insurance that reimburses providers on an FFS structure (see Chapter 2). The path has been laid out, however, to begin to transform this arrangement to one that will reflect an emphasis on value and quality.

While the details and effects surrounding financial incentives for motivating change are controversial, it seems critical that we at least stop disincentivizing the delivery of appropriate care. In a transformed medical system, clinicians should no longer be financially punished for providing care that does not translate into a specific "Current Procedural Terminology" (CPT) code (see discussion of RVUs and the Relative Value Unit Committee in Chapter 9). Keeping patients healthy requires care that often centers on noninvasive therapies. If we are to expect clinicians to take the time to appropriately counsel patients about the risks and benefits of undergoing a screening procedure (see Chapter 14), or to undertake true shared-decision making related to complex medical choices (see Chapter 12), or to discuss the best and most cost-effective individualized medication prescriptions (see Chapter 13), then it will be critical that there is some sort of compensation for these cognitive tasks. Whether or not it makes sense to provide specific financial incentives for "value-based care," the system needs to be calibrated so that the financial mechanics align with intended goals and outcomes. Clinicians are driven by intrinsic motivation and professionalism, but we should no longer counteract that impulse with financial incentives that run explicitly counter to care that may be best for patients.

"Payment reform should focus not on manipulating greed, but on dampening it," suggests Drs David Himmelstein and Steffie Woolhandler.[31] "Then the real motivations for good doctoring—altruism, social duty, and the glow we feel when we help our patients—can flourish."

KEY POINTS:

- The majority of healthcare payments in the United States are currently based on a fee-for-service (FFS) system, which results in separate fees paid for each distinct service rendered. Although there are some advantages for patients and clinicians to this system, FFS promotes (or at least does not discourage) the overuse of healthcare resources, by focusing solely on volume rather than value of services.
- Pay-for-performance (P4P) programs provide financial incentives, or bonuses, for meeting certain quality targets. Despite high face validity of this strategy, the results of these programs have been mixed thus far and there is a dearth of evidence that P4P actually improves patient outcomes.
- Financial incentives, when designed and used properly, can be a motivational tool to help drive behavior, but it is important that the incentives align well with the shared purpose of the organization and clinician.
- The Affordable Care Act (ACA) enacted a variety of Medicare "purchasing" strategies that include a value-based purchasing (VBP) program for all hospitals paid by Medicare and a physician value-based payment modifier (PVBPM) for individual physician services. These programs are intended to encourage physicians to work with their peers, systems, hospitals, other professionals, and their patients to hit quality targets while optimizing resource use.
- There is a recent drive to involve both physicians and healthcare systems in cost-sharing (or "risk sharing") via the development and promotion of accountable care organizations (ACOs) and bundled payments.

References:

1. Institute of Medicine. *Crossing the Quality Chasm: A New Health System for the 21st Century.* Washington, DC: National Academy Press; 2001. http://www.iom.edu/Reports/2001/Crossing-the-Quality-Chasm-A-New-Health-System-for-the-21st-Century.aspx. Accessed January 3, 2013.

2. Wachter RM. Pay for performance in healthcare—do we need less more or different. *Wachter's World.* 2012. http://community.the-hospitalist.org/2012/11/27/pay-for-performance-in-health care-do-we-need-less-more-or-different/.

3. Chernew ME. Reforming payment for health care services: comment on "physicians' opinions about reforming reimbursement". *Arch Intern Med.* 2010;170(19):1742-1744.

4. Reinhardt U. How Medicare Pays Physicians. Economix blog. *New York Times.* 2010. http://economix.blogs.nytimes.com/2010/12/03/how-medicare-pays-physicians/. Accessed August 30, 2013.

5. The 101st Congress (1989-1990). *H.R. 3299—The Omnibus Budget Reconciliation Act of 1989.* http://thomas.loc.gov/cgi-bin/query/D?c101:1:./temp/~c101XQ9YAH. Accessed August 30, 2013.

6. Berenson RA, Rich EC. US approaches to physician payment: the deconstruction of primary care. *J Gen Intern Med.* 2010;25(6):613-618.

7. Lepper MR, Greene D, Nisbett RE. Undermining children's intrinsic interest with extrinsic reward: a test of the "overjustification" hypothesis. *J Pers Soc Psychol.* 1973;28(1):129-137.

8. Wachter RM, Foster NE, Dudley RA. Medicare's decision to withhold payment for hospital errors: the devil is in the details. *Jt Comm J Qual Patient Saf.* 2008;34(2):116-123.

9. Epstein AM. Will pay for performance improve quality of care? The answer is in the details. *N Engl J Med.* 2012;367(19):1852-1853.

10. Lindenauer PK, Remus D, Roman S, et al. Public reporting and pay for performance in hospital quality improvement. *N Engl J Med.* 2007;356(5):486-496.

11. Werner RM, Kolstad JT, Stuart EA, Polsky D. The effect of pay-for-performance in hospitals: lessons for quality improvement. *Health Aff.* 2011;30(4):690-698.

12. Jha AK, Joynt KE, Orav EJ, Epstein AM. The long-term effect of premier pay for performance on patient outcomes. *N Engl J Med.* 2012;366(17):1606-1615.

13. Flodgren G, Eccles MP, Shepperd S, Scott A, Parmelli E, Beyer FR. An overview of reviews evaluating the effectiveness of financial incentives in changing healthcare professional behaviours and patient outcomes. In: *Cochrane Database of Systematic Reviews.* John Wiley & Sons; 2011. http://onlinelibrary.wiley.com/. Accessed July 28, 2014.

14. Scott A, Sivey P, Ait Ouakrim D, et al. The effect of financial incentives on the quality of health care provided by primary care physicians. In: *Cochrane Database of Systematic Reviews.* John Wiley & Sons; 2011. http://onlinelibrary.wiley.com/. Accessed July 31, 2014.

15. Houle SKD, McAlister FA, Jackevicius CA, Chuck AW, Tsuyuki RT. Does performance-based remuneration for individual health care practitioners affect patient care? A systematic review. *Ann Intern Med.* 2012;157(12):889-899.

16. Roland M, Campbell S. Successes and failures of pay for performance in the United Kingdom. *N Engl J Med.* 2014;370(20):1944-1949.

17. Campbell SM, Reeves D, Kontopantelis E, Sibbald B, Roland M. Effects of pay for performance on the quality of primary care in England. *N Engl J Med.* 2009;361(4):368-378.

18. Sutton M, Nikolova S, Boaden R, Lester H, McDonald R, Roland M. Reduced mortality with hospital pay for performance in England. *N Engl J Med.* 2012;367(19):1821-1828.

19. Kristensen SR, Meacock R, Turner AJ, et al. Long-term effect of hospital pay for performance on mortality in England. *N Engl J Med.* 2014;371(6):540-548.

20. Rosenthal MB. Nonpayment for performance? Medicare's new reimbursement rule. *N Engl J Med.* 2007;357(16):1573-1575.

21. Calikoglu S, Murray R, Feeney D. Hospital pay-for-performance programs in Maryland produced strong results, including reduced hospital-acquired conditions. *Health Aff.* 2012;31(12):2649-2658.

22. Lee GM, Kleinman K, Soumerai SB, et al. Effect of nonpayment for preventable infections in U.S. hospitals. *N Engl J Med.* 2012;367(15):1428-1437.

23. Woolhandler S, Ariely D. Will Pay For Performance Backfire? Insights From Behavioral Economics. *Health Aff.* Blog. http://healthaffairs.org/blog/2012/10/11/will-pay-for-performance-backfire-insights-from-behavioral-economics/. Accessed August 7, 2014.

24. Pink DH. *Drive: The Surprising Truth About What Motivates Us.* New York, NY: Riverhead Books; 2011.

25. Upton WE. *Altruism, attribution, and intrinsic motivation in the recruitment of blood donors.* New York, NY: Cornell University; 1973.

26. Cassel CK, Jain SH. Assessing individual physician performance: does measurement suppress motivation? *JAMA.* 2012;307(24):2595-2596.

27. Jain SH, Cassel CK. Societal perceptions of physicians: knights, knaves, or pawns? *JAMA.* 2010;304(9):1009-1010.

28. Ryskina KL, Bishop TF. Physicians' lack of awareness of how they are paid: implications for new models of reimbursement. *JAMA Intern Med.* 2013;173(18):1745-1746.

29. Rosenthal MB, Frank RG, Li Z, Epstein AM. Early experience with pay-for-performance: from concept to practice. *JAMA.* 2005;294(14):1788-1793.

30. Doran T, Kontopantelis E, Valderas JM, et al. Effect of financial incentives on incentivised and non-incentivised clinical activities: longitudinal analysis of data from the UK Quality and Outcomes Framework. *BMJ.* 2011;342(1):d3590-d3590.

31. Himmelstein DU, Woolhandler S. Global amnesia: embracing fee-for-non-service—again. *J Gen Intern Med.* 2014;29(5):693-695.

32. Pham HH, Schrag D, O'Malley AS, Wu B, Bach PB. Care patterns in Medicare and their implications for pay for performance. *N Engl J Med.* 2007;356(11):1130-1139.

33. Berenson RA, Kaye DR. Grading a physician's value—the misapplication of performance measurement. *N Engl J Med.* 2013;369(22):2079-2081.

34. Gratz DB. The problem with performance pay. *Educ Leadersh.* 2009;67(3):76-79.

35. Hickson GB, Altemeier WA, Perrin JM. Physician reimbursement by salary or fee-for-service: effect on physician practice behavior in a randomized prospective study. *Pediatrics.* 1987;80(3):344-350.

36. Lee TH, Cosgrove T. Engaging doctors in the health care revolution. *Harv Bus Rev.* 2014. http://hbr.org/2014/06/engaging-doctors-in-the-health-care-revolution/ar/1. Accessed July 30, 2014.

37. McCarthy D, Mueller K, Wrenn J. Geisinger health system: achieving the potential of system integration through innovation, leadership, measurement, and incentives. *Commonwealth Fund.* 2009. http://www.commonwealthfund.org/publications/case-studies/2009/jun/geisinger-health-system-achieving-the-potential-of-system-integration.

38. Vidyarthi AR, Green AL, Rosenbluth G, Baron RB. Engaging residents and fellows to improve institution-wide quality: the first six years of a novel financial incentive program. *Acad Med.* 2014;89(3):460-468.

39. Brown JR, Sox HC, Goodman DC. Financial incentives to improve quality: skating to the puck or avoiding the penalty box? *JAMA.* 2014;311(10):1009-1010.

40. Lee TH. Improving value is improving health care, not rationing. *JAMA Intern Med.* 2014;174(6):847-848.

41. Amabile TM. Motivational synergy: toward new conceptualizations of intrinsic and extrinsic motivation in the workplace. 1993. http://www.hbs.edu/faculty/Pages/item.aspx?num=2500. Accessed July 31, 2014.

42. Chien AT, Rosenthal MB. Medicare's physician value-based payment modifier—will the tectonic shift create waves? *N Engl J Med.* 2013;369(22):2076-2078.

43. Chassin MR. Achieving and sustaining improved quality: lessons from New York state and cardiac surgery. *Health Aff.* 2002;21(4):40-51.

44. Jha AK, Epstein AM. The predictive accuracy of the New York State coronary artery bypass surgery report-card system. *Health Aff.* 2006;25(3):844-855.

45. Werner RM, Asch DA. The unintended consequences of publicly reporting quality information. *JAMA*. 2005;293(10):1239-1244.

46. Totten AM, Wagner J, Tiwari A, O'Haire C, Griffin J, Walker M. *Closing the quality gap: revisiting the state of the science*. (Vol. 5) In: *Public Reporting as a Quality Improvement Strategy*. Rockford, MD: Agency for Healthcare Research and Quality; 2012.

47. Conway PH. Value-driven health care: implications for hospitals and hospitalists. *J Hosp Med*. 2009;4(8):507-511.

48. Medicare Hospital Compare Quality of Care. http://www.medicare.gov/hospitalcompare/search.html. Accessed August 7, 2014.

49. Medicare.gov Physician Compare Home. http://www.medicare.gov/physiciancompare/search.html. Accessed July 31, 2014.

50. Milstein A, Kocher R. Widening gaps in the wall obscuring physician performance differences. *JAMA Intern Med*. 2014;174(6):839-840.

51. Jha AK, Orav EJ, Epstein AM. The effect of financial incentives on hospitals that serve poor patients. *Ann Intern Med*. 2010;153(5):299-306.

52. VanLare JM, Blum JD, Conway PH. Linking performance with payment: Implementing the physician value-based payment modifier. *JAMA*. 2012;308(20):2089-2090.

53. James A III, Gellad WF, Primack BA. Implications of new insurance coverage for access to care, cost-sharing, and reimbursement. *JAMA*. 2014;311(3):241-242.

54. McWilliams JM, Chernew ME, Zaslavsky AM, Hamed P, Landon BE. Delivery system integration and health care spending and quality for medicare beneficiaries. *JAMA Intern Med*. 2013;173(15):1447-1456.

55. Mechanic RE, Santos P, Landon BE, Chernew ME. Medical group responses to global payment: early lessons from the "alternative quality contract" in Massachusetts. *Health Aff*. 2011;30(9):1734-1742.

56. McWilliams JM, Landon BE, Chernew ME. Changes in health care spending and quality for medicare beneficiaries associated with a commercial aco contract. *JAMA*. 2013;310(8):829-836.

57. Gold J. ACO's coordinated care savings may be contagious. *The Washington Post*, Published August 28, 2013. http://www.washingtonpost.com/national/health-science/acos-coordinated-care-savings-may-be-contagious/2013/08/28/28afa178-0fce-11e3-a2b3-5e107edf9897_story.html. Accessed August 31, 2013.

58. Centers for Medicare & Medicaid Services. Accountable Care Organizations (ACO). http://www.cms.gov/Medicare/Medicare-Fee-for-Service-Payment/ACO/index.html?redirect=/aco/. Accessed August 31, 2013.

59. Robert Wood Johnson Foundation. Accountable Care Organizations in Medicare and the Private Sector. RWJF. http://www.rwjf.org/en/research-publications/find-rwjf-research/2011/11/account able-care-organizations-in-medicare-and-the-private-secto.html. Accessed August 31, 2013.

60. Wilensky GR. Lessons from the physician group practice demonstration—a sobering reflection. *N Engl J Med*. 2011;365(18):1659-1661.

61. Colla CH, Wennberg DE, Meara E, et al. Spending differences associated with the medicare physician group practice demonstration. *JAMA*. 2012;308(10):1015-1023.

62. Berwick DM. ACOs—promise, not panacea. *JAMA*. 2012;308(10):1038-1039.

63. Guterman S, Davis K, Stremikis K, Drake H. Innovation in Medicare and Medicaid will be central to health reform's success. *Health Aff*. 2010;29(6):1188-1193.

64. Center for Medicare & Medicaid Innovation. About the CMS Innovation Center. http://innovation.cms.gov/About/index.html. Accessed August 7, 2014.

65. Rosenthal MB. Hard choices—alternatives for reining in medicare and medicaid spending. *N Engl J Med*. 2011;364(20):1887-1890.

66. Payment Models. http://www2.mitre.org/public/payment_models/. Accessed August 7, 2014.

67. Shrank W. The Center for Medicare and Medicaid innovation's blueprint for rapid-cycle evaluation of new care and payment models. *Health Aff*. 2013;32(4):807-812.

68. Delbanco S. Payment reform landscape: overview. Health Aff. Blog. http://healthaffairs.org/blog/2014/02/06/the-payment-reform-landscape-overview/. Accessed July 30, 2014.

69. National Commission on Physician Payment Reform. Report of the National Commission on Physician Payment Reform. RWJF 2013. http://www.rwjf.org/en/research-publications/find-rwjf-research/2013/03/report-of-the-national-commission-on-physician-payment-reform.html. Accessed January 7, 2014.

70. Selker HP, Kravitz RL, Gallagher TH. The national physician payment commission recommendation to eliminate fee-for-service payment: balancing risk, benefit, and efficiency in bundling payment for care. *J Gen Intern Med*. 2014;29(5):698-699.

Implementing Value-Based Initiatives: A New Challenge for Clinicians and Healthcare Systems

In the mid-1800s, giving birth could be dangerous. Ignaz Semmelweis worked as a house officer in an obstetrical ward in Vienna, Austria, where nearly one-in-six woman died following childbirth. In the other obstetrical clinic he worked in, the maternal mortality rate was less than half that, at 7%. He began to wonder why there was such a discrepancy in the outcomes between these two clinics. Ignaz noticed that doctors and medical students at the first clinic were often coming directly to the delivery room after performing autopsies, even frequently with a "disagreeable odor" on their hands. He began to hypothesize that there may be "cadaverous particles" that could be transmitted by the hands of these physicians resulting in harm for birthing mothers. He recommended hands be scrubbed in a chlorinated lime solution before every patient contact. Of course, we all know what happened. Hand-washing resulted in the mortality rate in the obstetrical ward to plummet to less than 3%.[1]

The experience of Ignaz Semmelweis and others across the globe around that time showed convincingly that hand-washing could dramatically save lives. So, naturally every clinician immediately began washing his or her hands prior to every patient contact, right? Well, incredibly this is not what happened. Over the next 150 years there was slow incremental progress in achieving universal hand-washing practices. It turns out that changing behaviors, especially in the traditions of medicine, is very challenging. Even when there is a mortality benefit, the availability of convincing evidence is generally not enough to ensure widespread changes.

Only recently have hand-washing practices improved substantially in most medical centers. This has been achieved through multidimensional strategies that connect available evidence with accountability, such as flagging nosocomial infections and providing 360-degree feedback, as well as with systems that address barriers to hand-washing, such as removing the need for a sink by strategically placing alcohol-based handrubs in clinical areas.

As we have stated previously, "When it comes to reducing healthcare waste, we may still be in the equivalent of the mid-1800s; we have convincingly identified the problem and some are now shouting from the mountaintops for change. But much like hand-washing, we may need to do a better job thinking about how to make it easier to do the right thing."[2]

Drawing on the lessons of hand-washing, our Costs of Care group has created a "COST" framework for designing multidimensional strategies to prevent harms from overuse: culture, oversight accountability, system support, and training. We introduced this framework in Chapter 11 in the context of educational efforts to teach value, but just as that discussion focused mostly on experiential learning and culture change, this structure also applies directly to implementation efforts. We believe that effective efforts need to target all four of these "COST" areas (Table 16-1 *includes a worksheet that can be used for designing interventions*).

This chapter will focus on the need for healthcare systems to operationalize the ideas behind value improvement into practice. We will consider how organizations can best support the efforts of frontline clinicians in creating change, highlighting some recent clinician-led efforts. We will also touch upon the translation of models from other industries to improve healthcare reliability and efficiency, such as the recent application of Lean management strategies to healthcare organizations.

IMPLEMENTATION SCIENCE TO TRANSLATE EVIDENCE INTO PRACTICE

Clinical research has led to remarkable medical breakthroughs that have saved and enriched countless lives. However, as discussed throughout this book, the delivery of such effective healthcare is extraordinarily uneven, leading to unconscionable disparities that result in some patients being given too little effective care whilst others receive too much—both situations creating unnecessary harm.[3] For us to realize the fruits of our research advancements, the uptake of the most reliable medical evidence will need to be enhanced. This requires strengthening the connections between the insights from science to the efficient delivery of evidence-based medicine, ultimately leading to better outcomes and superior patient experience (see Figure 4.5, page 88).

Remember from Chapter 10 that the use of aspirin by patients who have previously had a stroke greatly reduces the chances that they will have another stroke,[4] yet barely more than half of eligible patients are given aspirin.[3] While the pharmaceutical industry invested piles of money to create more efficacious medications such as clopidogrel (Plavix), much greater benefit may actually be gained by creating delivery systems that more reliably support patients taking aspirin after a stroke.[5] In other words, we need to not only study and

Table 16-1 COST framework for high-value care interventions

Interventions	Description	Example	List Predisposing Factors (Barriers or Assets) in Your Local Clinical Environment	List Potential Strategies to Apply in Your Local Clinical Environment
C	Culture	Valuing cost-consciousness and resource stewardship as practiced standards of medical professionalism at the individual and team level.	Hospital-wide campaign led by peer-champions to raise awareness regarding overuse of lab tests.	☐ ☐ ☐ ☐ ☐	☐ ☐ ☐ ☐
O	Oversight	Requiring accountability for cost-conscious decision-making at both a peer and organizational level.	Requiring an attending physician to review the labs that residents order to promote better stewardship.	☐ ☐ ☐	☐ ☐ ☐ ☐
S	Systems Change	Creating supportive systems to make cost-conscious decisions using institutional policy, decision-support tools, and evidence-based clinical guidelines.	Electronic health record displays costs of lab tests next to order for specific tests.	☐ ☐ ☐	☐ ☐ ☐ ☐
T	Training	Providing the knowledge, skills, and tools clinicians need to make cost-conscious decisions in their clinical environments.	Lecture or workshop on ordering of lab tests.	☐ ☐ ☐ ☐	☐ ☐ ☐ ☐

"COST" framework developed by the Costs of Care team, including Drs Andrew Levy, Neel Shah, Christopher Moriates, and Vineet Arora.

understand biology and medical therapeutics, but also how to best deliver health-care. The National Institute of Health (NIH) has recently recognized this gap and created a research agenda that focuses on advancing the "knowledge base related to disseminating and implementing evidence-based health strategies in real-world settings."[6] An entire multidisciplinary field of study in "implementation science" has now emerged, defining general design principles that include (1) application of individual and organizational behavior change theories, (2) identification and engagement of key stakeholders, and (3) commitment to rapid-cycle improvement with collaborative, bidirectional relationships between the intervention sponsor and the behavior change target.[7]

The success of implementation of a given target practice or system depends on a number of external and internal factors. People and systems must be prepared for change, and have the capacity for implementation.[8] Even if every single resident physician agreed that having in-depth goals of care discussions was a worthy and important goal for a defined group of hospitalized patients, if the residents are already working at the 80-hour-per-week limit there may not be any capacity to add yet another process to their work day.

In another example, when promoting a project to decrease transfusion rates in our hospital, I (CM) presented to our internal medicine resident physicians the evidence that supports a "restrictive" transfusion strategy. Following the educational session, many of the residents assured me they would change their practices and would encourage their colleagues and teams to do the same. These residents had the authority and leeway to make this change. But when I gave nearly the same presentation to a group of neurosurgical residents, who were very engaged and supportive, a hand went up from one of the residents at the table: "This is great and I believe in the evidence here that you provide," she said. "But unless you get my surgical attending to explicitly change what they want me to do, there is no way that I will be able to do anything about this." Heads across the room were shaking in agreement.

Building the will for change is clearly necessary but insufficient to make real differences. Once again, it is not enough merely to know what the right thing to do is, we must identify and tackle barriers to these practices, including factors that may be seen as predisposing, enabling, and reinforcing to the current and desired behaviors.[9] Just as the saying goes, "all politics is local," the same is often true when addressing barriers to implementation. While educational outreach—matched with appropriate enabling and reinforcing strategies—may be effective for internal medicine residents to change their transfusion practices, this may not be adequate for surgical residents even within the same institution. The "PRECEDE" model ("predisposing, reinforcing, and enabling constructs in educational diagnosis and evaluation") provides an example framework for thinking through the design of initial implementation strategies (Figure 16-1).[10] When planning a program to improve hand hygiene

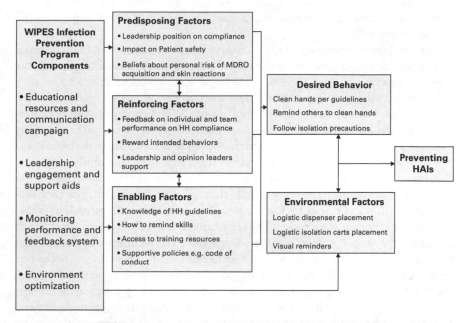

Figure 16-1. An example of applying the "PRECEDE" model for an Infection Prevention Program. (Reproduced, with permission of the University of Chicago Press. From Aboumatar H, Ristaino P, Davis RO, et al. Infection prevention promotion program based on the PRECEDE model: improving hand hygiene behaviors among healthcare personnel. *Infect Control Hosp Epidemiol.* 2012;33(2):144-151. © 2011 by The Society for Healthcare Epidemiology of America. All rights reserved.)

behaviors, the current leadership environment and personal beliefs related to infection control are predisposing factors that should be carefully considered and addressed.

By the way, what we did for our transfusion reduction project following our meeting with the neurosurgical residents was we focused on identifying local champions. We presented the information to the attending surgeons and recruited a bunch of prominent, well-respected surgeons from our institution to pose for a picture with a statement saying they supported the project. We hung this poster up prominently on the surgical ward. This helped the residents feel supported and enabled them to be more willing to follow the transfusion guidelines.

Engaging frontline clinicians

"If improvement is the plan, then we own the plan," said the Institute for Healthcare Improvement's Dr Donald Berwick in 2011.[11] "Government cannot do it. Payers cannot do it. Regulators cannot do it. Only the people who give the care can improve the care."

So how do healthcare organizations best engage clinicians in improving the care they provide?

For starters, as we discussed in Chapter 15, it is important that extrinsic incentives are well aligned with clinicians' internal motivations to provide the best possible care to their patients. The finest way to achieve this is to create a noble shared purpose. Clinicians nearly universally enter the medical profession with honorable ambitions to serve their patients. When the goals of an organization truly and explicitly align with this intention—rather than perhaps merely paying lip service in a mission statement—then it is more likely that clinicians will feel eager about pitching in to work toward that ideal. Currently, clinicians may be confronted with institutional oversight on whether their documentation maximizes billing, clinical "report cards" that focus on productivity or throughput, and quality indicators that are driven by national mandates such as indiscriminately reducing readmission rates, to name a few. When this is what floods clinicians' inboxes, the unintended message from the healthcare system is that these are the things that truly matter. Furthermore, clinicians may sense the tectonic plates beneath their feet shifting in response to various national reform efforts, creating an unstable environment that does not necessarily compel intrinsic motivations to improve care. "To help physicians move beyond grief and anger about what they might be losing as the healthcare system remodels, leaders must shift the conversation to something different—something positive, noble, and important," recommend health leaders Drs Thomas Lee and Toby Cosgrove.[12] "They must articulate a vision of what lies on the other side of the turmoil ahead: healthcare that will be better—maybe even great—for patients. Improved patient care has to form the core of any change agenda that clinicians will embrace." By laying out the hope ahead for the profession, we are more likely to generate an organic will for change.

The importance of key institutional leadership and role modeling cannot be stressed enough. An aligned mission empowers junior staff to pursue improvements in care delivery with a crisp overarching goal: make care better for our patients.

Another vital tool for creating behavior change is appropriately leveraging opinion leaders and peer pressure. Local opinion leaders can have profound impacts on the practices of their colleagues, oftentimes proving more effective at garnering changes in physician behavior than other tried-and-true methods. In one classic randomized trial at community hospitals in the early 1990s, some obstetricians obtained education from local opinion leaders about reducing cesarean section (c-section) rates, while others were given only audit and feedback.[13] The opinion leader education dramatically increased guideline-concordant care for trial of labor—resulting in significantly higher vaginal birth rates. The simple audit and feedback generated no measurable effect.

Thinking again about hand-washing, I know if I were to be seen entering a patient room without washing my hands by one of my colleagues, I would feel genuinely embarrassed. Do we feel embarrassed if our colleague sees us order an unnecessary test or procedure? Perhaps not yet. When used correctly, peer pressure can be a powerful motivator for behavior change. On an operational scale, sharing ratings or metrics internally and/or publically can generate perceived peer pressure and can drive behaviors.[14] Humans—and particularly physicians—are naturally competitive and will often respond to metrics that show them to be not performing as well as others. Thus, combining audit and feedback with role modeling from opinion leaders, creating suitable peer pressure, can be a potent strategy for inspiring change. Audit and feedback appear to be most effective when[15]:

- Baseline performance is poor, thus providing a lot of opportunity for change.
- The person providing the feedback is a supervisor or colleague.
- The feedback is provided more than once.
- The feedback is given both verbally and in writing.
- And the program includes clear targets with an action plan.

Although the engagement of frontline health workers is essential for improvement efforts, system changes nearly always require actions from management. Clinicians need the necessary tools to effectively study and design projects.[16] And many clinicians will need appropriate time and resources to stimulate and support proposed initiatives. Organizations can strategically invest in providing protected time to some individuals on the frontlines.

One common pitfall of utilizing "insiders" to develop change strategies is that ideas may be constrained by workers' own experiences. Leaders can help promote divergent thinking through providing analogies from outside healthcare (see below) and other creativity generating tools, which can stoke novel solutions and breakthrough ideas.[16,17]

The UCSF "caring wisely" program: an institutional program designed to spark and support initiatives from the clinical frontline

In 2013, the UCSF Center for Healthcare Value launched a "Caring Wisely" program, aimed at creating an organized process for engaging and supporting frontline clinicians in efforts to remove unnecessary costs from healthcare delivery systems (Figure 16-2). The idea was to create a model for translating the impetus behind initiatives such as the ABIM Foundation's "Choosing Wisely" campaign[18] into robust implementation strategies at the health system delivery level.

The underlying realization for this program was that top-down decrees for specific changes often did not align well with the interests or motivations of on-the-ground healthcare workers. A platform that could "pull" ideas and enthusiasm from the frontlines (rather than simply "pushing" programs out)—while simultaneously providing a bridge to institutional leadership and resources—may be more potent at generating behavior changes.

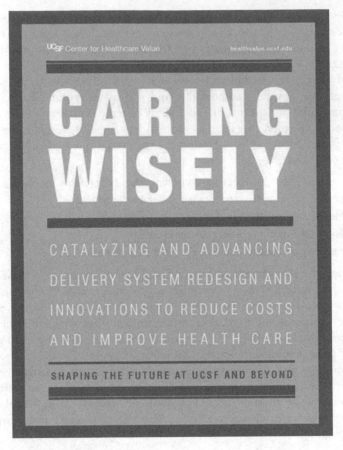

Figure 16-2. Caring Wisely at UCSF.

In an effort to provide a concrete example of this type of program, we will describe some of the details of how Caring Wisely works.

Phase I: Engage frontline staff to identify "hot spots"

The annual Caring Wisely campaign begins with an "ideas contest," a search for compelling ideas to identify key areas ("hot spots") for improving inefficiencies and reducing costs within the UCSF Health System. The announcement e-mail is sent by our chief medical officer to *all employees* of the UCSF Health System, implicitly displaying the buy-in from high-level hospital management to folks on the ground. Ideas are submitted by employees at all levels, including unit clerks, nurses, physicians, administrators, and researchers. Participants can submit an idea even if he or she does not intend to submit a proposal for implementation. Next, a selection committee that includes administrators, staff, and clinicians from each site reviews and ranks all ideas, choosing the top 5 to 10 ideas.

Criteria for selecting winning Phase I ideas include:

- Must be safe, and not cause harm, reduce quality, or adversely affect the patient experience.
- Must reduce costs to the UCSF Health System.
- Must reduce or not increase costs to the patient and their insurer.
- Problem must be under the direct control of providers and/or staff.
- Problem must be addressable in simple and straightforward ways.

Idea winners are announced in a system-wide e-mail and receive a modest gift card to their choice of a local fine dining establishment.

Phase II: Engage frontline staff to create implementation plans

Next, the Caring Wisely team sends out a call for proposals from the UCSF community, specifically highlighting the "hot spots" identified by the ideas contest. Proposals are collected via the UCSF Open Proposals system: a Web-based platform enabling transparent and collaborative proposal development. Up to $50,000 funding is provided by the UCSF Health System and is offered for each chosen proposal.

The Open Proposals system provides an iterative process that allows stakeholders to review proposals and provides the opportunity to ask clarifying questions, leave comments, or offer suggestions. This also fosters real-time multidisciplinary team building. Additionally, teams can promote their proposals and build further support from their community, with some teams encouraging their colleagues to go review their proposals and provide "likes" (similar to the like button on popular social media site, Facebook) to display support.

The review committee of Caring Wisely leadership and stakeholders evaluates proposals based upon a project's potential to:

- Measurably reduce costs from the perspective of the delivery system. (Should show potential savings of more than $200,000 within first year.)
- Ensure health outcomes are maintained or improved.
- Have demonstrated commitment and engagement of clinical leadership and frontline staff.
- Have potential to scale.

Two to three proposals were chosen during each of the first two rounds for funding and implementation.

Phase III: Support and build implementation

Chosen projects are funded for a one-year implementation phase and implementation is supported by the robust Caring Wisely program, which provides infrastructure support including delivery system leaders, the institutional finance team, and experts in implementation science. The partnership between project teams and the Caring Wisely team is a critical component of the program. The Caring Wisely team offers a director, program manager, data analysts, and implementation scientists to support project teams and to ensure institutional learning as the program matures.

Work-in-progress meetings are held with project teams and the Caring Wisely team every 2 weeks to support progress, troubleshoot issues, and foster collaborative learning between project teams. This ongoing support provides the frontline clinicians leading the efforts with the requisite expertise and institutional support to help generate successful implementation.

Geisinger's ProvenCare and other efforts to create continuous system-wide improvement

In 2006, Geisinger—a nonprofit, integrated health services organization serving over 2.5 million residents in central and northeastern Pennsylvania—did something that is generally unheard of in medicine. They made a "guarantee." Christening the program as "ProvenCare," Geisenger brought together their heart surgeons to review all class I and IIa recommendations—those recommendations that have the highest level of supporting evidence—from the 2004 American Heart Association/American College of Cardiology Guidelines for CABG surgery (coronary artery bypass graft, or "bypass surgery"), and to translate these recommendations into 40 verifiable behaviors.[19] They then assembled a multidisciplinary team to "hardwire" these best practices into everyday workflow, and to implement a robust program of real-time data collection and feedback.[19,20] So far, so good, sounds like many other quality improvement or clinical pathway initiatives. But, what Geisinger did was perhaps revolutionary: they guaranteed that all 40 benchmarks would be achieved for *every* patient that underwent elective CABG surgery within their health system—and they put their money where their mouth is.[21] They packaged all preoperative, inpatient, and postoperative care within 90 days into a single fixed price. If a patient suffered a postoperative complication, there would not be any additional charges from any Geisinger facilities. This part of the program is basically a provider-driven enactment of bundled payments (see Chapter 15). The *New York Times* famously referred to this as "surgery with a warranty."[22]

Taking responsibility for things that happen within 90 days of surgery—even when patients are no longer within a medical facility—requires not only care coordination and careful attention to quality practices, but also trust that patients will do their part. As part of the initial ProvenCare program, a Patient Compact was developed to highlight the importance of patient activation in their own healthcare (see Chapter 12).[19]

At the outset of the program, less than 60% of patients at Geisinger received all 40 best practice components, but shortly following implementation this rose to

100% and appeared to be sustained.[19] Nowadays, if any of the preoperative benchmarks have not been performed, surgery is delayed until this unfinished task is completed.[21] The benefits of performing these benchmarks were immediately obvious, with length of stay decreasing 16% and mean hospital charges falling more than 5% over the first year.[19] Operative mortality has also been declining. Leaders of the program have concluded that "frontline medical care providers, led by process design specialists, can successfully redesign episodic processes to consistently deliver evidence-based medicine, which may improve patient outcomes and reduce resource use."[20]

The ProvenCare model has now been expanded to other clinical areas, such as perinatal care,[23] and has even spread to include multiple institutions through a collaborative program to improve care for lung cancer patients.[24]

There are a handful of other well-known beacons for system-wide continuous improvement. In 2009, Intermountain Healthcare in Utah was highlighted by President Obama as a model for high-quality care at lower costs.[25] Applying evidence-based protocols and practice improvement methodologies to more than 60 clinical processes, Intermountain has now reengineered roughly 80% of all care that they deliver.[26] Intermountain has also actively addressed supply chain inefficiencies and resource utilization, cutting costs and ensuring that they are providing the best evidence-based tools and supplies to their providers and patients.[26] Over in Ohio, Cincinnati Children's Hospital has partnered with local physicians to create large-scale improvements in certain clinical areas, such as children with asthma, resulting in 92% adherence to best practices for asthma care, which has yielded many avoided hospital admissions and emergency department visits.[27] Cleveland Clinic, already renowned for state-of-the-art cardiac care, has recently risen as a leader in integrating team-based approaches and shared decision making, with an overarching focus on enhancing patient experience.[28]

Kaiser Permanente, based in California, is a massive integrated health system that has achieved a number of high-quality clinical indicators at low costs, primarily through coordinated efforts to provide population management to their large patient base.[29] For example, a blood pressure program by Kaiser involved a comprehensive hypertension registry, the sharing of performance metrics, the integration of evidence-based guidelines, the development of medical assistant visits for blood pressure management, and the promotion of single-pill combination pharmacotherapy, achieving hypertension control in more than 80% of their patients identified with high blood pressure.[30] Kaiser Permanente has been so successful that it now serves as a model for national health programs in various countries around the world.[29,31,32]

Many other examples of impressive healthcare system innovations exist. Later in this chapter, we will discuss how some institutions like Virginia Mason and Denver Health have successfully adopted Lean manufacturing methodologies to systematically cut waste. We will also outline the Institute of Medicine's

(IOM's) recommended strategies for creating "continuously learning healthcare systems."[33]

Centers and collaboratives for shared learning and organizational benchmarking

In 2008, the ThedaCare Center for Healthcare Value was founded in Appleton, Wisconsin, as a "small nonprofit with a big mission the help change the healthcare industry."[34] The ThedaCare Center for Healthcare Value provides a number of educational services and programs, partnering with health organizations to explore ways to improve quality and drive down costs in healthcare. Part of the program is dedicated to integrating Lean strategies (see below) within healthcare organizations to systematically root out waste and improve processes.

A number of academic health centers have also recently developed new institutes aimed at promoting innovation and value.[35] UCSF has established a Center for Healthcare Value to promote solutions for value throughout delivery systems, research, policy, and clinical training.[36] George Washington University opened an Office for Clinical Practice Innovation in 2013 with "the mission of engaging and educating faculty, fellows, residents, and students in clinical practice innovation," centering around new ways to deliver care that enhance value.[35]

In 2010, four leading health systems (Dartmouth-Hitchcock Medical Center, Denver Health, Intermountain Healthcare, Mayo Clinic) and The Dartmouth Institute for Health Policy and Clinical Practice formed the High Value Health Care Collaborative.[37] The core asset of the group is to provide a data trust with a number of supportive "marts" that are customized for specific purposes and easy analyses. The hope is to ultimately stimulate the identification and widespread adoption of best-practice care models. In 2014, the consortium included 19 healthcare delivery systems.

Story From the Frontlines: "Teaching Value—Arizona"

A little friendly competition is a good thing. We have seen it work in our residency programs. That is why we answered the "Teaching Value and Choosing Wisely Challenge" (see Chapter 11) with a competition of our own.

Unfortunately, it is not hard to find the waste and low value care in most hospitals. We reasoned that the best ideas to promote and teach high-value care would come right from our own residents and fellows. Our hospital, Banner Good Samaritan Medical Center, is among the largest teaching hospitals in the Southwest and a major teaching affiliate of the University of Arizona College of Medicine—Phoenix, where we are both faculty. Banner Health is among the more innovative health systems in the country and has jumped in with both feet to the "high-value" movement. Banner has incorporated high-value care into its major strategic objectives and is one of Medicare's Pioneer Accountable Care Organizations. It is not enough to just provide more care. We have to provide high-value care: better quality at less cost. Our contest was designed to educate house staff in high-value care, improve patient care, develop future leaders in healthcare, engage house staff in quality improvement activities, and disseminate findings to improve care throughout the system and beyond.

We challenged residents and fellows in our graduate medical education programs to enter our "high-value care" contest. Three project ideas would win $2500 each and the opportunity to design and implement their "high-value" idea with an interdisciplinary team in our hospital. The cash prize was donated by the medical staff. The entries were limited to 500 words and were judged based on: the impact on house staff education, the impact on patient outcomes, and the feasibility, scalability and alignment with the Choosing Wisely campaign and/or Banner Health strategic objectives.

We received a remarkable 46 entries from residents and fellows in 11 programs. Our first-round judges, engaged faculty from seven of our residencies and fellowships, selected 11 finalists. Our final judges were high-profile leaders from throughout the hospital and system including the system chief medical officer, the hospital chief executive officer, and the chief nursing officer. We thought including our system leaders as judges would be a great way to engage these leaders with our training programs and innovative efforts to improve care.

The final projects were as wide-ranging in their approach as they were high quality. The final projects included ideas to decrease admissions in cirrhosis, address end-of-life decision making, minimize imaging for duodenal tubes in the ICU, and increase the use of probiotics, to name a few.

The winning ideas from residents in our orthopedic, family medicine, and internal medicine programs were:

- Attempted reduction of unnecessary diagnostic testing by utilization of cost transparency.
- An evidence-based approach to reducing the incidence of catheter-associated urinary tract infections.
- Implementation of a hospital-wide system to increase the appropriate use of cardiac stress testing.

Now the hard work really begins for these winners. They have already assembled their multidisciplinary teams and received guidance from leaders in our system. These three presented their high-value project final results in May 2014 at our "Graduate Medical Education Quality and Safety Day" with a chance to win another $2500.

Our "high-value care" challenge at Banner Good Samaritan is off to a great start. We have had great support from hospital and system leadership, the program directors and faculty, and the medical staff. Our residents and fellows have great ideas on how to provide high-value care and have shown their dedication to this important effort. We look forward to seeing the impact of these innovative ideas across the system and to future years of our "high-value care" contest.

—Cheryl O'Malley and Steven R. Brown. "Teaching Value—Arizona."
Costs of Care, 2014. (www.costsofcare.org)

APPLYING TOOLS FROM OTHER INDUSTRIES TO HEALTHCARE ORGANIZATIONS

Oftentimes when entering an airplane I think, "Thank God this plane is not a hospital." The airline industry has achieved an astonishing safety record, making the drive to an airport much more dangerous than flying 30,000 feet above the Pacific Ocean. When travelling by plane, I can be quite confident that I will arrive in my predetermined destination, safe, and likely at—or reasonably near—my estimated arrival time. And when it comes to costs, despite gripes about airlines now charging fees for various services such as transporting luggage, the price of air travel has remained quite stable over the years; in fact, after adjusting for inflation and adding in baggage and change fees, domestic airfares (excluding taxes) are 39% lower in 2013 than they were in 1980.[38]

If only healthcare was as reliable and stable. Surely, you recall the infamous estimate by the IOM that medical errors result in the equivalent of a "jumbo jet crash each day."[39] None of us would feel nearly as comfortable entering a 747 if we knew that one would drop out of the sky every day. Considering this, it seems logical that the healthcare system could learn much from the airline industry. While this is clearly true, it is worth mentioning that healthcare is exceptional for a number of obvious and not-so-obvious reasons. Not least of all, when a plane crashes, the pilot is just as likely as the passengers to die, which clearly is not the case for a surgeon or physician treating a patient. Notwithstanding the best intentions in the world, it is inherently a different situation when one's own life is on the line. From an industry perspective, major aviation errors are immediately broadcast to the public with substantial financial and reputational ramifications. And even as airplanes become increasingly sophisticated and complex, the human body is many magnitudes more intricate and enigmatic. Aviation also has relatively few airlines and a single authoritative federal regulator.[40]

Despite these notable differences, many key principles of patient safety have been adapted from aviation, including teamwork training based on Crew Resource Management concepts,[41] nonpunitive reporting of errors,[42] and a focus on a "safety climate" or culture.[43] High reliability organizations—organizations or systems that operate in hazardous conditions but have fewer than their fair share of adverse events, such as aviation and nuclear power plants[44]—offer critical insights for enhancing the safety and dependability of healthcare. Thus, similarly, when it comes to considering efficiency and costs, it may make sense to look toward other industries outside of healthcare, particularly manufacturing.

In the city of Toyota, Japan, precise machines work side-by-side with people to build millions of vehicles each year. In 2012, Toyota sold about 9.75 million vehicles, making it the top auto manufacturer in the world.[45] Producing that many vehicles requires extreme efficiency. But, of course, to maintain a respectable reputation and to continue to sell so many cars, quality and safety is paramount. On a Toyota production line, if anything goes wrong, any member on the factory floor has the ability to "stop the line." This applies to the machines as well; if equipment malfunction or a defective part is discovered, affected machines automatically stop, allowing operators to correct the problem before it progresses through production. This practice of "jidoka" ("which can be loosely translated as 'automation with a human touch'"[46]) permits Toyota to apply their concept of "Just-in-Time" manufacturing, in which each process produces only what is needed by the next process in a continuous flow.[46] Since the principles and methods of the Toyota Production System focus on improving quality while reducing waste, they have been generically referred to as "Lean."

The five general principles of Lean are to define value from the customer's perspective, identify the value stream and remove any waste, make value flow without interruption, help customers pull value, and pursue perfection.[17]

Lean identifies three main categories of operational waste[17]:

- *Muda:* Anything that does not add value for the customer.
- *Muri:* Overburden, which occurs when one asks an individual, a piece of equipment, or a system to do that which it is not capable of doing.
- *Mura:* Unevenness. This concept is meant to focus attention on creating smooth and harmonious flow through processes.

The application of Lean management principles in healthcare

If it is not always entirely clear how efficiency better serves our patients, then perhaps we can turn to the "Father of Modern Medicine," Sir William Osler, who is quoted as stating in 1893, "Medical care must be provided with the utmost efficiency. To do less is a disservice to those we treat, and an injustice to those we might have treated."

Likewise, the leaders of Toyota have reportedly said, "Waste is disrespectful to humanity because it squanders scarce resources. Waste is disrespectful to individuals because it asks them to do work with no value." Dr Patricia Gabow, the chief executive officer at Denver Health, adds, "In healthcare... waste is disrespectful to our patients because it asks them to endure processes with no value."[47]

Since the philosophy of Lean is built on respect for people and continuous improvement, it translates incredibly well to healthcare. In fact, Lean has been increasingly adopted by medical centers across the country as a systematic approach for improving quality and efficiency.[48]

Perhaps the most prominent trailblazer in this movement has been Virginia Mason Medical Center in Seattle. Back in 2000, Dr Gary Kaplan became the CEO of Virginia Mason and, at that time, his board of directors challenged him by asking, "Who is your customer?" When he responded with a knee-jerk response, "our patient," he said the board did not accept it at face value. "We began to do a deep dive on our processes and came to realize that they were designed around us, the doctors, the nurses, the people working in the organization as opposed to our patients," Dr Kaplan explained.[49] "It all began with a desire to explore the redesign of processes around patients rather than caregivers."

So Virginia Mason began to look around for a better management system, but Dr Kaplan did not find any shining examples in American healthcare. "That is when we almost serendipitously discovered that Boeing just down the street was 7 to 8 years along in deploying the Toyota Production System," he said. "When we realized that Boeing was able to reduce the lead time to construct the 737 airplane from 22 days to 11 days, and in so doing build a safer aircraft at less costs, we said wow, this might have applications for healthcare."[49] So, in 2002, some of the leadership of Virginia Mason took their first trip to Japan to study "The Toyota Way." The trip was monumental for the future of Virginia Mason, which has led the way for integrating Lean methodologies to cut waste and improve healthcare, and has now become an exemplar for quality healthcare delivery. Now all leaders at

Virginia Mason attend mandatory leadership training, are required to lead formal improvement events each year, and are expected to coach and train staff in the use of production system tools and methods.[50]

One of the fundamental concepts of Lean is to go to where the actual work is done and observe firsthand the processes and how things work.[48] A representational flowchart called a current-state *value stream map* can be created to depict all of the individual steps in a process from beginning to end, providing a graphical tool for identifying and categorizing waste in the process, which include any non-value-added steps, delays, waiting times, and inefficiencies.[48] To ensure this current state is accurate, the honest insights and input from those that actually do the work in the process is required. With a current-state value stream map in hand, an experienced improvement team can systematically brainstorm potential solutions to identified issues, eventually devising a future-state value stream map that represents an improved and streamlined way to accomplish the processes.

Another key component of Lean is a commitment to rapid improvement cycles.[17,48] The goal is to quickly perform "small tests of change" and then to iterate and hone these changes until they neatly fit the needed improvement. Once a possible solution has been identified and needs detailed development and testing, a *kaizen event*—an intensive focused multiday effort—may be held.[17] Virginia Mason Medical Center says they conduct literally hundreds of these workshops annually.[17] A resident physician that took part in a week-long kaizen event as part of a quality improvement elective told me (CM) that he felt it was the most useful hands-on training in how to understand the inner workings of the hospital that he ever experienced. For the first time in his training, he sensed he could actually make a difference in the system. He noted that residents may have difficulty designing and implementing traditional quality improvement projects, due to a general lack of dedicated time and rotations that often do not provide longitudinal follow-through, but a dedicated event that lasts a few days to a week may be more easily carved out of their schedule and can provide an immersive experience. This is likely also true for many other frontline clinicians and healthcare staff.

Early success stories of Lean programs are emerging from different corners of the country. The application of Lean methodologies to a Joint Replacement Program at a Veteran's Affairs hospital cut length of stay for patients from about 5½ days to 3½ days[51]—just think, that is, two fewer nights sleeping in those uncomfortable hospital beds and being woken up during the middle of the night to have vitals checked! At the University of Michigan only about half of peripherally inserted central catheters (PICCs)—a long intravenous (IV) line that is inserted in the arm and terminates just above the heart—were not placed on the day they were requested. These delays resulted in postponed delivery of important medications and late discharges from the hospital. With the introduction of Lean production methods, now 90% to 95% of PICC lines are inserted within 24-hours of the request.[48] And at Virginia Mason there is a laundry list of metrics showing success. For example, the Virginia Mason Production System has freed an estimated 25,000 square feet of space by using better space designs, has reduced the time it takes to report lab results to patients by more than 85%, and reduced labor expenses in overtime and temporary labor by $500,000 in just one year.[50]

Denver Health has proven that Lean can be applied even in a resource-strapped safety net institution that includes an educational mission with medical students and resident physicians. Following the introduction of Lean, Denver Health achieved remarkable successes, resulting in more than $170 million in financial benefits, while simultaneously increasing their patient satisfaction ranking by almost 50 percentage points.[28]

FOMENTING CHANGE FROM WITHIN ORGANIZATIONS

Although many of the programs described above involve devoted institutional leadership and big-scale systemic transformations, there is an important role to be played by individual clinicians to work toward value improvement, and perhaps to even inspire bigger change within their own healthcare system. Clinicians generally "have the requisite drive, experience, and context to be productive innovators."[16] But obviously it takes more than drive and experience. Clinician innovators also need to possess some fundamental tools for innovation, such as an understanding of a *Plan-Do-Study-Act (PDSA) cycle* and how to create *"SMART" (specific, measurable, attainable, relevant, time-bound) goals* and project charters, which are described in further detail below.

Basic improvement tools

W. Edwards Deming—an American engineer, statistician, and professor that has become known as the "Father of the Science of Quality Improvement"—popularized the PDSA cycle that is widely used in business and medicine for the continuous improvement of processes (Figure 16-3).[52] The PDSA cycle is described as "the scientific method adapted for action-oriented learning."[53] The steps are simple: PLAN, or design, the experiment; DO the experiment; STUDY the results, outcomes, and unexpected problems; and ACT on the results by integrating learning generated throughout the process to make adjustments. The cycle is based on *continuous* improvement, which is why these steps are proposed to continue on *ad infinitum*, always leading to new insights and advancements.

But to even get started on the cycle, we need to first have a good plan. There are many different methods for recognizing a good target area for improving healthcare value. The first may be to simply reflect on personal anecdotal experiences—what things have you seen done or have you done yourself that you think might not make sense? Or, maybe there are areas of obvious variation

Figure 16-3. Plan-Do-Study-Act (PDSA) cycle for improvement.

within your own system. These practices may be easiest to identify and could be specific to your own environment. Does it seem like your hospital always orders carotid ultrasounds for patients admitted with syncope?[54] Does one of the attending physicians in clinic always recommend antibiotics for sinusitis, whereas the other one does not? These simple observations can be great for generating hypotheses to investigate. However, it is important to not base decisions on anecdotes, so once an area catches your interest, the next step is to collect the data and see if this is really a widespread problem warranting an intervention. Beside personal observations, another resource for generating potential practices to target are the ABIM Foundation's Choosing Wisely lists (www.choosingwisely.org). Once again though, it is critical that we use data to investigate whether or not the area highlighted by a Choosing Wisely list or guideline is actually applicable to local practices.

Sometimes investigating cost or utilization data can highlight outliers and identify potential areas of interest. In reviewing financial data at UCSF, the Division of Hospital Medicine discovered that they spent more than $1 million annually in direct costs for the administration of "nebs" (aerosolized breathing treatments) to patients admitted to the hospital on the medical service. An investigation found that they could be providing inhaler treatments for patients at a lower cost while having the benefit of teaching patients how to properly use their inhalers.[55] Still, not every area of high cost is a good target for intervention. For example, the use of recombinant factor VIII also cost more than $1 million per year at UCSF, but this was appropriately used for patients with hemophilia and appeared to be a necessary expenditure.[56]

Project ideas may be generated by many other mechanisms as well, including literature reviews, case reports, or national initiatives. For example, the Centers for Disease Control and Prevention ("the CDC") has recommended that every healthcare setting implement an "antimicrobial stewardship" program.[57]

If your practice setting does not include such a program then this could be a great goal.

Once an area for value improvement is identified, the next step is to create a clear aim statement. A good aim statement may follow the "SMART" criteria.[58] Say you want to decrease unnecessary blood transfusions in your hospital and that you have obtained baseline data confirming variation in practices and providing evidence of excess transfusions in some situations at your institution. A statement that claims your project aims to "reduce blood transfusions in our hospital" may capture the overall impetus but it is not very "SMART." How will you accomplish this goal? Is there a certain group that you are going to measure? How will anyone know if you succeeded in meeting your goals?

"By providing education, audit, and feedback, and creating a best practice alert in our electronic health record, we will reduce blood transfusions for all patients admitted on the orthopedic service by at least 25% over the next six months." This statement is specific, provides actionable items, is reasonably attainable (based on analysis of the baseline practices), is relevant, and includes a clear timeline.

The project team will also need to develop an overall measurement strategy. Consider using a balanced set of measures for all improvement efforts: *structure, process, outcomes,* and *balancing measures*.[59] As described in Chapter 4, process measures may be thought about as "what health professionals do to people," whereas outcome measures are "what happens to people."[60]

- *Structure measures:* The material, human, and organizational resources available in the settings in which care is delivered.[59] The number of MRI machines, hospital beds, and available staff may be important structural aspects to consider and measure. If a project seeks to deliver influenza vaccines to all eligible patients, then the number of nursing full time equivalents (FTE) required to deliver influenza vaccines could be a structural measure.
- *Process measures:* What is actually done in giving and receiving care? For a process measure to be valid, it must previously have been demonstrated to produce a better outcome.[61] For example, whether or not a patient is given an influenza vaccine during a hospitalization could be considered a process measure.
- *Outcomes measures:* The effects of care on the health status of patients and populations.[61] If fewer people die after receiving influenza vaccines, then this mortality benefit would be an outcome measure. Outcomes can be expressed as "the five Ds": death, disease, discomfort, disability, and dissatisfaction.[62]
- *Balancing measures:* Ensures that changes do not result in other unintended problems. For example, if efforts to discharge patients before noon actually resulted in increased length of stay because some patients were being kept until the next day to be discharged in the morning, this would be an important balancing measure that may not be captured if one is only measuring the percentage of patients discharged prior to noon.

A Project Charter can be a powerful way to bring together many of these steps and to compose a clear, concise overall plan that can be shared with the entire project team and other stakeholders. Figure 16-4 includes a Project Charter template that could be used or adapted by project teams during the early stages of project development.

Leveraging cost and quality data

Clinicians should know the basic lay of the land for what kind of data is available in their health system and where to look to obtain this data (Table 16-2). Analyzing healthcare data, and particularly cost data, often requires specific expertise and it is important to obtain the support of quality improvement, business, financial, and resource managers. Traditionally, costs are accounted for at a relatively high level, and are not routinely allocated to specific clinical processes. In Chapter 4 we describe a cost accounting method called *time-driven activity-based costing* that requires clinicians and financial managers to work together in order to understand how costs accrue in real time as patients receive care.

It is worth noting that cost reduction efforts in particular often require a certain level of diplomacy. Since a large proportion of healthcare costs go to labor, efforts to reduce cost may lead to cuts in the resources available to certain departments, or to individuals' wages. An initiative aimed at reducing inappropriate diagnostic imaging[63] could directly result in decreased revenue for the radiology department, which is partially paid based on volume of studies performed. Therefore, careful stakeholder recruitment is critical to successful value improvement initiatives. The support of senior leaders can make all the difference in negotiating these delicate situations.[56]

It is also often possible to find improvement opportunities that are financially beneficial to both patients and the radiology department (or another facet of the institution)—particularly for low-value clinical decisions where the institutional costs exceed the revenue. For example many ultrasounds that are ordered in pregnancy for "follow-up" testing do not inform patient care and the costs far exceed the Medicare reimbursement rates. At the same time, freeing up ultrasound machines or other forms of "excess capacity" can provide opportunities for higher value applications of institutional resources. By carefully measuring the costs of clinical processes, taking a diplomatic approach, and reapplying excess capacities, the University of Utah Health System was able to save $2.5 million in 2012 alone.[64]

Ready for implementation and dissemination

Once teams have trialed their improvement ideas through small tests of change and have a high degree of confidence that the changes are indeed an improvement, they are ready to progress to the "implementing and sustaining changes" phase. During this phase, change ideas are formally implemented into everyday practice in the unit or department where the work is done.

Project Name:		Date:

PROJECT PARTICIPANTS		
Executive Sponsor:	Champion:	Project Manager:
Stakeholders:	Core Team Members:	Ad Hoc Team Members:

PROJECT DESCRIPTION

Executive Summary

Business Case: captures the reasoning for initiating a project or task to convince a decision maker to take action (include what problem or situation triggered the initiative and what benefit, value or return is expected).

Problem Statement: a clear description of an issue facing an individual or group. The problem statement generally includes the scope and magnitude of the problem.

Project Objectives / Benefits (should be measurable):

OUTCOMES: (patient level benefits – e.g. cost, mortality, LOS)
-
-

PROCESSES: (changes in the steps of care delivery that are necessary to achieve those outcomes)
-
-

Current State Description / High Level Process Map

Current State Problems: Lists the issues identified with the current state and how they contribute to the overall problem.

Schedule (target date):

Start Date:
End Date:

Budget (amount):

Deliverables (different than objectives):

Deliverables are tangible things that will be created to support the project. They may include process maps, survey instruments or educational materials

Scope – Inclusions/Exclusions:

Stakeholders & Key Linkages/Dependencies:

Stakeholder are those that will be affected positively and negatively by the change. Often a stakeholder buy-in or commitment to change is necessary for project implementation

Known Risks/Issues:

Charter Sign-off:	
We agree that this is a clear definition of the project and approve the Charter.	
Signature	Date
Executive Sponsor:	Date:
"Champion" Lead:	Date:
Project Manager:	Date:

Figure 16-4. Sample project charter template. (Reproduced, with permission, from The UCSF High-Value Care Committee.)

Table 16-2 Finding data in your hospital

FINANCIAL DATA: Hospitals keep close records on all services that are billed for in the hospital. This can be very helpful if you are trying to understand utilization of a service such as transfusions or MRI scans.

Measures to consider

Direct Costs:	This is typically how much it costs your hospital to provide a particular service. It incorporates all the materials, labor, and expenses related to the production of a product.
Facility Charges:	This is what a hospital charges to a self-pay patient. This is the charge that would be listed on a hospital bill.
Facility Payment:	This is how much an insurer pays your hospital for a given service. Payment rates for Medicare are publically reported. One example is the website below which provides Medicare payments to physicians for certain services: http://www.cms.gov/apps/physician-fee-schedule/license-agreement.aspx
Cost Index:	Your hospital may be provided with a cost index for a particular service. This is the observed cost / expected cost, and can help your hospital know how its costs compare to others in the market.

Who to approach for this data

Decision Support:	Many hospitals have a "decision support" team that provides hospital departments with the tools, technology, and applications to access clinical, financial, and administrative information on a timely basis. A decision support analyst may conduct various types of specialized analyses, including cost-benefit analyses, financial analyses, and feasibility studies.
Service Line Director:	Other hospitals employ "service line directors" whose job is to ensure the financial success and productivity of a specific set of services in the hospital. They serve as a bridge between physician needs and hospital administration. They often have access to current data on the use and profitability of services in their domain.
Administrator/ Billing Department:	If your hospital does not have a decision support department, it is probably best to approach an administrator who can connect you to a friendly analyst in the billing department.

QUALITY DATA: This is a loosely defined term to encompass publically reported data like core measures and hospital acquired complications as well as other frequently measured performance data.

Measures to consider

Core Measures	Hospital core measures are CMS recommended treatments that the scientific evidence shows produce the best results. All hospitals are required to collect and report on these measures. These include treatment of perinatal

(Continued)

Table 16-2 Finding data in your hospital (*Continued*)

	care, stroke, VTE, Heart Failure, ED care, etc. A complete list of core measures and the requirements are found on http://www.jointcommission.org/core_measure_sets.aspx
Hospital Acquired Conditions (HACs)	In early 2010, Medicare implemented 11 categories of HACs for which they would no longer be paying hospitals. Hospitals had to develop a way to monitor, track, and report these conditions. Some states have additional penalties. For a list of conditions go to: http://www.cms.gov/Medicare/Medicare-Fee-for-Service-Payment/HospitalAcqCond/Hospital-Acquired_Conditions.html
Readmissions	Similarly, as part of the Affordable Care Act, payments to hospitals are reduced for hospitals that have excess readmissions in the category of heart failure, pneumonia, acute myocardial infarction. Penalties for COPD and large joint replacement started in 2014. In addition to tracking these rates, many hospitals are now tracking 7-, 14-, and 30-day readmissions for a variety of other groups. For post-acute care facilities, there are no readmission penalties as of yet and there is a lot of variation in the way this data is collected and monitored.
Mortality	Hospitals keep close track of mortality cases that occur in the hospital. Many hospitals even have a mortality review committee, responsible for reviewing the quality of care, documentation, and coding of in-hospital deaths. Mortality can be tracked as a raw percentage as well as a ratio of observed/expected (O/E). The O/E Mortality Index can be helpful in determining patients who had unexpected deaths based on their presenting severity of illness.
Sepsis	Given that many large hospitals have sepsis initiatives, many track prevalence of sepsis patients in their organization, mortality rates, and compliance with national best practices such as sepsis recognition and timely administration of antibiotics.
Who to approach for this data	
Director of Quality	The structure in every organization is different, but most hospitals have a quality department that is responsible for providing both the government and the organization with data regarding core measures and HAC performance. This person can be a wonderful source for your hospital's data.
Chief Quality Officer	A good link to the Quality Department will be the facility's chief quality officer. This is often a physician champion working with the quality department to monitor data and drive improvement.
Publically Reported Hospital Data Websites	The following websites contain publically reported data from multiple hospitals and can be a great way to compare your facility to others.

(Continued)

Table 16-2 **Finding data in your hospital (*Continued*)**

WhyNotTheBest.org

www.WhyNotTheBest.org was created and is maintained by The
Commonwealth Fund, a private foundation working toward a high
performance health system. It is a free resource for healthcare professionals and consumers interested in tracking performance on various
measures of healthcare quality. It enables organizations to compare
their performance against that of peer organizations, against a range of
benchmarks, and over a given period of time. A regional map shows performance at the county, state, and national levels. This site also includes
process-of-care measures, patient satisfaction measures, readmission
rates, mortality rates, and average reimbursement rates.

The Leapfrog Group

The Leapfrog Group, http://www.leapfroggroup.org/cp, started in 1998 by
a group of large employers. The Leapfrog Hospital Survey compares
hospitals' performance on the national standards of safety, quality, and
efficiency—areas of healthcare that are most relevant to consumers.
Hospitals that participate in The Leapfrog Hospital Survey achieve
hospital-wide improvements that translate into saving millions of
lives and cutting costs for hospitals and consumers. Leapfrog's
survey results are later used to inform key employees on purchasing
strategies.

Hospital Compare

The *Hospital Compare* website was created through the efforts of the
Centers for Medicare & Medicaid Services (CMS) along with the
Hospital Quality Alliance (HQA). The HQA was established to promote
reporting on hospital quality of care. This website can be found at:
http://www.hospitalcompare.hhs.gov

Public Data for Post-acute Facilities	Information regarding Skilled Nursing Facilities is obtained in cooperation with SNF Data Resources, an online source for SNF cost report data and Medicare survey findings.
Healthcare Collaboratives	You hospital may belong to a healthcare collaborative to which a group of similar hospitals submit data. These can be a rich source of data on your hospital's performance and comparisons to other hospitals. Some examples are University Health Consortium (UHC), NSQIP (National Surgical Quality Improvement Program), BEACON (Bay Area Patient Safety Collaborative). Ask about healthcare or patient safety collaboratives your hospital may belong to as a source of data.

PATIENT SATISFACTION: Increasingly patient satisfaction is being publically reported and tracked
by hospitals.

(*Continued*)

Table 16-2 Finding data in your hospital (*Continued*)

Hospital Consumer Assessment of Healthcare Providers and Systems (HCAHPS)	HCAHPS is a standardized instrument designed for measuring patient perspectives on hospital care. All hospitals are required to participate in HCAHPS data collection and public reporting. More information can be found here: http://www.hcahpsonline.org
MGMA, Press Ganey, SullivanLuallin Group	Three of the largest survey distributors and patient satisfaction consultants. These consultants will distribute the HCAHPS survey as well as other mandatory outpatient surveys, custom surveys, and provide dashboards, reports, and analytics with which to analyze the reports. All have a website that facilities use to access their data and can create custom reports that may be helpful in driving improvement.

Source: Adapted, with permission, from Michelle Mourad, MD, UCSF.

Consider: Do you have the buy-in and commitment from your stakeholders? Is there a high-degree of belief that your change will lead to improvement? *If so, you are ready to implement!*

Do not forget to consider all four areas of the "COST" framework:

- *Culture change:* How will you encourage a shift in the culture or the "hidden curriculum" that will support your project goals?
- *Oversight:* How will you most effectively provide audit and feedback or other methods for appropriate oversight?
- *Systems changes:* What changes to workflows or systems can you feasibly make that will make it easy for your target audience to do the right thing?
- *Training/Education:* Will your change require ongoing education? When new staff enter the world of your change, will they be ready to adopt your desired behavior?

There are many great resources for clinicians that want to learn more about the basic science and tools of improvement, including the free IHI Open School platform (http://www.ihi.org/education/ihiopenschool).

CREATING BETTER HEALTHCARE SYSTEMS

In his book, *The Checklist Manifesto*, Harvard surgeon and writer Dr Atul Gawande makes an important distinction between two sources of human fallibility, one that philosophers have termed "ignorance" and another they have termed "ineptitude."[65] Ignorance refers to a lack of knowledge, which science and medicine in particular are making great leaps in overcoming. Ineptitude refers to instances where knowledge exists but we fail to apply it correctly. Dr Gawande argues that science and medicine have a long way to go to overcome ineptitude. As healthcare systems become increasingly complex, this is the principle gap that we need to close in order to improve performance.

Dr Gawande goes on to describe three stages in our evolution to close the ineptitude gap: a "primitive" stage where we simply tell people "you should do X," a "medieval" stage where we use guidelines or regulations to tell people "you must do X," and a "modern" stage where we figure out how to make "X" the norm. Making "X" the norm is not trivial but many of the tactics we have described so far in this chapter are helpful aids in our early efforts. But to ensure that we do not remain inept in the long-term, we need to do more than implement the knowledge we currently have. We will also need healthcare systems that can adapt as we acquire new knowledge.

Continuously learning healthcare systems

Most health professionals are advised near the beginning of their training that being in healthcare is a commitment to lifelong education. Just as individual clinicians must continually adapt and learn to provide the best care, so do our health systems. In their report, "Best Care at Lower Costs," the IOM put forth a number of recommendations for creating "continuously learning healthcare systems" (Box 16-1).[33] The need for large-scale digital infrastructure with systems that allow for meaningful data collection and analyses is obvious. And easier said than done. As is better care coordination and continuity. However, now many different forces are working to integrate care both through clinical and payment models, such as the promotion of ACOs (see Chapter 15). These integrated systems need to optimize operations to make them efficient and reliable, perhaps borrowing tools from other industries. In addition, policy initiatives that support these ideals, including aligned payment reform and performance transparency (see Chapter 15), are critical to reinforcing sustainable systems.

Moving toward continuously learning healthcare systems will demand committed leadership. The executives of 11 leading healthcare delivery institutions created "A CEO Checklist for High-Value Health Care" that includes 10 key strategies based on their own experiences (Table 16-3).[26,28]

Clinicians and health systems are now tasked with concentrating on ways to support the best evidence in the care delivered to patients, while emphasizing patient-centered care and openly seeking patient preferences and input. This will require efforts at all levels from the bedside to the C-suite. Indeed it is the only way to ensure that we deliver on the promise of healthcare value for our patients. It is attainable. There are shining examples lighting up across the country, driven by dedicated people that come to work every day striving to help others feel better.

BOX 16-1: Institute of Medicine Recommendations for Continuously Learning Healthcare Systems

Foundational Elements

Recommendation 1: The digital infrastructure. Improve the capacity to capture clinical, care delivery process, and financial data for better care, system improvement, and the generation of new knowledge.

Recommendation 2: The data utility. Streamline and revise research regulations to improve care, promote the capture of clinical data, and generate knowledge.

Care Improvement Targets

Recommendation 3: Clinical decision support. Accelerate integration of the best clinical knowledge into care decisions.

Recommendation 4: Patient-centered care. Involve patients and families in decisions regarding health and healthcare, tailored to fit their preferences.

Recommendation 5: Community links. Promote community-clinical partnerships and services aimed at managing and improving health at the community level.

Recommendation 6: Care continuity. Improve coordination and communication within and across organizations.

Recommendation 7: Optimized operations. Continuously improve healthcare operations to reduce waste, streamline care delivery, and focus on activities that improve patient health.

Supportive Policy Environment

Recommendation 8: Financial incentives. Structure payment to reward continuous learning and improvement in the provision of best care at lower cost.

Recommendation 9: Performance transparency. Increase transparency on healthcare system performance.

Recommendation 10: Broad leadership. Expand commitment to the goals of a continuously learning healthcare system.

Source: Reproduced, with permission, from IOM (Institute of Medicine). *Best care at lower cost: the path to continuously learning health care in America.* Washington, DC.: National Academies Press; 2013.

Table 16-3 **A CEO checklist for high-value healthcare**

Category	Item
Foundational elements	Governance priority—visible and determined by leadership by CEO and board
	Culture of continuous improvement—commitment to ongoing real-time learning
Infrastructure fundamentals	Information Technology best practices—automated, reliable information to and from the point of care
	Evidence protocols—effective, efficient, and consistent care
	Resource use—optimized use of personnel, physical space, and other resources
Care delivery priorities	Integrated care—right care, right setting, right providers, right teamwork
	Shared decision making—patient-clinician collaboration on care plans
	Targeted services—tailored community and clinic interventions for resource-intensive patients
Reliability and feedback	Embedded safeguards—supports and prompts to reduce injury and infection
	Internal transparency—visible progress in performance, outcomes, and costs

Source: Reproduced, with permission of the National Academy of Sciences. From Cosgrove D, Fisher M, Gabow P, et al. A CEO checklist for high-value health care. In: *Institute of Medicine*; 2012. http://www.iom. edu/Global/Perspectives/2012/CEOChecklist.aspx. Washington, DC.: National Academies Press.

A CALL TO ACTION

We can all imagine a better American healthcare system. One that consistently delivers effective, efficient, safe care in humanistic ways and not only harnesses advancements in medicine and technology to heal physical ailments, but also truly supports health and happiness for all of us. A healthcare system that we all can be proud to work in. One that we could confidently send our family members into and trust they will get great care. Perhaps when we do not feel the need as health professionals to serve as personal advocates and watchful eyes for our own family members whenever they access healthcare, then we will know that the system is truly working.

Confronting such a large problem will require a concerted effort from individual clinicians along with systemic transformations. Together, we can take charge and help transform healthcare.

KEY POINTS:

- An "implementation science" field of study aims to help effectively translate evidence into practice. A key component of these efforts is to obtain authentic frontline clinician engagement in the design, implementation, and modification of projects aimed at changing behaviors.
- Many healthcare organizations have begun to apply methods and lessons from other industries to cut waste, improve efficiency, and enhance reliability. Lean management principles, chiefly emerging from the Toyota Production System, have proven to be powerful tools for some early adopters, including Virginia Mason Medical Center.
- Individual clinicians, equipped with the right tools and resources, can help provoke change within their own groups and institutions. There are a number of resources to obtain the foundational knowledge and supplies for improvement projects, including the free Institute for Healthcare Improvement (IHI) Open School.
- The future of healthcare improvement depends on creating continuously learning healthcare systems that can deliver on the promise of constant advancement in the delivery of healthcare that is safer, more efficient, less costly, and increasingly focused on the needs and experience of our patients.
- It is up to all of us to help create a healthcare system that we will consistently be proud to work in and that will reliably deliver better outcomes for our patients, families, and selves.

References:

1. Historical perspective on hand hygiene in health care. In: *WHO Guidelines on Hand Hygiene in Health Care: First Global Patient Safety Challenge Clean Care Is Safer Care*. Geneva: World Health Organization; 2009. http://www.ncbi.nlm.nih.gov/books/NBK144018/. Accessed June 3, 2014.
2. Moriates C, Shah N. Creating an effective campaign for change: strategies for teaching value. *JAMA Intern Med*. 2014;174(10):1693-1695.
3. McGlynn EA, Asch SM, Adams J, et al. The quality of health care delivered to adults in the United States. *N Engl J Med*. 2003;348(26):2635-2645.
4. Antithrombotic Trialists' Collaboration. Collaborative meta-analysis of randomised trials of antiplatelet therapy for prevention of death, myocardial infarction, and stroke in high risk patients. *BMJ*. 2002;324(7329):71-86.
5. Woolf SH, Johnson RE. The break-even point: when medical advances are less important than improving the fidelity with which they are delivered. *Ann Fam Med*. 2005;3(6):545-552.
6. Glasgow RE, Vinson C, Chambers D, Khoury MJ, Kaplan RM, Hunter C. National Institutes of Health approaches to dissemination and implementation science: current and future directions. *Am J Public Health*. 2012;102(7):1274-1281.
7. Gonzales R, Handley MA, Ackerman S, O'Sullivan PS. Increasing the translation of evidence into practice, policy, and public health improvements: a framework for training health professionals in implementation and dissemination science. *Acad Med*. 2012;87(3):271-278.

8. Braithwaite J, Marks D, Taylor N. Harnessing implementation science to improve care quality and patient safety: a systematic review of targeted literature. *Int J Qual Health Care.* 2014;26(3):321-329.

9. Langlois MA, Hallam JS. Integrating multiple health behavior theories into program planning: the PER worksheet. *Health Promot Pract.* 2010;11(2):282-288.

10. Aboumatar H, Ristaino P, Davis RO, et al. Infection prevention promotion program based on the PRECEDE model: improving hand hygiene behaviors among healthcare personnel. *Infect Control Hosp Epidemiol.* 2012;33(2):144-151.

11. Berwick DM. The moral test. 2011. http://www.ihi.org/knowledge/Pages/Presentations/The MoralTestBerwickForum2011Keynote.aspx. Accessed November 15, 2012.

12. Lee TH, Cosgrove T. Engaging doctors in the health care revolution. *Harv Bus Rev.* 2014. http://hbr.org/2014/06/engaging-doctors-in-the-health-care-revolution/ar/1. Accessed July 30, 2014.

13. Lomas J, Enkin M, Anderson GM, Hannah WJ, Vayda E, Singer J. Opinion leaders vs audit and feedback to implement practice guidelines. Delivery after previous cesarean section. *JAMA.* 1991;265(17):2202-2207.

14. Totten AM, Wagner J, Tiwari A, O'Haire C, Griffin J, Walker M. Closing the quality gap: revisiting the state of the science (Vol. 5). In: *Public Reporting as a Quality Improvement Strategy.* Rockford, MD: Agency for Healthcare Research and Quality; 2012.

15. Jamtvedt G, Young JM, Kristoffersen DT, Thomson O'Brien MA, Oxman AD. Audit and feedback: effects on professional practice and health care outcomes. *Cochrane Database Syst Rev.* 2003;13(6):CD000259.

16. Asch DA, Terwiesch C, Mahoney KB, Rosin R. Insourcing health care innovation. *N Engl J Med.* 2014;370(19):1775-1777.

17. Plsek PE. *Accelerating Health Care Transformation with Lean and Innovation: The Virginia Mason Experience.* 1 ed. Boca Raton, FL: Productivity Press; 2013.

18. Choosing Wisely. An initiative of the ABIM Foundation. http://www.choosingwisely.org/. Accessed October 7, 2013.

19. Casale AS, Paulus RA, Selna MJ, et al. "ProvenCareSM": a provider-driven pay-for-performance program for acute episodic cardiac surgical care. *Ann Surg.* 2007;246(4):613-621; discussion 621-623.

20. Berry SA, Doll MC, McKinley KE, Casale AS, Bothe A. ProvenCare: quality improvement model for designing highly reliable care in cardiac surgery. *Qual Saf Health Care.* 2009;18(5):360-368.

21. Lee TH. Pay for performance, version 2.0? *N Engl J Med.* 2007;357(6):531-533.

22. Abelson R. In bid for better care, surgery with a warranty. *The New York Times,* May 17, 2007. http://www.nytimes.com/2007/05/17/business/17quality.html. Accessed September 4, 2014.

23. Berry SA, Laam LA, Wary AA, et al. ProvenCare perinatal: a model for delivering evidence/guide line-based care for perinatal populations. *Jt Comm J Qual. Patient Saf.* 2011;37(5):229-239.

24. Katlic MR, Facktor MA, Berry SA, McKinley KE, Bothe A, Steele GD. ProvenCare lung cancer: a multi-institutional improvement collaborative. *CA Cancer J Clin.* 2011;61(6):382-396.

25. Daley J. Obama singles out Intermountain Healthcare as model system. *KSL.com,* September 10, 2009, Salt Lake City: Deseret Digital Media. http://www.ksl.com/?nid=148&sid=7873613. Accessed September 4, 2014.

26. Cosgrove D, Fisher M, Gabow P, et al. A CEO checklist for high-value health care. In: *Institute of Medicine;* 2012. http://www.iom.edu/Global/Perspectives/2012/CEOChecklist.aspx. Accessed November 15, 2012.

27. Mansour ME, Rose B, Toole K, Luzader CP, Atherton HD. Pursuing perfection: an asthma quality improvement initiative in school-based health centers with community partners. *Public Health Rep.* 2008;123(6):717-729.

28. Cosgrove DM, Fisher M, Gabow P, et al. Ten strategies to lower costs, improve quality, and engage patients: the view from leading health system CEOs. *Health Aff.* 2013;32(2):321-327.

29. Feachem RGA, Sekhri NK, White KL. Getting more for their dollar: a comparison of the NHS with California's Kaiser Permanente. *BMJ*. 2002;324(7330):135-143.

30. Jaffe MG, Lee GA, Young JD, Sidney S, Go AS. Improved blood pressure control associated with a large-scale hypertension program. *JAMA*. 2013;310(7):699-705.

31. Strandberg-Larsen M, Schiøtz ML, Silver JD, et al. Is the Kaiser Permanente model superior in terms of clinical integration? A comparative study of Kaiser Permanente, Northern California and the Danish healthcare system. *BMC Health Serv Res*. 2010;10:91.

32. Light D, Dixon M. Making the NHS more like Kaiser Permanente. *BMJ*. 2004;328(7442):763-765.

33. Institute of Medicine. *Best Care at Lower Cost : The Path to Continuously Learning Health Care in America*. Washington, DC: National Academies Press; 2012.

34. ThedaCare Center for Healthcare Value. http://createvalue.org/. Accessed August 31, 2014.

35. Pines JM, Farmer SA, Akman JS. "Innovation" Institutes in Academic Health Centers: enhancing value through leadership, education, engagement, and scholarship. *Acad Med*. 2014;89(9):1204-1206.

36. UCSF Center for Healthcare Value. http://healthvalue.ucsf.edu/. Accessed August 31, 2014.

37. High Value Health Care Collaborative. http://highvaluehealthcare.org/. Accessed August 31, 2014.

38. Barro J. Why you should pay frontier's carry-on bag fee. *The New York Times*, May 9, 2014. http://www.nytimes.com/2014/05/09/upshot/why-you-should-pay-frontiers-carry-on-bag-fee-with-a-smile.html. Accessed August 27, 2014.

39. Institute of Medicine. *To Err Is Human: Building a Safer Health System*. Washington, DC: National Academies Press; 1999.

40. Wachter RM. The end of the beginning: patient safety five years after "to err is human". *Health Aff*. 2004; Suppl Web Exclusives:W4-534-W4-545.

41. Oriol MD. Crew resource management: applications in healthcare organizations. *J Nurs Adm*. 2006;36(9):402-406.

42. Leape LL. Error in medicine. *JAMA*. 1994;272(23):1851-1857.

43. Sexton JB, Helmreich RL, Neilands TB, et al. The Safety Attitudes Questionnaire: psychometric properties, benchmarking data, and emerging research. *BMC Health Serv Res*. 2006;6:44.

44. Chassin MR, Loeb JM. High-reliability health care: getting there from here. *Milbank Q*. 2013;91(3):459-490.

45. Kageyama Y. Toyota sold nearly 9.75 million vehicles last year. *Yahoo News*. http://news.yahoo.com/toyota-sold-nearly-9-75-051532917.html. Accessed August 31, 2014.

46. Toyota Global Site. The origin of the Toyota Production System. http://www.toyota-global.com/company/vision_philosophy/toyota_production_system/origin_of_the_toyota_production_system.html. Accessed August 29, 2014.

47. Gabow PA. The promise of lean processes. *Institute of Medicine*. http://iom.edu/Global/Perspectives/2012/LeanProcesses.aspx. Accessed August 30, 2014.

48. Kim CS, Spahlinger DA, Kin JM, Billi JE. Lean health care: what can hospitals learn from a world-class automaker? *J Hosp Med*. 2006;1(3):191-199.

49. Robeznieks A. Virginia Mason Medical Center uses Lean production system to standardize processes, improve patient experience. *Modern Healthcare*. http://www.modernhealthcare.com/article/20140111/MAGAZINE/301119950. Accessed August 30, 2014.

50. Kaplan GS. The lean approach to health care: safety, quality, and cost. *Institute of Medicine*. http://www.iom.edu/Global/Perspectives/2012/LeanApproach.aspx. Accessed December 11, 2012.

51. Gayed B, Black S, Daggy J, Munshi IA. Redesigning a joint replacement program using lean six sigma in a veterans affairs hospital. *JAMA Surg*. 2013;148(11):1050-1056.

52. Deming WE. *The New Economics: For Industry, Government, Education*. 2nd ed. Cambridge, MA: MIT Press; 2000.

53. Institute for Healthcare Improvement. Science of improvement: how to improve. http://www.ihi.org/resources/Pages/HowtoImprove/ScienceofImprovementHowtoImprove.aspx. Accessed September 5, 2014.

54. Reyes D, Govindarajan R, Salgado E. A retrospective analysis of the clinical utility of carotid doppler ultrasound in evaluation of syncope (P06.256). *Neurology.* 2013;80(Meeting Abstracts 1): P06.256.
55. Moriates C, Novelero M, Quinn K, Khanna R, Mourad M. "Nebs no more after 24": a pilot program to improve the use of appropriate respiratory therapies. *JAMA Intern Med.* 2013;173(17): 1647-1648.
56. Moriates C, Mourad M, Novelero M, Wachter RM. Development of a hospital-based program focused on improving healthcare value. *J Hosp Med.* 2014;9(10):671-677.
57. Fridkin S, Baggs J, Fagan R, et al. Vital signs: improving antibiotic use among hospitalized patients. *Morb Mortal Wkly Rep.* 2014;63(9):194-200.
58. Yemm G. *The Financial Times Essential Guide to Leading Your Team: How to Set Goals, Measure Performance and Reward Talent.* Harlow: Financial Times; 2012.
59. Donabedian A. The quality of care: How can it be assessed? *JAMA.* 1988;260(12):1743-1748.
60. Brook RH, McGlynn EA, Shekelle PG. Defining and measuring quality of care: a perspective from US researchers. *Int J Qual Health Care.* 2000;12(4):281-295.
61. Mainz J. Defining and classifying clinical indicators for quality improvement. *Int J Qual Health Care.* 2003;15(6):523-530.
62. Lohr KN. *Medicare: a strategy for quality assurance* (Vol. 2). In: *Sources and Methods.* http://www.nap.edu/catalog.php?record_id=1548. Accessed September 5, 2014.
63. Neeman N, Quinn K, Soni K, Mourad M, Sehgal NL. Reducing radiology use on an inpatient medical service: Choosing Wisely. *Arch Intern Med.* 2012;172(20):1606-1608.
64. Appleby J. Utah hospitals try the unthinkable: Get a grip on costs. *USA Today.* June 28, 2014. http://www.usatoday.com/story/news/nation/2014/06/28/utah-hospitals-cost-of-medical-care/11416353/. Accessed October 26, 2014.
65. Gawande A. *The Checklist Manifesto: How to Get Things Right.* Reprint ed. New York, NY: Picador; 2011.

Glossary

Term	Definition
Acceptable/warranted variation	Variation in care related to aspects of health status or population demographics. This variation is expected in an efficient health system since it is driven by genuine health needs and is beyond the control of both providers and patients.
Accountable care organization (ACO)	Groups of doctors, hospitals, and other healthcare providers, who come together voluntarily to give coordinated care to a population. ACOs are characterized by a payment and care delivery model that seeks to tie reimbursements to metrics of quality and reduced costs for an assigned population.
Balancing measures	Measures that ensure changes designed to improve one part of the system or disease process do not cause new problems in other parts of the system or disease process.
Beneficiary	The person that receives any of the benefits of the insurance coverage.
Bundled Payment	A reimbursement method based on expected costs for a clinically defined episode of care that includes multiple services.
Capitation	The payment of a fee to a healthcare provider providing services to a number of people, such that the amount paid is determined by the number of total patients.
Charge	For purposes of this book, "charge" is used to signify the price asked for a healthcare good or service. The charge is the amount that would appear on a medical bill.

Chargemaster	A comprehensive listing of items billable to a hospital patient or a patient's health insurance provider.
Choosing Wisely	A campaign led by the ABIM Foundation seeking to improve doctor-patient communication related to over-utilization of medical resources.
Coinsurance	The amount a beneficiary must pay for medical care after they have met their deductible. For instance, the insurance company may pay for 80% of an approved amount, and the patient's coinsurance will be for 20%.
Consumer-driven health plans (CDHPs)	Health insurance plans that allow members to use specific accounts, such as health savings accounts or health reimbursement accounts or similar models, to pay directly for routine health expenses.
Copayment	The flat fee that a beneficiary must pay each time they receive medical care. For example, a patient may pay a $10 copayment ("copay") for every doctor visit, while the insurance plan covers the rest of the cost.
Cost	To providers: costs are the expense incurred to deliver healthcare services to patients.
	To payers: costs are the amount they pay to the provider for services rendered.
	To patients: costs are the amount they pay out-of-pocket for healthcare services.
COST framework	Framework developed by Costs of Care to categorize and guide educational and operational efforts to improve healthcare value. The acronym stands for: culture, oversight, systems, and training.
Cost-effectiveness analysis	A method of quantifying the value of care by comparing the relative costs and effects (clinical outcomes, patient experience, or both) of two different courses of action.
Cost-effectiveness acceptability curve (CEAC)	Graph of the probability that a technology will be cost-effective given different willingness to pay thresholds.
Coverage limits	The maximum amount that a health insurance plan may pay for certain healthcare services. Some health insurance policies may also have a maximum annual or lifetime coverage amount. After any of these limits are reached, then the policy-holder may have to pay for all remaining costs.

Deductible	The amount the beneficiary must pay each year before their health insurance coverage plan begins paying.
Defensive medicine	The practice of clinicians utilizing technology (ordering tests or providing treatments) to reduce malpractice liability.
Diagnosis-related group (DRG)	Payment categories used to classify patients based on their diagnosis for the purpose of reimbursing hospitals a fixed fee based on the diagnosis (known as a prospective payment). DRGs have been used by Medicare for hospital reimbursements since 1983. The classifications used to determine Medicare payments for inpatient care include primary and secondary diagnosis, primary and secondary procedures, age, and length of hospitalization.
Effective care	Medical interventions that provide clear net benefit for patients (the benefits far outweigh the risks).
e-Patients	A term coined by physician author Tom Ferguson in reference to patients who are "equipped, enabled, empowered, and engaged" in their health and health-care decisions.
Exclusions / Limitations	Services that are not covered by a plan. These must be clearly defined in the plan literature.
Extrinsic motivation	Motivation that arises outside the individual. Typically refers to monetary incentives.
False-negatives	A negative test result obtained in a case where the person *does* actually have the disease.
False-positives	A positive test result obtained in a case where the person *does not* actually have the disease.
Fee-for-service (FFS)	A payment system where healthcare services are unbundled and each paid for separately.
Fixed costs	Costs that are independent from the amount of care that is being delivered, typically related to organizational overhead and other resources that cannot be altered in the short term.
Formulary	An organization's or insurance provider's list of covered drugs.
Global payment	Fixed dollar payments for care that cover a given time period, such as a month or year.

GOT MeDS	A mnemonic created by Costs of Care for strategies to decrease medication costs for patients. The acronym stands for: Generic medications, Ordering in bulk, Therapeutic alternatives, Medication review, Discount drugs, and Splitting pills.
Health maintenance organization (HMO)	A form of managed care in which all care is received from participating providers within the network. A referral from a primary care provider needs to be obtained prior to seeing specialists.
Health reimbursement account (HRA)	An account established by an employer to pay an employee's medical expenses. Only the employer can contribute to a HRA.
Health savings account (HSA)	An account established by an employer or an individual to save money toward medical expenses on a tax-free basis.
Healthcare disparities	Population-specific differences in the presence of disease, health outcomes, quality of care, and access to healthcare services that exist across racial and ethnic groups.
Healthy volunteer effect	Volunteers for prevention or screening trials tend to be healthier than the overall population, which may result in concerns about the generalizability of results from these trials.
Hidden curriculum	Lessons that are not taught formally, but are learned through the transmission of norms, values, and beliefs conveyed in the classroom and the social environment.
High-deductible health plan (HDHP) or High-deductible insurance plan	A plan that provides comprehensive coverage for high-cost medical events but features a high deductible coupled with a limit on annual out-of-pocket expense.
High-risk, or selective, screening	Screening conducted only among populations at a particular risk for the disease.
High-value care	Providing the best health outcomes and patient experiences at the lowest costs.
High-value prescribing	Providing the simplest medication regimen that minimizes physical and financial risk to the patient while achieving the best outcome. Decreasing either cost, complexity, or risk of medications can improve value.
Incremental cost-effectiveness ratio (ICER)	A way of measuring value that is used in cost-effectiveness analysis. The ICER compares the change in cost to the resulting change in effect of two technologies or technology applications.

Individual health insurance	Insurance coverage purchased independently (as opposed to as part of a group), usually directly from an insurance company.
Intrinsic motivation	Motivation that arises inside the individual.
Kaizen event	A focused period devoted to process improvement and standardization of processes, often through waste reduction.
Lead-time bias	Overestimation of survival duration resulting from a test diagnosing a condition earlier, even if it does not change outcomes.
Lean	A management philosophy derived mostly from the Toyota Production System that focuses on consistently increasing quality while systematically eliminating waste.
Length-time bias	Overestimation of survival duration due to a screening test's overrepresentation of slowly progressive disease.
Mass screening	The screening of an entire population or a subgroup, offered to all, irrespective of the risk status of the individual.
Medicaid	A Federal program administered by individual States to provide healthcare for certain poor and low-income individuals and families.
Medicare	A Federal insurance program that provides healthcare coverage to eligible individuals aged 65 and older and certain disabled people (such as those with end-stage renal disease, or those that are blind).
Modifiable risk factor	Risks that can be reduced with a lifestyle change or medical intervention.
Moral hazard	Situation in which one has a greater tendency to take risks (or seek unnecessary care) because they are not exposed to the costs that could incur.
Multiphasic screening	A technique of screening populations that combines the application of two or more screening tests (a "battery of screening tests") to a large population at one time instead of carrying out separate screening tests for single diseases.
Negative predictive value	The proportion of negative results that are true-negatives.
Network	A group of physicians, hospitals, and other providers who participate in a particular managed care plan.

Out-of-pocket costs — Costs that come directly from the patient, or the share of expenses that the patient is directly responsible to pay. For insured patients, these costs can include deductibles, coinsurance, and copayments for covered services plus all costs for services that are not covered.

Out-of-pocket maxima — The maximum amount that an insured person can pay, after which the insurance plan pays all further covered costs. Out-of-pocket maxima may be limited to a specific benefit category (such as prescription drugs) or can apply to all coverage provided during a specific benefit year.

Outcome measures — A measure of a health state of a patient or population resulting from healthcare. Broadly, outcome measures may be thought about in terms of the "five Ds": death, disease, discomfort, disability, and dissatisfaction.

Overdiagnosis — The diagnosis of a "disease" that will not actually cause significant symptoms or death during a patient's lifetime.

Panel management — Also known as population management. A proactive approach to healthcare, where a healthcare provider constantly reviews a registry of assigned patients to identify overdue preventive care opportunities, such as cancer screenings and vaccinations, and chronic disease management opportunities, like overdue lab tests and diabetic foot screenings.

Patient-centered medical home (PCMH) — The original description of the PCMH required the following characteristics: a personal physician for each patient, physician-directed medical practice, whole person orientation, care coordination, enhanced access, and payment reform.

Patient-reported measures (PRMs) or patient-reported outcome measures (PROMs) — Any report of the status of a patient's health condition that comes directly from the patient.

Pay-for-performance — Reimbursement method based on paying providers for meeting defined healthcare delivery targets for quality and efficiency.

PDSA cycle — The Plan-Do-Study-Act framework is an iterative process for continuous improvement activities.

Polypharmacy — The use of five or more medications, often in an inappropriate context that leads to lower quality of life.

Positive predictive value	The proportion of positive results that are true-positives.
Preference-sensitive care	Situations when more than one generally accepted treatment option is available and thus choice should depend on patient preferences.
Preferred provider organization (PPO)	A form of managed care in which insurance policy-holders have more flexibility in choosing physicians and other providers than in an HMO. Both participating and nonparticipating providers may be seen; however, the out-of-pocket expenses paid by the policy-holder will vary.
Premium	The amount the insurance policy-holder pays to belong to a health plan. In general, under employer-sponsored health insurance, the employee's share of premiums is usually deducted from their pay.
Price	For purposes of this book, "price" is used to signify the amount of money requested for a given healthcare service or good. Used in this way, it is almost always synonymous with "charge."
Process measures	A measure of quality for a healthcare-related activity performed for, on behalf of, or by a patient. Often used in pay-for-performance programs.
Quality-adjusted life year (QALY)	A comprehensive measure of disease burden used in assessments of new technology. QALYs are often substituted for the effect when calculating incremental cost-effectiveness ratios.
Reimbursement	A payment made by a third party to healthcare organization or provider for repayment of services provided.
Relative value unit (RVU)	A measure of value used in the Medicare reimbursement formula to determine physician fees under the fee-for-service model.
Sensitivity	The ability of a test to detect people who actually have the disease.
Shared decision making	An approach where clinicians and patients share the best available evidence when faced with the task of making decisions, and where patients are supported to consider options, to achieve informed preferences.
SMART goals	An acronym for setting effective project goals, that are: specific, measurable, attainable, relevant, and time-bound.

Specificity	The ability of a test to detect people who do *not* have the disease.
Supply-sensitive care	Activities for which the frequency of use relates to the capacity of the local healthcare system. This includes doctor visits, diagnostic tests, and hospital admissions.
Technological progress	Changes in clinical practice that enhance the ability of providers to diagnose, treat, or prevent health problems.
Time-driven activity-based costing (TDABC)	A cost accounting model that considers the unit cost of supplying capacity and the time required to perform a transaction or an activity. In healthcare, TDABC connects institutional costs to the clinical processes of care.
Triple aim	A framework developed by the Institute of Healthcare Improvement that aims to simultaneously improve the patient experience of care, improve the health of populations, and reduce per capita costs of care.
Unacceptable/ unwarranted variation	Variation in healthcare services due to aspects of system inefficiencies, such as overuse of low-value services and unnecessary service duplication. This variation cannot be explained by differences in patient illness or patient preferences.
Underinsurance	"Underinsurance" occurs whenever there are potential barriers to healthcare access due to out-of-pocket costs of care for people who have health insurance.
Unnecessary services	Medications, tests, and procedures that are not evidence-based and/or are not supported by guidelines, and do not make patients healthier.
Value-based Purchasing	See *Pay-for-performance*. Often used in the context of the Medicare hospital Value-Based Purchasing (VBP) initiative that will provide incentives and penalties for hospitals based on metrics related to quality and costs of care.
Value-stream map	A lean management method that uses a visual flow chart to depict and analyze the current state and design a future state for the entire series of events in a given process.
Variable costs	Costs that depend on the amount of care that is being delivered, typically includes items such as supplies or medications.

Index

Acknowledgments

The authors would like to thank and acknowledge the many people that have contributed to the creation of this book. This book was born from the suggestion of **Dr Robert M. Wachter**, who provided us not only with the courage to pursue the enormous task of writing this book—all while still maintaining our clinical "day jobs"—but who also gave us constant support and encouragement throughout the process. Indeed, his book from this same series, "Understanding Patient Safety," helped provide a model goalpost for us to strive toward. Our editor at McGraw-Hill, **Jim Shanahan**, similarly encouraged us along our way and consistently helped guide the making of this book. We are very grateful for his help, input, and enthusiasm. The **staff at McGraw-Hill**, particularly **Christina Thomas**, and the staff at **MPS Limited**, especially **Ruchika Abrol**, are responsible for turning hundreds of pages of Word document manuscripts into the finished product that we now have. We are very lucky to have worked with such a fantastic and professional crew. **Victoria Valencia, MPH** created and managed all of the tables and figures seen throughout this book. She also read through each manuscript chapter and provided thoughtful edits and input. Victoria is a remarkable project manager and we are extremely thankful for her significant contributions to this book.

We also would like to thank our colleagues that directly contributed writing for this book. **Dr Steven E. Weinberger**, President of the American College of Physicians (ACP), was generous enough to write a foreword for us, as well as help coauthor *Chapter 10*. It is truly an honor to work with someone that has delivered such thoughtful and inspirational leadership nationally on high-value care. **Dr Cynthia D. Smith**, also from the ACP, coauthored *Chapter 10*. As the leading force behind the ACP's groundbreaking high-value care curriculum, Daisy has been a true leader in the work of educating our profession about high-value care and we are thankful for her input and mentorship. When looking for someone to help write a chapter about primary care, we could not have been luckier than getting to work with **Drs Andrew F. Morris-Singer** and **David Margolius**, who are a force to reckon with in the world of primary care redesign, chiefly through their extraordinary grass-roots organization, Primary Care Progress. We sincerely thank them for their writing of *Chapter 9*.

We are thankful to many of our colleagues at our nonprofit organization, Costs of Care, that have helped create and shape some of the frameworks and tools that we have used in this book. **Dr Andrew Levy** led the development of our "COST" framework and has been an excellent partner in Costs of Care. **Dr Rupali Kumar** helped lead the development of the "GOT MeDS" acronym for reducing medication costs for patients. **Jordan Harmon, MHA** has done an amazing job leading the advocacy initiatives for Costs of Care, and has been especially helpful with the vignettes that we feature as "Story From the Frontlines" in this book. We also would like to thank and acknowledge the other members of the Costs of Care team, including: **September Wallingford, RN, Michele Rhee, MBA, MPH, Jonathan Gordon, MBA**, and **Dr Mark Kelley**.

We are eternally grateful to **Daniel Wolfson, MHSA** and **Leslie Tucker** from the ABIM Foundation for bringing together the "trio," for their tireless support of our work, and for their invaluable partnership in our shared initiatives, including the annual "Teaching Value and Choosing Wisely Challenge," which greatly informed aspects of this book. The **ABIM Foundation** has provided our Costs of Care organization with funding to pursue some of these projects. We are thankful for the entire **ABIM Foundation staff**.

We are very appreciative to **Dr David C. Goodman** from the Dartmouth Institute for his review of a draft of *Chapter 7*, and for his suggestions, which helped improve this chapter.

A major focus of this book was to provide voice to the many folks—patients and caregivers—directly affected by issues related to healthcare costs and value. We thank the more than 500 people who have submitted stories to Costs of Care over the past few years, particularly those that we used in this book for our opening vignettes and our "Story From the Frontlines": **Erin Plute, Morgan Congdon, Linda Burke-Galloway, Grayson Wheatley, Karan Chhabra, Ingrid Stobbe, Lissy Hu, Eijean Wu, Paul Abramson, Andreas Mauer, David Mou, Robert Gray, Sarah Jorgenson, Padma Kandadai, Amy Berman, Ann Rabinow, Luisa Kontoules, Lauren Demosthenes, Kathy Day, Cheryl O'Malley**, and **Steven R. Brown**.

Chris Moriates would also like to specifically thank the following people: **Dr Michelle Mourad** has had a profound impact on my professional career through her committed mentorship and enthusiastic inspiration. I am also indebted to the personal mentorship from my UCSF colleagues including **Drs Andrew Lai, Bradley Sharpe, Bradley Monash, Alvin Rajkomar, Niraj Sehgal, Sumant Ranji**, and **Diane Sliwka**. **Maria Novelero** has been a brilliant partner in our work launching the UCSF High-Value Care Committee, which has helped shape much of my perspectives on high-value care. Similarly, the knowledge and experience that I have gained through my involvement with the **UCSF Center for Healthcare Value** and the **Caring Wisely Program**, particularly the mentorship and leadership of **Drs Ralph Gonzales, George Sawaya, Deborah Grady**, and **Adams Dudley** is invaluable to me.

Thank you to **Vinny and Neel** for seeing this project through with me and for filling my work life with exciting opportunities to work on one of the most important healthcare issues of our time. You are amazing work partners and even better friends.

I am forever lucky to have the astonishing support of my loving family. Thank you **Mom** and **Dad** for teaching me about feeling good by doing good for others, and for instilling in me the drive to pursue my interests—even when they come in the form of late nights spent writing. **Andrew, Danielle, Matthew**, and **Taran**, thank you for always cheering me on and inspiring me in your own wonderful ways. **Mark and Pam Bauer**, thanks for your steadfast support. To my loving wife, **Jessica**—as with everything that I have done, this was completed only because of your undying support, sacrifice, and love. Thank you. And my son, **Julian**, thanks for wanting to spend some Sunday mornings at the coffee shop with me while I wrote and you "worked" on your cartoons. I will cherish that time. You are a remarkable young boy and I am very proud.

Vineet Arora would like to specifically thank the following people: I am forever indebted to the friendship, mentorship, and support of my loving husband, **Dr David Meltzer**, who has had a major impact on both my personal and professional life. As an MD with a PhD in economics, he is a national expert on this topic and has, of course, contributed to my interest and ideas on high-value care. We are so fortunate to share a beautiful daughter, **Sonia Leann Meltzer**, whom I was pregnant with while I was doing the bulk of the writing for this book. I am grateful every day for her entry into our lives and the joy she brings us. I would certainly be remiss if I did not acknowledge her nanny, **Marcele Castel**, whose impeccable care for Sonia gave me the moments I needed to make the "final push" and assist with reading and editing chapters. I also wish to thank **Dr Jeanne Farnan**, my professional partner in our educational work, who was able to "hold down the fort" while my attention was directed elsewhere. Likewise, I also wish to thank **Laura Ruth Venable, Lisa Spampinato**, and **Samantha Ngooi**, our research project managers, who have not only supported Neel, Chris, and me in our endeavors, but who always rose to the occasion and were able to manage our many projects fairly independently while I was focused on this project. In addition, I am indebted to the mentorship of **Dr Holly Humphrey**, who has been an amazing role model and inspiration for how to push the envelope in medical education to be more aligned with patients' needs. Last but not least, I wish to acknowledge my wonderful and visionary coauthors, especially **Chris Moriates**, for being our fearless leader and keeping us honest and on task!

Neel Shah would like to specifically thank the following people: Thank you to my dad, **Tushar**, for teaching me to be curious, my mom, **Dipika**, for teaching me to be persistent, my brother, **Niral**, for teaching me how to take the road less traveled, and my wife, **Julie**, for taking every step with me along the way (even when I had a broken leg). Thank you to my dear friends and intellectual partners in this effort—**Vinny** for first taking me seriously even when I was an intern living in a different corner of the country, and **Chris** for stretching our ideas from coast to coast and completing what we now affectionately refer to as the "trio."

Thank you to **Drs Toni Golen**, **Hope Ricciotti**, and **Atul Gawande** for helping me design my dream job, and for collectively serving as my role models and life coaches. Thank you to **Riki MacKillop** for helping me manage my life at Beth Israel Deaconess Medical Center, and to **Grace Galvin** for helping me build and manage our research program at Ariadne Labs. While the ideas in this book took time to grow in popularity, I have relied on many additional, wise mentors to keep me on course, specifically: **Drs Phillip Gruppuso** and **Eli Adashi** at Brown University, **Drs Ross Berkowitz** and **Michael Muto** at Brigham & Women's Hospital, and **Drs AnneKathryn Goodman** and **Whitfield Growdon** at Massachusetts General Hospital. Finally, many of the ideas in this book came from inspiring conversations with colleagues around the United States who are leading the way in bringing value-based care to the clinical frontlines. Thank you for all that you have done and will do. There is much work ahead.